'Tom Linehan here reaffirms his reputation as one of Britain's foremost historians. *Scabs and Traitors* takes us deep into the formative class struggles of the eighteenth and nineteenth centuries, uncovering the treatment afforded to those who resisted the call to collective action. An important book: wonderfully researched and engagingly written.'

— *Professor Matthew Worley, University of Reading*

'This beautifully written and deeply researched monograph casts an empathetic and judicious eye over an all too often hidden aspect of modern labour history, the conflict between collectively-bound and individual workers. It is a compelling and fascinating history from a historian at the height of his powers that deserves a wide readership.'

— *Professor Ian Thatcher, Ulster University*

'This volume brilliantly exposes the nature of class struggle in an industrialising British society over the course of the late eighteenth and nineteenth century. Linehan reveals the ways working class communities sought to protect themselves from the perpetual threat of employers using non-union labour to undermine their livelihoods, and by extension, their families and communities. This is compulsive reading and a major addition to our understanding of the history of British trade unionism.'

— *Dr Peter Wilkin, Brunel University*

SCABS AND TRAITORS

In its broadest sense, this book is concerned with the attempt by workers in Britain during the period 1760–1871 to engage in collective action in circumstances of conflict with their employers during a time when the nation and many of its traditional economic structures and customary modes of working were undergoing rapid and unsettling change. More specifically, the book principally focuses on the attempt by those workers favouring a collective approach to struggle to overcome what they felt to be one of the main obstacles to collective action, the uncooperative worker. At times during these decades, the sanctions directed by collectively inclined workmen at those workers deemed to have engaged in acts contrary to the interests of the trade and customary codes of behaviour in the context of strikes and other instances of friction in the workplace were severe and uncompromising. Stern and unforgiving, too, was the struggle between the collectively inclined worker and the uncooperative worker in a more general sense, a contest that occasionally took a violent and bloody form. In exploring the fractious and hostile relationship between these two conflicting parties, this book draws on concepts and insights from a range of scholarly disciplines in an effort to shift the perception and study of this relationship beyond many of the conventional paradigms and explanatory frameworks associated with mainstream trade union studies.

Thomas Linehan is Lecturer in History, Brunel University. He is the co-editor (with John Roberts) of the Routledge Studies in Radical History and Politics book series. His previous publications include *Modernism and British Socialism*. Palgrave Macmillan (2012), *Communism in Britain, 1920–39: From the Cradle to the Grave*. Manchester University Press (2007), *British Fascism 1918–39: Parties, Ideology and Culture*. Manchester University Press (2000), *East London for Mosley: The British Union of Fascists in East London and South-West Essex 1933–40*. Routledge (1996).

ROUTLEDGE STUDIES IN RADICAL HISTORY AND POLITICS

Series editors: Thomas Linehan, *Brunel University*, and **John Roberts**, *Brunel University*

The series *Routledge Studies in Radical History and Politics* has two areas of interest. Firstly, this series aims to publish books which focus on the history of movements of the radical left. 'Movement of the radical left' is here interpreted in its broadest sense as encompassing those past movements for radical change which operated in the mainstream political arena as with political parties, and past movements for change which operated more outside the mainstream as with millenarian movements, anarchist groups, utopian socialist communities, and trade unions. Secondly, this series aims to publish books which focus on more contemporary expressions of radical left-wing politics. Recent years have been witness to the emergence of a multitude of new radical movements adept at getting their voices in the public sphere. From those participating in the Arab Spring, the Occupy movement, community unionism, social media forums, independent media outlets, local voluntary organisations campaigning for progressive change, and so on, it seems to be the case that innovative networks of radicalism are being constructed in civil society that operate in different public forms.

The series very much welcomes titles with a British focus, but is not limited to any particular national context or region. The series will encourage scholars who contribute to this series to draw on perspectives and insights from other disciplines.

For a full list of titles in this series, please visit http://www.routledge.com/Routledge-Studies-in-Radical-History-and-Politics/book-series/RSRHP

Titles include:

Challenging Austerity
Radical Left and Social Movements in the South of Europe
Edited by Beltrán Roca, Emma Martín-Díaz and Ibán Díaz-Parra

Contemporary Trotskyism
Parties, Sects and Social Movements in Britain
John Kelly

Scabs and Traitors
Taboo, Violence and Punishment in Labour Disputes in Britain, 1760–1871
Thomas Linehan

SCABS AND TRAITORS

Taboo, Violence and Punishment in Labour Disputes in Britain, 1760–1871

Thomas Linehan

LONDON AND NEW YORK

First published 2018
by Routledge
2 Park Square, Milton Park, Abingdon, Oxon OX14 4RN

and by Routledge
711 Third Avenue, New York, NY 10017

Routledge is an imprint of the Taylor & Francis Group, an informa business

© 2018 Thomas Linehan

The right of Thomas Linehan to be identified as author of this work has been asserted by him in accordance with sections 77 and 78 of the Copyright, Designs and Patents Act 1988.

All rights reserved. No part of this book may be reprinted or reproduced or utilised in any form or by any electronic, mechanical, or other means, now known or hereafter invented, including photocopying and recording, or in any information storage or retrieval system, without permission in writing from the publishers.

Trademark notice: Product or corporate names may be trademarks or registered trademarks, and are used only for identification and explanation without intent to infringe.

British Library Cataloguing-in-Publication Data
A catalogue record for this book is available from the British Library

Library of Congress Cataloging-in-Publication Data
Names: Linehan, Thomas P., author.
Title: Scabs and traitors : taboo, violence and punishment in labour disputes in Britain, 1760-1871 / Thomas Linehan.
Description: First Edition. | New York : Routledge, 2018. | Series: Routledge radical history and politics series | Includes bibliographical references and index.
Identifiers: LCCN 2017058563| ISBN 9781138926523 (hardback) | ISBN 9781138186057 (pbk.) | ISBN 9781315680538 (ebook)
Subjects: LCSH: Labor disputes--Great Britain--History--18th century. | Labor disputes--Great Britain--History--19th century. | Labor movement--Great Britain--History 18th century. | Labor movement--Great Britain--History 19th century.
Classification: LCC HD5365.A6 L56 2018 | DDC 331.892/94109034--dc23
LC record available at https://lccn.loc.gov/2017058563

ISBN: 978-1-138-92652-3 (hbk)
ISBN: 978-1-138-18605-7 (pbk)
ISBN: 978-1-315-68053-8 (ebk)

Typeset in Bembo
by Taylor & Francis Books

To my daughter, Ciara

'And what is a Scab? He is to his trade what a traitor is to his country'
(Articles of the Friendly and United Society of Cordwainers. 4 June 1792)

CONTENTS

Acknowledgements   *x*
Abbreviations   *xii*
Preface   *xiii*

   Introduction   1
1 Blackleg economics   24
2 Tabooed persons   46
3 Vows and sacred lines   73
4 The call to arms   94
5 Carnivalesque rituals   112
6 Magic rituals and tabooed things   132
7 Shaming and degradation rituals   152
8 Retribution   178

Conclusion   212

Index   *223*

ACKNOWLEDGEMENTS

I would like to express my gratitude to the following individuals who have helped in some way in the preparation and completion of this book. To begin with, may I express my sincere thanks to the commissioning and editorial staff at Routledge for their encouragement and professionalism in supporting and assisting this project, particularly Craig Fowlie and Rebecca McPhee. I would also like to thank Emma Chappell for assisting this book project at an earlier stage of the editorial process at Routledge. I would also like to thank and acknowledge the support of Brunel University for providing me with a period of research leave to enable me to conduct much of the fieldwork and writing for this book, as well as Mark Neocleous and Matthew Seligmann for providing some constructive feedback on my initial research proposal.

I am also very grateful to Ian Thatcher and Matthew Worley, both of whom provided invaluable and incredibly constructive comments on my initial book proposal. I would also like to thank the various archivists and librarians who assisted me during my visits to their establishments. My thanks here go to those at the Archives Division of the LSE; the Bishopsgate Institute in London; the Bodleian Library; the British Library of Political and Economic Science (LSE); Brunel University Library; the Modern Records Centre at Warwick University; the National Archives at Kew; the National Library of Scotland Manuscripts Division in Edinburgh; and the National Archives of Scotland in Edinburgh.

I would also like to thank those work colleagues and friends for their much appreciated words of support and encouragement for this project along the way. These include Alison Carrol, Gareth Dale, Philip Davies, Filippo del Lucchese, Martin Folly, Stanley Gaines, Martin Hansen, John MacMillan, John March, Marian March, John Roberts, Peter Thomas, Varun Uberoi and Peter Wilkin. If I have forgotten to mention any names, I do apologise to those individuals concerned. I would also like to acknowledge the rich scholarship on Britain's trade union history. I am grateful to those historians for their painstaking efforts in helping to build this invaluable body of knowledge which greatly helped my understanding of important areas of British labour and trade union history.

Finally, I would like to thank my family for their love, support, patience and encouragement during the course of writing this book, particularly my wife, Janet, and two children, Ciara and Michael. My daughter Ciara is deserving of a special mention. She has always shown tremendous interest in this project throughout the research and writing of this book. For this unwavering support, I am exceedingly grateful and I dedicate this book to her.

ABBREVIATIONS

GNCTU	Grand National Consolidated Trades' Union
HO	Home Office, National Archives, Kew
ILP	Independent Labour Party
LSE	London School of Economics
MRC	Modern Records Centre, University of Warwick
NAS	National Archives of Scotland, Edinburgh
SDF	Social Democratic Federation

PREFACE

The history of Britain's trade unions between 1760 and 1871, the period covered by this book, is in many respects a history of the struggle of Britain's labouring classes to adapt to a rapidly changing economic, technological, spatial and temporal environment during a phase of history when traditional structures and boundaries in society had become particularly unstable and precarious. This struggle took many forms. These included the struggle to adapt to the arrival of de-skilling machinery and a labour market in seemingly constant flux, the struggle against emerging philosophies which clearly favoured the masters and capital over labour, and the struggle against unjust and punitive laws arising from a legislature which seemed in thrall to the new economic and individualistic doctrines of the age. All of the above will feature at various stages in this book. However, there was another very important struggle in this period which forms the principal subject of this book, and is one which has not always received the detailed attention it deserves in earlier histories of Britain's trade unions. This is the struggle of those workers who believed that the effort to improve the wages and conditions of labour was best undertaken as a collective endeavour to overcome what they felt to be one of the principal obstacles to collective action, the uncooperative worker. The term 'uncooperative worker' is of course a euphemism. To the collectively inclined workman, the uncooperative worker was a scoundrel and a traitor to his brethren, trade and community. The former expressed their disapprobation of the latter's behaviour by assigning him an array of epithets such as 'scab', 'rat', 'blacksheep', 'knobstick', 'black-neb' and 'blackleg', the use of which was intended to convey intense disapproval and even disgust.

This struggle between the collectively inclined worker and the uncooperative worker during these decades was invariably acrimonious, frequently coercive, often ugly, and occasionally violent and bloody. Indeed, violence became one of the dominant frames through which this relationship has been understood and portrayed in both contemporary mainstream commentary and some later influential scholarly literature. In saying this, and as this book will seek to demonstrate, the interpersonal violence on display during these decades was never straightforward, uniform, or one-dimensional. Without question, acts of violence committed against non-compliant workmen could on occasions be unequivocally direct, physical and uncompromising, which bring to mind punishments meted out to deserters or traitors in times of war. At other times though, the measures used to encourage compliance with collective norms could be hedged in with caution and restraint. On such occasions, the anger felt towards offending workmen and the aggressive behaviour which flowed from this resentment could be consciously stylised and mediated through ritual.

Offering an exploration of a controversial topic in labour history outside the comfort zone of many of the standard histories of British trade unionism, this book will appeal to a wide audience. This includes specialist scholars and postgraduates working in the field of labour and trade union history, and undergraduate students studying courses or modules which deal with modern British history or the broader themes of social and political unrest, conflict and violence. This book will also appeal to anyone interested in the history of labour relations in Britain.

INTRODUCTION

Broadly speaking, this book is about the attempt by workers in Britain during the period 1760–1871 to engage in collective action in circumstances of conflict with their employers during a time when the nation was undergoing rapid and unsettling economic, industrial and technological change. More specifically, the aim of this book is to explore the efforts by those workers favouring a collective approach to struggle to overcome what they felt to be one of the principal obstacles to collective action, the uncooperative worker. The term 'uncooperative worker' is of course a euphemism. To the workmen who felt that the struggle to improve the conditions and wages of labour was best undertaken as a collective endeavour, the uncooperative worker was a scoundrel and a traitor to his brethren, trade and community. As such, the former expressed their disgust at the latter's behaviour by assigning him an array of disagreeable epithets such as 'miscreant', 'blacksheep', 'scab', 'rat', 'knobstick' and 'blackleg'. But more of this later.[1]

The non-compliant worker came in a number of forms and guises. Most obviously, he was the fellow who refused to join his brethren during a turnout. In other, though related, circumstances, he was the workman who undercut his brethren by accepting work below that of an agreed, established or sought-after price or wage, whether during turnouts or in other situations where 'speculation' on the price of labour was rife and unregulated.[2] In some trades, as with stonemasonry for example, a workman could also incur the displeasure of the union Lodge if he engaged in acts which contravened the union's 'laws' and codes of conduct regarding working practices, such as taking work by the piece, procuring sub-contracted work, agreeing to work by candle light, or working 'over hours', the latter of which could include working beyond 4.00pm on Saturdays (on the latter three misdeeds, see MRC. Friendly Society of Operative Stonemasons of England, Ireland and Wales. MSS.78/OS/4/1/6/45–8. Fortnightly Return.

16–30 Nov. 1843; MSS.78/OS/4/1/1/284–7. Fortnightly Return. 17–31 Aug. 1838; and MSS.78/OS/4/1/10. Fortnightly Return. 19 July–7 Aug. 1849).[3] Other modes of behaviour could also be deemed objectionable, such as when an individual avoided paying union contributions, or obstinately refused to join the union Society.

An uncooperative worker could hail from within the shop, works, factory, trade or community, or he could be a 'new hand' who came from afar to fill a position vacated by a striking worker during a turnout. Nor, it should be said, were undercutting workers and strike-breakers exclusively male. Not infrequently in Britain's evolving industrial economy during the early decades of the nineteenth century, the masters, often cynically, sought to undercut, or replace altogether, skilled male workers with cheaper female labour, including in strike situations (Clark 1995: 133–40).[4]

During the decades covered by this book, there was general unanimity within the ranks of collectively inclined workers that the uncooperative worker presented a serious problem in matters relating to wages and conditions of work. Many union-inclined workers also believed that a workman of this type represented their most dangerous adversary in a world of work that was abounding with new challenges and multiple threats to the very idea of union itself. Let us listen to a few voices from this era from one union alone, the Operative Stonemasons' Society. For the then Secretary of the Society, Angus McGregor, writing in June 1836, 'refractory' members such as those who refused to pay their union arears, or engaged in actions contrary to union 'rules', 'act in open and avowed hostility to our Union'. As such, 'those miscreants who thus oppose us are our most powerful enemies, and either directly or indirectly occasion the principal part of our expenditure, and are the only weapons in the hands of a tyrant by which he can oppress us' (MRC. Friendly Society of Operative Stonemasons. MSS.78/OS/4/1/1/79–81. Fortnightly Return. 9–23 June 1836). The same message could be heard over ten years later, when in June 1848 the stonemasons' union opined that 'our greatest opponents are a set of unprincipled characters, who dare not stand up for their undoubted rights' (MRC. Friendly Society of Operative Stonemasons. MSS.78/OS/4/1/10. Fortnightly Return. 25 May–8 June 1848).

Blackleg labour drafted in from other places to defeat a turnout, or 'Blacks' in the language of the stonemasons' union, were deemed to represent the most serious problem. When, in October 1836, a building contractor in Huddersfield, Yorkshire, 'placarded the town and surrounding country for a number of good, steady men, unconnected to the Union' to defeat a strike of masons in the town, it was evident to the then Society Secretary, James Rennie, that the contractor's 'motive for introducing the Blacks was to undermine the power of his men and make them suppliant to any infringement he might think proper to impose on them' (MRC. Friendly Society of Operative Stonemasons. MSS.78/OS/4/1/1/103–5. Fortnightly Return. 30 Sept.–14 Oct. 1836). Similar concerns about the effect of blackleg labour were expressed a decade later by the Scottish United Operative Masons:

There were a great number of utterly shameless scoundrels scattered over the country, who on every assertion of right involving a collision with our employers, threw themselves on us crushing us and impeding our movements, or went bodily over to our oppressors assisting might and main in our overthrow.
(Extract from the Scottish United Operative Masons' Circular. Cited in MRC. Friendly Society of Operative Stonemasons. MSS.78/OS/4/1/6/214–4. Fortnightly Return. 2–16 Oct. 1845)

While there was general unanimity as to the threat to wages, working conditions and the union ideal posed by the uncooperative worker, there was less unanimity as to how to deal with the problem. One response was to use 'kindness' and 'moral persuasion' in an attempt to win over uncooperative workmen. Take the following example from the Iron Moulders' union in 1851. At one level, the Iron Moulders' Society recognised the serious threat to union posed by non-Society strike-breakers in particular. As the Chairman of the Executive Committee put it:

How often have we been struggling with our employers against oppression, and in many instances with every rational appearance of success, when just on the point of gaining what we have been struggling for, the non-clubman has stepped in, and at once put aside all the good we had already achieved, and debarred us from any further progress for some time in that direction.
(MRC. MSS.41/FSIF/4/2/7. The Twenty-Eighth Half-Yearly Report of the Friendly Society of Iron Moulders of England, Ireland and Wales. From 7 Jan. to 7 July 1851)

This being recognised, the Society's Executive Committee urged unionised workers to be magnanimous in their dealings with 'non-clubmen'. Thus, in order to accomplish the crucial task of winning the latter over to the cause of union:

let us excite their respect for us by acts of kindness and acts of sympathy for aggressions made upon us by them, and by so doing we shall break down the hardness of their obstinacy, and bring them into the Society. Acts of kindness and moral feeling will do more towards their subjugation than all the physical force that can be applied.
(MRC. MSS.41/FSIF/4/2/7. The Twenty-Eighth Half-Yearly Report of the Friendly Society of Iron Moulders of England, Ireland and Wales. From 7 Jan. to 7 July 1851)

The leadership of other unions also favoured moral persuasion over other more aggressive forms of enticement. Hence the same year, 1851, the leadership of the Amalgamated Society of Engineers commended the tactics adopted by their brethren in Leeds during a labour dispute in the town. Apparently the Leeds unionists were of the view 'that the moral influence at their command is much more powerful than lawless violence can be; and they denounce the conduct of men who, to satisfy a personal vindictiveness, would bring them into disrespect with their fellows' (MRC. MSS.259/ASE/4/1/1. Amalgamated Society of Engineers. Monthly Report for December 1851). Others were of the view that 'miscreant' workmen would be won over to the cause of collective endeavour by being made aware of the eminent reasonableness of the union project itself. According to this narrative, the 'sun' of union would shine the light of reason, truth and natural justice to dispel the 'darkness' caused by ignorance and self-interested behaviour. An example of such thinking can be seen from the following sentiment expressed by the Executive Committee (EC) of the London Society of Compositors in March 1834. Criticising those trade unions that relied for their 'success' on 'physical force', 'cunning' and 'brutal strength', the compositors' EC instead urged the artisans of England to eschew such methods and 'employ only the irresistible weapons of truth and reason' to advance the cause of unionism (MRC. MSS.28/CO/1/8/1/1. Report of the General Trade Committee to the Compositors of London. 4–11 Mar. 1834).

As can be seen above, in all such responses rank-and-file unionists were urged to turn their back on physical violence. Even in the midst of the heightened tension of a turnout, the leadership of unions frequently spoke out against the use of violence by their fellow unionists. It is well known that the highly regarded leader of the Lancashire cotton spinners, John Doherty, was 'strongly opposed to violence, advocating moderation, respect for employers and compliance with the laws' (Kirby and Musson 1975: 32). So, too, with Thomas Hepburn, the respected leader of the mineworkers of the Tyne and Wear during the efforts to establish unionism in the region's coalfields in the early 1830s. Hepburn's exhortations to striking pitmen during the strike of 1831 to abstain from violence were reiterated at every gathering 'with almost wearisome emphasis' (Hammond 1995: 35). Indeed, one does not have to look long and hard in the written record to find instances of trade union leaders and union committees during strike situations condemning violence or urging unionists to refrain from violence.[5]

All the above being said, there was another response to the issue of uncooperative workmen which forms the essence of this book. On some occasions, this response emanated from the formal leadership of the workers' combination, while on other occasions the impetus came from the rank-and-file members of the collective. At the core of this response was the conviction that the most effective and sometimes only means of ensuring correct behaviour on the part of uncooperative workmen was compulsion and a system of penalties to punish wrongdoing. In this regard, observe the following argument from September 1836 by the Secretary of the stonemasons' union, Angus McGregor, where he outlines the case for compulsion and punishments in regard to uncooperative workmen during strikes, which included those who deliberately evaded paying strike contributions:

> [We] state with regret, that there are members who would pay nothing unless compelled to do so, and they have only to refer to the strikes at Preston,

Liverpool, Blackburn, and lately at Bury, as a proof of this statement. The fact is, that in general those who do not pay are our decided enemies, and we find, that impelled by a strange infatuation their ranks present the only formal barrier to the success of our cause. The Blacks cost us nearly all the expense of strikes, and cause our defeat in all cases of defeat. They ruin themselves as well as the Union. We have therefore a right to compel them to abandon a course of procedure so hurtful to society; for the principle on which the welfare of every community depends is, that the general rights of its members being protected by equitable laws, the observance of which is inculcated by reason and justice, while the experience of all ages testifies the universality of punishing the aggressions of individuals against the general rights of society, hence it is our undeniable right to prevent Masons from persisting in conduct which ruins the Masons' trade. Experience has shewn [sic], that there are Masons who will not act as they ought unless compelled; and further that compulsion has the effect of causing their adherence to their duty, even when persuasion and reason will not, for the state of the Union where it flourishes is mainly attributable to the strict enforcement of its rules and penalties.

(MRC. Friendly Society of Operative Stonemasons. MSS.78/OS/4/1/ 1/94–6. Fortnightly Return. 18 Aug.–1 Sept. 1836)

Lest we think these sentiments peculiar to Angus McGregor alone, let us listen to a later Secretary of the masons' union, James Rennie, in June 1837. 'We', the stonemasons' Society, he asserted:

consider a man who has the turpitude to discomfit those who are supporting his rights ought to suffer the full penalty of his transgression, whenever we have the power of compelling him, and thereby teach the dastardly miscreants that whatever time may elapse before they are brought to justice we will not allow them to escape their just reward.

(MRC. Friendly Society of Operative Stonemasons. MSS.78/OS/4/1/1 /169–72. Fortnightly Return. 9–23 June 1837)

Lest we think as well that such sentiments were peculiar to the stonemasons' union alone, note the following from the Secretary of the Filesmiths' Union, Henry Cutts, a view he expressed in April 1862: 'No state of society that I ever heard of could exist together without regulations, and more or less of coercion made use of to enforce them' (*Sheffield Independent*, 8 Apr. 1862: 6. See also Downing 2013: 177). As to those workmen who would not comply with the spirit of union or pay his union dues, Cutts added that: 'I say honestly that I would use a certain amount of force to make him comply in a reasonable manner' (*Sheffield Independent*, 8 Apr. 1862: 6).

In regard to the wider universe of Britain's trade unions in this era, acts of coercion and punishment could take many forms. In terms of coercion, this could be quite indirect and understated. In this regard, it could involve the adoption of military-like rituals such as the muster 'by the list' in an effort to build unity and discipline in the collective and to ensure that all held fast to their place in the ranks in times of the most acute conflict with the employer. In terms of punishments, this could involve quite straightforward penalties such as punitive fines or expulsion from the union. This could also involve more controversial measures, such as the use of a range of shaming punishments to encourage compliant behaviour. At its most extreme, and despite the best efforts of some union leaderships to steer unionists onto a different path, acts of coercion and punishment could sometimes entail the use of direct physical violence against non-compliant workmen. The issue of interpersonal violence of this nature has proved to be a quite delicate topic in labour history scholarship. Indeed, some strands of trade union scholarship have tended to suggest that violence of this kind was something external to the authentic history of Britain's trade unions, that it did not form a part of trade unionism's 'true' history. This viewpoint has proved to be quite resilient in this earlier scholarship, so it is worth examining it and the assumptions on which it is based at greater length.

In some of these earlier classic trade union histories, there was a tendency to view the formative period of trade unionism through the prism of an over-arching 'grand narrative' of political development. This grand narrative sketched a line of continuity between these earlier forms and the eventual emergence of labour institutions into the mainstream of British politics, culminating in the formation of the Labour Party (examples of this earlier historiography would include Webb and Webb 1920; Cole 1948; Pelling 1963; and Pelling 1965). In so doing, these grand narrative histories were prone to look at the more fractious early history of workers' struggle through the lens of these later developments. Those adopting such evolutionary perspectives too often assumed that the emergence of 'legal' trade unionism into the mainstream was somehow pre-determined and inevitable, being the inescapable consequence of an unfolding sequence of historical circumstances which logically favoured the advance of labour.

One by-product of this teleological, historicist approach was the tendency to view some forms of labour militancy in these earlier disputes as exhibiting pre-modern traits, behavioural characteristics thought to be fundamentally at odds with responsible, rational and peaceful trade unionism or even the mainstream, liberal values of the age. Thus, the more aggressive methods employed by unionists in these earlier labour disputes, such as acts of violence against non-compliant workmen, were viewed as the regrettable by-product of an earlier more barbaric time and an earlier more primitive phase of labour agitation. Hence, when welcoming the decline in the 'crude' labour violence that he felt had particularly marred the decades prior to the 1840s, which involved acts of violence against non-union 'knobsticks', 'rats' and 'blacklegs', and its replacement with the peaceful, constitutional collective bargaining of late nineteenth and early twentieth-century trade unionism, Albert E. Musson saw this as 'part of the progress from primitive barbarism to a more civilised society' (Musson 1972: 14–5).

Even when violence against non-compliant workmen was again in evidence during the 1850s and 1860s in the Manchester brickmaking trade and the light metal trades in Sheffield, the latter involving the blowing up of a workman's home with gunpowder, this was viewed as a hangover or residue from that earlier more violent age of labour agitation, an unfortunate and unwelcome echo of those times (on the 'Sheffield Outrages', see Downing 2013). To the Webbs, for example, the 'criminality' on display during the 'Outrages' in Manchester and Sheffield represented 'the survival among such rough and isolated trades as the brickmakers and grinders of the barbarous usages of a time when working men felt themselves outside the law, and oppressed by tyranny' (Webb and Webb 1920: 269). For the Webbs, the task for the 'enlightened and respectable' moderate 'New Model' unionism that they felt had come into focus during the 1860s therefore, was to disassociate itself from the 'the ignorant turbulence of the old-fashioned unions' along with the 'outrage-mongers' in their ranks (Webb and Webb 1920: 264).

On occasions, the scholarship has claimed that the physical violence on show during the labour disputes of the middle decades of the nineteenth century had its roots in an even earlier age. Thus, when chastising England's weavers for their acts of 'pointless physical violence' during the late 1830s, which involved incidents of interpersonal violence, Duncan Bythell saw these 'old-fashioned' modes of action as 'a throwback to the disorganised activities of a pre-industrial age, and not a forerunner of modern collective bargaining' (Bythell 1969: 180).

The relationship between the collectively inclined worker and the uncooperative worker has been comprehended in related, though still other ways. In these particular characterisations, the highly fractious relationship between the two parties is depicted as a reflection of rudimentary and unsophisticated forms of workers' action, of a trade unionism in its infancy. In other words, the tendency towards violent behaviour on the part of collectively inclined workmen is represented as a form of behaviour emanating from groups of workers in trades and industries where permanent union organisation had not yet been established (these attitudes can be discerned in Pelling 1963: 27 and 40–1). Charles Tilly, too, was apt to characterise earlier forms of workers' collective action as unsophisticated (see Tilly 1995). As such, aggressive and particularly violent behaviour towards non-compliant workmen is portrayed as being unrepresentative, as being outside the realm of formal or 'real' trade unionism and destined to disappear once workers 'had acquired the discipline and training in trade-union principles' (Pelling 1963: 41). Hence, as Adrian Randall has pointed out, historians like Malcolm Thomis were inclined to explain such violence as being due to an absence of effective trade union machinery, which apparently would have acted to contain the aggression and divert it down more formal channels (see Thomis 1970; and Randall 1982). Again, the image of the early nineteenth-century labouring classes thus presented is that of 'industrial primitives' who had not yet quite progressed to the next, more mature and rational stage of a modern trade union consciousness.

Another, though related, narrative is to suggest that collective violence directed at non-compliant workmen is not only an unfortunate symptom of a more primitive age or a more rudimentary trade unionism but is also indicative of an individual, when engaged in collective action, reverting backward to a more primitive condition. Thus, Duncan Bythell put the many and numerous acts of 'riot' and 'pointless physical violence' engaged in by England's weavers during labour unrest in the late 1830s down to the unreasonableness of the weavers themselves:

> Such pathetic demonstrations were the admission of weakness by men in the last extremes of demoralisation and incapable of pursuing a course of industrial bargaining with their employers. This aimless, despairing, desultory violence of the last years of handloom weaving was epitomised in such events as the riot in Colne in June 1837, when a crowd of unemployed weavers attacked a few of their fellows who had had the good fortune to obtain a little work.
> (Bythell 1969: 181)

As well as being present in some segments of labour history, this equating of workers' collective action with acts of 'mindless' and essentially irrational violence can be observed in much of the contemporary commentary on the workers' combinations of the era covered by this book. Indeed, in this contemporary mainstream discourse, the theme of mindless irrational violence became one of the dominant frames through which workers in collective action has been understood and portrayed. During this period it became routine for members of the governing and employing classes, the intellectual elite, and the mainstream press to bracket workers in combination with 'unreasonable' extreme violence to such an extent that all forms of workers' collective action became virtually synonymous with terrorism. Adam Smith, for example, in his *magnum opus*, the *Wealth of Nations* (1776), had the following to say on workers' combinations. Whether the aim of these combinations be offensive or defensive, Smith opined, 'in order to bring the point to a speedy decision, they have always recourse to the loudest clamour, and sometimes to the most shocking violence and outrage' (Smith 1904: 60–1).

Even when the notorious 1799–1800 Combination Acts were eventually repealed in 1824, the issue of workers' collective action and violence continued to engage the attention of mainstream commentators (regarding 'The Combination Acts of 1799 and 1800', see Cole and Filson 1967: 90–3). Lurid accounts of extreme and unreasonable union violence were commonplace. In late 1825 a contributor to *Blackwood's Edinburgh Magazine* complained that since the repeal of the Combination Acts, the system of combination 'has been rendered more pernicious, the demands of the workmen have been more unreasonable' and 'outrages' and 'atrocious murders' have increased in number (*Blackwood's Edinburgh Magazine*, Oct. 1825: 463). According to another contemporary voice, this from 1831, trade union rules in regard to the workman were not voluntary but were 'enforced by threats and terror, by blows, maiming, and murder' (The Society for the Diffusion of Useful Knowledge: 6).[6] The same year, the prominent political economist Nassau William Senior submitted a report to the then Home Secretary Lord Melbourne on the subject of combinations and strikes, with particular stress on their relationship to trade, commerce and the law. The most material portions of this report would eventually form part of the Royal Commission of Inquiry into the Condition of the Hand-Loom Weavers in England and Wales of 1837–41. The expanded report as eventually appeared in the later Royal Commission Inquiry report expressed in the most lurid language Nassau Senior's hostility towards workers' combinations and particularly the methods used by unionists to secure loyalty within their own ranks (the report featured in Senior 1865: 116–72). According to Senior, workers in combination direct against such workmen that pursue a contrary path, or do not fall in line, 'the dread of bodily sufferings more severe than those which any civilised tribunal inflicts' (Senior 1865: 119). The 'obnoxious workmen' so defined thus 'suffer in their persons the punishments rising from simple assaults to blinding with vitriol and beating to death' (Senior 1865: 118).

The vituperative tone of much of this commentary had hardly eased during the later Victorian decades. Reflecting back on the trade unionism of the 1830s, a writer in the *Edinburgh Review* in October 1859 referred to the sanction of 'torture and murder' deployed by unionists in that decade, which apparently involved 'burning out a man's eyes, or breaking his bones, or shooting him in the back' (*Edinburgh Review*, Oct. 1859: 526). As Patrick Brantlinger informed us, such was the extent of Victorian middle-class anxiety about trade unions that a stream of invective against combinations and the related phobia of working-class insurrectionary violence can be discerned in a number of works of Victorian fiction and political polemic, albeit with varying degrees of intensity. These works included Thomas Carlyle's *Chartism* (1839), Elizabeth Gaskell's *Mary Barton* (1848), Charlotte Brontë's *Shirley* (1849), Benjamin Disraeli's *Sybil* (1849), and Charles Reade's *Put Yourself in his Place* (1870) (Brantlinger 1969).

As we have seen above, such negative representations of workers in collective action during this earlier era of trade unionism have proved resilient in some later scholarly studies and many contemporary accounts, so it is worth exploring some of the assumptions underpinning these views. In all such interpretations there is a tendency to stress the supposedly negative traits of 'crowds' or 'mobs' and acts of collective behaviour. Such assumptions cannot be disentangled from the wider culture and political horizon associated with the period covered by this book. As Clive Emsley has pointed out, a new perspective began to dominate the thinking of elites and the rising middle classes in Britain in the early nineteenth century, which inclined these groups to look with contempt on those engaged in acts of collective violence. This perspective was partly rooted in emerging discourses associated with ideas concerning rational behaviour, propriety and self-restraint, and was partly borne of the fear of the supposedly barbarous violence unleashed by the French revolutionary 'mob'. These ideas and fears would help spawn a mind-set which tended to characterise collective violence as a form of behaviour engaged in by primitives and deviants who operated outside the mainstream of civilised society (Emsley 2005: 12 and 107). In all such characterisations, the rights and values of the individual trumped those of the collective or the 'mob'. This situation had barely eased in the later decades of the nineteenth century as the highly individualistic 'Victorian values' of respectability, self-help, temperate behaviour, earnestness and respect for law and order became the common currency of the bourgeois middle-class code of behaviour (on 'Victorian values' more generally, see Sigsworth 1988).

In all such accounts, these negative traits are said to be much in evidence when these so-called mobs make their appearance in times of heightened socio-economic and political tension, as during incidents of labour unrest in the case of the former. One variant of this perspective is to depict the 'mobs' which materialised during times of conflict as inherently chaotic, disorderly, unstable, as somehow indicative of a reversion backward to a more primitive condition and mode of behaviour (for a critique of such views, see Davis 1973). Another variant maintained that a collective gathering when roused to anger was a reflection of the low level of intelligence of its constituent elements. According to the final report of the 1867 Royal Commission of Inquiry into trade unions, acts of labour violence, as committed by miners in Wales, Wigan and Derbyshire during the middle decades of the nineteenth century, 'appear when a rude population has been brought to a pitch of irritation' and that these 'riots of a rough population' are 'proofs of an unhappily low state of intelligence, and of an unsettled industrial condition' (*Eleventh and Final Report of the Royal Commissioners Appointed to Inquire into the Organisation and Rules of Trades Unions and Other Associations. Volume 1.* 1869: xxxiv).

Certain explanations emanating from the discipline of psychology may help shed additional light on the persistence of negative characterisations of crowds and collective behaviour in contemporary mainstream anti-trade-union discourse and some segments of labour history. For instance, some pathological and deprivation theories of collective violence have claimed that crowd behaviour, particularly if this took a violent form, was a product of individuals acting out their frustration and aggression. In such frustration-aggression models of collective violence, which seemed overly concerned with the psychological makeup of the individuals who made up the collective gathering, it was too readily assumed that violence was a product of individual or collective pathology, even madness, and was most certainly irrational (for a critique of this approach, see Snyder and Kelly 1976; and Mider 2013). As such, violence was deemed to be a digression from standard behaviour, an aberration from the norm. At other times, the supposed psychopathology and violent leanings of crowds has been put down to something akin to a 'group mind' acting on individuals participating in mass gatherings which renders them susceptible to the manipulative designs of the more cunning or aggressive members of the crowd, in our case supposedly manipulative trade union leaders. We can obtain a glimpse of such thinking as applied to purportedly 'dictatorial' trade union delegates manipulating gullible rank-and-file unionists from the following account from the 1830s on the subject of workers' combinations:

> Selected at moments of party excitement, of rancorous feelings, of raised expectations – the brawler, the factious man, the specious scoundrel, have too often become the dictators of the misguided people, and to maintain their evil pre-eminence, they [the union delegates] have spared no pains to distort and

garble facts, to blacken and destroy the reputation of the masters, and to keep open the breach from which they alone can derive advantage.

(Gaskell 1836: 274)

In such perspectives, which tend to resurrect 'the ghost of Gustave Le Bon', it is claimed, or at least implied, that individuals on entering the crowd are highly vulnerable to 'mass suggestion' and too readily yield to the irrational, impulsive and aggressive side of their nature (for a critique of such approaches, see Senechal de la Roche 1996). Those who subscribed to this view of crowds and crowd behaviour were also inclined to claim that individuals could lose their sense of moral perspective in a crowd, as individual personalities dissolved into the 'mass'.

Some strands of thought of a more sociological persuasion also viewed the collective violence emanating from mobs or crowds as irrational, as a 'wrong turn' or departure from an essentially harmonious, ordered and efficiently functioning social structure. Again, collective violence is cast as an aberration from the norm, engaged in by marginal, socially isolated, disturbed or anomic persons at odds with society and its system of values and laws (see Sewell 1990 for a critique of these particular sociological perspectives). Such negative judgements extended to theories of collective movements and behaviour more generally, as with Smelser's theory that collective behaviour was engaged in by irrational actors in thrall to generalised beliefs who opt to circumvent society's more formal institutional channels for change (Smelser 1962. For a critique of Smelser's position, see Buechler 1993: 218). In a related sense, crowd behaviour when it becomes aggressive or lapses into violence is viewed through these particular sociological perspectives as a form of deviancy, which is judged to be not only unwelcome, misguided and unreasonable, but blameworthy and criminally inclined (Senechal de la Roche 1996: 99–100).

Taking all of the varied strains of contemporary commentary and later scholarship discussed above into account, it is important at this point to set out the position adopted by this book. Before this is done, it is important to flag up that some scholars of labour history, some of these studies having been influenced by the work of E.P. Thompson in particular, have approached the question of labour violence in Britain during the decades covered by this book with a much greater degree of understanding and sensitivity (examples of this scholarship include Chase 2012; Downing 2013; Linebaugh 2003; Navickas 2011a, 2011b; and Randall 1982. Regarding Thompson, see Thompson 1968; and Thompson 1971). In these histories, much of the labour violence of this period can hardly be viewed as irrational or deviant. Thus, in analysing the 'moral economy' of food riots in eighteenth-century England gradually giving way to the laws of the political economy of the unregulated free market, Thompson argued that those participating in crowd action in this period did so in the belief that their actions had a moral legitimacy which was rooted in the understanding that they were upholding traditional rights and customs supported by the wider community (Thompson 1971). Moral considerations of a similar nature were also discerned in contemporary labour disputes. According to Clive Emsley, weavers in eighteenth-century Gloucestershire 'moved easily from food riots to industrial action and back. In both kinds of protest their actions suggest elements of the thinking associated with the moral economy' (Emsley 2005: 105). In a similar vein, for Adrian Randall the industrial violence of the journeymen shearmen of the west of England during the labour unrest of 1802 was 'specifically directed against men who in the workers' eyes were engaging in immoral and illegal practices' (Randall 1982: 302).

In terms of the position taken by this book, it is important to point out in the first instance that this book distances itself from those lurid and alarmist accounts stemming from contemporary mainstream commentary of the type referred to in the paragraphs above, whereby all forms of workers' collective action became virtually synonymous with extreme mob violence, riot and terrorism. That being said, this book recognises that compulsion did play some part in the attempt by collectively inclined workmen to maintain unity in the ranks and ensure that all complied with collective norms. It also recognises that on occasions this involved acts of direct physical violence against uncooperative workmen. In stating this, this book sees the acts of compulsion in the various forms they assumed as a fundamental and intrinsic part of the history of Britain's trade unions. In other words, it does not view the inclination to forcefully bring waverers into line or punish strike-breakers, even when this assumed a violent form, as an aberrant phenomenon somehow unconnected to the 'true' history of trade unionism. These more aggressive forms of persuasion should thus not be relegated to the status of a passing footnote in the history of the struggle of collectively inclined working people to advance the cause of labour unions in Britain during those formative decades of growth.

As the reader will see in the following chapters, while being rightly critical of some of the violent methods used by collectively inclined workmen to address the threat posed by the uncooperative workman, this book adopts a more empathetic approach when seeking to understand the motivations of those engaged in such actions. As such, this book aims to give a qualitative sense of the experiences and challenges faced by working people as they sought to maintain a living wage at a time when the price of labour was determined almost exclusively by the master and when a hostile legislature had, in the eyes of the worker, unequivocally lined up on the side of the latter. Given these difficult circumstances, it would have been remarkable if some degree of compulsion and violent confrontation did not play some part in labour relations during the decades between 1760 and 1871. To take the circumstances of the law and employer-worker relations alone, the belief that the legislature was failing them and that they had no recourse to formal legal sanctions to redress grievances was a recurring motif in the response of union-inclined workmen to the new circumstances in the world of work and labour relations brought about by the new impersonal, market-driven economics of political economy. Let us listen to a voice from the time on this matter. In April 1834 the trade union newspaper *The Tradesman* had the following to say on the nature of the legislature and the law as applied to the nation's labouring classes:

> A corrupt legislature and wicked laws, have made it next to impossible for us to emancipate ourselves without coming in contact with some cruel enactment, which either stops us altogether, or comes upon us with the fury of revenge.... You are so situated that to move either hand or foot becomes fatal to you; and not to move is to sink into the most horrible state of slavery and suffering that can be conceived.
>
> (The Tradesman, *19 Apr. 1834: 2*)

This reluctance on the part of the legislature to temper the structural violence visited upon workers' livelihoods and communities by the new economics was well understood by the late-nineteenth-century socialist Annie Besant. For Besant, the English worker in the early decades of that century had:

> reached the nadir of political and social degradation. He was voiceless in the State, a bond-slave in industrial life. Gripped by the law of settlement, his wages fixed by those who lived on his labour, forbidden to associate with his fellows for his own improvement, gagged if he tried to advise with his mates on the conditions of their labour, he was ringed round by laws that bruised him at his lightest movement. The Government was his tyrant. The law his worst enemy.
>
> (Besant 1890: 10)

The plight of Scottish, Welsh and Irish labour in particular during the same decades was hardly better, it should be said. Miners in Scotland up to the process of emancipation, which began in 1775, for instance, worked in conditions of virtual serfdom under the yoke of the long-service bond, whereby they even formed part of the capital invested in the work and could be sold by the master as such (Trant 1884: 22). In some mining districts in Scotland, the children of miners could also be drawn into servitude (Raynes 1928: 20).

In such circumstances, where there was a perceived void in the law and where the legislature was seen to have clearly aligned itself with capital, the masters, and non-union workmen, many in the beleaguered labouring classes, brought forth their own system of regulation and justice to fill the vacuum. This proposition should not startle us. To the workers' mind, there was an absence of a properly functioning legal system to regulate the labour market and mediate disagreements between unionised workmen and workmen averse to collective action in a considered and balanced manner which took account of the concerns of the former. In addition, history has shown us on many past occasions that subaltern groups in a range of different national contexts have turned to extra-legal actions in an effort to remedy perceived wrongs and thereby compensate for deficiencies in the official law of the land (in relation to rural subaltern groups, see for example Frank 1987; and Simms 1978).

In regard to the labouring classes which feature in this book, it needs to be recognised that the informal justice that they fell back on in times of crisis was never a single unified 'system' in any formal sense. Rather, it came in many forms and guises and could be shaped by a variety of factors, which included local traditions, customs peculiar to the trade, the 'laws' of a particular union Society, and the particular circumstances of the moment. Nevertheless, as with the formal mainstream legal system, this alternative system of justice and 'law' enforcement had certain features recognisable in a system of law in all its various forms. For instance, in the broadest sense, this system provided a regulatory framework to maintain the stability of the social structure or society and ensure individual and collective compliance with the society's core values and norms of behaviour, the 'society' in this case being the trade and working community. It should be said in this regard that no effective legal system seeking to uphold the values and norms of the social structure can function without attempting to bring forth modes of behaviour consistent with these standards. At the same time, it would be naïve to imagine that such a system could function effectively without some measure of compulsion to ensure compliance with the core standards of the social structure.

As you will see in this book, this informal 'system' of popular justice included a range of measures and penalties to deter potential wrongdoers, discourage bad habits, impart moral lessons, and retributively punish those behaviours adjudged to have seriously violated these standards. It could embrace quite indirect methods of deterrence, such as the recourse to the use of binding and mystical oaths of allegiance to forewarn individuals of the implications of wrongdoing. There was even scope for the rehabilitation of offenders. Thus in June 1838 the stonemasons' union inform us that a mason in Carlisle who had erred by 'going to work in opposition to our society' was welcomed back into the union fold as a result of having 'paid all the demands our society had against him' (MRC. Friendly Society of Operative Stonemasons. MSS.78/OS/4/1/1/267–70. Fortnightly Return. 8–22 June 1838). Indeed, all such measures and penalties involved a rite of passage format which sought to bring about a transformed status in the offender. To a large extent, it was this broader quasi-judicial context which ensured that much of the compulsion deployed to help guarantee that all complied with collective norms would be so nuanced and varied in form. Some of the 'rules' and penalties in operation during these years would be elaborately staged and performative in that they sought to send a strong message regarding correct behaviour to the wider community. In regard to the relationship between compulsion and violence for example, we should note the important observation made by the anthropologist David Riches that all violence is a performance in that it harbours an intention to send a message to an audience (Riches 1986. See also Accomazzo 2012).

In saying the above, the approach taken in this book thus seeks to acknowledge the context, circumstances and 'situational' factors which played some part in contributing to the conflict between the collectively inclined worker and the uncooperative worker. The sometimes violent conflict that ensued between these antagonists was therefore contingent on the presence and interplay of these other factors in the wider society. By factoring in the wider structural, interactionist and social situational variables, this allows for the establishment of a more reliable framework within which to analyse the particular form of conflict that is the concern of this book (on the advantages of including these wider variables in violence research, see Zahn, Brownstein and Jackson 2015: 10). In flagging up the importance of these wider contextual and circumstantial factors, this book thus seeks to go beyond behavioural or motivational units of analysis, such as focusing on an individual's personal makeup or mind-set. As such, the approach taken in this book distances itself from those accounts, whether appearing in scholarship or in other outlets, which have been preoccupied with the supposedly negative traits of collective gatherings and behaviour.

It is here claimed, therefore, that the labour violence which preoccupies this book cannot be adequately explained by reference to the supposed backwardness, psychopathology, irrationality or innate deviancy of those who engaged in such actions. Nor can it be adequately understood by viewing those participating in these acts of collective aggression as mere dupes of manipulative and aggressively inclined leaders, in this case supposedly 'dictatorial' trade union leaders. Equally unsatisfactory is the contention that when they enter the collective gathering of the crowd, individuals somehow manage to slip down the evolutionary scale to arrive at a more infantile, irresponsible, immoral and brutal state. Seeing such gatherings as inherently chaotic, unstable and fundamentally out of control is also a barrier to greater understanding. Neither is it really helpful to view the incidents of compulsion which occurred during the labour unrest in the decades covered by this book, even when such incidents took a collective and violent form, as a primitive and reactionary phenomenon out of keeping with a society on a forward journey in the direction of modernisation, reason and peaceful progress.

It follows from all of the above, and taking account of context and circumstances in particular, that the various acts of compulsion against non-compliant workmen, even when this took an aggressive and even violent form, had a definite purpose which, from the perspective of those engaged in such acts, was decidedly rational in terms of matters of calculation and execution. In seeing the rational intent behind these acts of aggression and violence, one should acknowledge those theories of violence which define most instances of violence as intentional and instrumental acts which seek to achieve a certain aim (Thomas 2011. See also Arendt 1969: 51). Within this instrumentalist framework, violence can assume a range of forms, the most obvious being the use of direct physical violence to attain a particular aim (Thomas 2011: 1833). Undoubtedly at times, acts of compulsion against non-compliant workmen could be unambiguously direct, physical and violent, as in the overt and sometimes extreme acts of retributive violence witnessed in some turnouts in our period.[7]

Seeing all acts of coercion to ensure compliance with collective norms through the lens of direct physical violence takes our understanding only so far, however. For instance, as we will see in some of the following chapters, the careful avoidance of direct physical violence was often the norm in the turnouts in our period. As conflict behaviour theorists point out, efforts at conflict resolution, where adversaries perceive that they have conflictual or incompatible goals, can take a variety of forms and it does not necessarily follow that direct violence of a physical nature is sanctioned as a legitimate course of action in such scenarios (Demmers 2017: 6). Indeed, parties usually deploy a range of strategies in an effort to prevail in a conflict situation which seeks to avoid direct physical attacks on people. Hence, in the conflict situations that we will be looking at in this book, the strategies used to encourage compliance with collective norms could often be hedged in with caution, discretion and restraint. Here, anger and aggression would be implied, latent, deferred, mediated, regulated, bounded, and often sublimated into ritual. Indeed, as we will see in many instances in this book, ritual often provided an indispensable frame through which anger, aggression and more violent impulses could be better controlled and managed. On such occasions, the anger felt towards offending workmen and the aggressive behaviour which flowed from this resentment could be consciously stylised, and even assume the form of theatre or pantomime with its own repertoire of a villain, stylised behaviours and gestures, and accompanying props. In such scenarios, the hostility towards the other party assumed the form of parody or even play, or, to put it more precisely, anger and hostility dissipated into these latter forms.

We need to apply a similarly nuanced and flexible approach where acts of direct physical violence are concerned, too. In all such situations we need to see violence directed at uncooperative workmen during the decades between 1760 and 1871 as a sliding scale of aggression which could take multiple forms ranging from 'soft' to 'hard', with many gradations in between. The latter could include, as mentioned in relation to the 'Sheffield Outrages', acts of extreme violence like the blowing up of the home of an uncooperative workman with gunpowder, whereas the former could include acts of 'soft' violence which were mockingly jocular as when strikers threw snow-balls at 'scabs' during the 1857–9 strike of boot and shoe makers in Northamptonshire (Ball 1860: 3).[8] In short, this form of labour violence was never uniform, one-dimensional or straightforward. In terms of the need to understand violence as complex and multi-dimensional, it is also worth reflecting on the observation by Randall Collins that violence can be 'short and episodic as a slap in the face; or massive and organised as a war. It can be passionate and angry as a quarrel; or callous and impersonal as the bureaucratic administration of gas chambers' (Collins 2008: 1).

There is also a need to view violence as part of a shifting and mutating scenario, rather than as a static product. In so doing, this book identifies with that branch of scholarship which conceptualises violence as 'dynamic and processual' (Demmers 2017: 8). Also, it follows from this proposition that the path to more extreme acts of hard violence was not inevitable or pre-determined in advance. As we will see on many occasions in this book, the decision by workers to engage in more extreme acts of physical violence was often only taken when all other strategies had failed to achieve the desired outcome and a resolution to the conflict could not be achieved via more moderate means. In such a scenario of downwardly cascading tensions and options, the decision to sanction acts of more extreme violence emerged towards the latter stages of a conflict situation, at the 'eleventh hour' so to speak.

It is with some irony, therefore, that we should note that in many strike situations for instance, the more extreme forms of violence made their appearance when all reasonable hope for victory had dissipated, when the dreadful prospect of a potentially ruinous defeat for the workers' cause seemed imminent.

There is a further factor that we need to consider when analysing acts of physical violence. However disturbing to contemplate, research into violence in past times and across different cultural zones has shown that moral sentiments often underpin individual and collective motivations for engaging in acts of violence. As Fiske and Rai explain it, 'across cultures and history, most violence is morally motivated to regulate relationships in a culturally prescribed manner' and that 'people are violent when they feel that violence is necessary to constitute essential social relationships' (Fiske and Rai 2015: 16). This being said, a focus on moral imperatives only provides a partial picture of the motivational impetus behind the labour violence of our era. Certainly, the concept of 'moral economy' as discussed earlier in this Introduction, with its notions of fairness, justice and traditional rights, and its emphasis on the collective defence of custom, community and a just price, goes some way to aid understanding of the motivations of those who participated in the informal 'system' of popular justice erected by the labouring classes in this period. In order to take our understanding a step further, however, we need to go beyond straightforward moral considerations and recognise that the motivations of those administering punishment sanctions against transgressors of the collective code were varied and complex. Hence, while it seems evident that a sense of moral indignation and a desire to correct a wrong done did indeed play some role in these matters, we also need to take account of other motivational factors which seemed to grow out of more forbidding fears. Looked at from this angle, it was the dread of highly pernicious influences seeping into the community having breached sacred taboo boundaries which sometimes contributed to the decision to opt for compulsion over more moderate forms of persuasion, along with an associated impetus to stem the contagion through whatever means, however aggressive. The role played by taboo in the troubled labour relations of this period will be explored in later chapters.

There is a further dimension to the more extreme forms of violence witnessed during this period that we also need to recognise. In some strikes during this period, the violence deployed against non-compliant workmen bring to mind a society in the grip of war. Here, the violence was certainly not implied or latent, or hedged in with caution and restraint. Rather, the violence here assumed an almost military-like character in its directness, decisiveness, severity and unforgiving nature. In this respect, the motivation to bring the non-compliant into line seemed driven by a desire to punish individuals deemed to be nothing-less than traitors or cowards who had fled the field of battle and, in so doing, abandoned their comrades-in-arms in their hour of greatest need. This latter mind-set and disposition can only be properly understood by appreciating that on those occasions of the most acute tension and conflict between labour and capital during the decades under consideration in this book, organised labour saw itself as a community almost at war with its adversary. On such occasions, unionised labour effectively put itself on a war-footing in preparation for a battle of attrition and survival with a well-resourced, powerful and often uncompromising opponent.

For all his faults in seeming to promote violence, Georges Sorel is one of the very few scholars to recognise the analogy between a workers' strike and war. For Sorel, a strike was never simply about a temporary cessation of commercial relations between those disagreeing about an appropriate price for goods or for labour. Rather, for Sorel, 'the strike is a phenomenon of war' (Sorel 1941: 297). A strike brought clarity to the wider class struggle and had the capacity, particularly if tenaciously fought over a long duration, and as in situations of war, to introduce a heroic quality into the contest and even evoke an 'epic state of mind' amongst the combatants. To imagine that such a struggle, akin to war, could unfold without acts of violence being committed by both sides in the contest was naïve in the extreme for Sorel and showed a lack of understanding of the true nature of strikes. Sorel even likened the heroism, discipline and epic qualities on show in the proletarian strike to the heroic exploits and 'extraordinary enthusiasm' of the soldiers who took part in the wars of Liberty in the early stages of the French Revolution (Sorel 1941: 282–90). This analogy between soldiers in war and workers on strike is particularly apt in regard to the uncompromising stance taken by combatants in both scenarios, a war and a strike, towards those who failed to do their duty. Thus, the soldier in the revolutionary army 'was convinced that the slightest failure of the most insignificant private might compromise the success of the whole and the life of all his comrades' (Sorel 1941: 284). Accordingly, and due as well to 'the high sense of responsibility felt by the soldier about this own duties, and the extreme thoroughness with which he carried out the most insignificant order, made him approve of rigorous measures taken against men who in his eyes had brought about the defeat of the army and caused it to lose the fruit of so much heroism. It is not difficult to see that the same spirit is met with in strikes; the beaten workmen are convinced that their failure is due to the base conduct of a few comrades who have not done all that might have been expected of them' (Sorel 1941: 289). This contrast between the call of war and the person who failed to abide by the call is well illustrated by the following account of a mass picket of unionists during the 1869–70 lock-out of Thorncliffe mineworkers:

> Someone in the crowd carried a flag, on one side of which was the representation of a black sheep, surmounted by the words 'Look here at your brother'; there being on the other side a red sheep, over which was painted the word 'War'.
>
> *(The Sheffield Daily Telegraph, 14 Apr. 1869: 4)*[9]

Finally, there are still other strands to the violence that we will be looking at in this book that we should also note, some of which are not so easily traceable to a particular or clearly identifiable context, as with a context of social injustice or a skewed legal system. Thus, while acknowledging that violence should certainly not be severed from context, this should not prevent us from identifying these other strands which are less discernible to the eye and less easily traceable to an obvious source. For instance, the purpose of this violence could sometimes be cathartic for the community, allowing for a release of aggressive energy and anger and a corresponding decrease of emotional tension. This discharging of aggressive energy could act to alleviate the pressure on the system, allowing it to regulate and manage tensions more effectively, particularly during moments of profound instability and crisis, as when a working community is undergoing a phase of unsettling change.

In a similar manner, the rites of violence in labour disputes could be expiatory, as well as cathartic. To the often religiously motivated, collectively inclined workman, the uncooperative workman had betrayed his brethren. His transgressions were sinful and had shamed the trade and community. There had to be atonement and a sacrifice. By punishing the transgression therefore, the community sought to spiritually 'cleanse' itself, expiate the wrong done, which, if not addressed, threatened to 'infect' the entire social body with the contamination of self-interested conduct. Moreover, the expiatory ritual punishment of the transgressor, while exposing the sin of self-regarding behaviour to the fulsome gaze of communal judgement, stridently proclaimed the purity of the collective and in so doing sin was expunged and unity and harmony was restored to the community.

In terms of methodology, this book is eclectic in its approach, drawing on a range of thinkers, concepts and theoretical perspectives to help examine the range of matters and issues referred to above. In adopting this more nuanced approach, this book is sensitive to recent calls within labour history for the production of more histories of labour which are less reliant on the over-arching, historicist explanatory frameworks of grand narratives, such as those which feature in some of the classic heroic 'forward march of labour' histories of trade unionism mentioned earlier in this Introduction (scholars calling for this different approach include Navickas 2011b and Kirk 2012). In line with this more nuanced, time-specific approach, historians of labour history also need to be mindful of conceptual and theoretical insights generated by other scholarly disciplines. In seeking better understanding of the issues under consideration in this book, this study therefore draws on concepts and insights from disciplines such as social anthropology and cultural studies where relevant and as appropriate. In so doing, this book will seek to tease out the presence of more esoteric elements at work in the labour disputes of this period by exploring their relationship to concepts and paradigms of thought relating to sympathetic magic, sacralisation, ritual, and taboo. In relation to the latter, and as touched on above, an important contention of this book is that the alternative system of workers' popular justice in play during this period can only be properly understood by appreciating that some of its roots lay in trade and community taboos, some of which were deeply entrenched. In exploring this matter, this book will take account of the principal theories on taboo, including those emanating from the writings of Sir James Frazer, Sigmund Freud, Franz Steiner and Mary Douglas.

These invaluable theoretical perspectives aside, it should also be stressed that this book is a research monograph based on extensive work in the primary sources. During the course of the research and writing for this book, a substantial body of primary evidence was drawn from a number of archival collections in the UK. These included the manuscript records and printed materials relating to English, Scottish, Welsh and Irish trade unions held at the National Archives at Kew; the Bishopsgate Institute in London; the Archives Division of the LSE; the Bodleian Library at Oxford; the Modern Records Centre at Warwick University; the National Library of Scotland Manuscripts Division in Edinburgh; and the National Archives of Scotland in Edinburgh. Along with the archive-based materials, this study has also benefitted from being able to access various digitised online primary materials. These wonderfully accessible sources range from the Royal Commission and Commons Select Committee reports and investigations into trade unions which took place at various stages during the nineteenth century, to contemporary newspapers held by the British Newspaper Archive.

It remains to be stated that the following chapters have been arranged in such a way as to more adequately explore the main concerns of this book. Chapter 1 will consider some of the key economic, political and legislative developments of the period under investigation in order to provide an appropriate contemporary context for the chapters which follow. In particular, this chapter will consider the implication for the wages and livelihoods of Britain's labouring classes arising from the shift from a relatively regulated pre-industrial economy to the more de-regulated industrialised market economy of the late eighteenth and nineteenth century. Chapter 2 will then go on to probe more deeply into the fractious and hostile relationship between the collectively inclined workman and the unco-operative workman in this new de-regulated and highly competitive market environment. In so doing, it will seek to gain some understanding of the mind-set, sentiments and fears underpinning this hostility. Chapter 3 will then look at the various efforts of unionised workmen to shore up their defensive structures and networks against potential acts of disloyalty or betrayal in this era of rapid and unsettling economic change, such as through the recourse to emotive Christian religious rhetoric or the administering of mystical oaths. The various methods and strategies deployed by unionised workmen to help ensure unity, discipline and loyalty in the ranks during the initial and early phases of a turnout will then form the focus of Chapter 4. The remaining chapters, Chapters 5, 6, 7 and 8, will address the issue of those workers who refused to obey the initial call to arms once battle had been joined with the adversary, or who broke ranks and fled the field of battle once hostilities had got underway. To these perceived deserters we should add a more reviled foe, those adjudged to have cynically thrown in their lot with the enemy, the hated blackleg stranger from afar. As we will see in these chapters, the response of unionised workmen to these challenges emanating from within their own ranks during a time of acute strain and danger for the labouring classes was never uniform or one-dimensional. Nor is this response free of controversy, particularly when looked at from the moral standpoint of the twenty-first century and twenty-first-century trade unionism. Nevertheless, it is important that the historian should not shy away from engaging with such matters, however sensitive and unsettling.

Notes

1. See chapter 2.
2. 'Speculation' on the price of labour was certainly not uncommon during the decades when liberal political economy was in the ascendency, as in the first half of the nineteenth century.
3. The Friendly Society of Operative Stonemasons of England, Ireland and Wales was founded in 1833. For ease of reference, and to avoid excessive duplication in the notes, the Society will hereafter be referred to in the notes in those chapters which make mention of the stonemasons as the 'The Friendly Society of Operative Stonemasons'.
4. Such 'female encroachments' could sometimes lead to inexcusable instances of violence against women strike-breakers. Indeed, it took some years for the more entrenched male fraternities associated with some artisan trades to set aside traditional masculine notions of solidarity and 'overcome simple misogynist techniques of fighting women in favour of patriarchal cooperation with women' (Clark 1995: 135). A few such instances of violence towards female strike-breakers involving male cotton spinners occurred during labour disputes at mills in Glasgow in late 1824 (see *Fife Herald*, 23 Dec. 1824: 3). This being said, and as we will see in the following chapters, and as Clark also points out, women would often be at the forefront of efforts to advance trade unionism in the nineteenth century and could often be the most formidable opponents of strike-breakers.
5. In this regard, see HO42/178/111. Letter 20 July 1818, in relation to the 1818 Manchester cotton spinners' strike; HO40/19/64. Proclamation from the Committee of the Silk Weavers of Macclesfield. 28 February 1820, condemning 'riotous proceedings' in the town; HO45/5244B/97. Proclamation from the Preston Spinners' Committee, c. March 1854, which condemned 'persons violating the peace of the town' during the Preston lock-out of October 1853 to May 1854 by 'surrounding the entrances of the various mills working, or calling the parties therein employed certain names'.
6. The Society for the Diffusion of Useful Knowledge was founded in 1826 and aimed at the self-improvement of the working masses and the aspiring middle classes. It ceased its activities in 1848.
7. See chapter 8.
8. The strike was triggered by the attempt in November 1857 by some local shops to introduce machinery to the manufacture of boot and shoes. The strike was coordinated by the Northamptonshire Boot and Shoe Makers' Mutual Protection Society, which the striking operatives established in April 1858. The strike ended in defeat for the strikers in early 1859.
9. The term 'blacksheep' was often used in the nineteenth century to describe strike-breakers and other categories of 'obnoxious' workmen. See chapter 2 regarding the various epithets in use during these decades. For a detailed discussion of the Thorncliffe lock-out, see chapter 8.

References

Accomazzo, Sarah (2012) 'Anthropology of Violence: Historical and Current Theories, Concepts, and Debates in Physical and Socio-cultural Anthropology', *Journal of Human Behavior in the Social Environment*, 22: 535–552.

Arendt, Hannah (1969) *On Violence*. London: Harcourt Brace.

Ball, John (1860) 'Account of the Strike of the Northamptonshire Boot and Shoe Makers in 1857–1859', in Report of the Committee on Trades' Societies Appointed by the National Association for the Promotion of Social Science, *Trades' Societies and Strikes*. London: John W. Parker & Son: 1–9.

Besant, Annie (1890) *The Trades Union Movement*. London: Freethought.

Buechler, Steven (1993) 'Beyond Resource Mobilization? Emerging Trends in Social Movement Theory', *The Sociological Quarterly*, 34(2): 217–235.

Brantlinger, Patrick (1969) 'The Case Against Trade Unions in Early Victorian Fiction', *Victorian Studies*, 13(1): 37–52.

Bythell, Duncan (1969) *The Handloom Weavers. A Study in the English Cotton Industry During the Industrial Revolution*. Cambridge: Cambridge University Press.

Chase, Malcolm (2012) *Early Trade Unionism. Fraternity, Skill and the Politics of Labour*. London: Breviary.

Clark, Anna (1995) *The Struggle for the Breeches. Gender and the Making of the British Working Class*. Berkley: University of California Press.

Cole, G.D.H. (1948) *A Short History of the British Working-class Movement, 1789–1947*. London: Allen & Unwin.

Cole, G.D.H. and Filson, A.W. (eds) (1967) *British Working Class Movements. Select Documents 1789–1875*. New York: St Martin's Press.

Collins, Randall (2008) *Violence. A Micro-Sociological Theory*. Princeton, NJ: Princeton University Press.

Davis, Natalie Zemon (1973) 'The Rites of Violence: Religious Riot in Sixteenth-century France', *Past & Present*, 59: 51–91.

Demmers, Jolle (2017) *Theories of Violent Conflict. An Introduction*. London: Routledge.

Downing, Arthur (2013) 'The "Sheffield Outrages": Violence, Class and Trade Unionism, 1850–1870', *Social History*, 38(2): 162–182.

Emsley, Clive (2005) *Hard Men. The English and Violence since 1750*. London: Hambledon.

Fiske, Alan Page and Rai, Tage Shakti (2015) *Virtuous Violence*. Cambridge: Cambridge University Press.

Frank, Stephen (1987) 'Popular Justice, Community and Culture Among the Russian Peasantry, 1870–1900', *The Russian Review*, 46(3): 239–265.

Gaskell, Peter (1836) *Artisans and Machinery. The Moral and Physical Condition of the Manufacturing Population*. London: John W. Parker.

Hammond, J.L. and Hammond, Barbara (1995; first published 1919) *The Skilled Labourer 1760–1832*. Stroud: Allan Sutton.

Kirby, Raymond and Musson, Albert (1975) *The Voice of the People. John Doherty, 1798–1854. Trade Unionist, Radical and Factory Reformer*. Manchester: Manchester University Press.

Kirk, Neville (2012) 'Taking Stock: Labour History during the Last Fifty Years', *International Labour and Working Class History*, 82: 156–173.

Linebaugh, Peter (2003) *The London Hanged. Crime and Civil Society in the Eighteenth Century*. London: Verso.

Mider, Daniel (2013) 'The Anatomy of Violence: A Study of the Literature', *Aggression and Violent Behavior*, 18: 702–708.

Musson, Albert (1972) *British Trade Unions 1800–1875*. London: Macmillan.

Navickas, Katrina (2011a) 'Luddism, Incendiarism and the Defence of Rural "Task-scapes" in 1812', *Northern History*, 48(1): 59–73.

Navickas, Katrina (2011b) 'New Histories of Labour and Collective Action in Britain', *Social History*, 36(2): 192–204.

Pelling, Henry (1963) *A History of British Trade Unionism*. London: Macmillan.

Pelling, Henry (1965) *The Origins of the Labour Party, 1880–1900*. Oxford: Clarendon Press.

Randall, Adrian (1982) 'The Shearmen and the Wiltshire Outrages of 1802: Trade Unionism and Industrial Violence', *Social History*, 7(3): 283–304.

Raynes, John (1928) *Coal and Its Conflicts*. London: Ernest Benn.

Riches, David (1986) 'The Phenomenon of Violence', in David Riches (ed) *The Anthropology of Violence*. Oxford: Blackwell: 1–27.

Senechal de la Roche, Roberta (1996) 'Collective Violence as Social Control', *Sociological Forum*, 11(1): 97–128.
Senior, Nassau William (1865) *Historical and Philosophical Essays. Volume 2*. London: Longman Green.
Sewell, Willam H.Jr (1990) 'Collective Violence and Collective Loyalties in France: Why the French Revolution Made a Difference', *Politics & Society*, 18(4): 527–552.
Sigsworth, Eric (ed) (1988) *In Search of Victorian Values. Aspects of Nineteenth-Century Thought and Society*. Manchester: Manchester University Press.
Simms, Norman (1978) 'Ned Ludd's Mummers Play', *Folklore*, 89(2): 166–178.
Smelser, Neil (1962) *Theory of Collective Behaviour*. New York: Free Press.
Smith, Adam (1904; first published 1776) *An Inquiry into the Nature and Causes of the Wealth of Nations. Book 1*. London: Methuen.
Snyder, David and Kelly, William (1976) 'Industrial Violence in Italy, 1878–1903', *American Journal of Sociology*, 82(1): 131–162.
Sorel, Georges (1941; first published 1905) *Reflections on Violence*. New York: Peter Smith.
The Society for the Diffusion of Useful Knowledge (1831) *A Short Address to Workmen, on Combinations to Raise Wages*. London: Charles Knight.
Thomas, Claire (2011) 'Why Don't We Talk about 'Violence' in International Relations?', *Review of International Studies*, 37(4): 1815–1836.
Thomis, Malcolm (1970) *The Luddites. Machine-breaking in Regency England*. Newton Abbot: David & Charles.
Thompson, E.P. (1968) *The Making of the English Working Class*. London: Penguin.
Thompson, E.P. (1971) 'The Moral Economy of the English Crowd in the Eighteenth Century', *Past & Present*, 50: 76–136.
Tilly, Charles (1995) *Popular Contention in Great Britain, 1758–1834*. Cambridge, Mass: Harvard University Press.
Trant, William (1884) *Trade Unions. Their Origin and Objects, Influence and Efficacy*. London: Kegan Paul, Trench & Co.
Webb, Sidney and Webb, Beatrice (1920) *The History of Trade Unions*. London: Longman.
Zahn, Margaret, Brownstein, Henry and Jackson, Shelly (2015) *Violence. From Theory to Research*. London: Routledge.

1

BLACKLEG ECONOMICS

> That many employers have an evil desire to reduce the workmen's wages far below anything like an adequate reward, is as evident, as it is certain that the workmen ought to oppose it.
>
> *(Scottish Trades' Union Gazette, 9 Nov. 1833: 6)*

Although the roots of modern trade unions can be traced back to the English medieval craft Guilds, the more immediate precursors of trade unions are the journeymen fraternities and trade societies of seventeenth and eighteenth-century England and Wales, and Scotland after the Act of Union in 1707 (on the craft Guilds, see Brentano 1870). These journeymen worked in various skilled handicraft trades such as tailoring, felt-making, currying, hosiery, silk-weaving, and wool-combing. Still others worked as compositors, brushmakers, cabinet-makers, coopers, hatters, bakers, potters, watch and clockmakers, shoemakers, papermakers, printers, painter-stainers, bookbinders, dyers, sawyers, wire-drawers, masons, millwrights, sail-makers, riggers, rope-makers, and shipwrights.

As with the craftsmen of the medieval Guilds, these journeymen fraternities identified with a set of core principles and beliefs from which emerged a series of strict internal rules and codes of behaviour for those associated with their trade. These rules and codes of behaviour were meant to help fend off efforts by antagonistic masters to degrade their way of life by imposing what the journeymen considered to be unjust rates of pay and conditions of work. To some extent, at least during the seventeenth century and the earlier part of the eighteenth century, the journeymen were afforded a measure of protection by the laws of the land for the maintenance of a fair rate of pay for their labour and the protection of long-established, customary working practices. Thus, the Elizabethan Statute of Artificers of 1563, which would establish the legislative framework governing labour law for the next two centuries, while containing a number of punitive provisions hostile to labour, also aimed to 'yield unto the hired person, both in the time of scarcity and in the time of plenty, a convenient proportion of wages' (*An Act containing divers Orders for Artificers, Labourers, Servants of Husbandry and Apprentices*. 5 Eliz. C. 4 (a)). These wages were to be set by the justice of the peace in a particular locality. Failure to comply with the decisions of the justices would bring a heavy penalty. The Statute of Artificers of 1563 also established firm guidelines for the working man to practise a skilled craft. Before attaining the status of journeyman, he would need to 'serve his time' in an apprenticeship spanning at least seven years. The apprenticeship system was viewed by the journeymen of the time as both a mechanism to ensure quality and standards in the trade, and as a means of establishing a measure of control over the supply of labour and rates of pay. The threat to trade standards and rates of pay in the decades of the seventeenth century and the earlier part of the eighteenth century usually came in the form of 'illegal men' or un-apprenticed labour, 'those not of his club' who had taken work below an agreed price or wage rate, and the small independent master one step removed from the journeyman who contrived for reasons of self-interest to contravene the established customs or piece rates of the trade.

These threats to standards in the trade and rates of pay, however, were set to increase in intensity and range during the later decades of the eighteenth century and early nineteenth century, as Britain slowly but inexorably shifted from a pre-industrial and proto-industrial economy to a more industrialised or 'modern' society and economic system. The journeymen artisans were not the only category of worker caught in the eye of this storm. By the later part of the eighteenth century, and increasingly so as industrialisation gathered pace during the nineteenth century, they had been joined by other groups of workers associated with newer or expanding trades and industries that reflected Britain's changing economic profile. These included coal, tin and copper mineworkers, boiler-makers, plate-makers, nail-makers, riveters, cutlery and file makers, dockworkers, railway-workers, building and construction workers, and puddlers, shinglers and various categories of engineers in the expanding metal industries (for a detailed discussion of Britain's changing occupational profile in this period, see Rule 1986: 7–13).

In terms of threats to standards in the trade, the apprenticeship system favoured by the journeymen, which had hitherto benefitted from the protective framework of the apprenticeship clauses of the Statute of Artificers of 1563, was facing mounting criticism by the later decades of the eighteenth century. To the increasingly influential supporters of the new philosophy of liberal political economy, an arrangement which set up stringent regulations as to the necessity of apprenticeships within certain trades, the number of apprentices to be hired by the master, and the length of the term of apprenticeship, amounted to unnatural interference in the natural laws of the market and free competition. In a similar vein, the long-established and related custom of barring those who had not been through a proper apprenticeship from following a trade was considered contrary to the values of personal liberty and a 'free' labour market. In a letter of July 1802 to the Whig Home Secretary Lord Pelham, the Lord Lieutenant of the West Riding of Yorkshire, Earl

Fitzwilliam, expressed a view held by many amongst the governing classes in regard to the apprenticeship system:

> I am inclined to think that every man is at liberty to weave, to dress cloth, to perform any of the processes in the manufacture, without having gone through any apprenticeship; it is a trade open to all. If it is so, others will come in and do the work the persons in question refuse to do.
> *(Letter 28 July 1802. Document in Aspinall 1949: 45)*

For their part, the skilled artisans felt that in defending the apprenticeship system they were upholding a system which afforded the working man a degree of respectability and freedom in a usually hostile and unforgiving economic market. Moreover, the skill acquired was the working man's 'property' or 'capital' in the parlance of the age, which bore comparison with other forms of property within the state. As such, the worker's labour and skill should be afforded the same rights and protection in law as other forms of property in the state. The time and money spent by the artisan acquiring his skill are his capital, stated a defender of the apprenticeship system, 'which he is equally entitled to preserve and improve as the members of the church or the law; and it is an invasion of natural right to prevent him from doing so, until all laws, conferring special privileges, are abrogated' (Richmond 1824: 4).[1] The artisans also believed that all benefitted, workmen and masters, from their efforts to maintain standards of craftsmanship and skills in the trade. In 1792, the shoemakers' union, the Friendly and United Society of Cordwainers, justified their practice of allowing only those who had served a legal apprenticeship to follow the trade on the grounds that:

> We are determined to raise the trade to a more respectable rank among mechanical professions, by excluding unqualified intruders, by procuring proper and legal journeymen for the masters, and more constant employment for the men who are entitled to it.
> *(Articles of the Friendly and United Society of Cordwainers, instituted at Westminster on 4 June, 1792. Document in Aspinall 1949: 83)*

For the journeymen artisans, their attempts to preserve the apprenticeship system was not just about issues relating to property in a skill, respectability, the need to maintain regular employment, and trying to secure a measure of control over the supply of labour and the composition of the workforce. When strictly adopted in trades and professions, it was felt that apprenticeship agreements helped maintain a high price for labour and kept wage fluctuation at bay (Richmond 1824: 4). Preserving the apprenticeship system, then, offered the artisan some control over the price of labour and rates of pay in an environment that by the later decades of the eighteenth century was becoming increasingly unsympathetic to wage regulation in any form. The system of wage regulation as established by the Statute of Artificers of 1563 had become almost redundant by this period, with labour increasingly left to find its price in a competitive struggle with the masters as 'free bargaining' between the two parties became the principal method of establishing rates of pay or wage levels. This would not be a meeting of equal parties in the market, however. In the new circumstances of political economy, labour found itself confronted by a philosophy which clearly favoured capital and the masters. Labour also, as we will see below, came up against an increasingly hostile and unresponsive legislature as it sought to redress this imbalance. In these new circumstances, workers felt that they were being denied a fair and proper remuneration for their labour from the masters and that the latter used every opportunity to press down on wages.

When considering the question of wages in the decades covered by this book, we need to guard against viewing wages, particularly in the earlier decades of industrialisation, in terms of a simple notion of a money wage. Some groups of workers like fishermen in Cornwall had some stake in 'the share' of the profit extracted from the work, albeit a small stake, while still others received wages partly paid in goods or 'truck', usually through the 'tommy shop' system present in a number of trades and industries in our period, as in the coal-mining industry. Workers could also receive part remuneration for their labour in 'waste' materials from the manufacturing or work process, as with waste timber remunerated to the shipwright by custom or waste cloth to the tailor (see the discussion on the wage and its form in Rule 1986: 107–29).

Two modes of remunerating labour tended to predominate by the early to middle decades of the nineteenth century, however, the piece-rate wage and the time wage, though it was the former that was more commonplace. Work produced by the piece, that is, in accordance with the piece quantum either agreed between master and workman or, as was more prevalent, that which was established by the master, featured in many trades and industries. This would include framework knitters in the east Midlands; weavers in Gloucestershire, Essex and Wiltshire; tailors, shoemakers, print-workers and hatters in London; tin and copper miners in Cornwall; shipwrights in Portsmouth; and stonemasons everywhere (Rule 1986). The piece system of payment by results also featured in the newer trades and industries, as with engineers in Birmingham and with skilled male spinners in the early cotton mills of the north-west of England (Rule 1986). In 1833, John Rule informs us, around half of all cotton-mill workers were on piece work (Rule 1986: 124).

This more nuanced and complex picture of the wage form has implications for our understanding of wage trends during the decades when Britain underwent industrialisation. As Eric Hobsbawm pointed out when questioning the statistical basis of J.H. Clapham's 'optimistic' contention that real wages rose between 1790 and 1850, the then available figures for money wages were chiefly for time rates for skilled artisans. 'About piece workers', Hobsbawm stated, 'we know very little' (Hobsbawm 1964: 67). For the 'optimistic' view, see Clapham 1926–1938). Moreover, 'the absence of adequate data on the British income structure' for the period 1790 to 1840 in particular, Hobsbawm went on to say, rendered it highly problematic to make over-optimistic claims about rising national wage levels (Hobsbawm 1964: 69). In a similar vein and writing in the same period, E.P.

Thompson pointed out that 'wage-series derived from the rates paid in skilled trades do not give us the awkward, un-statistical reality of the cycle of unemployment and casual labour' characteristic of these decades (Thompson 1968: 275).

Nonetheless, these complicating factors have not prevented later economic historians, post-Clapham and post-Hobsbawm, from attempting an estimate of national trends in wages during the decades of the Industrial Revolution. Writing in 1983, the 'optimists' Peter Lindert and Jeffrey Williamson stated that prolonged wage stagnation characterised the earlier decades of industrialisation up to the end of the Napoleonic Wars (Lindert and Williamson 1983). Lindert and Williamson went on to claim that matters improved quite markedly in the decades after 1815, with the average real wages of adult male workers in England almost doubling between 1820 and 1850 (Lindert and Williamson 1983: 11). A number of categories of adult male workers were included in these findings, including 'artisans' and 'farm labourers'. This over-optimistic assessment was later revised downward by Lindert and Williamson in response to criticism of their data and findings, though their claim that adult male workers' average real wages showed strong improvement from the end of the Napoleonic Wars to 1850 remained firmly in place. Charles Feinstein, however, writing over ten years later in 1998 from within the 'pessimist' camp, was highly critical of Lindert and Williamson's findings. Feinstein did not have an issue with that part of the argument which pointed to wage stagnation for the decades between the 1780s and 1815, though he did part company quite sharply with Lindert and Williamson in regard to their assessment of the decades between 1820 and 1850. In respect to wage rates and earnings pertaining to both male and female 'blue-collar' workers in Britain from 1770 to 1880, Feinstein stated that in the decades that followed the long phase of wage stagnation between 1781 and 1815, wage earners' average real incomes remained broadly stagnant until the mid-1830s, improved marginally at that point, dipped again during the cyclical depression of 1838–42, before starting to climb after the mid-1840s (Feinstein 1998). This halting and moderate progress registered in the 1820s, 1830s and 1840s was only checked by the 1850s, and it was only towards the latter end of that decade 'that the average British worker enjoyed substantial and sustained advances in real wages' (Feinstein 1998: 642). Feinstein concluded his analysis of this 'long plateau' in income and material standards on an unsurprisingly pessimistic note, stating that for the majority of Britain's working class 'the historical reality was that they had to endure almost a century of hard toil with little or no advance from a low base before they really began to share in any of the benefits of the economic transformation they had helped to create' (Feinstein 1998: 652).

Even if the optimists can show statistically that average wage rates for workers did indeed rise between 1790 and 1840, and being mindful that there remain profound disagreements amongst scholars regarding the validity of these claims or the degree of this rise, as we saw above with the work of Charles Feinstein, we can at least conclude that this process was unquestionably uneven in terms of regions, specific occupational groups, and particular categories of worker. As E.P. Thompson pointed out, 'progress was not as smooth nor as continuous as is sometimes implied' (Thompson 1968: 268). Thus, in terms of particular categories of worker, while it could be claimed that cotton spinners in north-west England in times of economic upturn enjoyed relatively high wages, due to a large extent to their high levels of union organisation as much as their skills it should be said, the same cannot be said for other groups of workers like handloom weavers for example.[2] By the early decades of the nineteenth century, with the processes of mechanisation and de-skilling accelerating at an ever-faster pace, the increasingly displaced handloom weavers saw their wages fall from £1 in 1806 to 8s. 3d. in 1820, and to 6s. 3d. in 1830 (Kirby and Musson 1975: 12).

Additionally, and as already mentioned, much of the information available on wages for the decades in question did not always capture those who found themselves on the margins of mainstream or 'official' economic activity, such as the self-employed, the under-employed, or short-time workers, the latter of which includes those involved in seasonal short-time working. Much of the wage data as well refers to adult male incomes and is less forthcoming in regard to child and female labour. Neither is wage data which aims to speak to national trends or issues particularly sensitive to the uneven effect of industrialisation as applied to particular occupational groups. Also, wage data which seeks to speak to national trends or issues obscures the uneven impact of industrialisation and change on the different regions of England or the United Kingdom and is not always sensitive to wide regional differences in earnings. Long hours for workers and the irregular payment of wages were other factors which complicate the picture on wages. Another complicating factor, for some categories of worker at least, was the seemingly incessant fluctuation in the price of labour during the early decades of the nineteenth century when political economy was in the ascendency.[3]

We can thus state with some certainty that at particular stages in these uncertain decades there was a periodic and ongoing squeeze on the 'price of labour', with workers often struggling to hold the line on wages. Beyond the statistics, we just have to listen to the voices of the workers themselves to understand this. In March 1795, the journeymen fullers of Exeter petitioned the merchants and master dressers of the woollen 'manufactory' of the city to highlight 'the small and inadequate hire of our weekly labour' at a time 'when every Article necessary to the support and comfort of human life is considerably enhanced' (HO42/34/265. Petition. 28 Mar. 1795).[4] The records are very scanty on this friction between the journeymen fullers and master dressers of Exeter on the issue of wages, but we do know that by April 1795 the fullers had struck work on account of the low rate of wages. The journeymen fullers had a history of organisation and struggle in the city of Exeter, having withdrawn their labour in 1784 on issues relating to working practices and control over the number of apprentices entering the trade (Hoskins 1935: 61).

Moving forward a few years to the aftermath of the bitter eight-week-long cotton-spinners strike in Manchester in 1818 over the issue of wages, we find the following judgement on the town's cotton masters by a journeyman cotton spinner. Writing in the radical newspaper the *Black Dwarf*, the journeyman stated that the cotton masters were 'petty monarchs, absolute and despotic', whose whole time is 'occupied in contriving how to get the greatest quantity of work turned off with the least expense' (*Black Dwarf*, 30 Sept. 1818. Cited in Thompson 1968: 218). A similar note was struck by a speaker at a meeting which took place during a turnout of calico-printers in Lancashire in July 1831 'occasioned by the determination of twenty masters to reduce the wages of their men' (*Manchester Times*, 16 July 1831: 6). It was becoming evident to the striking calico-printers and other operatives, declared the speaker:

> that nothing would satisfy the masters but the whole produce of their labours: at present they got the greatest part of it, by which they were enabled to accumulate princely fortunes and to live splendidly in halls and palaces; and yet they were not satisfied, and would never be satisfied until they obtained the whole, and left the poor man without the means of subsistence.
> (*Manchester Times*, *16 July 1831: 6*)

Autobiographical sources tell of a similar story. The Owenite socialist and Chartist George Holyoake recalled that piece-workers and day-workers at the Eagle Foundry engine works, where he had worked as a young boy learning the trade of whitesmith in the early 1830s, 'were so continually subjected to reduced prices and wages that they never felt certain on Monday morning what they would receive on Saturday evening' (Holyoake 1900: 21). 'The arbitrary and continual reduction of prices by the master' to steal 'the earnings of all the men' was not confined to this particularly foundry workshop in Birmingham according to Holyoake, it being 'the way in which employers behaved generally so far as I knew them' (Holyoake 1900: 22). William Kiddier, of the journeymen Brushmakers' Society, recalled that the all-too-numerous business 'adventurer' within the trade during the 1800s, 'paid what wages he liked and, in bad times, little enough, God knows' (Kiddier 1930: 56). For Kiddier, wages justly paid to workers gave money a moral, even sacred, standing, stating that 'if money has ever a sacred attribute it is in the weekly earnings of the manual worker' (Kiddier 1930: 138).

Wage reductions could have devastating consequences for workers and their families. In 1831 the pro-labour journal *Voice of the People* decried the all-too-prevalent 'practice of reducing workmen's wages' amongst masters which had reduced 'the poor weavers of Rochdale' to such a state of starvation 'that they have not a dram weight of flesh on their bones to spare' (HO52/14/307. Extract from the 'Voice of the People', which was reprinted in an 8 Oct. 1831 edition of the *Poor Man's Guardian*).

Wage compression continued to remain a serious issue for the weavers of north-west England in the Victorian period. When weavers at the Hollow Factory in Hyde struck work in May 1859, they did so on account of the incessant 'nibbling' at their wages by the masters, declaring that if they did not prevail in the turnout 'their wages would be nibbled to nothing' (*Kentish Mercury*, 21 May 1859: 2). Even those who promoted the cause of political economy and free trade were prone to admit that there was an issue in this regard. Adam Smith in the *Wealth of Nations*

(1776) stated that 'masters are always and everywhere in a sort of tacit, but constant and uniform, combination, not to raise the wages of labour above their actual rate', and that they 'sometimes enter into particular combinations to sink the wages of labour even below this rate. These are always conducted with the utmost silence and secrecy till the moment of execution' (Smith 1904: 60–1). In another, though related, context, the leading advocate of free trade, William Huskisson, is said to have 'blurted out' in the House of Commons in 1825 during a debate on Corn Law repeal, in what may or may not have been an unguarded moment, that 'the object of free trade was to keep down the price of labour' (mentioned in Webb Trade Union Archive. LSE. A/1/4143. 1825).

Why was there this seemingly constant tendency to press down on wages during our period? We can identify a number of reasons why some masters were inclined to favour low wages for workmen. The eminent Scottish engineer James Watt believed that the more moderate the wage, 'the better servants they will prove for they will have less to spend in idleness' (Letter from James Watt to John Rennie. 2 July 1786. Doc. 9 in Ward and Fraser 1980: 9). Watt was not alone amongst members of the eighteenth-century educated elite in believing that high wages were an inducement to idleness and bad habits on the part of the 'hands' and that, alternatively, lower wages acted as a stimulus to increased labour productivity. When he took time off from berating the 'insufferable behaviour', 'insolence' and 'saucy tongue' of apprentices and 'menial servants', Daniel Defoe in 1724 castigated England's labouring classes for their attitude and behaviour during times when trade was brisk and wages were buoyant. Instead of inspiring diligence and thrift:

> this prosperity introduces sloth, idleness, drunkenness, and all manner of wickedness; instead of making hay while the sun shines, they flight their work, and bully their employers; perhaps they will work two or three days, or it may be a week, till they find a few shillings jingle and chink in their pockets; but then, as if they could not bear that kind of music, away they go to the Alehouse, and 'tis impossible to bring them to work again, while they have a farthing of it left.
>
> *(Defoe 1724: 84)*

For his part, Dr Samuel Johnson believed that 'raising the wages of day labourers is wrong; for it does not make them live better, but only makes them idler, and idleness is a very bad thing for human nature' (Boswell 1830: 531). Another concern for the eighteenth-century elite in this idleness narrative was that the supposedly idle and feckless would be thrown onto the parish, thereby becoming a burden on the parish rates. Though ruling elites favoured wages being kept to a low necessary minimum, it was felt that they should not be kept too low lest this could provoke unrest and riots borne of penury and desperation. So, not content to just keep wage levels low, the need was to ensure that wages remained in a situation of 'quantitative equilibrium' in order to reconcile seemingly 'opposite purposes', neither too intolerably low and certainly not too high (as noted by Linebaugh 2003: 54–5).

Those on the receiving end of wage pressures often attributed their plight to nothing other than the avarice, scheming, and self-aggrandising instincts of the masters. In March 1827 the woollen weavers and spinners of Rochdale spoke of 'the great disadvantages under which we labour' in consequence of 'the unjust, unprincipled and unmanly conduct pursued by a number of mean, selfish, and tyrannical Manufacturers who resort to all manner of clandestine Plans in reducing the workman's wages, when there is no real necessity for it except their own selfishness' (H040/22/62. Notice of Public Meeting. 27 Mar. 1827). On occasions, variations on the vampire trope were evoked to represent the behaviour of covetous, self-interested masters. In late 1837, a Spitalfields weaver lamented that his brethren in the weavers' community had 'become the prey, alas! the easy prey, of those heartless and rapacious Manufacturers, who fatten upon our labour, upon our sweat, and upon our blood' (*Spitalfields Weavers' Journal*, Oct. 1837: 23). In the view of the hard-pressed labouring classes, the covetous master had much to gain in terms of material reward and personal advancement from pocketing the surplus. In April 1832, *The Poor Man's Advocate* had this to say on the matter:

> for it is what the workpeople receive *less* [sic] than their labour is *worth*, that makes up the profits of their employers, and enables them to become baronets… or aspire to the honour and dignity of legislators… or retire from business with princely fortunes, like many we could name.
>
> (The Poor Man's Advocate, *28 Apr. 1832: 115*)

At other times, it was felt that low wages stemmed from a conscious desire on the part of the masters to sap the spirits and will to resist of the operatives. The Manchester journeyman cotton spinner whom we met above stated that the master spinners in the town were 'anxious to keep wages low for the purpose of keeping the spinners indigent and spiritless' (*Black Dwarf*, 30 Sept. 1818. Cited in Thompson 1968: 219). Whether or not there was a concerted attempt to use low wages to keep the workers dispirited and apathetic, we can certainly detect a degree of concern within the ranks of the governing classes about the effect of high wages on the workers' disposition and capacity to organise. This was particularly the case if these workers had a demonstrated a strong and persistent resolve to combine to protect the interests of their trade. Writing in September 1802, the Lord Lieutenant of the West Riding, Earl Fitzwilliam, attributed the supposed truculence of the croppers or shearmen, then agitating on a range of issues relating to wages, the introduction of de-skilling machinery and the hire of 'illegal' apprenticeships, to high wages and the scope that this gave to the croppers to build up a bank of money to advance their combination. The Earl's solution to the problem of the croppers, who he described as 'the tyrants of the country', was uncompromising and brutal. They are, he informed Lord Pelham, 'an order of men not necessary to the manufacture, and if the merchants had firmness to do without them, their consequence would be lost, their banks would waste, their combinations would fall to the ground, and we should hear no more of meetings of any description' involving them (HO42/66/312–6. Letter from Earl Fitzwilliam to Lord Pelham. 27 Sept. 1802).

While the cultural prejudices of members of the elite towards plebeian behaviour and the avaricious nature of some masters certainly helped contribute to the squeeze on wages, we should not ignore other contributory factors. These would include the periodic trade fluctuations experienced during the decades of the so-called 'Industrial Revolution', as well as the innate tendency of capitalism to boom and slump, both of which also impacted on wage levels. Thus, for instance, trade dipped or slumped in 1825–6, 1831, 1837–42, and 1847–8 (Thompson 1968: 228–9). Prior to this later economic turbulence, the impact of the Napoleonic Wars and its immediate aftermath on economic confidence, trade, commerce and prices also need to be considered. Account also has to be taken of fluctuations in trade peculiar to specific trades and industries, which could also injure the master's profit. These fluctuations could be particularly acute in those trades at the high sharp end of competition and technological innovation like handloom weaving for example. Competition and selling below price by masters seeking to undercut rival manufacturers also acted as a stimulus to pay the lowest rate of wages.

All this being said, masters inclined towards paying low wages usually did not need to wait for wider economic trends and developments to whittle away at workers' incomes. In this endeavour they were much assisted by certain economic theories of the age which lent considerable weight to the myth that high wages constituted a problem. The perception mentioned above that high wages encouraged indolence and loss of effort was a hangover to some extent from English mercantilist theory (on mercantilist thinking on wages, see Wiles 1968). At the beginning of the period covered by this book, that is, 1760, the British economy was gradually shedding its mercantilist character and orientation and moving albeit tentatively to a different stage of production in keeping with the changed circumstances associated with the capitalist free market and the philosophy of liberal political economy. There was another take on the supposed benefits of a low-wage economy prevalent in mercantilist theory. This was the view, particularly evident amongst mercantilist commentators during the seventeenth century and early eighteenth century, that in a trading nation heavily predisposed towards exports, wages should be kept as low as possible so as to see off trade rivals. This arrangement, so ran the argument, would thus help facilitate the best possible relationship between exports and international markets.

For its part, political economy had much to say on the question of wages. At a general level, labour was viewed as one of the factors of production which required that wages as a cost of production should remain competitive at all times in order to benefit trade. This meant that excessive labour costs in the form of high wages represented a risk to trade and were therefore to be avoided. More specifically, those in the political economy camp drew on prevailing economic theories to inform and justify their thinking on wages. One particularly prominent theory was wage fund theory, which held sway in thinking on economics for the better part of the nineteenth century up to the early 1870s (on wage fund theory, see Clements

1961; and Breit 1967). Wage fund theory held that wages depended on the available fund of capital, which was pre-determined in accordance with past production and was fixed at any one moment. The point at which the wage fund was fixed, moreover, was determined not just by past production but conformed to the natural laws of supply and demand and free competition in the market. Because the wage fund at any one time was fixed and could not be increased by 'unnatural' or artificial stimulus during that particular period, the apostles of wage-fund theory asserted that wages could only be increased if there was a rise, 'absolutely and relatively', in the fund of capital. The corollary of this was that the workman should thus show restraint and prudence in his dealings with the master in regard to wages, thereby allowing the profits of the capitalist to increase which, in turn, would enable the latter to augment the wage fund. All would then benefit, labourer, master and ultimately society, from the augmented wage fund once increased through these means, as well as through the enhanced investment that followed from the increase in aggregate profits.

If restraint and low wages were necessary to help augment the wage fund, the quest for high wages in a relationship of mutual antagonism with the master would have the opposite effect. Higher wages meant reduced profits, which served to diminish the sum of capital that could be added to the wage fund. In this scenario, where the laws of political economy were deemed akin to the laws of nature and gravity, combinations of workers and particularly strikes were adjudged to be a dangerous check on the vital accumulation of capital and an impediment to economic well-being and trade. In such a scenario, capital and the master clearly held the whip hand in that labour was deemed 'naturally' dependent on capital or capital formation for its basic requirements, that is, employment, wages and subsistence.

To the advocates of political economy and their supporters amongst the employing classes then, there were three main obstacles to an efficiently functioning economy in accordance with the liberal principles by which trade was meant to be conducted. The first was adjudged to be the customary restrictive working practices in the skilled journeymen trades relating to the supply and employment of labour, particularly in the form of the apprenticeship system. The second perceived obstacle to healthy trade was the wage level that did not conform to the elementary principles of political economy, such as those principles associated with wage fund theory. The third obstacle arose when workers combined in a quest to 'regulate' this wage level without regard to the sensitivity of market forces, particularly when attempting to raise wages through strike action.

How then, from the perspective of the supporters of political economy, to remove these obstacles to healthy trade? In terms of applying restraints to wage levels, one option was to attempt to lower labour costs at the point of production. This often led to crude attempts to 'pilfer' the earnings of the operatives. Cotton spinners working in the emerging factory system of the early nineteenth century in the north-west of England frequently complained of the petty 'contrivances' by which the little that the workmen 'are *permitted* to earn is filched from them' by the master (*The Poor Man's Advocate*, 17 Mar. 1832: 67). Punitive fines would be imposed by the 'cotton lords' for such 'misdeeds' as the operative standing on a dirty floor, accidentally damaging a wheel-ring or other machine implements, leaving waste 'in the necessary', or being ten minutes' late for work. As well as compulsory deductions, there would also be additional enforced payments for the use of power such as gas and lighting, while supplying the hands 'with hot water for tea afforded a pretext for deducting a few more pence from their wages' (*The Poor Man's Advocate*, 17 Mar. 1832: 67). In one cotton-spinning mill at Bollington near Macclesfield, fines were imposed for washing one's hands and face in the mill and being caught during 'mill hours' eating food, reading and speaking when one 'ought not to speak' (*The Poor Man's Advocate*, 29 Apr. 1832: 113–5). To this system of 'extortion' and 'petty pilfering', we should add the 'tommy shop' system set up by some masters, whereby the hands would receive wages partly paid in goods or 'truck'. Outworkers working in small workshops or the home economy were also exposed to compulsory deductions calculated to reduce labour costs, curb wages and enhance profits. Enforced out-payments along the manufacturing chain could include excessive rent for machinery, premises or 'services'. The former could include the rent of the stocking-frames used by framework knitters in the east Midlands. Or, consider the case of the handloom weavers in Gloucestershire. When giving evidence in a letter to the Royal Commission inquiring into the condition of the handloom weavers in England and Wales, the chairman of the Delegates of Weavers stated that following the defeat of weavers in Gloucestershire during the 1828 strike over wage reductions, the triumphant masters:

> to be further revenged on the poor weavers, many of them built large factories, filled them with looms, and made the weavers work as journeymen under them; and many of the weavers were compelled to take their looms to the factory, and pay a shameful rent for the standing of their own looms in the factory; so they had rent at home, and rent to pay to the master; and many an industrious man has been brought to the parish by this conduct.
>
> *(see Miles 1837–41: 457)*

Abatements, that is, fines imposed for supposedly shoddy work or 'short-weight' work, was another means of imposing a 'tax' on workers' earnings (Rule 1986: 114). Earnings could also be held down through other, more subtle, means, as when the master increased the piece quantum arrangement with the journeyman, which involved increasing the output of work for the same pay (Rule 1986: 115).

Should more comprehensive measures be required to impose restraint on labour costs and wage levels during the decades when political economy was in the ascendency, employers could always look to what E.P. Thompson has described as the 'partiality of the law' (Thompson 1968: 221). At the most extreme end, this could entail the wholesale dismantling of the workers' defensive networks by supressing the 'evil' of workers' combinations and strikes. As the eighteenth century unfolded and morphed into the nineteenth century, we can see a hardening of attitude towards labour on the part of the legislature as the latter become more and more taken with the arguments of the political economists. Even before political economy won over the legislature, the capacity of working men to act collectively to protect what they perceived to be their long-established right under the Elizabethan system to a fair and just proportion of their earnings was being constrained by Acts of Parliament. In 1718 a Royal Proclamation was issued against the 'lawless Clubs and Societies' of weavers and woolcombers which had established an effective and widespread combination in the southern counties of Somerset and Devon and were 'unlawfully conspiring' to dictate terms to the masters on a range of matters pertaining to trade (Cole and Filson 1967: 82). The tailors' Combination Act, applicable to the Westminster and Greater London area, was passed in 1721. This was followed in 1726 by a Combination Act directed at journeymen weavers throughout the country. A further Combination Act followed in 1749, targeted at journeymen workers in the clothing trade, such as felt-makers, hatters, dyers and hot-pressers and those involved in the production of silk, fur, mohair, flax, hemp, cotton, linen, fustian, and leather. Moving into the second half of the eighteenth century, the journeymen papermakers were hit by a Combination Act in 1796 (on the various Combination Acts, see Orth 1991: 5–24). Some of these trades were also the recipients of additional Combination Acts whose purpose was to clarify, amend, or improve a number of the provisions in the earlier acts. In this respect, a second tailors' Combination Act was passed in 1768, two Combination Acts regulating the silk-weaving trade in Spitalfields were passed in 1773 and 1792, and a hatters' Combination Act in 1777.

Even worse was to follow for labour with the appearance during 1799–1800 of the infamous Combination Acts, a single statute applicable to all trades. While the main spur to the passing of the 1799–1800 Combination Acts was a desire on the part of Parliament to accede to the wishes of the supporters of political economy to unshackle trade from the supposedly harmful restrictions imposed on it by combinations, we should be aware of another influence. This was the general aversion exhibited by the governing classes of the day towards all forms of confederacies of the 'people' in the wake of the political convulsions of the French Revolution.

Lest labour was in any doubt as to Parliament's determination to remove obstacles to capital and trade, the various Combination Acts referred to above came with heavy punishment sanctions. These sanctions came in different forms and exhibited a number of characteristics. At one level, there were the punishments imposed for simply combining for the purpose of raising wages, reducing hours, or indeed regulating the working of the trade in any way. A draconian punishment of two months' hard labour in a 'bridewell' house of correction or two months' imprisonment in a common gaol, as in the tailors' Combination Act of 1721, was the usual penalty imposed by the state (Orth 1991: 5–24). Similar punishment sanctions, though sometimes with extended sentences, against combining for the aims mentioned above would feature in the eighteenth-century Combination Acts subsequent to the tailors' Combination Act. An absence of display and formal legal ritual usually accompanied these prosecutions. Justices of the peace were empowered to pass sentence by summary procedure, without the performance of indictment rites and the associated legal rituals of pleading and trial by jury.

At another level, there were the even more draconian punishments imposed for violent acts against persons arising from strikes and other forms of labour dispute. The 1726 weavers' Combination Act included a section imposing a punishment of seven years' transportation for violence against a master. An act of violence thus carried out did not just have to be physical. The act of threatening a master carried a similar penalty of seven years' transportation. At still another level, and even more draconian, were the punishments imposed for violent acts against property. These are arguably the most significant of the state's punishment sanctions against journeymen during this earlier phase of our study, in that they were indicative of increasingly more determined efforts on the part of the employing class and their supporters in the legislature to stamp out the more militant attempts to impede the process of manufacture and trade. Again, it was the weavers' Combination Act of 1726 which placed these additional sanctions on the statute book. A section of the 1726 act decreed that breaking into a workshop with the aim of destroying tools or goods therein was to be a capital crime, that is, punishable by death. Even first offenders were to be subjected to the terrifying ritual of the gallows. Those charged with such punishments against persons and property would be subject to a further set of imposing rituals established by the state. There was to be no trial by summary procedure by justices of the peace, as in the sections of the Combination Acts dealing with combining for the purpose of raising wages or reducing hours. Instead, offenders would be tried and convicted in a court of law utilising all the formal ritual of court procedure.

When considering punishments imposed by the state for violent acts against property, we should also be mindful of legislation which aimed at specific acts of militancy which arose in the context of a particular labour dispute. Thus, an Act passed in 1765 in response to labour unrest in the silk-weaving industry in the Spitalfields district of London meant that those convicted of breaking into a house or shop with intent to cut or destroy silk in the loom in the process of manufacture faced death at the hands of the hangman (see Page 1911: 132–7). Subsequent to the 1765 Act, in 1769, a number of journeymen silkweavers charged with 'cutting' the work in the looms would be condemned to death.[5] Mention should also be made of the way that the common law of criminal conspiracy could supplement the punishments imposed by special statute. As the Radical Joseph Hume pointed out in 1824, if all the penal laws against workmen combining to raise wages were removed from the statute book, there would still remain ample scope for the state to clamp down on workers' efforts to secure a better wage by recourse to the common law of the land (cited in Capet 2009: 41–2).

For the propertied classes, however, the wholesale dismantling of labour's defences through punitive legislation such as the combination laws could never provide an adequate means to hold down labour and wages, even when enforced by the terror of harsh punishments. Such a response was disproportionate, overly confrontational, cumbersome and ultimately ineffective in that labour continued to turn out in defence of wages and working conditions during the years when the combination laws were operational.[6]

Another, more astute and ultimately more effective, means of cultivating a more compliant workforce and wage environment favourable to capital was to exploit a labour market that was undergoing rapid and substantial change. By the early decades of the nineteenth century, the labour market in Britain was becoming increasingly volatile and over-stocked in many sectors, partly as a result of the sharp rise in the UK population. The sharpest rise was in England, which saw its population increase from less than 6 million in 1750 to 8.3 million by the first Census of 1801, then rising to almost 17 million by the time of the 1851 Census. This sharp upturn in population created an abundance of labour in most trades, mostly unskilled or semi-skilled workers entering a labour market recently prised open by the waning of the apprenticeship safeguards protecting the skilled journeymen. Many in this 'reserve army' of the unskilled and semi-skilled were juveniles and women. Technological developments, which included labour-saving machinery and techniques, further encouraged this growing tendency to draw on juvenile labour and women. 'In those employments which are carried on under shelter, and with the assistance of that machinery which affords power, and requires human aid only for its direction,' stated Nassau William Senior, a vocal advocate of political economy, 'the industry of a woman, or a child, approaches in efficiency to that of a full-grown man. A girl of fourteen can manage a power-loom nearly as well as her father' (Senior 1830: 8). Downgraded or displaced altogether by technological innovation and the unskilled 'new hands' who worked the new machinery, the adult male skilled journeymen could find himself, in turn, entering the pool of surplus labour. Compelled to seek work in the same trade, or in other trades, in other places, the displaced journeyman could then find himself, paradoxically, forcing other workers out of employment by taking work under price or during a turnout.[7]

Other factors contributing to Britain's changing and volatile labour market were those more intangible underlying forces associated with the capitalist mode of production. Here one has in mind the extraordinary dynamism and inventiveness of the capitalist economic model, with its restless energy and voracious appetite for capital accumulation and new markets, and its role as a key driver of the modernisation process. Once set in motion, the modernisation processes associated with technological change, scientific development, industrialisation, innovations in transportation and communication, and modes of thinking related to the new mantra of 'progress', ushered in a frenetic new world which assumed a 'state of perpetual becoming', in the words of Marshall Berman (Berman 1981: 16). In such an atmosphere and environment of perpetual change and 'creative destruction', traditional journeymen trades and skills, along with many customary ways of working, were ruthlessly swept away.

Another source of pressure during these decades contributing to this changing labour market was the supply of 'cheap' unskilled migrant labour at the disposal of Britain's employing classes. These labour flows were often the product of extreme economic distress on the part of the migrants. A notable example here would be the flow of labour from Ireland emanating from the situation of extreme rural poverty and later famine conditions in that distressed country, which spawned an exodus of uprooted and mostly unskilled labourers into various parts of the United Kingdom. The economic advantage accrued to the employers of labour by this abundance of 'cheap' labour was obvious. 'The ragged Irish peasants', lamented the English socialist Thomas Hodgskin in 1825, 'are suffering under a more grievous system even than the one that afflicts us', though 'by them also we are destined to suffer; for they are imported here in crowds, and beat down the wages of our labour' (Hodgskin 2013: 11). We should add to the labour flow from Ireland, the movement of migrant labour from and within other parts of the United Kingdom. The cotton manufacturing trade in Glasgow and Paisley during the late eighteenth century, for instance, drew in unskilled labourers from adjoining counties and the West Highlands, as well as Ireland. Some of the former were cottagers and small farmers displaced by the establishment of 'the system of large farms' which left them no alternative but to migrate to the towns in search of work. The 'unrestricted freedom of admission' which henceforth prevailed, and which saw the new arrivals being taught the trade 'for a few pounds without any apprenticeship', had a debilitating effect in terms of the Glasgow and Paisley cotton workers in general, this being 'a tendency to reduce the price of labour, by producing a redundancy of hands' (Richmond 1824: 6–7).

Though there were undoubtedly powerful underlying forces propelling these changes to Britain's labour market, we should not assume that such changes came about as if through a process of natural necessity guided by the 'invisible hand' of the market and a particular set of economic laws which logically favoured the advance of capital. Given the many advantages to be gained by a 'free' and competitive labour market of this type, the masters and supporters of political economy also sought to expedite this arrangement whenever possible. The legislature certainly assisted them in this endeavour. By the early part of the nineteenth century, a number of important statutes had effectively swept away what remained of the Elizabethan system of paternalistic regulation as regards traditional work practices and wages. Thus, the system of wage regulation as established by the Statute of Artificers of 1563 was finally abandoned in 1813. This was followed a year later by the repeal of the apprenticeship clauses of the Elizabethan statute. All such additions and amendments to labour law struck at the capacity of the skilled journeymen trades in particular to resist the increasingly competitive and fluid labour market that was coming into view during the later decades of the eighteenth century and the early decades of the nineteenth century.

Nor were the masters and supporters of political economy idle in extolling the supposed virtues of an unregulated labour market and the free movement of labour in its various aspects. Thus, there was increasing prominence in these decades of the narrative of the 'free labourer', the 'well-disposed' workman with supposedly 'good habits of industry', free to sell his labour in an open and competitive labour market unhindered by regulation. This was hailed as a worker of a new type, attuned in instinct, emotion and consciousness to the new world of competition, fluid labour markets and possessive individualism. In spatial terms, it was felt by those seeking to liberalise the labour market that hitherto the individual workman had been overly regulated, static, and fixed due to an unreasonable attachment to trade fraternities, community, place, and custom. Rather, according to the 'free labourer' ideal, the worker needed to be less fettered and place-bound, and more responsive to a labour market with widening spatial horizons. All this would entail the reconceptualising of the working man as an individual exercising his free will in the disposal of his labour within a market arrangement according to the doctrine of *laissez-faire*. In the name of personal liberty, Adam Smith had declared in the *Wealth of Nations* (1776):

> the property which every man has in his own labour, as it is the original foundation of all other property, so it is the most sacred and inviolable. The patrimony of a poor man lies in the strength and dexterity of his hands, and to hinder him from employing this strength and dexterity, in what manner he thinks proper, without injury to his neighbour, is a plain violation of this most sacred property. It is a manifest encroachment upon the just liberty, both of the workman, and of those who might be disposed to employ him.
> (Smith 1904: 67)

By the time the nineteenth century arrived, this championing of the right of the workman to dispose of his 'free labour' as deemed appropriate to his individual self-interest hardened into a fundamental tenet of political economy. The strength and skill of the working man is his 'property', declared Nassau William Senior, and 'the right of the working man to employ that property in the way which he considers most for his interest, so far as he does not interfere with the exercise of a like free will on the part of another, is a right as sacred as any right for the protection of which laws are maintained' (Senior 1865: 121). Senior went on to stress the importance of giving 'freedom to the labourer: and we firmly believe that, as soon as he is made master of his own conduct, he will use his liberty in the way most useful, not only to himself, but to the rest of the community' (Senior 1865: 172). The right of the free workman to dispose of his labour in accordance with his individual self-interest and personal liberty would also, at least for libertarian fundamentalists in nineteenth-century Britain, form an important element of the doctrine of freedom of contract. In terms of our concerns in this book, the principle of free labour would certainly influence the attitude of governments and the employing class towards those who sought to interfere with the free movement of labour during strikes and other forms of labour unrest.

The ideal workman to those eulogising the open and competitive labour market was not just the 'new hand' who came from distant places to help a master 'beat down the wages' of his operatives, or fill a position vacated by a trade-union-affiliated worker during a lock-out. The ideal workman or 'free labourer' could also hail from within a particular shop, works or factory who declined to join his brethren during a strike to resist a wage reduction or secure a raise in pay. In a related sense, the ideal workman was also the fellow prepared to accept work below that of a price or wage agreed by the collective, whether during a turnout or in other work situations.

An open, de-regulated and competitive labour market of the type mentioned above would place a powerful weapon in the hands of the masters and the supporters of political economy in their efforts to subordinate wages to the interests of capital and profit. At a general level, the free movement of labour provided a means of challenging and undermining customary working practices in the drive to create new, more compliant work disciplines more favourable to capital accumulation and wage restraint. At moments of the most acute tension between labour and capital during our period, both the free movement of labour and the self-interested free labourer could also help the master defeat strikes, destroy workers' defensive networks in the form of combinations, clubs and unions, and even drive 'refractory' workers and their families from the community by evicting them from company dwellings. Indeed, it was in such arenas and often brutal circumstances that workers and their families most frequently came 'face to face' with political economy and its agenda.

Even before the decades covered by this book, we can observe masters both favouring and exploiting a more open and flexible labour market in order to press down on labour costs. In 1752 it was reported that 'many Master Taylors, in order to have their work done cheap, get a great number of young, raw, and unexperienced lads out of the country, who, for better instructions, are glad to work at low prices' (The Case of the Journeymen Taylors and Journeymen Staymakers, Residing within the Cities of London and Westminster, and Weekly Bills of Mortality. 28 Jan. 1752. Doc. 9 in Ward and Fraser 1980: 8). Bringing in the young unskilled 'new hands' could have a devastating effect on the circumstances of the skilled journeymen tailors and their families. 'By such means, great numbers of the best and most experienced journeymen taylors [sic] are forced to go into all parts of the kingdom, to the great prejudice of themselves, their wives and children' (The Case of the Journeymen Taylors and Journeymen Staymakers, Residing within the Cities of London and Westminster, and Weekly Bills of Mortality. 28 Jan. 1752. Doc. 9 in Ward and Fraser 1980: 8).

It was when faced with outbreaks of militancy within their trade, however, whether on the issue of wages or other contentious matters, that an open and flexible labour market underpinned by the free movement of labour could prove to be such a devastating weapon in the masters' armoury. As frequently occurred in such instances, young, unskilled or partly trained new hands were to be procured from other places. In a letter written on 2 July 1786, James Watt urged fellow engineer John Rennie to hire 'tractable' hands rather than members of the journeymen millwrights' union lately in 'rebellion', as Watt described it, at Rennie's works at Birmingham. Watt further advised Rennie to ensure that all the journeymen millwrights 'while they are your servants' sign an article of Agreement not to join the union nor attend its meetings under pain of a heavy penalty should they not comply (Letter from James Watt to John Rennie. 2 July 1786. Doc. 9 in Ward and

Fraser 1980: 9). Should these measures not have the desired effect, Watt assured Rennie that 'there are many young Scotch Cabinet Makers and joiners who have not completely learnt their trade' willing to work at 'more moderate' rates that could be brought down to replace the more intractable of the Birmingham journeymen (Letter from James Watt to John Rennie. 2 July 1786. Doc. 9 in Ward and Fraser 1980: 9). During the early and middle decades of the nineteenth century, this method of encouraging wage restraint was becoming best practice in many sectors of the economy. Thus, when the journeymen shoemakers turned out in Shrewsbury in August 1818 it sparked the following observation:

> The Master Shoe-makers of Shrewsbury have adopted an efficacious mode of bringing their workmen to their senses, by employing others who are willing to labour at the usual rate of wages. Wherever it can be done, it is of all remedies the best, as it puts an end to irritating negotiations between the employers and the employed, while it saves the former from any serious injury in their business.
> (Dublin Evening Post, 13 Aug. 1818: 2)

In a related sense, employers of labour were also able to exploit regional disparities in earnings, the latter consequent, to some extent, on the uneven impact of industrialisation on the different regions of the United Kingdom. As the Operative Stonemasons' Society pointed out in early 1847:

> in cases of strikes, the places most feared for supplying men to supplant turn-outs are those where low wages are paid. The low wages of the west of England, Wales, and Scotland have been the cause of us losing almost every strike of magnitude we have entered into.
> (MRC. Friendly Society of Operative Stonemasons. MSS.78/OS/4/1/10. Fortnightly Return. 7–21 Jan. 1847).

The response to these pressures by workmen favouring a collective approach to the struggle to maintain a just rate of wages was predictably rational. To their thinking, the legislature had abdicated its traditional role of regulating wages and the labour market in an equitable manner which took account of the interests and concerns of the labouring classes. As a representative of the stonemasons' union put it in 1837:

> not only are employers hostile to our society, but all those who administer the laws are notoriously opposed to the poor man if he attempts to raise the price of his labour, and thus exemplify their arbitrary disposition by inflicting the severest punishment the law allows on all those who transgress it.
> (MRC. Friendly Society of Operative Stonemasons. MSS.78/OS/4/1/1/156–9. Fortnightly Return. 14–28 Apr. 1837)

Nor to unionised workmen did the nation's law-makers seem concerned to restrain the structural violence visited upon workers' livelihoods and families by a de-regulated labour market and the competition between workers that such an arrangement encouraged. Most alarmingly for collectively inclined workmen, the legislature, the bulk of the intelligentsia and the organs of mainstream public opinion, had taken on the role of arch-defenders of the cause of non-union workmen. Because of this confluence of negative factors, the beleaguered collectively inclined workmen felt that they had been left with no alternative but to attempt to gain some semblance of control over an increasingly dangerous situation. Some of the measures eventually adopted could be harsh, even brutal, and bring to mind a society mobilised for war. We can only properly appreciate this if we listen to the voices and empathise with the concerns of those engaged in this struggle. In this regard we should consider the following, where an operative writing in August 1831 likened what seemed to be a relentless attempt on the part of the masters everywhere to lower workers' wages to a war of extermination:

> The oppression of workmen is now become quite systematic – a mere matter of course. The ear of the public are now become so familiar with facts and complaints of starvation, that reductions of 20 and 50 per cent are accounted a mere bagatelle… The late and present attempt to reduce, by wholesale, the wages of workmen is a war of extermination. A war, in which capital, and the influence it confers are arrayed against the flesh and blood – the bones and sinews – the rights and the liberties – the present comforts, and the future prospects of the working man.
>
> *(Cobbett's Weekly Political Register, 6 Aug. 1831: 380)*[8]

Most tellingly in terms of the concerns of this book, the operative concluded his account of the workers' plight by urging his brethren to let the message be heard everywhere that 'He that is not for us, is against us'. It is to this matter, that is, the struggle against uncooperative workmen and the threat they posed to the security of the collective and the price of labour that we shall now turn to consider in the following chapters.

Notes

1 According to some accounts, Richmond, a weaver and strike-leader during the high-profile 1812–13 turnout of Glasgow weavers, later became a government informer. Richmond's fall from grace is said to have been brought on by his falling into debt. See Wilkes (2015).
2 It has been estimated that between 1814 and 1822 the average weekly wage of fine spinners for instance who worked in the mill districts in and around Manchester was 32s. See Kirby and Musson 1975: 15.
3 For instance, the Scottish weaver Alex Richmond told the 1824 Parliamentary Committee on artisans and machinery that 'fluctuation was a greater evil' than the 'lowness' of the wage rate, adding that at certain points during these years fluctuations 'to the extent of thirty per cent took place in the course of a month in the price of labour' in the handloom weaving trade (Alexander Richmond. *Evidence to the Committee. Second Report from the Select Committee on Artisans and Machinery*. 10 Mar. 1824: 60). This 'speculation'

regarding the price of labour was compounded by the economic uncertainty engendered by the French Revolutionary wars, it should be said.
4 Fullers were responsible for cleansing the woollen cloth of impurities during the manufacturing process.
5 The importation by the masters of cheaper French silks to cater for the higher end of the consumer market in the form of silk ribbons, stockings and gloves, and the implications these imports had for weavers' wages and employment, formed much of the background to the labour unrest in Spitalfields.
6 As in the eight-week-long cotton spinners' strike in Manchester in 1818.
7 It was particularly this type of situation that was witnessed during the infamous lock-out of workers belonging to a trade union instigated by the masters of Derby in late 1833 and early 1834. That is, some of the 'new hands' who filled the places of the locked-out unionists were displaced, unemployed journeymen smallware weavers from Spitalfields. See *Derby Mercury*, 22 Jan. 1834: 2.
8 The operative made his remarks against the background of the Lancashire calico-printers' strike mentioned above.

References

Aspinall, Algernon (1949) *The Early English Trade Unions. Documents from the Home Office Papers in the Public Record Office*. London: Batchworth.

Berman, Marshall (1981) *All That is Solid Melts Into Air. The Experience of Modernity*. London: Verso.

Boswell, James (1830) *The Life of Samuel Johnson*. London: John Sharpe.

Breit, William (1967) 'The Wages Fund Controversy Revisited', *The Canadian Journal of Economics and Political Science*, 33(4): 509–528.

Brentano, Lujo (1870) 'On the History and Development of Gilds and the Origins of Trade-Unions', in Lucy Toulmin Smith and Joshua Toulmin Smith (eds), *English Gilds*. London: N. Trubner & Company: 65–199.

Capet, Antoine (ed) (2009) *The Representation of Working People in Britain and France. New Perspectives*. Newcastle-Upon-Tyne: Cambridge Scholars.

Clapham, John Harold (1926–1938) *The Economic History of Modern Britain. Volumes 1–3*. Cambridge: Cambridge University Press.

Clements, R.V. (1961) 'British Trade Unions and Popular Political Economy 1850–1875', *The Economic History Review*, 14(1): 93–104.

Cole, G.D.H. and Filson, A.W. (eds) (1967) *British Working Class Movements. Select Documents 1789–1875*. New York: St Martin's Press.

Defoe, Daniel (1724) *The Great Law of Subordination Considered*. London: S. Harding and W. Lewis.

Feinstein, Charles (1998) 'Pessimism Perpetuated: Real Wages and the Standard of Living in Britain during and after the Industrial Revolution', *The Journal of Economic History*, 58(3): 625–658.

Hobsbawm, Eric (1964) *Labouring Men. Studies in the History of Labour*. London: Weidenfeld and Nicolson.

Hodgskin, Thomas (2013; first published 1825) *Labour Defended Against the Claims of Capital*. New York: Prism.

Holyoake, George (1900) *Sixty Years of an Agitator's Life. Volume 1*. London: T. Fisher Unwin.

Hoskins, William (1935) *Industry, Trade and People in Exeter, 1688-1800*. Manchester: Manchester University Press.

Kiddier, William (1930) *The Old Trade Unions. From Unprinted Records of the Brushmakers*. London: George Allen and Unwin.

Kirby, Raymond and Musson, Albert (1975) *The Voice of the People. John Doherty, 1798–1854. Trade Unionist, Radical and Factory Reformer.* Manchester: Manchester University Press.

Lindert, Peter and Williamson, Jeffrey (1983) 'English Workers' Living Standards during the Industrial Revolution: A New Look', *The Economic History Review*, 36(1): 1–25.

Linebaugh, Peter (2003) *The London Hanged. Crime and Civil Society in the Eighteenth Century.* London: Verso.

Miles, William A. (1837–41) *Royal Commission of Inquiry into the Condition of the Hand-Loom Weavers in England and Wales. Gloucestershire Section.* Sessional Papers of the House of Lords. Volume XXXVIII.

Orth, John V. (1991) *Combination and Conspiracy. A Legal History of Trade Unionism, 1721–1906.* Oxford: Clarendon Press.

Page, William (ed) (1911) 'Industries: Silk-weaving', *A History of the County of Middlesex. Vol. 2*: 132–137. London: Victoria County History.

Richmond, Alexander B. (1824) *Narrative of the Condition of the Manufacturing Population and the Proceedings which led to the State Trials in Scotland.* London: John Miller.

Rule, John (1986) *The Labouring Classes in Early Industrial England, 1750–1850.* London: Longman.

Senior, Nassau William (ed) (1865) 'Combinations and Strikes', *Historical and Philosophical Essays. Volume 2*. London: Longman Green: 118–171.

Senior, Nassau William (1830) *Three Lectures on the Rate of Wages.* London: John Murray.

Smith, Adam (1904; first published 1776) *An Inquiry into the Nature and Causes of the Wealth of Nations. Book 1.* London: Methuen.

Thompson, E.P. (1968) *The Making of the English Working Class.* London: Penguin.

Ward, J.T. and Fraser, W. Hamish (eds) (1980) *Workers and Employers. Documents on Trade Unions and Industrial Relations in Britain since the Eighteenth Century.* London: Macmillan.

Wiles, Richard (1968) 'The Theory of Wages in Later English Mercantilism', *The Economic History Review*, 21(1): 113–126.

Wilkes, Sue (2015) *Regency Spies. Secret Histories of Britain's Rebels and Revolutionaries.* Barnsley: Pen & Sword Books.

2

TABOOED PERSONS

> This was one of the worst features that trades' unions had to contend with; the designs of unprincipled men in their own ranks.
> (Secretary of the South Yorkshire Miners' Association. Reported in the Sheffield Independent, 26 May 1869: 5)[1]

As we saw in the previous chapter, those who identified with political economy and *laissez-faire* viewed the ideal working man as a 'free labourer' exercising what was felt to be his undoubted right to sell his labour on his own terms and as deemed appropriate to his individual self-interest. As such, this ideal worker was a non-union workman who eschewed a collective approach to struggle. The increasing liberalisation of labour law and the labour market during the decades of the late eighteenth and early nineteenth century would create the appropriate environment to help facilitate the proliferation of this ideal-type worker. This was an environment that prized unchecked competition, and where many of the regulatory obstacles perceived to have hitherto hampered the effective operation of trade, commerce and capital accumulation had been removed. Those workmen favouring a collective approach to the struggle to maintain a just rate of wages had a different perception of the 'free labourer', however. In his history of the 'old trade unions', William Kiddier, a former member of the brushmakers' union the Brushmakers' Society, remarked that the morality of those working in the world of business and commerce, particularly the larger employers of labour, was governed by narrow utilitarian concerns relating to business success (Kiddier 1930: 137). In this world, where it was deemed morally acceptable for individuals to 'purposely cut against one another' and where ruthless cut-throat competition 'is the soul of business', the 'brotherly feeling' that held workers together posed a threat and was hated. As such, those wedded to the philosophy of competition 'encouraged the traitor', and made him a hero. This was the non-Society man 'who betrayed his fellow workmen' and 'cut in against another' (Kiddier 1930: 137). The charge of being a traitor would be one of many such accusations levelled at the 'free labourer' during our period, as we will see in this chapter.

In the Articles of the shoemakers' union, the Friendly and United Society of Cordwainers, issued on 4 June 1792, the question 'And what is a scab?' was posed. To this question, the Articles went on to say that:

> He is to his trade what a traitor is to his country....When help is wanted, he is the last to contribute assistance, and the first to grasp a benefit he never laboured to procure. He cares but for himself, but he sees not beyond the extent of a day, and for a momentary and worthless approbation, would betray friends, family and country. In short he is traitor on a small scale.
> *(HO42/79/55–61. Articles of the Friendly and United Society of Cordwainers, instituted at Westminster. 4 June 1792)*

Official union Articles were rarely so frank on such matters. This being said, we find the same scathing commentary almost word for word in the Preamble to the 1839 Rule Book of the London Operative Tin-Plate Workers. The only difference is that in this case, rather than 'scab', the perceived miscreant is assigned the equally disagreeable epithet 'rat', which hardly diminishes the contempt felt for the hated 'traitor'. Thus, the Preamble to the Rule Book opened with the words 'A rat is to his trade, what a traitor is to his country' (cited in Kidd 1949: 26–7).

It was indicative of the contempt felt towards so-called traitors within their ranks that unionised workmen chose to frame their displeasure within the language of bodily or health disorders like 'scab', or by deploying other epithets which aroused feelings of aversion and disgust such as 'rat'. 'Scab', in particular, is an instructive and apt metaphor in that it is a sore growing where it is not wanted, an unwanted intrusion on the healthy body, in the same manner as the 'scab' worker is viewed by the union-inclined workmen as an unwelcome presence blighting the healthy body of the trade or collective. For its part, the epithet 'rat' was rarely in use in labour discourse in the decades covered by this book. Even the epithet 'scab', which was in common usage by the late nineteenth and twentieth century, was infrequently used in this earlier period of labour history and may have been confined to certain combinations of working men. We saw above that the journeymen cordwainers certainly used the term, it appearing in their Articles of 1792, and it may have originated with this group of workers. Indeed, what seems to be the first recorded usage of the term, which appeared in an edition of *Bonner & Middleton's Bristol Journal* in 1777, relates to a labour dispute involving the cordwainers. The Bristol journal stated that matters in a recent cordwainers' turnout had been 'amicably settled' between the masters and the men but that 'the Conflict would not been [sic] so sharp had not there been so many dirty Scabs; no Doubt but timely Notice will be taken of them'. It seems that the cordwainers continued to use the term into the following century. In order to understand this continuity we need to recognise that cordwainers were sometimes referred to as shoemakers in this period. If a distinction is to be made it is a very fine one, in that a cordwainer claimed to make shoes from only the finest new leather for the high end of the market. In any case, the two terms are often used interchangeably in this period to describe this form of work.

We also find journeymen shoemakers drawing on the language of 'scabs' at the start of the nineteenth century, as we can see from an 'anonymous letter' to the Home Office in September 1804, which seems to have emanated from a government informer. Writing on the subject of what appears to be a clandestine meeting of unionised shoemakers in a public house probably in the London area, the informant stated in regard to the shoemakers that 'if every man is not of their way they will call them Scabb and fine them' (HO42/79/32. Anonymous Letter. 3 Sept. 1804).

The most frequent epithet of opprobrium used to describe the miscreant worker, however, a term particularly prevalent during the earlier decades of the nineteenth century, was 'blacksheep'. As with other figurative language like 'scab' and 'rat', the use of the term blacksheep was meant to convey strong disapproval and disgust, it being a term with a long ancestry used to describe an atypical, anomalous, unwelcome and usually disreputable member of a group. Along with the term blacksheep, the other most commonly used epithet of opprobrium in use during the earlier decades of the nineteenth century to describe the obnoxious worker was 'knobstick', along with its associated permutations such as 'nob-stick' or 'nob'. As with 'scab', 'rat' and 'blacksheep', the term knobstick had negative connotations for the target of the labelling exercise. The origins of this particular term though, is less easy to discern. One explanation is that it originated at a printworks in Stockport at a date described as 'the early nineteenth century', when an elderly unemployed block-printer was offered a position at the works only to be undercut the following day by a younger worker who struck an agreement with the master to undertake the same work at an inferior price. Such treachery brought forth an enraged response from the undercut block-printer. On hearing of it, he was said to have heaved up the walking stick which he had in his hand and cried out to the master in an emphatic manner, in the presence of other workmen, that the undercutting worker was 'no better than this Nob-stick' for his act of treachery (*Chester Courant*, 14 Dec. 1824: 3). Whether this can be ascribed more to legend than to fact, what is indisputable is that henceforth the appellation 'knobstick' was applied to all workers in any trade who undercut their fellows by taking up work for an inferior price or wages, particularly during a strike. This could apply to workers from within the workshop, factory, trade or community who undercut their fellows by foul means, and it could apply to the 'new hands' who came from afar to take up work during a strike or lock-out.

It should be noted that it was only by the later decades of the nineteenth century that the equally pejorative term 'blackleg' came to be almost exclusively applied to the 'new hands' who came from afar to fill the places of unionised workmen during labour disputes. As with that other term 'scab' extracted from the language of bodily or health disorders, 'blackleg' denoted disagreeable characteristics which invariably aroused a negative reaction. A much more frequent term in use during the early decades of the nineteenth century to make sense of what appeared to be the waves of 'new hands' appearing in local communities and trades was 'stranger'. There are also those appellations which are more peculiar to particular regions. Thus, we have 'black-neb', a term more likely to be uttered by Scottish trade unionists. As with the aforementioned epithets, 'black-neb' was a derogatory term which denoted roguishness and skulduggery.

We should note as well the deployment of the word 'black' in the pejorative term 'black-neb', as well as its role as a stem in the compound words 'blacksheep' and 'blackleg', in regard to the historic association forged between the word black and wickedness, evil and pollution. The use of the word and colour black as a symbolic representation of something wicked, evil and foul, as opposed to white as a symbolic representation of purity, innocence and cleanliness, can be traced to the medieval period. From the Medieval Age, a word which had hitherto in its earlier Indo-European usage meant light and shining now became associated with more malign and ominous aspects of life (see Joyce 1981). Some unions in our period, such as the Operative Stonemasons' Society and the Society of Operative Bricklayers, frequently used the contracted form 'blacks' to refer to strike-breakers and other types of offending workmen (on the former, see for example MRC. Friendly Society of Operative Stonemasons. MSS.78/OS/4/1/4/152–5. Fortnightly Return. 10–24 Feb. 1842. On the latter, see George Howell Collection. Bishopsgate Institute. Howell/23/12. Rule Books, 1859–1885. General Laws of the Metropolitan Society of Operative Bricklayers. 1859).

The colour black evidently had powerful symbolic value for unionised stonemasons in particular. When, in July 1836, a number of masons broke ranks during a strike in Carlisle over issues relating to low pay rates, irregular payment of wages, the master's 'tommy shops' and the deduction of eight pence per month from every workman's wages to pay doctor's expenses in the event of accidents, the remaining strikers greeted this act of betrayal by hoisting a black flag as the strike-breaking 'blacks' proceeded to return to work (MRC. Friendly Society of Operative Stonemasons. MSS.78/OS/4/1/1/85–7. Fortnightly Return. 7–21 July 1836).

Then there are those more general terms used by Society or union men to deride non-Society men or those who worked below price, such as 'foul' men, 'dishonourables', and 'illegal' men (on 'dishonourables', see Webb Trade Union Archive. LSE. A/14/60. *Tailors. London.* 1833). In relation to the latter, and to cite William Kiddier again:

> The brushmakers called their body a Society [and] called themselves legal men; and the master that paid List wages and conformed to Trade regulations as to the number of apprentices was a legal master and a legal shop. In like manner the word illegal was used to define the opposite. So we hear of the illegal Shop, illegal apprentice, illegal man.
>
> *(Kiddier 1930: 52)*

To these we should add those terms more specific to particular trades which were used to describe perceived wrongdoers, such as 'corks' in the hat-making trade and 'dungs' in the tailoring trade who usually worked by the piece and under price (on flints and dungs, see Webb Trade Union Archive. LSE. A/14/35. *Tailors*. 1818). All the aforementioned epithets, whether 'blacksheep', 'knobstick', 'scab', 'rat', 'black-neb', 'blackleg', 'foul' men, 'dishonourables', 'illegal' men, 'dungs' and 'corks', were in use at one stage or another during the decades covered by this book. However, for ease of recognition the following chapters will use the more familiar terms 'scab' and 'blackleg', and particularly the latter, when discussing these matters, unless the primary evidence specifically uses one or other of the more time-specific or trade-specific terms.

Just to clarify then, the so-called 'scab', more often than not in the late eighteenth and first half of the nineteenth century known by the name of 'blacksheep', 'knobstick' or 'black-neb', was usually an individual local to a particular workshop, factory, trade, village, town or community. As such, the 'scab' usually emanated from the community and was often known to his fellow workmen. The 'blackleg', on the other hand, was a more amorphous and mysterious being. His individual identity was usually unknown to the workmen attached to a particular workshop, factory or local community, in that he was a 'stranger' newly arrived from other places often as part of a group of strangers, and sometimes from other trades and industries not even associated with the labour dispute in question. These other places could vary. During the 1832 lock-out in the coalfields of the Tyne and the Wear when the coal-owners resolved to destroy the mineworkers' union, the 'Pitmens' Union of the Tyne and Wear', the blacklegs came from far and wide. The 'Pitmens' Union' was the offspring of the 'Colliers' United Association', which sprang up in the Durham and Northumberland coalfields in 1825 in the immediate aftermath of the repeal of the Combination Acts. The Union had proved objectionable to the coal-owners when it sought redress on a range of issues adjudged obnoxious to the mineworkers and their families. These issues included the colliery 'tommy shop' system where the collier was obliged to buy necessaries for work and home such as candles, meat and drink; the yearly bond system of 'virtual serfdom', which bound the miner in service to the master under a substantial penalty at a certain rate of pay pleasing to the latter; the often seventeen-hour working day for boys; the punitive system of 'fraudulent fines' imposed on the pitman by the coal masters for a range of alleged infringements; and the system of colliery houses which the bonded miner and his family were obliged to rent from the master and which they were usually forced to vacate to the blacklegs during strikes (Hammond 1995: 12–33). The blacklegs imported to displace the unionised colliers during the dispute of 1832 were part of the 'punishment' imposed on the mineworkers of Durham and Northumberland for their refractory behaviour, and the influx was vast and unrelenting:

> Great numbers of persons, particularly from Wales, left their homes, removed their families and went to work in the North. The northern coaches were

crowded with the adventurers, and the stage-waggons were piled with their bedding and boxes. Many from the shorter distances of Staffordshire and Yorkshire walked or hired light vehicles.

(cited in Webb 1921: 35–6)

This flow of non-union labour had the desired effect, the Pitmens' Union being formerly dissolved on 20 September 1832. The pitmen of Durham and Northumberland could not be kept down for long and resumed their long-standing conflict with the coal-owners on the issues of the yearly bond, the system of punitive fines, and guaranteed weekly pay, amongst other grievances, during the strike of 1844. On this occasion, the influx of strangers imported to break the strike came from even further afield, most notably from Ireland (see HO45/644/177. Letter 12 June 1844; and HO45/644/217–8. Letter 12 July 1844).

The pitmen of Durham and Northumberland were not the only group of workers in Britain's evolving industries who resented the influx of Irish labour into their workplace and communities, particularly blackleg Irish labour. The iron trade in Wales was another point of arrival for Irish workers, and native workers often took great exception to their presence. In March 1826, a manager at the Tredegar Iron Works in south-east Wales reported 'that several thousand men had assembled at Tredegar and were on their march over the hills to assist in driving away the Irishmen' who worked at the iron works (HO40/19/60–1. Letter 7 Mar. 1826). Tensions between native workers in Wales and new arrivals from Ireland invariably increased during periods when trade and wages became depressed. We should therefore set the 1826 unrest at the Tredegar Iron Works against the wider economic background of 1825 and 1826, which were years of economic difficulty, wage cutting and severe hardship for the labouring classes in many trades across the United Kingdom. Following the relative upturn in investment confidence and some sectors of overseas trade which came in the preceding years, albeit haltingly and unevenly as the British economy sought to extricate itself from the negative effects of the Napoleonic Wars, the mid-1820s would witness a financial panic, bank failures and a slump in the export market.

Wage cutting and economic hardship provided the backdrop to a later dispute in Wales involving native Welsh iron workers and Irish migrant labour. In early June 1850, a 'superintending constable' residing in the County of Brecon informed the Home Office that the workmen employed in works located in the several parishes of Llanelly, Llangattock and Llangynidr 'are dissatisfied with the lowering of the wages and the presence of Irish labourers and that a determination has been expressed by several of the persons employed in the works to drive all the Irish labourers away' (HO45/3134/40–1. Correspondence. 1 June 1850). At around the same time, a report emanating from Newport stated that 'the Welsh people residing at the iron works on the hills seem determined to drive all the Irish from amongst them. We have had large numbers of the expelled Irish flocking into the town' (*Hereford Times*, 8 June 1850: 8).

England's stonemasons, too, feared the arrival of migrant Irish blackleg labour. In June 1848 the Operative Stonemasons' Society had the following to say on the matter:

Most unfortunately at this time an influx of characters into this country from Ireland, in the garb of masons, are attempting to support what we have endeavoured by our united exertions to resist, namely, all unjust encroachments on the part of the employers, who are endeavouring to oppress us during this season. Whenever any dispute has taken place these serfs have hastened to the locality and obtained employment, on the employers' terms, setting our members at defiance; or they have demanded sums of money with card and strike cheques, or go to work they would.
(MRC. Friendly Society of Operative Stonemasons. MSS.78/OS/4/1/10. Fortnightly Return. 8–22 June 1848)

The contentious issue of blackleg Irish labour was witnessed a few years later during the great Preston lock-out of October 1853 to May 1854 (for a comprehensive study of the lock-out, see Dutton and King 1981). The dispute had its origins in the trade and commercial downturn of 1847 when the wages of workers in the cotton industry were cut by ten per cent, to be restored, on the understanding of the operatives, when trade revived. When by 1853 trade had recovered, cotton workers sought the restitution of the ten per cent which was granted in some cotton towns such as Blackburn and Stockport, though denied by the Masters' Association in Preston. This decision by the latter precipitated turnouts at a number of cotton mills in Preston followed by the lock-out applicable to all mills in Preston from 15 October. A few months into the lock-out and in response to the refusal of the Preston cotton workers to yield, blackleg labour began arriving in Preston. Many amongst the new influx hailed from Ireland, and the reception they received on arrival in Preston was hardly convivial. When 'a large number of Irish' arrived in Preston on 3 March 1854 to blackleg at a cotton mill in the town, it was reported that 'upon their arrival in Preston it was found impossible to remove them from the railway station' due to the throng of Preston operatives 'amounting to several thousands' gathered to halt their passage into the town (HO45/5244B/61. *Telegraph*. 3 Mar. 1854). The impasse was only overcome following the three times reading of the Riot Act. Despite these efforts, the 'soft' tactic of blockading the railway station failed to halt the flow of blacklegs. In one newspaper report it was stated that in one week alone in late March 1854 'nearly 500' new hands had been imported into Preston, making an aggregate of some 1,000 'who have been introduced to the town since such tactics were adopted by the masters' (*Huddersfield Chronicle*, 25 Mar. 1854: 2). Though the bulk of the mainstream press saw no problem with the influx of blackleg labour, attitudes towards the new arrivals from Ireland could be condescending. As a columnist in the *Huddersfield Chronicle* put it, 'of the strange hands introduced' into Preston 'many take very readily to their newly adopted calling; and even amongst the Irish immigrants there are numbers who exhibit a surprising aptitude for the various employments to which they have been put' (*Huddersfield Chronicle*, 25 Mar. 1854: 2).

It should be said that migrant Irish labour had been arriving in various parts of Britain before the middle decades of the nineteenth century of course, as we saw above in regard to the 1826 Tredegar incident. Two developments in this later period though helped to further facilitate the arrival of these 'strange hands'. The first was the improvements in transportation which marked these decades, particularly the arrival of the railways in the 1830s and 1840s. The revolutionary technology of the railway and its significance for time and space acted as a fillip to internal migration and encouraged the free movement of labour and blackleg strangers should the latter's services be required by a strike-breaking master. The other development which made the arrival of strangers from Ireland into other parts of the United Kingdom more likely by the middle decades of the nineteenth century and beyond were the circumstances of acute poverty and distress in rural Ireland arising from the Great Famine of c. 1845 to 1852. Many of the unskilled labourers or 'hands' flowing into Britain's various coalmines, iron works and cotton mills from Ireland from the mid-1840s onwards would have been emigrants fleeing the famine which ravaged the Irish population during these decades. Trade unionists in other parts of the United Kingdom generally recognised this and were often deeply sympathetic to the plight of the Irish migrant, even, at times, the blackleg Irish migrant. A speaker at a rally of union cotton operatives at Cottam during the later stages of the Preston lock-out in March 1854 spoke in sympathetic terms of the 'half alive and half dead' Irish men and women being shipped into Preston by the unscrupulous masters. The same speaker put a rhetorical question to his audience:

> If the people of Ireland had got proper wages in their own country would they have come here?… The men and women of Ireland are brought down to such a pitch of wretchedness that the finger of all the world is pointed at them as specimens of a miserable existence. Don't blame them therefore but feel sorry for them.
> *(HO45/5244B/138–59. Report of a meeting at Cottam, 4 Mar. 1854)*

Another speaker at the same rally told the audience that it 'grieved' him to see 'a set of innocent women and children driven from their own country and brought to Preston, gulled by a set of Preston masters' who are well satisfied 'when they have got them' (HO45/5244B/138–59. Report of a meeting at Cottam, 4 Mar. 1854).

It should be said as well of course that blacklegs were certainly not exclusively Irish, as we saw above with the influx of 'new hands' from Wales, Staffordshire and Yorkshire during the lock-out of the unionised pitmen of the Tyne and the Wear in 1832. A couple of additional examples from the primary evidence for one group of workers in one town alone will demonstrate this further. In September 1853, Wigan colliers and their drawers struck work over pay. The following month saw blacklegs being imported into the district by the masters. In late October, the Home Office received a communication from the authorities in Wigan saying that 'great excitement has been created amongst the colliers in consequence of Lord Crawford's agent having brought about 120 Welshmen into this township of Haigh….and that it was the intention of the colliers to have the Welshmen's blood' (HO45/5128/150–3. Letter 31 Oct. 1853).[2] In a later dispute involving striking colliers at Wigan in early to mid-1868 it was the importation of blacklegs from another region of the United Kingdom, this time by the Wigan Coal and Iron Company, which provoked the ire of the turnouts. During the by then eight-week-long strike, a local magistrate reported on 26 April that 'much angry feeling prevailed between the "Turnouts" and those who being anxious to secure their work had done so at the reduced rate of wages'. The report continued that 'this feeling was embittered by the Wigan Coal and Iron Company introducing a number of "foreigners" into the District', the blackleg 'foreigners' on this occasion hailing from Staffordshire (HO45/8110/80–7. Letter 26 Apr. 1868).

If trade unionists in the United Kingdom during the nineteenth century and particularly during the decades that followed the Great Famine exhibited compassion towards the plight of the Irish poor, which sometimes even translated into sympathy for Irish blacklegs, there was little sympathy shown towards the blackleg as a general character type. So, too, with the hated 'scab'. Before we turn to consider these responses, it would be helpful to reflect on the theoretical insights of Mary Douglas in regard to boundary transgressions (Douglas 1991). For Douglas, society and the idea of society has form, in that it has internal structure and external boundaries. However, this bounded system also has margins and unstructured areas that lay outside and which emit danger and threaten harm to the system. Douglas makes this point elsewhere in her analysis when she describes the idea of society as 'a complex set of Chinese boxes, each sub-system having little sub-systems of its own, and so on indefinitely', joined or separated by lines or boundaries which help to maintain the system or social structure and which need to be respected and protected (Douglas 1991: 138).

Nevertheless, these boundaries are often precarious and porous and likely to be breached by forces or elements which threaten the integrity and 'purity' of the social structure. As we will see below, structures are particularly at risk of being breached during moments of heightened societal instability and change. It is from the more 'inarticulate', ambiguous and formless regions that danger emanates, then, whether this be the formlessness which lays outside the structure, the 'unstructured crevices' of the structure, or at the structure's 'margins'. For Douglas, in relation to the latter, 'all margins are dangerous. If they are pulled this way or that the shape of fundamental experience is altered. Any structure of ideas is vulnerable at its margins' (Douglas 1991: 121). Douglas makes the point that the margins and the unstructured regions which carry the threat of danger, or what she refers to as 'pollution', as well as being ambiguous, are usually understood to be 'dark, obscure areas'. To emphasise the dangers and mysteries of the margins, she refers to the vulnerable, danger points at the margins of the human body, at the orifices of the body, as the body spills forth 'marginal stuff of the most obvious kind' (Douglas 1991: 121). This marginal stuff is the spittle, blood, milk, urine, faeces, tears, sweat and bodily parings which both traverse and escape the boundary of the body. Vulnerability and danger also reside on the margins of the social body of society, an observation by Douglas which has particular relevance for our study in this chapter. Finally, when reflecting on the aversion aroused by 'stuff' which escapes the places it usually inhabits, we should add Douglas's famous dictum that 'dirt is matter "out of place"' (Douglas 1991: 189).

The themes of form, boundaries, margins, formlessness, danger, pollution, and being out of place, all of which feature in Douglas's analysis, help shed light on the attitudes of unionised workmen towards scabs and blacklegs. As we saw above, the use of the term 'scab' aptly captured the aversion felt by unionised workmen towards the unwelcome appearance of the 'sore' of the deviant workman on the healthy body of the trade or collective. In a similar manner, from the perspective of the collectively inclined workman, the scab and the blackleg dwelt in 'the threatening non-structure against which barriers must be erected' (Douglas 1991: 123). We can appreciate this if we take account of the almost spiritual attachment of many workmen to their trade in this period, as well as the defensive organisations which helped guarantee the security of the trade. These bodies were the fundamental source of group solidarity and identity. Loyalty to the trade and its defensive networks became the source and meaning of group existence, its life-blood and sustaining force. In a similar vein, these attachments became the foundation of the moral and social obligations of the journeyman attached to that trade.

To some extent, these loyalties and attachments can be traced to the value system of the English medieval craft Guilds (for an interesting account of the links between the Guilds and 'modern' trade unions, see Brentano 1870). This value system was bound up with established customs relating to a just wage and rules relating to apprenticeships, though it went beyond the mere forging of an association for the protection of earnings and maintenance of fair and regulated conditions of work. Even more sacrosanct, and one of the higher and more sacred principles of the medieval craft Guild, was the idea of brotherhood and mutual support as a habit of life. Another, and related, principle was the belief in common or reciprocal obligations which were 'legally', in terms of the Guild's internal rules, and morally, binding on all members of the Guild collective. Attachment to these sacred principles was usually secured by a sworn pledge partaken by a Guild brother to abide by the Guild's internal rules and codes and protect the rights of others in the collective. The idea of brotherhood and mutual support as a habit of life would become one of the enduring myths which helped sustain the solidarity and sense of fellowship of the journeymen trades and trade unions of the eighteenth and nineteenth century. We can get a sense of this myth from the following rousing address written by a kindred spirit to his brother trade unionists in 1829:

> The principles which drew workmen together, to combine for their mutual security, were among the noblest of which the human heart is susceptible – an honest regard for their own welfare and independence, a kind and generous sympathy in the condition and comforts of their friends and neighbours, a prudent forethought for the future, a magnanimous self-denial, and sacrifice of present comforts, a noble public spirit, expanding and spreading itself over distant individuals, unknown even by name, whose only recommendations was that they wore the same form and lineaments, carried the same heart in

their bosom, were heirs of the same fleshy pangs, and had none to whom to cry for help but their own humble, poor and suffering fellow workmen.

(King 1829: 3)

As with other forms or structures in society, however, the trade, and the workers' defensive organisation which protected it had vulnerable external boundaries, crevices, cracks in the edifice, darkly obscure margins, unstable elements 'out of place', and a mass of formless chaos laying outside. In November 1833, in a metaphorical flourish, *The Pioneer*, a champion of the Grand National Consolidated Trades' Union (GNCTU), likened disunity, division, disloyalty and betrayal in the workers' ranks to 'a mouldering fragment, that has crumbled from a rock of granite', the latter being representative of workers in glorious solidarity (*The Pioneer*, 16 Nov. 1833: 84). All such 'unstructured' parts and areas warned of encroaching fragmentation or corrosion, emitting danger or 'pollution' which threatened the integrity, stability and 'purity' of the structure. As a consequence, and as with other forms or structures in society, the trade and combination had to be 'fenced in' with safeguards, prohibitions, and particularly pollution preventions, which worked to preserve the integrity of the social fraternity and spirit of brotherhood within its borders.

We should flag up at this point that the period covered in this study, namely 1760 to 1871, was a time when traditional structures, boundaries or 'lines' in society had become particularly precarious, unstable and porous due to the vicissitudes of industrial and economic change. These included the rapid development of technology, the introduction of new machinery, and the determination of the devotees of political economy to sweep away impediments to free trade, the latter to include those associated with the labour market, labour law, and workers' defensive networks. In such an atmosphere of heightened uncertainty and change, workers in the 'margins' of the structure, 'out of place', or in the formlessness laying outside, like scabs and blacklegs, appeared to the unionised workman as a particularly potent source of danger, to the extent of posing a mortal threat to the very idea of union itself. One does not need to look long and hard in the primary sources to find evidence of this. As the *Poor Man's Guardian* stated in April 1834, 'black sheep are the ruin of all combinations of workmen' and 'every such recreant' who refuses to join the union of working men or 'takes inferior wages to those agreed on by the body' is the 'mortal enemy' of the unionised working man (*Poor Man's Guardian*, 19 Apr. 1834: 1).

On occasions, metaphors associated with the work process were used to help explain the crucial importance of union to the integrity of the structure and thus the safety and well-being of all, as well as the dangers to the edifice posed by weakness, wavering, falling away, straying from the right course, being out of place, and all the other 'deviations' thought to be associated with blacksheep behaviour.[3] During the protracted lock-out of union-associated mineworkers at Denaby Main colliery, Mexborough, in the Rotherham district of south Yorkshire in 1869, a miners' union official addressed a gathering of locked-out workers and their supporters in the following way:

Mr Brown said the position of those in employment would be regulated by the terms upon which the struggle would be concluded. They all stood and fell together. The union was the prop which prevented their grievances from overpowering them. If they saw any part of the prop giving way or getting out of the perpendicular, drive it up to its proper place.

(reported in the Sheffield Daily Telegraph, 9 Apr. 1869: 4)[4]

If the union was the prop guaranteeing the integrity of the structure, then the scab and blackleg was the worker 'out of place', threatening its stability and the security of all.

In some trades where the particular spatial geography and structure of work made it difficult to build a viable and solid basis of worker organisation, the prop of unionism often gave way due to the sheer weight of the external pressure of non-union labour pressing in on it from the dangerous 'margins' and 'formless' regions beyond the structure, particularly during turnouts. Masonry was one such trade. During a strike in the Summer of 1848 by stonemasons at Sheffield seeking to maintain 'the tea half-hour at four o'clock' in accordance with the Society rules, the turnouts reluctantly had to concede their ground as they found themselves overwhelmed by blackleg labour. As a sympathetic national union representative explained it:

They have done their best to gain their object, but all has been of no avail. They have been overpowered by a set of unprincipled serfs, who have no regard either for the benefit of themselves or the interests of the trade. Had there been no interference by these parties the object would have been gained in a few days.

(MRC. Friendly Society of Operative Stonemasons. MSS.78/OS/4/1/10. Fortnightly Return. 6–20 July 1848)

The masons had an acute awareness of the threat posed by the formless danger laying outside the union structure. In nearby Rochdale around the same time, that is, in early June 1848, local stonemasons found themselves having to accept a wage reduction of 1s. per week. Although there were additional mitigating circumstances, such as a contracting labour market in the region, the national union concluded that their brethren in Rochdale were stricken by an even more intractable problem, in that 'the worst feature they had to contend with was that they were surrounded by a great number of non-members. Under these circumstances they were obliged to submit to the reduction' (MRC. Friendly Society of Operative Stonemasons. MSS.78/OS/4/1/10. Fortnightly Return. 25 May–8 June 1848).

The individual who turned his back on, deserted, or betrayed the union and the workers' cause was thought to emit danger in many respects. As well as being the carrier of the virus of non-unionisation, he was seen to represent harmful unchecked competition within the trade; a low-wage economy; insecurity of work and income that came with a de-regulated, de-unionised economy; de-skilling and the loss of status arising from the erosion of craft skills; loss of control in the face of seemingly uncontrollable market forces; a drain on union funds as turnouts became fractured and thus protracted; a means of disciplining the workforce on behalf of the master; and displacement arising from the loss of work, place and home, which in some sectors often followed in the wake of defeat in a strike or lock-out. In regard to the understandable dread of displacement, the blackleg in particular loomed large. This was a person not of the 'community', the community here being understood as the trade and locality associated with the workplace and labour dispute in question. As such, he was the quintessential outsider, 'not of this place', an unknown, even mysterious, 'stranger' who could not be trusted and was feared and loathed in equal measure. Indeed, the blackleg stranger fits one of the four kinds of 'social pollution' identified by Mary Douglas, that is, the 'danger pressing on external boundaries' (Douglas 1991: 122).

The danger of the stranger 'pressing on external boundaries' and the threat of displacement was omnipresent during the heightened uncertainty that workers experienced in the decades covered by this book. In late 1845, journeymen bakers in Belfast, seeking to have their hours of daily labour lessened from its average high of eighteen hours, struck work. As the struggle ensued into late December, a journeyman baker lambasted the 'strangers' who would 'supplant their brethren', and particularly the masters who 'prefer strangers and turn Belfast men adrift on the world entirely' (*Banner of Ulster*, 19 Dec. 1845: 2). An 'obnoxious' master so inclined could also punish his truculent workmen by turning them and their families adrift of their homes, an ever-present dread in pit communities in particular. There are numerous examples from the primary evidence of this ultimate sanction being applied, though one should suffice for now. In November 1839, following a turnout of colliers protesting a wage reduction at the Poynton and Worth collieries near Stockport, Lancashire, it was reported that 'strangers, such as spadesmen, calico printers' and others 'have been induced to work some of the pits' and that permanent accommodation was being sought for them, 'which was to be obtained by ejecting the old colliers from the cottages, and introducing the new ones as the future occupiers' (*Northern Liberator*, 9 Nov. 1839: 6). The instalment of the blackleg 'occupiers', most of whom were from Staffordshire, had an inevitable knock-on effect in terms of further distress for the evicted colliers and their families. The Chartist newspaper the *Northern Liberator* reported that 'large bodies having been ejected, have this week been obliged to quit the grounds, to go in search of work into Lancashire; and, therefore, the knobsticks are, comparatively speaking, unmolested in their avocations' (*Northern Liberator*, 9 Nov. 1839: 6).

As well as representing a 'danger pressing on external boundaries', the blackleg, though more likely the scab, could also hover around and emit danger from 'the margins of the lines', identified by Mary Douglas as another of the four kinds of 'social pollution' (Douglas 1991: 122).[5] Historically, deviancy and threat have invariably been located in the non-structure, at the margins. Thus, witches, Douglas tells us, 'are social equivalents of beetles and spiders who live in the cracks of the walls and wainscoting. They attract the fears and dislikes which other ambiguities and contradictions attract in other thought structures' (Douglas 1991: 102). Wherever form has been threatened or attacked, therefore, usually by 'malevolent persons in interstitial positions, anti-social, disapproved, working to harm the innocent', pollution danger comes to the fore (Douglas 1991: 104–5). Persons with anomalous characteristics or persons occupying ambiguous roles or having an ambiguous status were historically perceived to dwell in the margins of the social order and were often assumed to be the source of dangerous and mysterious powers, like witches.

The 'deviant' uncooperative worker, too, in the various forms he assumed, was imagined to be an anomalous and ambiguous individual dwelling on the borders of the established order. For the London Union of Compositors in February 1835, there were certain individuals employed in the book-trade who, 'flitting from house to house', were disdainful of union and went out of their way to avoid paying union subscriptions. Such types, in the view of the compositors' union, are 'like other noisome creatures, they dwell in holes and corners, shunning alike the association of their fellow workmen in public and private' (MRC. MSS.28/CO/1/8/1/1. Annual Report Of The Trade Council To The Members Of The London Union Of Compositors. 15 & 22 Sept. 1835). For the collectively inclined workman, such a miscreant defied easy categorisation, appearing almost 'liminal' in that he was perceived to occupy an 'in between' state, being neither genuine workman nor master but something more indefinable in between.

On occasions this indefinable type morphed into a monster lacking even the most basic human qualities and characteristics. In the strike literature published by power-loom weavers in Oldham, Lancashire, in the late Summer of 1845, then in dispute with local cotton masters 'who employed knobstick men' on inferior wages, a knobstick was deemed to be:

> not a human being, but a two-legged animal, that has the world shut out, and is the slave of self: a being void of reason and common sense; a heartless monster: one who in a court of justice would swear anything, provided only that it is false enough; he hates all honest men, and all honest men hate him; he is invariably an inferior workman, and none but the knobstick masters will employ him.
>
> *(reported in Manchester Courier and Lancashire General Advertiser, 25 Apr. 1846: 6)*

On another occasion, this time across the Pennines in Leeds during a meeting of unemployed workmen in early August 1832, a speaker complained of the erosion of the apprenticeship system and the tendency of skilled journeymen to lose their positions in the 'manufactories', with their places filled 'by inhuman beings, things not made of flesh and blood, and consequently devoid of human feelings' (*Leeds Intelligencer*, 2 Aug. 1832: 3). When in the Summer of 1842 a seven-week-long wage strike of stonemasons in Glasgow was defeated, it was, in the words of a member of the Operative Stonemasons' Society, because they 'have been inundated, as it were, with swarms of black locusts from Dundee, who, despite every exertion, took their places at the reduced wages' (MRC. Friendly Society of Operative Stonemasons. MSS.78/OS/4/1/4/199–200. Fortnightly Return. 28 July–11 Aug. 1842). Using similar language, the stonemasons' union complained in October 1846 that 'the West of England swarms with blacks', which placed their brethren in nearby locations taking strike action in a potentially precarious situation (MRC. Friendly Society of Operative Stonemasons. MSS.78/OS/4/1/6/357–60. Fortnightly Return. 1–15 Oct. 1846).

When considering such hostility towards the scab and blackleg, which could be so uncompromising in tone, we need to recognise that this antipathy transcended simple issues relating to right and wrong. In other words, this was never a straightforward moral question, though this is not to say that moral issues did not play a part in these interactions. If we briefly return to Mary Douglas's thinking on pollution we can understand this more fully. For Douglas, 'a polluting person is always in the wrong. He has developed some wrong condition or simply crossed some line which should not have been crossed and this displacement unleashes danger for someone' (Douglas 1991: 113). Douglas stresses this important point further on in her analysis when pointing out that 'the polluter becomes a doubly wicked object of reprobation, first because he crossed the line and second because he endangered others' (Douglas 1991: 139). This notion of the polluting person as committing not just a moral offence, but posing a threat which endangered others becomes more apparent if we see the line that has been crossed as a taboo boundary. To understand this further, we need to clarify the meaning of taboo and thereby establish its relationship to the study in hand.

Theorists of taboo flag up the relationship between taboo and *danger*. As Franz Steiner states, 'one might say that taboo deals with the sociology of danger itself' (Steiner 1956: 20). Taboos sanctioned by a community were put in place to mark off certain things and activities as either being sacred to the community and its core values, or which threaten to cause harm, distress or offence to a community. In breaking a sacred taboo sanctioned by the community, the taboo-breaker invariably puts himself or herself in some danger, whether from a 'supernatural' source, or from human agency in the form of a penalty imposed by a disapproving community.

There is a further aspect to the link between taboo and danger. In failing to abide by the customary observances of the taboo, the offender puts the entire community at risk by the 'delinquent' behaviour which was thought to have the capacity to spread like an infection throughout the social body of the group. The bad behaviour was thus treated like a *contagion* which had to be checked lest it contaminated the entire group. The relationship between taboo and contagion is recognised by the leading theorists of taboo, who also acknowledge the relationship between contagion and impurity. The assumption that impurity, with its association with uncleanliness and danger, is contagious seemed to be prevalent in the taboo customs of most traditional pre-modern peoples. Moreover, in regard to contagion, the most perceptive scholars of taboo inform us that those who violate a taboo themselves become taboo and thereby a source of the potentially dangerous contagion. As Sigmund Freud explained the taboo prohibition and its violation, 'the most peculiar part of it is that anyone who has violated such a prohibition assumes the nature of the forbidden object as if he had absorbed the whole dangerous charge' (Freud 1919: 37). From there, because this 'dangerous charge' carried transmittable properties, it followed that henceforth no one may come into contact with the tabooed person lest he or she also became contaminated.

It is within this additional framework of analysis in relation to taboo that we can more fully understand the reaction exhibited by collectively inclined workmen towards those judged to have violated sacred principles of the trade associated with the myth of brotherhood and the ideal of mutual support as a habit of life. What we are witnessing in these reactions is a combination of both loathing *and* fear. The loathing speaks to the contempt felt for the individual who, through his behaviour and actions, had violated a core taboo of the union brotherhood by betraying his brethren and turning his back on the sacred principles which drew working people together. In so doing, in committing this act of betrayal and renunciation, fear gripped the collective as the miscreant worker had himself become taboo, the carrier of the 'dangerous charge' or contagion of anti-unionism and self-interested individualism which threatened to contaminate the entire social body of the trade or community of workers.

It was not uncommon for this perception of the betrayal of one's brother to be framed in language borrowed from religion and scripture. In August 1858, Coventry's ribbon weavers attended a public meeting to protest against the efforts of a local master to circumvent the list of prices for weaving and winding which during the previous seventeen years had protected wages and standards in the trade. While a relay of speakers denounced the miscreant master, one speaker focused on those within the weavers' ranks who procured work below the list price, 'those cringing and crawling weavers who barter away their own independence and their children's birth-right for some supposed momentary advantage'. For the speaker, 'the conduct of Judas was more dignified than theirs. He sold his Lord for twenty pieces of silver, but they sacrifice their neighbours for a few pence' (*Coventry Weekly Times*, 4 Aug. 1858: 3). For other unionists, however, references to Cain, the slayer of his brother Abel, the first born of Adam, seemed a more fitting way to describe such betrayals. During a turnout in Stockport between January and June 1829 involving some ten thousand cotton spinners seeking to resist a reduction in wages, 'strangers', who included blacklegs from Glasgow, were brought into the town by steam boats. On their arrival, many were greeted by awaiting 'picquets' calling to them that 'Caine's mark is upon you' (HO40/23/407–9. State of matters at Stockport as regards Masters and Labourers. 29 May 1829). This was a common refrain. In another turnout, this time in early 1834 involving machine and engine makers, though in an unspecified location, a contributor to the trade union journal *The Tradesman* said of the blacklegs who came to fill the places of the turnouts that 'these modern Cains, who have injured their brothers, are more to be pitied than envied, for all will know them by the mark which they have put upon themselves'

(*The Tradesman*, 22 Feb. 1834: 5).[6] The language of Cain also turned up in the following 'sermon' on the 'brotherly' principles of the union, which appeared in another of the pro-trade union publications a few months earlier:

> It behoves everyone who has the welfare of his fellow creatures at heart, to put his shoulder to the wheel, and to devote his best energies to a cause, which, if properly directed, will have the effect of bringing into operation all the best feelings of our nature, and fulfilling the commandment, "though shalt love thy neighbour as thyself"; whilst the bad passions of our nature, which find so many lurking corners in the irregular fabric of society as at present constituted, will be held up to the desecration of mankind, and the wretch who has harboured them in his bosom become a second Cain, shunned by all, a fugitive and vagabond shall he be on the earth.
> (The Pioneer, 28 Sept. 1833: 28)

One should note here as well, *à la* Mary Douglas, the awareness on the part of the writer of the vulnerable and porous nature of the structure of society, with its 'irregular fabric' and 'so many lurking corners' harbouring the potentially dangerous pollutants represented by the 'bad passions of our nature'. References to the blackleg as Cain also cropped up during the widespread unrest in the mining industry in 1844 over low pay and long hours. At a mass meeting of striking Derbyshire and Nottinghamshire colliers and ironstone-getters near Chesterfield in early April, a speaker representing the Miners' Association issued a warning to the blacklegs brought in by the masters to break the strike. With the colliers' victory, inevitable because righteous in the speaker's view, would come retribution for the blacklegs. Compelled by circumstances the masters would have no recourse but to dismiss the blacklegs, 'and then they would wander like Cain, a nuisance and pestilence to England', and all would know them in their wanderings by their mark of treachery (*Derbyshire Courier*, 6 Apr. 1844: 2).

Trade unionists found in the fratricidal myth of Cain and Abel, with its parable of betrayal and the slaying of one's own flesh and blood, the ultimate taboo, a powerful frame to illustrate the fall into sin and ignominy of the miscreant worker, the reviled scab and blackleg who betrays his brother worker. Unionists found in the complementary myth of the mark of Caine, too, a powerful image to elucidate other displeasing features associated with the miscreant worker. The fallen worker, forever 'marked' like Cain with the sin of betraying his brethren, was tabooed and contagious, shunned by all as if a pestilence. As with Cain, he was a renegade and deserter from all that was humane and virtuous, doomed to perpetual wandering and exile from all that was deemed good in society. For the unionised workman, too, the 'modern Cains' appeared alarmingly as the harbingers of a new economic and political order, the new world of political economy that was coming into view, whose 'fratricidal' instincts and inclination towards self-interested individualism threatened to unravel the long-established fraternal bonds, rights and protections of the journeymen Clubs and Societies.

Commentary on the scab and blackleg emanating from unionised workmen is shot through with references to the betrayal of one's brother. One of the principal reasons why unionised workers mistrusted those workmen who stayed aloof from the union, according to a journeyman engineer writing in the early 1870s, was that the former considered the latter 'ignobly selfish; men without brotherly sympathy, and therefore little deserving of the sympathy of others should evil days come upon them' (Wright 1969: 13). Such types were thought to be a traitor to their kind. We saw above that to the journeymen cordwainers the scab was at heart a traitor. In his 1891 reflections on trade unionism 'new and old', the bricklayer and prominent trade union activist George Howell likened blackleg behaviour to the treachery of those who deserted their country in times of war. To Howell, those who refuse to partake in union with their fellows and are inclined to blackleg:

> hang on the outskirts of the Union as a drag, and, in times of dispute, they go in to take the places of men who are fighting, not for themselves only, but for the whole trade. Under military law a deserter is severely punished; the man who fled into the enemy's camp to fight against his own comrades would be shot without mercy. This, and much more, can be urged in palliation of the bitterness displayed by Unionists against those whom they term "blacklegs".
>
> (Howell 1973: 84)[7]

Others, too, were inclined to view blackleg behaviour through the prism of patriotism and national duty. 'Those on strike', observed the barrister and trade union sympathiser Henry Crompton, 'naturally regard any one acting contrary to the general interests of the trade with disfavour; just as an unpatriotic man is condemned by those imbued with a higher sense of national duty' (Crompton 1875: 17). Part of this higher sense of duty for the working man was to aspire to the ideal of social fraternity and not forsake one's fellows in the struggle to secure a living wage and decent working conditions. The blackleg was accused of habitually scorning these higher duties of the trade. Drawing on a host of nature metaphors, George Howell remarked that the non-unionists who go on to desert their comrades and blackleg were 'always ready to take advantage of the fruits of others' labours; they ought to partake of some share in sowing the seed, tilling the ground, and promoting the growth and maturity of the harvest, as well as reaping it and gathering it in' (Howell 1973: 84).

The inclination to betrayal was thought to course through the veins of the scab and blackleg. As well as betraying his brother the working man, as with Cain, he betrayed his wife and family. During a strike of seamen in Hull in March 1845 on the issue of pay, a representative of the Mariners' Union referred to the 'half man, or scabbed sheep, that would undermine us, and rob his own and our families of a bare subsistence' (*Northern Star*, 28 Mar. 1846: 12). Furthermore, many of the 'new hands' or 'strangers' who 'stole our berths from us' by accepting low pay are men 'who have run away from their wives and family, leaving them on the parish' (*Northern Star*, 28 Mar. 1846: 12).

In the 1893 novel, *The Knobstick*, by the socialist Charles Allen Clarke, a morality tale of love, labour, strikes and blacklegging in the Lancashire engineering industry, the story plays hard on the image of the knobstick Andrew Rugden, the principal villain of the plot, as a notorious philanderer. Rugden appears in the novel as a 'gambler, drunkard, blasphemer and God knows what else beside', as well as a fellow with 'a shifty look of deceit and cunning lurking in his eyes'. Even more than this though, and to underline and reinforce his inherent roguishness, he is represented as an inveterate womaniser who had deserted his wife and 'led other men's wives astray' (Clarke 1893: 180–2).[8] For the stonemasons' union, this inclination to betrayal had even wider implications, for those who turned their backs on union betrayed not only themselves and their working brethren, but also the next generation. 'What will he who has made masons of his children', stated a union-inclined mason in June 1845:

> say to them should they have to upbraid him in his old age, for having allowed the very trade he doomed them to live by, to become wretched and down-graded? Will he not then feel the anguish of a guilty conscience after such a life, and that past redemption?
> *(MRC. Friendly Society of Operative Stonemasons. MSS.78/OS/4/1/6/209–12. Fortnightly Return. 12–26 June 1845)*

Everywhere one looks in the language used by the unionised workman in these decades to describe the behaviour of the scab and blackleg, one is presented with the image of a character, like Cain, suffused in wretchedness and moral turpitude. At the August 1832 meeting of unemployed workmen in Leeds mentioned above, the behaviour of 'those men, commonly called Black-Sheep' who take the work of other workmen to work at a lower wage, which had the effect of 'depriving thousands of bread', was conduct so base it was 'far beyond the nature of savage beasts, and deserves the execration of every industrious community' (*Leeds Intelligencer*, 2 Aug. 1832: 3). When around seventy 'new hands' were brought in to fill the places of striking colliers at the White Hill colliery in Scotland's mid-Lothian region in November 1842, the former were described as 'a most wretched set, consisting of some of the worst characters in the county of Edinburgh!' Moreover, 'the great part of these miserable, cowardly Black Nebs' were 'the very refuse of society' brought in to intimidate the turnout colliers to return to work (*Northern Star*, 4 Nov. 1842: 11).

A frequent charge levelled at those who broke ranks and lined up alongside the employer was that they were sycophantic and overly deferential towards the master. In early 1837, a group of stonemasons at Little Haywood in Staffordshire struck work in protest against a cut to their customary hour for dinner to half an hour. When two of their number refused to join the turnout, the latter were described by unionised masons as 'deceitful fawning slaves, who would lick the dust from their tyrant's shoes rather than follow the example of their shop-mates, by standing up for their rights' (MRC. Friendly Society of Operative Stonemasons. MSS.78/OS/4/1/1/113–6. Fortnightly Return. 11–25 Nov. 1837).

The charge that a workman of this type was imbued with an innate deference towards the master and authority was commonplace. Such a disposition was thought to incline such a workman to become a 'talebearer' to the master. According to the stonemasons' union, once they are ensconced in a workplace following the defeat of the union in a strike, blacklegs then do all in their power to ensure that the works in question remained non-union, to the extent of informing on workmates attached to the union. Thus, following the defeat of a masons' strike at Grimsby Docks in mid-1850, the newly installed 'Blacks' then proceeded to 'use their utmost endeavours to learn who are members of the Society, then away they go to their employers with the information, and a discharge is the consequence' (MRC. Friendly Society of Operative Stonemasons. MSS.78/OS/4/1/13. Fortnightly Return. 13–27 Mar. 1851). The unionised masons seemed perplexed by the deference displayed by the blackleg talebearers at the Grimsby Docks:

> It is astonishing to behold with what tenacity they cling to their tyrant lords for leave to toil under such oppression as this job is surrounded with; having all the horrors of piece-work, at miserably low prices – Tommy tickets – Sick money – Funeral money – and Monthly pay. And all these disadvantages these serfs tamely submit to.
> (MRC. Friendly Society of Operative Stonemasons. MSS.78/OS/4/1/13. Fortnightly Return. 13–27 Mar. 1851)

To these forms of oppression one should add those iniquities which initially prompted the stonemasons at the Grimsby Docks to strike work, namely the masons having to pay for their own tools to be sharpened, having eighteen pence deducted each week from their pay for the use of the crane, weekly payments to the doctor, and paying 'for the stamp to the agreement which each man is required to sign previous to entering on the job' (*Derbyshire Courier*, 23 Mar. 1850: 2).

Similar sentiments regarding overly deferential tale-bearing workmen were expressed at a meeting of Scottish union delegates in the Summer of 1859 convened to discuss a colliers' strike in the west of Fife. The 'black-nebs' or 'turn-ins' who continued to work at the local Oakley colliery were described as being 'neither remarkable for skill, intelligence, nor spunk', as well as being imbued with a 'spirit of subserviency [sic]' towards the coal masters and their supervisory 'oversmen' even though the latter 'treated them like dogs'. Some of the black-nebs 'were such low fellows', and such was their endemic 'subserviency', that they acted as 'spies' at union outdoor meetings where 'they would skulk behind a hedge, or down into a ditch, if there was one at hand, to overhear what was said, and to repeat it to the oversmen' (*Fife Herald*, 9 June 1859: 3).

In the privately owned spaces of Britain's collieries, the 'black-nebs' were seen to pose an ever-present threat to turn out colliers defending pay and working conditions. During a dispute between colliers and the Dukinfield Coal Company in Cheshire in mid-1845, the blacklegs were referred to as 'creatures' and the 'very scum of society' who 'go prowling about the country in search of places where the men are on strike, in order that they may have "good money" for doing nothing for a few weeks, and then they are off again' (*Northern Star*, 10 May 1845: 4). There are parallels between the rootless blackleg 'parasite' roaming the country in search of a host on which to settle and the unwanted and marked Cain, the perpetual wanderer. The representation of the blackleg as rootless and parasitic was commonplace. For the Glasgow cotton spinners of the 1830s, imported hands or 'nobs' were 'a low class who wandered about the country living on the strikes of others, by getting employment, in spite of their worthlessness as workmen, from the masters, in emergency, or being brought out by the unionists' (cited in Lushington 1860: 401). For knobsticks and blacklegs, stated the *Northern Star* in May 1844, 'a strike of those at work is generally a Godsend, as it is the unnatural means by which they now and then come in for a scramble in the labour market' (*Northern Star*, 25 May 1844: 1). In the opinion of a striking mineworker speaking during the lock-out which took place at the Thorncliffe colliery in the south Yorkshire coalfield between 1869 and 1870, all imported knobsticks 'were the same'. The characteristic that all these 'blacksheep' shared in common is that they 'were men who were totally unprincipled', dishonest men 'who could knowingly steal the bread from the mouths of their fellow workmen' (*Sheffield Independent*, 14 May 1869: 3).[9]

For the Operative Stonemasons' Society, there was collusion between the masters and the 'rootless' parasitic workmen who preyed on strike situations, a situation rendered easier by the seemingly vast reserves of migrant Irish labour at the disposal of cynical employers. Writing in the Summer of 1848, the masons declared that these Irish 'serfs' were 'unprincipled men' who were:

> scouring the fields and lanes eagerly awaiting a dispute to arise amongst our members in order to supplant them. They are not in general, however, qualified to perform a day's work on jobs where the perfection of masonry is to be displayed; but, in cases of strikes the employers do not look to qualification if they can get numbers; no matter the pecuniary loss they suffer if they can obtain the object in view, namely, the oppression of the fair workman and honest man.
> (MRC. *Friendly Society of Operative Stonemasons*. MSS.78/OS/4/1/10. *Fortnightly Return*. 8–22 June 1848)

A sub-text of this narrative of the rootless parasitic blackleg workman was the charge that the latter was an 'inferior' workman lacking the necessary skills which were fundamental to those standards in the trade and pride in workmanship that were at the heart of the labour ethos. When a Glasgow cotton master in 1818 tried to impose a wage reduction and the cotton-spinner operatives struck work in protest, their places were filled by blackleg labour. For a member of the Glasgow Cotton Spinners' Operative Association reflecting on the 1818 strike some years later, the new hands:

> were characters which would not get employment in ordinary times. In all trades there were dissipated characters and bad workmen, and amongst the

cotton spinners there were as many as in any other; but when a strike took place, these persons were lauded as the best possible men – they were armed and privileged – they were considered as the advocates of free labour.

(*Morning Advertiser*, 2 Feb. 1838: 3)

When, during the strike of boot and shoemakers in London in 1838, the masters brought in new hands, many of whom were secured 'at a great distance' by the masters' representatives scouring the countryside 'in cabs and omnibuses', a striking journeymen complained that:

these masters were now employing men who, had they brought home work, while those who were now on strike were in employ, they would have thrown it in their faces. They have emptied cobblers' bulks, and brought up inferior workmen from the country, but they had made no reduction in their prices to the public.

(*The Operative*, 25 Nov. 1838: 4)

The operative stonemasons, too, despaired of those 'inferior workmen' who preyed on disputes between the skilled journeymen and the master. In late 1841 extending into 1842, masons loyal to the union became embroiled in a strike with their employers, Messrs Grissell and Peto, over the 'tyrannical' behaviour of a 'notorious' foreman which affected construction at the new Houses of Parliament, Woolwich Dockyard and Nelson's Column. According to the standard contemporary mainstream narrative, the new hands drafted in to replace the turnouts were described as being 'almost entirely from the country, most of them young, active men, and anxious not only to give satisfaction to their employers, but also to improve themselves in the London mode of working' (*Morning Post*, 4 Dec. 1841: 2). The stonemasons' union, however, was less gracious in its opinion of the new arrivals. The new men were 'scoundrels' brought to the works in an underhand manner 'in omnibuses and cabs, so that we could not get sight of them', 'black serfs' who were 'as inferior in skill as they are in character' and whose names 'should be known through the length and breadth of the land' on account of their treachery (MRC. Friendly Society of Operative Stonemasons. MSS.78/OS/4/1/4/133–6. Fortnightly Return. 2–16 Dec. 1841).

Supporters of the masons' cause were equally disparaging of the craft skills of the new hands. According to a trade union delegate speaking at a meeting in support of the strike, the new arrivals were 'persons not hardly able to manage a tool' (*Northern Star*, 29 Jan. 1842: 3). When a few years later, in early 1849, there was an attempt by the masters to cut the wages of stonemasons constructing a new Catholic Chapel in Liverpool from 4s. 6d per day to 4s. 4d per day, and the latter struck work in response, the strikers complained that 'the struck job has been infested with a set of unprincipled characters, who can only get work on such occasions' (MRC. Friendly Society of Operative Stonemasons. MSS.78/OS/4/1/10. Fortnightly Return. 4–18 Jan. 1849). It appears that the masters' tactic of drawing on 'inferior workmen' to defeat the turnouts paid off, when a few weeks later the stonemasons' union announced that:

> The strike at the new Catholic Chapel in Liverpool is totally lost, in consequence of the unprincipled serfs we have been surrounded with from the country. As fast as they were taken out, others went in... We may attribute the loss of this strike in a great measure to the depression of trade, and the number of the craft out of employment; but those that did supplant our members were of that character that would not have an opportunity of working only where disputes of this description arise.
> (MRC. *Friendly Society of Operative Stonemasons. MSS.78/OS/4/1/10. Fortnightly Return. 18 Jan.–1 Feb. 1849*)

In the context of the new economic times, it was felt that no trade or industry was immune from the 'blight' of the 'new hands' from whichever locality they derived. In November 1832, a dispute broke out at the works of Messrs Thomas Bury and Sons in Salford, Manchester, between the operative silk dyers and their employers. The origins and sequence of the dispute as it unfolded exhibited features that were all too familiar in regard to labour disputes in the era of political economy. Firstly, the master silk dyers announced a reduction in the wages of the operatives. This was then followed by a turnout of the operatives resisting what the Committee of the Silk Dyers' Union referred to as the latest attempt by the master to 'defraud the labourer of his wages' and 'take the necessaries of life from the poor man's table' (*The Poor Man's Advocate*, 10 Nov. 1832: 7). The third stage in the sequence of events was the step taken by the master to press home the wage reduction and defeat the strike by discharging the turnouts and 'treacherously and assassin-like' hiring 'a lot of fresh men at a reduced price' in their stead. Fourthly, came the outraged response by the displaced workmen as they witnessed their places being filled by a set of 'strangers' from other places. As ever, the language used by the operative silk dyers to describe the usurper is damning of the blackleg character. 'Since the strike', declared the Committee of the Silk Dyers' Union:

> there have gone to work a set of vagabonds, complete thieves, mere wretches, the scum of the country, villains, some of whom have more than once graced the inside of the New Bailey; they go to work guarded by a set of thief-catchers; and Bury's dye-house is literally turned into a den of thieves.
> (*The Poor Man's Advocate*, 10 Nov. 1832: 7–8)

The older, longer-established journeymen trades also had to reckon with the so-called scab and blackleg. The unflattering image of the strike-breaker as the master's weak-willed cringing servant, which we saw bestowed on the black-nebs during the 1859 Oakley colliery strike mentioned above, also featured in the following account of a strike by journeymen print-workers and their apprentices in the printing trade in the early nineteenth century. 'Should some pusillanimous wretch pretend to be troubled with qualms of conscience, or fear of ingratitude to a kind and generous master, and return to his work', opined the writer:

> he must work *solus*; and, when the other gentlemen have agreed upon certain terms with their master, and return to theirs, this obnoxious wretch must immediately be turned adrift, under the opprobrious epithet of *knobstick*, as the *uni qua non* of their condescending to work again. Happy it is for these poor knobsticks if they be able to work at any other business; for their characters are up, and their notoriety is in every print-shop in the United Kingdom.
>
> (Jackson 1805: 442)

For the journeymen shoemakers of London in the mid-1830s, those who refused to join their brethren, in the fight against 'the determined and destructive system of competition' pursued by the master shoemakers, were less than men, whose betrayal could have far-reaching consequences for those whose labour was their sole property. These 'wretches', it was stated, are 'so lost to every sense of honour, and so besotted with ignorance, as not to see that they are paving the way to the ruin of their own families, as well as the class to which they belong' (*Bell's Weekly Messenger*, 12 June 1836: 6).[10] The journeymen bookbinders, too, were scathing of those miscreants in their ranks who served the master rather than the higher 'God' of the trade, the former described as being lustful of worldly goods to excess. As such, the miscreants and their masters carried within their soul the contagion of self-interest and avarice, which threatened to infect not just the trade but the entire labouring class with a fatal malady.

In March 1839, a number of 'black-neb' Edinburgh journeymen bookbinders accepted a situation with an 'obnoxious' London bookbinding company during a dispute between the c. 800 members of the journeymens' Society and the master bookbinders on the issues of rising apprenticeship scales, time-work, and union recognition. The betrayal prompted a representative of the journeymen Bookbinders' Society of Edinburgh to state that the black-nebs:

> not only robbed the London journeymen of the common necessaries of life, but they became instruments in the hands of servile and fawning vagabonds, whose sole aim, at this moment, is to sacrifice the best and dearest interests of working men, on the altar of blood-sucking Mammon!
>
> (The Charter, 31 Mar. 1839: 1)

As with unionised workers in other trades as we saw above, the union-inclined Edinburgh journeymen bookbinders also despised the 'talebearer', that 'pest of all societies', the master's informant. For the Edinburgh bookbinder, the talebearer was the 'low and worthless' workman 'equally ready at all times to protect the interests of employers, when that is threatened or placed in jeopardy' by those of a collectively inclined nature who sought to promote the welfare and happiness of all members of the trade (MRC. Introduction To The Laws Of The Edinburgh Union Society Of Journeymen Bookbinders. Sept. 1846. MSS.39/50/E/3/1/1.).

In these dangerous times, then, the threat of contagion was ever-present. As such, there was the need for constant vigilance to guard the entrances and exits of the union against the contagion of dangerous habits and behaviours which carried the seed of betrayal. 'There are a set of scamps who have no principles', declared a contributor to *The Tradesman* in March 1834:

> and who, in case of strikes, take airs upon themselves; they go to the lodges and they threaten to go to work, if not bought off... Brothers attend to this: send all these rotten rascals to their proper place, and let them spread a moral plague in the enemy's camp... Let public hate bear hard on wolves like these, and clear the country of their nuisance. We hope our Union will consider this, and act with judgement in such cases; for let it be remembered, that he who threatens treason, is in heart a traitor.
>
> *(The Tradesman, 8 Mar. 1834: 6–7)*

How, then, should those who believed that a collective approach to struggle offered the labouring classes the best hope of seeking redress in dangerous times resolve the issue of the perceived unprincipled 'scamp', the 'rotten rascal', the 'wolf', the 'traitor' and the 'moral plague' within their ranks? Many unionists in this period, given the circumstances then prevailing in society, believed that some degree of compulsion was unavoidable if this matter was to be properly addressed. In this regard, let us listen to the words of the Sunderland Shipwrights' Society expressed in 1857:

> It is true there is an indirect species of compulsion in trade societies which the present state of society renders absolutely necessary. It consists in this. Society men refuse to work with those who are utterly regardless of their own interests – men who never look beyond the hour in which they are living; often drunken reprobates, selfish, unfeeling, greedy men, who cannot feel in their hearts to contribute their mite towards the support of their fellow men. Such men have often constant work, and are utterly regardless of their suffering brothers... If this compulsion be tyranny in the eyes of others, it is for the working man "Freedom's best and bravest friend".
>
> *(Rathbone 1860: 516–7)*

The hope was, though, that compulsion could be avoided and should be the weapon of last resort. In the meantime, it was hoped that other regulatory mechanisms would work to address the problem of the uncooperative workman. One such means was to shore up the workers' defensive structures and reinforce the stability of the world inside the confines of the union brotherhood. This effort at collective reinforcement will be addressed in the following chapter.

Notes

1 Comment made at a meeting held in the village of Kilnhurst in May 1869 to discuss the labour unrest in the south Yorkshire coalfields.
2 The strike ended in defeat for the Wigan colliers the following month when they returned to work 'on the terms offered, to save themselves from absolute starvation'. See the *Huddersfield and Holmfirth Examiner*, 19 Nov. 1853: 7.
3 I am grateful to Dr Peter D. Thomas for alerting me to the role of workplace metaphors in political discourse.
4 The lock-out began in February when the colliery owners announced that Denaby Main was to be a 'free labour colliery' devoid of unions. The union men and their families held out until mid-September 1869, their fortitude being rewarded when the unionists were re-employed at the colliery as part of the settlement to end the dispute.
5 The two remaining kinds of social pollution for Douglas were the 'danger from transgressing the internal lines of the system' and, secondly, the 'danger from internal contradiction'.
6 The article in *The Tradesman* was silent as to the location of the turnout, though it likely relates to the strike of machine and steam-engine makers in Glasgow which commenced circa September 1833. The dispute arose, in the words of the journeymen, due to the 'dictatorial manner' by which the Association of Master Machine and Steam-engine Makers of Glasgow 'assert their determination of employing at our business whom they choose, and for what length of time they think proper, in defiance of the long established rights and privileges of the trade'. Such actions, the journeymen continued, placed the mechanic 'in a scale of society little removed from that of the colonial slave'. See *Poor Man's Guardian*, 5 Oct. 1833: 320.
7 Howell became Secretary of the Trade Union Congress in 1871.
8 Clarke was a member of the ILP and the Marxist SDF at various points during his time as a socialist activist.
9 The 1869–70 Thorncliffe dispute pivoted on issues which included the length of the working day, low wages and the right to join a union. The lock-out and its causes and consequences are discussed at greater length in Chapter 8.
10 The rebuke was sparked by a dispute in the summer of 1836 relating to a number of shops in Oxford Street and Tottenham Court Road in central London. The rebuke appeared on a printed bill alongside a 'Black-List' of strike-breakers' names. The bill was pinned to shop windows in the vicinity of the strike.

References

Brentano, Lujo (1870) 'On the History and Development of Gilds and the Origins of Trade-Unions', in Lucy Toulmin Smith and Joshua Toulmin Smith,(eds) *English Gilds*. London: N. Trubner & Company: 65–199.
Clarke, Charles Allen (1893) *The Knobstick. A Story of Love and Labour*. Manchester: John Heywood.
Crompton, Henry (1875) *The Labour Laws Commission*. London: Parliamentary Committee of the Trades Union Congress.
Douglas, Mary (1991; first published 1966) *Purity and Danger. An Analysis of the Concepts of Pollution and Taboo*. London: Routledge.
Dutton, H.I. and King, JohnEdward (1981) *Ten Per Cent and No Surrender. The Preston Strike 1853–1854*. Cambridge: Cambridge University Press.
Freud, Sigmund (1919) *Totem and Taboo*. New York: Moffat, Yard & Co.
Hammond, J.L. and Hammond, Barbara (1995; first published 1919) *The Skilled Labourer 1760–1832*. Stroud: Allan Sutton.

Howell, George (1973; first published 1891) *Trade Unionism New and Old*. Brighton: Harvester Press.
Jackson, Samuel (1805) *Harvest Home*. London: Richard Phillips.
Joyce, Joyce A. (1981) 'Semantic Development of the Word Black: A History from Indo-European to the Present', *Journal of Black Studies*, 11(3): 307–312.
Kidd, Archibald T. (1949) *History of the Tin-Plate Workers and Sheet-Metal Workers and Braziers Societies*. London: National Union of Sheet-Metal Workers and Braziers.
Kiddier, William (1930) *The Old Trade Unions. From Unprinted Records of the Brushmakers*. London: George Allen and Unwin.
Lushington, Godfrey (1860) 'Abstract of Parliamentary Report on Combinations, 1838. Glasgow Cotton-Spinners', in Report of the Committee on Trades' Societies Appointed by the National Association for the Promotion of Social Science, *Trades' Societies and Strikes*. London: John W. Parker & Son: 396–402.
Rathbone, Philip H. (1860) 'An Account of Shipwrights' Trades' Societies in Liverpool, the Tyne and Other Ports', in Report of the Committee on Trades' Societies Appointed by the National Association for the Promotion of Social Science, *Trades' Societies and Strikes*. London: John W. Parker & Son: 479–520.
Steiner, Franz (1956) *Taboo*. London: Cohen & West.
King, William (1829) *An Important Address to Trade Unions*. Manchester: W. Jackson.
Webb, Sidney (1921) *The Story of the Durham Miners*. London: The Labour Publishing Company.
Wright, Thomas (1969; first published 1873) *Our New Masters*. New York: Augustus M. Kelley.

3

VOWS AND SACRED LINES

> Strangers within our sacred walls we have admitted you, expecting you will prove honest, faithful, just, and true.
> (Lines of a verse read at a cotton workers' union initiation ceremony in north-west England in 1834. See Manchester Times and Guardian, 7 June 1834: 3)

We saw in the previous chapter the fear engendered in the minds of collectively inclined workmen by those workers who dwelt in the 'dangerous' world outside the confines of the union brotherhood, those 'inarticulate' regions of the structure, the 'crevices', the 'cracks' in the edifice, the darkly obscure margins, and the mass of formless chaos laying beyond. The workmen who inhabited this dangerous world outside or on the edges of the structure were the so-called 'blacksheep', 'knobsticks', 'scabs', 'black-nebs', 'blacklegs', 'foul' men, 'dishonourables' and 'illegal' men, as well those specific to particular trades like 'dungs' in the tailoring trade and 'corks' in the hat-making trade. How, then, to address this problem? In particular, how to address this problem during a period of far-reaching economic and technological change of a type and intensity which characterised the late eighteenth and nineteenth-century British economy and society? Added to these stresses emanating from rapid and unsettling structural and temporal change were those pressures stemming from a changing and increasingly fluid labour market, an employing class inclined to press down on wages, an unsympathetic legislature which consistently favoured capital over labour, and an increasingly dominant philosophy of life and economics which valorised the individual at the expense of the collective.

When there are pressures on boundaries, margins, thresholds and other vulnerable regions of the social structure, when there is a concern about 'transgressions' destabilising the system, 'it is only by exaggerating the difference between' seemingly dichotomous and contradictory regions such as 'within and without' and 'with and against' that a semblance of order can be created (Douglas 1991: 4). We can see evidence of this at work in union attempts to exaggerate the difference between the world of the unionised workmen and the world outside. This was realised by marking off the union world as a distinct sphere, a special, even sacred realm, separate and morally superior to the world beyond the 'threshold'. Union narratives, both written and verbal, frequently reminded members and initiates of the sacred nature of the union world, as well as the threat posed by the profane world outside. Inducements replete with religious references were made in an effort to encourage the uninitiated to cross the threshold and enter the sacred world of the union. The Articles of the 'Colliers' Commercial and Benefit Union', for instance, this Union being formed in November 1833, promised the colliers:

> that the day of your redemption draweth nigh – The Almighty has seen your affliction – He has heard your cry by reason of your task-masters, and he has seen your sorrows, and the affliction wherewith you have been afflicted, and you must, you will, you shall be delivered – the Union is formed, and we exhort every one of you to take refuge within its precincts, and thereby throw off the galling chain of tyranny and oppression that fetters your every thought and limb.
>
> *(HO44/29/31–42. Articles of the Colliers' Union. c. Jan. 1834)*

Most tellingly in relation to this book, lines from scripture and parables borrowed from the Bible also helped exaggerate the difference between the 'with and against'. We saw in the previous chapter how the powerful myth of Cain and Abel, with its chronicle of fratricide and betrayal, served as a convenient frame to illustrate the fall into sin of the miscreant worker, the forever-shunned scab and blackleg who betrayed his brother unionists.

It is important to make the point here that the trade unions of the early decades of the nineteenth century probably inherited some of their Christian rhetoric from Biblical terms and references passed down to them by the journeymen fraternities and trade societies of the seventeenth and eighteenth centuries. It is also likely that these fraternities and societies would have inherited the same from the language, myths and 'mysteries' which permeated the world of the English medieval craft Guilds. Here one would have in mind the references in Guild and journeymen discourse to 'brethren', 'brotherhood', 'fellowship', 'brotherly aid and charity', as well as the enduring myth of 'the trade as a moral community' (on the likely Guild origin of this myth, see Chase 2012: 15–6 and 91–6). This being said, the prevalence of Biblical language and the attempt to invest the union project with a sacred aura evident in later trade union discourse cannot be explained simply by alluding to past forms and earlier medieval discourses. Malcolm Chase has shown that many of the trade union societies, clubs and fraternities which sprang up in the immediate aftermath of the repeal of the Combination Acts in 1824 sought to deliberately invest their projects with an 'air of solemnity' as evidenced by the 'strictly religious tone' in certain of their written rules and regulations (Chase 2012: 91–2).

Nor should we assume that such religious sentiments were not genuinely felt. In 1831, the mineworkers of the Durham and Northumberland coalfield struck work. The grievances of the pitmen were manifold and included the yearly bond, the 'tommy shop' system, the excessive working day for boys, and the system of punitive fines.[1] According to reports from the authorities in the Tyne and Wear, the most alarming feature of the strike was the 'religious fanaticism which prevails amongst the pitmen', a disposition fomented by union delegates who were 'chiefly Ranter preachers' who infuse all their speeches to the 'ignorant' multitude 'with large quotations from scripture' (HO40/29/89–90. Letter 8 June 1831). These so-called Ranter preachers were usually Primitive Methodists. Primitive Methodism, from its humble beginnings as a breakaway sect from mainstream Wesleyan Methodism formed in Staffordshire in 1811, began to makes its presence felt in the Tyne and Wear mining districts during the first half of the 1820s. By 1845, Primitive Methodism had become an established part of life in the coalfield (Colls 1987: 118). Primitive Methodism and Ranter preachers spreading the Word infused the pitmen and the colliers' union project with passion, the light of revelation, a sense of communalism, egalitarian fervour and evangelical enthusiasm for the union cause, along with a heightened sense that this cause was just and righteous and had the blessing of God. Moreover, fulsome engagement in the union mission held out the hope of salvation in a sinful world. More tellingly from the point of view of the concerns of this book, Primitive Methodism harboured an acute sense of grace and the fall from grace in the form of saints and sinners. In this sense, God could be invoked both 'as a redeemer of the pledge to the union and as a punisher of those who broke it' (Colls 1987: 190). In punishing the blackleg sinner who had betrayed his brethren, therefore, striking colliers were merely carrying out the judgement of the Almighty (Colls 1987: 190–1).

Proselytising preachers were not just spreading the Word of the Union in the Tyne and Wear coalfield. In June 1831, at the same time as the strike of pitmen in the north-east, concerns were expressed by the authorities in the mining district of Ruabon in Denbighshire, north Wales, about 'itinerant preachers' travelling around the coalfields of the United Kingdom 'for the sole and avowed purpose of instigating the colliers to form themselves into Societies for the purpose of fixing the price of wages' (HO52/16/103–6. Letter 29 June 1831). Specific concerns were expressed about the 'sermons' and 'preaching' in Ruabon itself of one such itinerant preacher, a man said to be of 'slender make and exceedingly effeminate' and a former affiliate of the Church of England, whose conversation with the pitmen was of 'the most insidious and dangerous kind, and likely to destroy that subordination, deference and respect which they owe to their employers' (HO52/16/103–6. Letter 29 June 1831). 'Ranter preachers' were also reported to be active in Whitehaven, Cumbria, in the same period. On this occasion, the preachers were supporting the efforts of the colliers employed at pits owned by the Earl of Lonsdale to form a 'Combination Society' (*Morning Post*, 17 Aug. 1831: 3).

Clearly, in a time of increasing stress brought on by rapid economic change, the recourse to religious language and conviction certainly helped in the effort to sacralise the world of the union and demarcate it from the dangerous world beyond its borders. As such, the use of Biblical references helped in some measure to address the issue of those 'ambiguous' workmen who lurked in the 'margins' and in those uncertain realms in other spaces and places in the profane world outside. This being acknowledged, written and verbal forms of persuasion drawing on religious sentiment and imagery often had to be supplemented by other means of encouraging individuals to cross the threshold and 'take refuge' within the precincts of the union. These other means could also be deployed to discourage actions which betrayed the union. One of the most oft-used means, relative to both the aforementioned ambitions, was the oath-taking ritual. Oath-taking was a central component of the quite formalised trade union initiation rituals which were such a customary feature of union life in these decades. It is important to point out, though, that while all forms of initiation into the union world involved some form of oath-taking, not all oath-taking was concerned with initiation, as we will see below.

In regard to initiation rituals, the first point to make is that they were complex and esoteric in nature. An example of this can be seen from an incident in Exeter in January 1834 when a contingent of policemen forced their way into an initiation ceremony involving the bricklayers' union at an Inn in the town. On entering the premises, the Exeter police were shocked to discover a man with a drawn sword guarding the entrance to the ceremony, initiates with their eyes bandaged, a painting of Death, and a range of 'paraphernalia' arrayed on a table in the club-room, which included a 'formidable looking battle-axe', a wooden war-hatchet, two judges' wigs, a white surplice, and a Bible (*Morning Chronicle*, 23 Jan. 1834: 3). Similar elements and symbols were present during initiation ceremonies conducted by trade unions at Worcester in the same year. According to a Home Office report of March 1834, the candidate for membership was taken to a secluded room in a public house, at the entrance of which stood a man with a drawn sword. The initiate was then blindfolded before being led into the room, whereupon a man in a mask administered the union oath. The ensuing rite involved the removal of the blindfold in order that the initiate could be confronted with what the Home Office report described as 'a hideous representation of death', to be followed by a drawn sword being pointed at the initiate's breast by an attending officiate (HO44/29/21–30. Correspondence from Lord Lyttelton to Lord Melbourne on the subject of trade unions. 4 Mar. 1834). As to the form of oath sworn, it was said to be of a 'very strong' nature 'and implies submission to whatever the managers of the society dictate' (HO44/29/21–30. Correspondence from Lord Lyttelton to Lord Melbourne on the subject of trade unions. 4 Mar. 1834).

A similar air of mystery and menace pervaded the initiation ceremonies of the trade unions in Huddersfield the same year, where initiates encountered a union Vice President in a white robe, a white wig, 'a terrifying mask upon his face', and a hatchet in his hand (HO52/25/189–91. Mode of Initiating Members into the Trade Union. Huddersfield. 15 Feb. 1834). Around the same time, a report reached the mainstream press of a trade union initiation ritual involving machine-makers in Wakefield. On this occasion, the rite was carried out in the trade union

Lodge rather than in a public house in the town. Apart from a few variations, many of the elements and symbols which featured in the Exeter and Worcester ceremonies were in evidence at the Wakefield ceremony. Thus, the intended member was blindfolded, ordered to kneel prior to the administering of the oath, and confronted with a transparency of a Death's head and a skeleton following removal of the blindfold. In attendance at the ceremony was a man in a surplice bearing a sword who read the words of the Trinitarian formula 'in the name of the Father, the Son, and the Holy Ghost' as the rite unfolded. The words of the oath, though perfunctory, left little room for ambiguity, the initiate declaring 'before Almighty God, that I will not divulge the secrets of the Lodge; and if I do, may that sword be plunged through my body, and my soul sent to hell' (*Morning Post*, 14 Apr. 1834: 1).

A few years previously in March 1829, a report arrived at the Home Office from Francis Fagan concerning the 'union clubs' then operating in the weaving districts in the neighbourhood of Stroud in Gloucestershire. Fagan had been sent to Gloucestershire by the Public Office in Bow Street to investigate the union clubs and 'to obtain evidence of their illegality'. Fagan's report told of union Lodge meetings held at various Inns in the district guarded by men with drawn swords. As to what unfolded in these inner sanctums, Fagan told of blindfolded initiates and oath-taking ceremonies which were accompanied by hymn singing and prayer recitals, all of which was presided over by men with wooden axes 'painted to resemble Battle Axes', a union President clothed in a white robe and turban, and a union Vice President wearing a black robe, turban and mask. As with the initiation rituals mentioned above, the rite concluded with a chastening experience for the new member. On removal of the blindfold he was made aware of 'a transparency in the room resembling a skeleton sticking a man with a dart in the head'. Fagan's report revealed other details concerning the rite. These included the prospective initiate being turned round several times just prior to swearing the oath until he became 'giddy', the laying of the right hand on a Bible as the oath was administered, and wooden battle axes being waved over the new member's head as the President repeated the oath. At the closing of the ceremony, another element of 'mystery' was added to the proceedings when the new member was given the secret passwords and secret signs of the club, the former being 'The Tower of David' and 'I Will Prove True'. Once bestowed, the new member was thereby granted entry both literally and symbolically into the sacred inner world of the union brotherhood (HO40/23/107–9. The Report of Francis Fagan. 30 Mar. 1829).

Before we attempt to make sense of strange rites such as those described above, it would be helpful to consider how these union rituals have been viewed by contemporary opinion, and later historians. The usual response from those in authority, as well as those who aligned themselves with the established order, ranged from bewilderment to outright revulsion. In a damning account written in 1834, the Lancashire factory commissioner Edward Tufnell described the ceremonies of admission into the trade unions in Yorkshire as being of 'the most awful description', whereby 'every accessory device is employed to strike terror into those who go through these inaugural rites' (Tufnell 1834: 65–6).

The association between trade union rites and 'terror' made by Tufnell was not untypical of the times. A statement issued a year earlier in 1833 by the master tradesmen of Liverpool associated with the building trade spoke of the growing presence of trade unions in such towns as Leeds, Liverpool, Manchester, Bradford, and Bolton. For the concerned Liverpool master tradesmen, these unions were 'promulgating doctrines of the most dangerous tendency' and 'establishing a system of dictation to masters' which was breaking down all manner of distinction and control in trade and industry. Even more alarming for the Liverpool masters was that 'nearly the whole of the working classes by threats, intimidation, or enticement, have been virtually compelled to join them. An oath is administered upon the sacred scriptures to every member upon his entrance, binding him to obey the mandates of the Club' (Anon. 1833: 4–5). A few years later in 1838, a contributor to the *Annual Register* struck a similarly alarmist note regarding trade unions and their attendant rituals:

> The promoters, therefore, of the confederacies under consideration, find themselves compelled to carry their designs into effect by the instrumentality of much coarser means. Terror becomes the main foundation of their authority. Like all secret associations, they begin by the institution of certain mystic and superstitious rites, which not only impose upon the imagination of their neophytes, but give a dramatic interest to their proceedings, and a dignity to their lawless schemes.
>
> (Annual Register *1838: 204*)

Another, related response was to characterise the oath-taking rituals as an exercise in deliberately contrived and cynical obfuscation designed to subvert rational thinking and render individuals more malleable to persuasion by manipulative and malevolent leaders. As the masters of Derby put it in December 1833 just prior to their concerted attempt to purge the entire town and its workplaces of trade union members and influence:

> The members of the Union are bound by a secret oath, and their admission is accompanied by mistical [sic] ceremonies, calculated and designed to impose upon and overawe the minds of credulous and unsuspecting men, and render them the unconscious slaves, and ready tools, of their more crafty masters.
>
> (Derby Mercury, *11 Dec. 1833: 3)*

Another response to union oath-taking rituals by those in authority during these years was to characterise them as being indicative of seditious behaviour and divided loyalties. Thus, it should come as no surprise to hear that efforts were made to charge the fifteen Exeter bricklayers apprehended at the January 1834 initiation ceremony mentioned above with administering an illegal oath, though the authorities were unable to make the charge stick, it should be said. This characterisation of union initiation rituals as seditious behaviour received its most potent expression two months following the Exeter incident, when six Dorset agricultural labourers were sentenced to seven years' penal servitude in Australia for swearing a secret oath in connection with the Tolpuddle Lodge of the Agricultural Labourers Friendly Society. It was the recourse to an earlier statute, the Unlawful Oaths Act of 1797, which enabled the state to banish the soon-to-be martyrised Tolpuddle labourers.

Another reaction to the 'mystic and superstitious rites' of trade unionists during these years was to cast them as primitive and irrational, as barbaric relics of a past age. This view was not just confined to those who considered themselves loyal defenders of the settled order, as with Edward Tufnell. Robert Owen considered the more esoteric union rites, particularly with their obsession with secrecy and opacity, as survivals from an earlier barbaric age and thus an impediment to more rational forms of political engagement such as socialist cooperation, the latter of which he championed of course (Behagg 1982: 159).

A variation on this theme of union rituals as backward and irrational was to portray them as immature, even puerile. Before inviting his readers to peruse the extensive and elaborate theatre of the initiation rites of the Yorkshire woolcombers' union, Edward Tufnell forewarned them that they would find in the performance 'much to disgust, and something to laugh at' (Tufnell 1834: 66). Again, such views were not just the preserve of the mainstream defenders of the established order. There was much that William Lovett admired about trade unions, though he chastised them and even the Owenite-inclined general unionism of the 1830s for copying 'a great number of the forms, ceremonies, signs, and fooleries of freemasonry' (Lovett 1920: 89). The pro-union publication *The Tradesman* also thought the more esoteric and mystical rites of the unions immature and unbecoming of a movement seeking meaningful social and political advancement in a world that was becoming ever-more rational and modern. Better that the unions 'should act like men seeking their rights', proclaimed *The Tradesman*, and 'let no childish means be resorted to by them, no secret oaths, no paraphernalia of lodges, or pass-words be used, but let all their movements be open and honourable' (*The Tradesman*, 18 Jan. 1834: 1).

This characterisation of the more esoteric and mystical rituals of Britain's early nineteenth-century trade unions as immature, even childish, and unsuited to the modern industrial and political world that was coming into being would also seep into the later historiography. In their classic study of the history of trade unions, Sidney and Beatrice Webb could write of the prevalence amongst the early trade unionists of 'fearful oaths, mystic initiation rites, and other manifestations of a sensationalism which was sometimes puerile and sometimes criminal' (Webb 1920: 87). For historians like the Webbs, the persistence of these 'puerile' and backward practices acted to stall or impede the transition to the next level of trade union consciousness, a more mature and higher stage of awareness in line with modern circumstances and the trajectory of Britain's economic and political development.

Clearly, the Webbs tended towards an evolutionary perspective when seeking to make sense of the early years of trade unionism in the United Kingdom. As such, their approach to the study of labour history was tinged with historicism and teleology, which disposed them to make sense of these earlier expressions of trade unionism in terms of a 'grand narrative' of economic and political change, which saw an evolutionary line existing between these earlier forms and the later appearance of more advanced and 'modern' labour organisations such as mainstream 'legal' trade unions. It should not come as a great surprise to us, then, that the Webbs would be disdainful of the strange, esoteric rites and ceremonies of early trade unionism, treating them as reflections of a backward, immature, and even pre-modern mind-set.

A more sensitive response to these rituals in the historiography was provided by William H. Oliver. In a well-informed and detailed account of trade union oaths which is particularly sensitive to the ecclesiastical and symbolic dimensions of union initiation rites, Oliver highlighted the prevalence of oath-taking rites in a range of contemporary trade unions, including woolcombers, builders, tailors, compositors and cotton spinners (Oliver 1966: 5–12). For Oliver, the principal functions of the union rites were to secure internal discipline, protect union secrets, and 'impose religious sanctions' on would-be informers or embezzlers of union funds.

As the Webbs and some of the contemporary critics of these trade union rituals were at least willing to recognise, these rituals were quite extraordinary affairs. This much being true, it does not aid understanding to view them with consternation and disgust, as did detractors like Edward Tufnell. Rather, the historian needs to adopt a more empathetic approach which is sensitive to the particular context and circumstances of the times, as well as the many pressures that working people were experiencing at this time. Nor is it helpful to interpret these rituals one-dimensionally as crude instruments of seduction imposed on credulous workmen, or as brutal instruments of terror imposed on petrified souls. Nor should they be viewed as 'so many relics of barbarism', as irrational survivals of a more primitive age. In a similar vein, these esoteric and mystical rituals should not be simply dismissed as the 'puerile' and sometimes comical antics of workmen unable to progress to the next, more mature and rational stage of trade union consciousness. Nor do the union rituals simply mimic the 'fooleries of freemasonry', as William Lovett claimed. Of course, it would be hard to deny the overlap between some of the components in trade union rites, particularly those in the rituals of the older journeymen craft unions, and some of the elements in the rituals of Freemasons. Both placed a strong emphasis in their initiation rituals on secret oaths and passwords, the need to preserve secrets, and the potency of symbols and dramatic intensity to convey the appropriate message (on freemasonry rituals, see Cohen 1971). Nevertheless, to see the trade union rituals as mere replicas of freemasonry rituals would be to misunderstand the nature of the former and risk not seeing elements that were unique to union rites.

Clearly, a more empathetic and nuanced approach to the early trade union rituals is called for. If we turn to look more closely at these rituals, we can observe that they were intricate and performed a number of functions, many of which were consistent with all rituals. In terms of our earlier discussion of union efforts to invest their world and project with a sacred aura, rituals have a capacity to bring the sacred to the fore. As Catherine Bell informs us, all the leading scholars of ritual have demonstrated that ritual activities 'effectively sacralise things, people, or events', thereby reinforcing ritual as 'a universal category of social life' (Bell 1992: 15). Emile Durkheim, too, put the sacred at the heart of his theory of ritual. Thus, the repeated or ritual veneration of sacred things and objects by a community aids the organisation of social life, and helps forge group solidarity and enhance social cohesion within the collective (Durkheim 1965).

Another of the functions of ritual is to help communities understand their condition and environment, help bring meaning and structure to an otherwise confusing world. In praising the imaginative creativity of ritual, Mary Douglas observed that they are 'more wonderful than the exotic caves and palaces of fairy tales', displaying a magic which 'creates harmonious worlds with ranked and ordered populations playing their appointed parts' (Douglas 1991: 72). In this sense, rituals can help address the many ambiguities that life throws up. In their inimitable manner and style, the trade union initiation rituals sought to bring some form, structure and meaning to what seemed to working people to be an increasingly chaotic, confusing and threatening world and working environment. In this sense, and at one level, these rituals can be viewed as a creative response to the manifold pressures that union-inclined workmen were experiencing during the era of industrialisation and modernity of the late eighteenth and nineteenth century. These were the pressures mentioned above relating to changes in the economy and labour market, pressure on wages, an unresponsive legislature, and the primacy of *laissez-faire* thinking on economics and political life. Given these multiple pressures, union rituals would help provide a frame through which these tensions could be better controlled and managed. As Mary Douglas tells us, ritual framing has the capacity to 'shut in desired themes, or shut out intruding ones' (Douglas 1991: 63). Thus, in the face of life's multiple pressures, ritual can help restore one's balance and equilibrium and help dissipate some of the uncertainties thrown up by life.

In a related sense, rituals can also help address the many contradictions that life presents. In this sense, 'ritual is a type of critical juncture wherein some pair of opposing social or cultural forces comes together' (Bell 1992: 16). These opposing elements, and which speak to the issues addressed in this book, would include order and chaos, the individual and the group, unity and disunity, the inside and the outside, and even the seemingly irreconcilable realms of 'within and without' and 'with and against' that we looked at earlier in this chapter. In such scenarios, ritual has a dialectical function, resolving apparent contradictions or dichotomies. Or, as Catherine Bell puts it, ritual in this sense serves as a 'paradigmatic means of sociocultural integration, appropriation, or transformation' (Bell 1992: 16).

Rituals also have the capacity to alleviate anxiety in times of acute emotional stress brought on by rapid temporal change. According to this take on ritual, communities often fall back on ritual when their experience of time undergoes a fundamental change, when they feel that time is pressing in on them and that their survival is threatened by deadly external powers, a threat perceived to be imminent (Fenn 1997). Ritual thus helps the threatened community to both control the temporal anxiety and regenerate itself in preparation for the struggle to combat the external threat. Temporal anxiety, the fear that time was pressing in on them, certainly gripped many of those working people and their families associated with Britain's beleaguered journeymen craft trades during the modern era of industrialisation and *laissez-faire* economics. These tradesmen in particular, such as those labouring in trades such as felt-making, currying, hosiery, brush-making, cordwaining, rope-making, book-binding, hat-making and wool-combing to name but a few, were being hit hard by structural economic change, technological innovation, increasing specialisation, rapidly changing working methods and practices, and particularly the arrival of the machine. These feelings of anxiety and time pressing in can be exacerbated still further if the threatened community perceives that the institutions of mainstream society are failing them. In such circumstances, the threatened community looks for sanctuary within ritual frameworks of its own making, as with the quite distinctive trade union initiation rituals. This scenario becomes even more likely if the beleaguered community felt that the state's legal system had forsaken it, and that it had no recourse to law to seek redress of grievances. 'Ritual is also likely to assume greater importance relative to law when the apparatus of legal enforcement is ineffective', as in circumstances where there existed corruption, weak government, or disrespect for the law (Miller 2005: 1229). This perception of the law as 'ineffective', indeed one could say openly hostile when it came to combinations of workmen up to 1824 and trade unions thereafter, certainly applied to working people during the era of political economy and *laissez-faire*. As we saw in an earlier chapter, those whose only 'capital' was their labour felt that the legal system was not working for them and that they were being denied access to a legislature which clearly prioritised the masters.[2]

As mentioned earlier in this chapter, a threat perceived by unionised workmen to be just as lethal as a hostile legislature in these troubled times was the threat from within their own ranks. This threat from within had the potential to endanger the survival of the social structure itself. This was the threat posed by the miscreant workmen, the hated 'scabs' and 'blacklegs', who inhabited the 'dark' regions and dangerous borderlands of the structure, as well as the realm of formless chaos laying outside. Averting this threat from within their own ranks would be an important function of the unions' initiation rites, as well as those oath-taking rites which occurred in contexts outside the formal initiation ceremonies. Therefore, in terms of the former, we should avoid viewing the initiation rites as simply a means of protecting union secrets, discouraging would-be informers, or forestalling embezzlement. While the union rituals most certainly sought to speak to such issues, their function also extended to addressing the matter of potential waverers and traitors in the ranks, particularly during times of heightened tension between labour and capital. This additional dimension has been recognised by some historians. Malcolm Chase has stated that while trade union ritualism was concerned with the 'practical issues of financial security' and 'confidentiality', the rituals also addressed 'a need to reinforce loyalty and solidarity that might be tested under the duress of strike action and employer hostility' (Chase 2012: 137). That union oaths varied in their nature, wording and range of concerns, and thus were not restricted to preserving union secrets and ridding the union of informers and embezzlers, can be seen from the following few examples from the primary evidence.

Some unions would make quite specific reference to potential waverers or traitors in their oaths and initiation ceremonies. The oath of the Scottish cotton spinners in 1823 spoke of the need to further 'our common welfare', as well as the 'chastisement of knobs' (Webb Trade Union Archive. LSE. A/1/289. Oath of Cotton Spinners in Scotland. 1823). The initiation ritual of the Sawyers' Union in Lancashire in the early 1840s featured blindfolded initiates, a man in a mask, a skeleton, hymn singing, Bible kissing, and words said to be 'of a threatening character to all knobsticks' (*Perthshire Advertiser*, 14 Jan. 1841: 1). The oaths of other unions could be less explicit in their wording, though the intended message to potential traitors and strike-breakers was the same. Thus, new members to the 'Weavers' Union' in the Rochdale area of Lancashire in the late 1820s swore on oath 'to stand firm to one another and to perform whatsoever is commanded to reveal everything they know or learn to each other' (HO40/23/347–8. Report on system of Combination. Rochdale. 16 May 1829).

The wording of some union oaths was framed quite specifically with potential strike-breakers in mind. In the latter part of 1827, probably around December of that year, a union designating itself 'The Saddleworth Weavers and Spinners Union' was founded in Saddleworth, a cotton and weaving district lying between the West Riding of Yorkshire to the east and the town of Oldham to the west. Many of the elements we have discerned in the practices of other trade unions existing at this time were present in the Saddleworth Union. The new union held weekly 'secret' meetings of the Lodge and initiation ceremonies at various Inns in the parish. Present at the latter ceremonies were men with swords guarding the meeting, psalm singing, a copy of the Bible, and kneeling blindfolded initiates swearing an oath to keep union secrets and obey union orders. Failure to abide by these pledges would bring forth 'some horrid penalty'. The sworn oaths of the Saddleworth Union were clearly not just confined to securing pledges to preserve union secrets, however. Thus, a blindfolded member was obliged to swear on a Bible 'That he would not work under a certain price, nor work till all went in'. After making this pledge, the member 'was made to hold his right hand up and lay his left hand on the Book, and then wish his right hand might drop from his body if he went in before all went in – then he kissed the Book' (HO40/22/423–5. Correspondence. 22 Dec. 1828).

We also have a record of an oath of a similar nature sworn by cotton workers during the wage strike in Stockport and Manchester in 1818 (on these disputes, see Hammond 1995: 94–109). According to a report sent to the Home Office by an informant operating under the alias 'B', the cotton operatives 'took not less than three oaths, one in Ludissm [sic] and the other not to work under such a price and the third to be faithful to one another' (HO42/179/159–160. Letter from the spy

'B'. 3 Aug. 1818).³ It is likely that this particular oath was forged under the duress of the strike and the seemingly ever-present threat posed by the importation of blacklegs by the factory owners. In certain instances this threat became a reality, as when blacklegs from Burton-on-Trent were drafted in by one of the factory owners during the turnout of Stockport power-loom weavers (Hammond 1995: 95).⁴

Oaths forged in the 'heat of battle' during a turnout, with the oath-taking message tailored to the particular stage at which the strike had arrived, were not uncommon during these decades. We can find evidence of this even during the early years of political economy. In April 1789, it was reported that journeymen papermakers in Edinburgh, then in dispute with their masters over wages, had entered into a combination 'to carry their point by force, and with this view bound themselves, by an oath to one another, not to work at the present wages' (*Whitehall Evening Post*, 25–28 Apr. 1789: 2). Further south, during a turnout of weavers in Carlisle in 1819, sparked in the weavers' words 'because the wages we have been in the habit of receiving are quite inadequate for our existence', oaths were administered at union gatherings binding those present not to work for particular manufacturers in Cumberland under a certain rate of wages (*Public Ledger and Daily Advertiser*, 8 June 1819: 3). On occasions during this dispute, the Carlisle weavers resorted to more forceful measures to administer the oath. Weavers reluctant to swear the oath to support the strike were sometimes visited in their homes, with some 'even surrounded in bed, and there made to swear against their will' (*The Carlisle Patriot*, 3 July 1819: 3).

Colliers, too, were not averse to using the oath-taking rite as a strike weapon to discourage potential waverers and traitors. During a strike in Radstock and Paulton, near Bath, in March 1817, the turnout colliers, having taken possession of several of the works, 'sent persons down into the pits to compel those who worked in them to be drawn up'. Once drawn up from the pit, the waverers were then obliged to swear an oath which bound them not to return to work until the colliers' grievances had been met (*Cambridge Chronicle and Journal*, 7 Mar. 1817: 4). A similar, though more robust method of persuasion was used by Welsh colliers in the neighbourhood of Wrexham and Ruabon a few years later, in December 1830, during a turnout over wages. Pitmen showing reluctance to participate in the strike action were encouraged by the turnout colliers to exit the pit one by one. Once ascended, the waverers were then made to swear an oath on the Bible not to work for less than the price stipulated by the strikers. In such circumstances oath-taking and compulsion often went hand-in-hand, as those pitmen reluctant to comply were threatened with being dragged into the engine pool or being left stranded down the pit by the rope being cut (HO52/16/66–72. Correspondence and depositions. Dec. 1830 to Jan. 1831). We encountered the 1831 strike in the Durham and Northumberland coalfield earlier in this chapter. The oath-taking rite was also to the fore during this stoppage. The numinous power of the oath to persuade and bind was reluctantly recognised by the Duke of Northumberland, who wrote to the Home Office in April lamenting the stoppage and the fact that 'the men are sworn in to the union and all hopes of them being persuaded to return to labour seems now quite at an end' (HO52/14/215–6. Letter 23 Apr. 1831).[5]

The oath-taking rite was prominent in other contexts involving mineworkers, as when it was deployed to recruit pitmen to the colliers' union. In October 1830, William Hulton, one-time High Sheriff of Lancashire and the owner of Hulton colliery on the Lancashire coalfield, wrote to Robert Peel complaining of the 'serious dangers' posed by the colliers' combination then gaining influence amongst the Lancashire pitmen. Amongst the many practices of the union that alarmed Hulton was that of unionist colliers traversing the coalfields administering on-the-spot union oaths to pitmen. For instance, at some pits on the coalfield, complained Hulton, 'a number of men belonging to the Union compelled the Banksmen and Engineers to absent themselves and then ordered all the colliers to desist from work and take the oaths of the Society' (HO40/26/79–81. Letter 22 Oct. 1830).

The more elaborate oath-taking rituals which featured in the formal setting of a union initiation ceremony also sought to address the threat posed by potential traitors and strike-breakers within the ranks. We can more fully appreciate this if we consider some of the insights on ritual provided by Richard Fenn. In his study of ritual, Fenn presents a typology of ritual forms, two of which are 'rituals of transformation' and 'rituals of aversion'. According to Fenn, rituals of aversion become operational at critical junctures, times of stress, or moments when it appeared that the 'enemy was at the gates' (Fenn 1997: 48–53). As with all initiation rituals, the individual initiate stood at the heart of the process. Fenn likened rituals of aversion to those rituals engaged in by an army prior to battle which aimed to stiffen the resolve of the combatants. During rituals of aversion, which apply to a range of contexts military or otherwise, the initiate is made to appreciate the importance of holding fast to his place in the ranks, maintaining his nerve in the face of the enemy and, above all, not to betray his comrades-in-arms. The initiate is also made aware in the ritual that to flout these fundamental requirements and expectations would be to seriously threaten the unity and even survival of the social structure. Fenn makes the related point that in order to maintain discipline in the ranks, stiffen resolve, and 'keep people in formation' in the tense liminal moment before the commencement of battle, rituals of aversion seek to impress on the initiate the need to conform to 'the formal and informal expectations of the society in question, even in the face of death'. The ritual works to bring about this result, that is, ensuring that the individual can be 'counted on to hold up even in the face of death' by magically and symbolically creating for the initiate an 'existential encounter with death' that is both tangible and terrifyingly close (Fenn 1997: 51). We can more fully understand this need within aversion rituals for an 'existential encounter with death' if we turn to consider Fenn's other ritual type, that is, 'rituals of transformation'.

Rituals of transformation feature many of the standard rite of passage characteristics of all rituals as recognised by Arnold van Gennep in his pioneering work on ritual (van Gennep 1960). This is the notion of ritual as transition to a different state of being or status. This transition comprises a three-stage passage which involves separation from one's original state, a liminal stage of suspension prior to incorporation into the new state, and integration into the new identity. The latter stage marks the conclusion of the rite and signals the re-entry of the individual into society, albeit in a new form. These standard rite of passage elements are certainly evident in Richard Fenn's notion of 'rituals of transformation', though the transformative rituals that he writes about are informed more by Maurice Bloch's analysis of ritual in *Prey into Hunter* (Bloch 1992).

The themes of the omnipresence of death in life, the evanescence of life, and the vulnerability of the individual in the face of these existential threats, play an important part in Fenn's and Bloch's understanding of ritual. In Bloch's well-known analysis of the initiation ritual of the Orokaiva of Papua New Guinea, he observed that the rite placed much stress on mortality and used aggressive symbolism to evoke in the living initiate 'a terrifying closeness to death' as well as a sense of the immanence of death (Bloch 1992: 8–23 for an extensive discussion of Orokaiva initiation). This 'existential encounter with death' experienced by the initiate aimed to bring into being a person of a new type, a person more mature, steadfast and courageous than had been present at the initial 'separation' phase of the ritual. A key mechanism of such rituals is to bring initiates to an enlightened awareness of their new state of being, whereby they perceive themselves to be reinvigorated and superior to their original state. At this point, they are then ready to play a constructive part in the social life of the community. No longer prey, the initiates emerge from the ritual as hunters with all the vitality and strength that this condition entails. The transformative rituals of Bloch and Fenn thus have a strong transcendental quality which place much emphasis on the 'regeneration' or 'rebirth' of the participant. In other words, having overcome the symbolic encounter with death encountered during the initiation test, the participant re-enters the world re-revitalised having 'consumed' the 'vitality' served up by the ritual. The ritual thus marks a new beginning, a new chapter in the life of the individual. The community, too, gains benefits from these initiation rites. 'Those who have passed these tests of initiation presumably will not be petrified – will not "turn into stone" – at the hideous prospect of the enemy arrayed in armour on the battlefield, or in the face of any other trials that life indeed may offer that try the soul' (Fenn 1997: 44).

The work of Richard Fenn and Maurice Bloch provide some valuable insights into the workings of the more formalised union oath-taking rituals, particularly the symbolism on show in these ceremonies. As discussed earlier in this chapter, these symbols have usually been interpreted as aspects of a crude apparatus of terror and intimidation by Edward Tufnell and other like-minded defenders of the established order. On the surface, it is difficult to deny that this apparatus did have the capacity 'to stimulate terror and awe' in the initiate, as well as those witnessing the proceedings. Certainly, the presence of swords, axes and representations of death, the latter usually in the form of a skeleton or a 'picture of death', offered up an awe-inspiring spectacle for the participants. Nevertheless, we need to discern the more complex, multi-layered function of the ritual, as well as the symbolism which accompanied it. The first, more general point to make here is that it is important to recognise that during the decades under consideration in this book, Britain and its economy and labour relations were in transition as the nation slowly mutated to a new economic order. As such, it was a time of acute stress and danger for the labouring classes in particular. During these threatening and dangerous liminal decades, unionised labour effectively mobilised for war against a well-resourced and determined adversary in the form of capital, the masters and their powerful supporters in the political establishment, the legislature and law enforcement. As 'rituals of aversion', therefore, the elaborate trade union initiation and oath-taking rituals sought to foster a sense of duty, loyalty and unity within the ranks, stiffen the resolve of members new to the union cause, and forestall acts of betrayal or desertion borne of treachery or cowardice in times of heightened conflict between labour and capital, as during turnouts. The ritual process would work to achieve this outcome through the deployment of an aggressive symbolism committed to extracting maximum benefit from the potential of particular representations and images of mortality and the ever-present spectre of death. On conclusion of the rite, a workman of a new type was to emerge, equipped with the identity and consciousness of one no longer gripped by fear and weakness of a kind which only aided the oppressor. As the lines of a verse read at the initiation ceremony of the 'Friendly Society of Operative Cotton Manufacturers', which took place in their union Lodge in north-west England in the Summer of 1834 stated:

> Where the weak are slaves the stronger bear command;
> When tyrants rule with uncontrolled sway,
> Degraded subjects must their will obey.
>   (*Manchester Times and Guardian*, 7 June 1834: 3)

The emergence of this workman of a new type certainly seemed to alarm the defenders of the settled order. In February 1829, a report arrived at the Home Office from the authorities in Briscombe, near Stroud, in the weaving districts of Gloucestershire, telling of secret union Lodge meetings held at night, 'mysterious' initiation ceremonies, and of operatives 'impetuously' flocking to the union cause. Equally concerning for the authorities was that 'becoming an associate' of the union 'seems in many instances to produce a very unfavourable change of demeanour', producing in the workman a 'calm, confident and determined' bearing even under questioning by those in authority, which 'is as remarkable as it is alarming' (HO40/23/77–80. Letter 20 Feb. 1829). The evident disinclination of workmen to break their oath once sworn also frustrated the authorities. The authorities in Scotland, for instance, complained in 1818 that the culture of secrecy and silence amongst the colliers, and their general reluctance to betray their brothers resulting from the oath-taking system, made it extremely difficult to secure convictions against 'illegal' combinations and other forms of union activity (NAS. AD14/18/112/16. Letter 27 Oct. 1818. See also NAS. AD14/18/112/18. Declaration of Robert Martin. 13 Oct. 1818; and NAS. AD14/18/112. Declaration of Thomas Hay. 22 Oct. 1818).

The more formalised trade union initiation and oath-taking rituals also bear comparison to Richard Fenn's 'rituals of transformation'. This can be seen in the emphasis in the latter on the strong transcendental dimension to the initiation process, whereby the pre-liminal, less robust nature of the initiate is symbolically expunged through a ritual encounter with death in its various representations so as to make space for the rebirth of the new revitalised and more resolute individual. In terms of the trade union initiation rite, it is the worker who transitions to the new state of being, revitalised and now ready to pass over the threshold into the union brotherhood and join with his fellows in defence of the collective and the trade.

Following Maurice Bloch, we may also wish to view the trade union initiation rite as a reconfiguration of the standard three-stage rite of passage sequence of birth-life-death involved in the transition to the higher state of being. For Bloch, ritual violence, or what he calls the two stages of 'rebounding violence' in ritual, entailed the initiate, in a strange inversion of the birth-life-death cycle, being symbolically 'slain' before rising from the dead to take his place once more in the mundane world, though now revitalised, imbued with spirit, and aware of being part of something that transcends the individual self (Bloch 1992: 18–20). Bloch believed this to be generic to many initiation rituals:

> Initiation frequently begin with a symbolic "killing" of the initiates, a "killing" which negates their birth and nurturing. The social and political significance of such a passage is that by entering into a world beyond process, through the passage of reversal, one can then be part of an entity beyond process, for example, a member of a descent group. Thus, by leaving this life, it is possible to see oneself and others as part of something permanent, therefore life-transcending.
>
> *(Bloch 1992: 4)*

Union initiates, too, transitioned to the new state of being following a journey which reconfigured the standard rite of passage sequence of birth-life-death. As with the rites of passage observed by Bloch, the union rites followed a pattern of life-death-rebirth in the course of which the prospective member symbolically died in his former identity following an 'existential encounter with death', before being reborn into a new consciousness as a fraternal brother of the union. Here it seems as well, that in blurring the boundary between life and death, the union initiation ritual had that capacity unique to some rituals to create a sense of what Edward Carpenter called a 'mystical oneness' with all things fundamental in life, nature and the cosmos (Carpenter 1920: 47).

Despite some differences in emphasis and form, with both Fenn and Bloch as well as with the trade union initiation rituals, the theme of death and rebirth is a fundamental and powerful component of the initiation process. So, too, is the theme of violence. Initiation ritual ceremonies as a rule tend to incorporate some element of violence, whether physical, emotional or symbolic. This is particularly the case with initiation rituals which seek to bring about a profound identity transformation which effectively turn a boy into a warrior or, for Maurice Bloch, transform prey into a hunter-cum-warrior. As we have just seen with Bloch, violence in ritual could assume quite extreme forms, with the initiate being symbolically 'slain' in the ritual before rising from the dead to re-enter the world of the living. We can observe elements of violence in the trade union initiation rituals, too, though of an emotional and symbolic nature, as they sought to turn individuals into loyal and hardened warriors ready to give all for the collective and the trade 'even in the face of death'. It is likely as well that those administering the initiation ceremonies were fully aware that the initiate's emotional encounter with the symbols of violence on show in the rite, whether this be the swords, battle axes, or the 'picture of Death', should be of an intensity commensurate with the vital task of ridding the community and trade of the deadly malaise of treachery and cowardice.

Transforming individuals into loyal and hardened warriors was not the sole function of the trade union initiation rituals. We know from the work of Victor Turner in particular, and Roy Rappaport, that ritual symbols are multivocal in that they have multiple meanings and significations (Turner 1967; and Rappaport 1999). As Rappaport put it, 'at any moment an array of "meanings" may be represented simultaneously by the same object or act' (Rappaport 1999: 170). Indeed, the ritual process in its entirety should be understood as an event which can carry a number of meanings simultaneously, which mean that different people can interpret these meanings in different ways. With this qualification in mind, we should not confine our understanding of the more formalised union initiation rituals to the meanings and significations discussed above. In seeing these union rituals as 'rituals of aversion' and 'rituals of transformation', much has been made up to now of the representations and symbols of death which featured in these ceremonies. Less has been said, however, of the presence of other items and symbols at these ceremonies which are suggestive of other meanings and which sought to communicate other messages during the rite. Here one has in mind, for instance, the judges' wigs and the Bible seized by the authorities when they broke up the initiation rite conducted by the bricklayers' union in Exeter in January 1834.[6] Before we attempt to comprehend the meaning of such items, it is important to preface our analysis by making the obvious point that one of the key functions of ritual is to communicate the values and moral code of the community to those participating in the ritual. Secondly, and in a related sense, an additional function of the ritual is to assign the initiated individual a role in the social order which encourages acceptance of these values and morals. Thirdly, the ritual should also seek to instil an awareness in the individual that the said values and morals are fundamental to the life and well-being of the community. Fourthly, rituals also work to impress upon the initiate the importance of remaining true to his or her role in the established social order and holding fast to its moral code.

We can explore this function of ritual further by considering the relationship of ritual to law. In an interesting analysis, Geoffrey Miller likened rituals to law. According to Miller, law, as with ritual, seeks to assign the individual a social role consistent with the needs and requirements of the wider community and its system of values and moral code. In so doing, the law 'imposes on people certain conventional and obligatory forms of behaviour', and forms 'part of the essential constitution of human societies' relating to a set of shared understandings concerning the proper allocation and exercise of power in society (Miller 2005: 1181). Law, like ritual, also discourages behaviours deemed to be harmful to the society and ensures that the members of society are made aware that acts of behaviour which flout accepted norms will not be tolerated. Elsewhere, Miller refers to 'the legal function of ritual'. Rituals:

> like law and norms, control behaviour by encouraging beneficial actions and discouraging harmful ones. The role of ritual in influencing behaviour in the service of an ostensibly broader good can be termed its "legal function" – that is, the idea of law is employed generally to describe attempts by the broader society, enforced if necessary by compulsion, to impose social controls on behaviour.
>
> *(Miller 2005: 1182–3)*

Taking our cue from Miller, and being mindful of the multivocal nature of ritual, we need to see that an important, though not exclusive, function of trade union initiation rituals was to perform a 'legal' role. In other words, as with law, the union initiation rite worked to assign the initiate a social role which ensured recognition of the values and moral code of the community and trade, impress on the initiate the obligations that came with the role, and make the initiate aware of society's disapproval of those acts which may contravene this code. Indeed, it could be postulated that the initiation ceremony functioned as a court of popular justice of a type that marginal groups were likely to establish, having been forced by circumstances and pressures to work outside the formal legal framework. There were a number of items in evidence at these ceremonies strongly suggestive of the ritual's legal function. We have already mentioned the presence of the judges' wigs at the January 1834 Exeter bricklayers' initiation ceremony. One should also mention the almost universal presence of the Bible at union initiation ceremonies. The Bible, as we know, was the enduring symbol of discernment, truth and justice in the Christian world to which late eighteenth and nineteenth-century Britain belonged. For the many union members of a Christian faith, the Bible functioned as the ultimate arbiter concerning fundamental questions of right and wrong, good and evil, and truth and falsehood. The Bible performed a similar role in law environments, symbolising truth and justice and the importance of remaining true to one's word. One could even interpret the almost universal presence of a sword at union initiation ceremonies as signifying 'truth combatting' or 'divine truth', or even as a symbol of purification, as seen in numerous passages in Biblical scripture (as in Isaiah 66:16: *By fire and by the sword will Jehovah judge all flesh, and the slain of Jehovah shall be many*).

As we have already seen in this chapter, many workers in this period of unsettling economic and social change looked to scripture and reassuring messages from itinerant preachers to help them make sense of the difficult times, and to find a pathway through the confusion. We have also seen that to a considerable degree the union rites, whether the formal initiation rites or the more perfunctory and often improvised oath-taking rites staged in the heat of battle during a turnout, were seeped in rhetoric and symbolism derived from Christian belief. During the former ceremonies, prospective members would encounter union officers in sacred garments, swear solemn oaths on a Bible, and heard or recited invocatory passages from scripture. They were also made aware of enduring Christian mythologies and truths concerning righteous behaviour, sinfulness, duty, sacrifice, the sacred nature of the pledge, brotherhood, divine judgement, and the omniscience of scripture and the Word. In this way, and certainly in the more elaborate of the trade union ceremonies, the rites conferred on the initiates a sense of the sacred nature of the fraternal brotherhood whose ranks they had entered and whose principles they had sworn to uphold. Indeed, the trade union rituals and ceremonies should be seen as part of that wider process whereby the union world was sacralised and rendered a separate sphere to that of the dangerous world beyond its borders. Such rhetoric and symbolism also melded with the language and cherished myths of many journeymen trades, 'mysteries' which as we have seen probably reached back to the belief system and practices of the medieval craft Guilds.

Pointing up the strong presence of the sacred in the trade union initiation rituals alerts us to another dimension to these rituals. This is the role played by the ritual in imparting the taboos of the trade union world. As scholars of taboo recognise, individuals are more likely to avoid engaging in a course of action which flouts society's established rules, traditions and codes of behaviour if it is believed that these rules, traditions and codes have the endorsement of a sacred authority which is inviolate. To cross these sacred lines, moreover, would be to incur divine wrath, with all the potential perils for the transgressor that this implies (Rossano 2013: 38). Thus, while at one level the trade union initiation ritual brings awareness of the community's established rules, traditions and codes, at another level the ritual makes known the sacred nature of this established framework and the dangers that would befall the community should this framework be undermined. A breach of this framework risked unleashing a host of unpalatable dangers on the community which threatened its very survival. In bringing awareness of the taboo, moreover, this latter function of the ritual also issued a grave warning to the initiate not to engage in behaviour which threatened the established order of things.

This was no longer a straightforward moral issue, a simple matter of an individual exercising his or her independent judgement in choosing between a right or a wrong course of action. With the taboos transmitted through the union initiation ceremony there was to be no ambiguity, no ambivalence, no grey areas, no confusion, no hesitation, no vacillation, no latitude for individual contemplation and reflection. Nor would there be scope for the individual to indulge the selfish side of his nature, to fall into temptation or, to cite Freud on taboo, arouse his forbidden unconscious desires (Freud 1919: 54–7). In regard to the latter, taboo prohibitions check 'the sway of contrary tendencies' within our nature, discourage feelings of ambivalence, and impose restraint on forbidden wishes and selfish impulses (Freud 1919: 60). To cross these sacred lines, then, was taboo, and the warnings not to breach these lines were clear and unambiguous. As the closing line of a verse read at the initiation ceremony of the 'Friendly Society of Operative Cotton Manufacturers' of north-west England, a north-west of England trade union we met above, put it: 'Woe! woe! and dishonour attends the faithless and unjust!' Lines contained in another verse read at the same ceremony conveyed a similar message: 'Strangers, hear me, and mark what I say; Be faithful to your trust, or you may rue the day' (*Manchester Times and Guardian*, 7 June 1834: 3). The ceremony and rite concluded with a similar warning:

> Say ye to the righteous, it shall be well with him.
> Behold the heir of heavenly bliss,
> His soul is filled with conscious peace;
> A steady faith subdues his fear,
> He sees the happy Canaan near.
> But who to the wicked, it shall go ill for him,
> For the reward of his hands shall be given him.
> Tormenting pangs disturb his breast,
> Where here he turns he finds no rest;
> Mount Sinia's thunders stun his ears,
> And not one ray of hope appears;
> Death strikes the blow, he groans, he dies,
> And in dispair [sic] and horror flies.
>
> (*Manchester Times and Guardian*, 7 June 1834: 3)

Retribution, divine or otherwise, however, was for the future. In the immediate term, the expectation was that the power of the taboo would keep the danger 'outside the gates'. That is, the worker would remain true to his vows, obey the call to arms when it came, and stand firm once battle with the adversary had been joined. It is to this next phase of the struggle that we shall now turn.

Notes

1 The pitmen won a number of concessions on these issues as a result of the 1831 stoppage. This proved to be a pyrrhic victory, however, as the following year the mineworkers' union, the 'Pitmens' Union of the Tyne and Wear', was defeated following a long and bitter confrontation with the coal-owners.
2 See chapter 1.
3 This correspondence is rather vague on accurate detail and seems to suggest that the operatives in question were Manchester cotton spinners. It is highly probable that the informant 'B' was a cotton dealer turned spy named John Bent. See Wilkes (2015: 85).
4 The factory owner in question was one Mr Garside.
5 The Duke had coalmines on his large landed estates from which he accrued rent income.
6 The 1834 union initiation ceremony in Exeter featured earlier in this chapter. See this earlier section for additional details on this incident.

References

Anon. (1833) *An Impartial Statement of the Proceedings of the Members of the Trades' Union Societies*. Liverpool: J. & J. Mawdsley.
Behagg, Clive (1982) 'Secrecy, Ritual and Folk Violence: The Opacity of the Workplace in the First Half of the Nineteenth Century', in Robert Storch (ed), *Popular Culture and Custom in Nineteenth Century England*. London: Croom Helm: 154–179.
Bell, Catherine (1992) *Ritual Theory, Ritual Practice*. Oxford: Oxford University Press.
Bloch, Maurice (1992) *Prey into Hunter. The Politics of Religious Experience*. Cambridge: Cambridge University Press.
Carpenter, Edward (1920) *Pagan and Christian Creeds. Their Origin and Meaning*. New York: Harcourt, Brace and Company.
Chase, Malcolm (2012) *Early Trade Unionism. Fraternity, Skill and the Politics of Labour*. London: Breviary.
Cohen, Abner (1971) 'The Politics of Ritual Secrecy', *Man*, 6(3): 427–448.
Colls, Robert (1987) *The Pitmen of the Northern Coalfied. Work, Culture, and Protest, 1790–1850*. Manchester: Manchester University Press.
Douglas, Mary (1991; first published 1966) *Purity and Danger. An Analysis of the Concepts of Pollution and Taboo*. London: Routledge.
Durkheim, Emile (1965) *The Elementary Forms of the Religious Life*. New York: Free Press.
Fenn, Richard (1997) *The End of Time. Religion, Ritual, and the Forging of the Soul*. London: Society for Promoting Christian Knowledge.
Freud, Sigmund (1919) *Totem and Taboo*. New York: Moffat, Yard & Co.
Hammond, J.L. and Hammond, Barbara (1995; first published 1919) *The Skilled Labourer 1760–1832*. Stroud: Allan Sutton.
Lovett, William (1920) *Life and Struggles of William Lovett in his Pursuit of Bread, Knowledge and Freedom*. New York: A.A. Knopf.
Miller, Geoffrey (2005) 'The Legal Function of Ritual', *Chicago-Kent Law Review*, 80(3): 1181–1233.
Oliver, William H. (1966) 'Tolpuddle Martyrs and Trade Union Oaths', *Labour History*, 10: 5–12.
Rappaport, Roy (1999) *Ritual and Religion in the Making of Humanity*. Cambridge: Cambridge University Press.
Rossano, Matt (2013) *Mortal Rituals. What the Story of the Andes Survivors Tells Us About Human Evolution*. New York: Columbia University Press.
Tufnell, Edward Carleton (1834) *Character, Object and Effect of Trades' Unions. With Some Remarks on the Law Concerning Them*. London: James Ridgeway & Sons.
Turner, Victor (1967) *The Forest of Symbols. Aspects of Ndembu Ritual*. Ithaca, NY: Cornell University Press.
van Gennep, Arnold (1960; originally published 1909) *The Rites of Passage*. Chicago: University of Chicago Press.
Webb, Sidney and Webb, Beatrice (1920) *The History of Trade Unions*. London: Longman.
Wilkes, Sue (2015) *Regency Spies: Secret Histories of Britain's Rebels and Revolutionaries*. Barnsley: Pen & Sword Books.

4

THE CALL TO ARMS

> The [master's] establishment is meanwhile carefully watched by parties summoned by the union from a distance, who are called piquets, and, under their captains, exercise, in a strange town, their assumed authority, without any dread of the law.
>
> *(Anon. 1831: 37)*

In early December 1844 the mill town of Rochdale, Lancashire, witnessed an interesting set of proceedings arising from a turnout in the town. During the incident in question, a procession of boys from fourteen to sixteen years of age were seen parading the streets of the town with fife and drum. The boys making up the musical procession were doffers who had recently turned out with other 'hands' for an 'advance of wages' at the mill of Edmund Howard at Cheetham Street (*Preston Chronicle*, 14 Dec. 1844: 3).[1] As the procession of young doffers made its way through the streets, it stopped at the various mills in the town in turn whereupon the young operatives proceeded 'to play their music opposite the factories'. The purpose of these musical serenades was to summon the workers in these mills to join their strike. Other strike processions in the decades covered by this book, much larger in scale than the Rochdale parade, also had music at the heart of the performance. During a wage dispute involving seamen in the north-east of England in the Spring of 1768, a procession of some four to five hundred striking sailors marched from North Shields to Sunderland 'with colours flying'. On arrival at their destination, the turnouts 'went on board the several ships in that harbour, and lowered down their yards to prevent them from going to sea' (*Leeds Intelligencer*, 19 Apr. 1768: 3). A musical atmosphere returned to the proceedings when the striking sailors disembarked from the incapacitated ships. Now joined by seamen from Sunderland, they paraded the town's streets with drums beating and colours flying.

It appears that the seamen of Shields never lost the habit of adding music and colour to their strike proceedings. Decades later, in the Spring of 1854 in response to local ship-owners manning their vessels with blackleg labour and seeking to break up the seamen's combination, around three thousand Shields seamen took to the streets 'with three bands of music, and an immense variety of flags' and paraded the towns of North and South Shields followed by a large crowd. Even the usually hostile mainstream press complimented the turnout seamen on their 'conduct', stating that 'the whole of the proceedings were conducted with the greatest order and decorum' (*The Examiner*, 1 Apr. 1854: 12).

Although these strike processions were set apart in time and varied in size and in certain aspects of their performance, they did exhibit a number of common features. The proceedings took place in the public space of the street, included a strong performative component, featured a procession which had an audience in mind, and unfolded in a disciplined and ordered framework, while the playing of music was at the forefront of the performance. Street processions of this type, which creatively utilised the public space of the street, assumed greater importance for groups in society that found themselves marginalised from the mainstream of political power, as with trade unions during much of the era covered by this book.[2] As such, the highly visible nature of street processions enable such groups to resist efforts by those monopolising power to render them and their concerns invisible.

Street processions also help marginalised groups to convey their various messages to a target audience, particularly if alternative forms of communication are less readily available, or have been closed down altogether by entrenched and more powerful political opponents holding sway over the means of communication and political power. Carefully choreographed street processions, particularly the more elaborate affairs like those performed by the seamen of Shields, also help a group to forge a collective identity. Being part of a well-staged and occasionally festive street procession in the context of the drama of a turnout, to hear the drums beating and see the colours flying, can exert a powerful emotional hold on the participants and help bind the individual to the group, the part to the whole. In this regard, we also need to be mindful of the important role played by street processions in assisting trade unionists to maintain the cohesion of the social structure and community in circumstances where there had been a build up of acute pressure arising from new methods of working and economic organisation. These particular strike processions thus had characteristics similar to other rituals we have been looking at in this book up to now, in that they brought a degree of control and order to potentially threatening situations which had arisen in the wider environment.

All the above being said and noted, there are some further aspects to the trade union street processions of these decades that need to be identified. If staged in the right manner, a street procession could perform a vital role in the early stages of a struggle with an adversary. In other words, and as shown in the turnout of the Rochdale doffers, a procession could issue a call to arms to other workers to join the fray. The street procession could also help maintain unity and enthusiasm in the ranks once battle had been joined with the adversary. Just as importantly, a procession could also impress itself upon the minds and senses of potential waverers in the ranks, help maintain discipline, and 'keep people in formation' in the heat of the battle. Strike processions thus worked to instil in the minds of those participating in the struggle the imperative of observing the codes of behaviour and rules of discipline judged to be necessary to achieve victory in the struggle.

The defenders of the established order certainly recognised the power of a union street procession to impress itself on individual minds. This can be seen in the response of the ship-owners of the Tyne to the musical processions of the seamen of Shields during the 1854 turnout mentioned above. One concerned member of the Sunderland Shipowners' Society informed Lord Palmerston that large processions of seamen 'march from Sea Port, to Sea Port, with Bands and Banners – by these means they cause many a decent man with a large family, against his will, to take part with them to the ruin of himself and his family' (HO45/5244N/2–7. Letter to Lord Palmerston. 1 Apr. 1854). This evident capacity of striking workers to call people to arms, maintain unity in their ranks, and discourage waverers had much to do with the military atmosphere which often pervaded trade union processions in this era. Thus, it was not uncommon for such processions to feature a repertoire of instruments and manoeuvres which appeared to knowingly call to mind military combat and war. The structure of these processions tended to mimic the style and form of rituals drawn from the military and war, with their emphasis on military precision, colours flying, stirring sounds emanating from musical instruments, and particularly the steady beat of the drums making plenty of noise in relation to the latter. This was evident during the turnout of Rochdale doffers in December 1844, with fife and drum much to the fore. Fife and drums had long been the preferred mode of 'turning out' the troops or militias during times of conflict and war. Rousing tunes and sounds deriving from the fife and drums heralded the onset of an engagement, put combatants on alert, helped instil discipline in the ranks, and aimed to impress upon the minds and emotions of potential waverers the necessity of standing firm in the heat of the battle to come.

There is another dimension to these musical sounds of which we should also be aware. Music has a unique capacity to impress itself on the mind and emotions and thereby elicit a response that is often far more effective than other forms of communication. In a similar vein, music has that unique quality, often numinous, to convey a message. This has much to do with the nature of the senses. As Kirsten Wood tells us, learned philosophers and popular writers alike in past and present ages have long believed that hearing is 'the most powerful of the senses. Far more than sight, touch, or taste, hearing kindled strong, immediate responses in the body, mind, and spirit' (Wood 2014: 1087). As such, music has that capacity to stir feelings and arouse strong emotions which suit those seeking to convey political messages of various kinds, such as those looking to stir patriotic emotions. Music could stir feelings and emotions so effectively as well because the transmission of the message to the recipient of the message was direct and instantaneous. This was because the power of music, as some philosophers believed, 'stemmed from the fact that auditory sensations travelled through the nerves of the body more quickly and were felt more intensely than other stimuli' (Wood 2014: 1094).

From our point of view in this chapter, music thus seemed uniquely placed to convey messages, influence thinking, and elicit required responses in the context of labour disputes. Music could stir one to action or, from another perspective, deter one from acting in ways contrary to the social ideal. In terms of the latter, music possessed that arresting power to promptly remind potential waverers of their duty to the collective, and could also convey a sharp and immediate warning to those contemplating engaging in acts of betrayal. Finally, it should be noted that music in labour disputes came in many forms. This included the playing of 'rough music' by strikers and their supporters when the need arose, usually when a strike had entered a later phase beyond the initial call to arms. We shall encounter more of 'rough music' in subsequent chapters.

It should not surprise us then to find that musical sounds were much in evidence in the early phase of a turnout. As already mentioned, fife and drums were particularly prominent in this early phase. Fife and drums called to mind for all concerned the muster and the sound of the approaching confrontation, and helped facilitate the mobilisation of the personnel necessary to successfully prosecute the strike.[3] As evident with the Rochdale doffers, cotton workers certainly recognised the value of musical sounds and musical processions which included fife and drums as a means of issuing a call to arms during a turnout. We can see this in other labour disputes in the cotton districts of north-west England. In one particular dispute in mid-November 1831, it was reported that a 'large mob' had gathered in the cotton districts of Preston and Blackburn with the intention of turning out the spinners. To this end, the 'mob' then 'marched in procession through the streets, with drums, fifes, and banners, and proceeded to the different manufactories, and public works, bearing down all opposition, and insisting on the men turning out' (*Dublin Evening Mail*, 14 Nov. 1831: 3). Another newspaper account of the same dispute reported that the highly mobile procession, said to number about two hundred marchers with drum and fife to the fore, halted before a 'machine manufactory' in Preston whereupon they 'summoned the men to turn out, and drummed before the yard' (*Preston Chronicle*, 12 Nov. 1831: 3).

Similar methods of persuasion can be observed in another labour dispute in the north-west in August 1842 involving cotton operatives, on this occasion in the mill town of Congleton in Cheshire. This particular dispute needs to be seen in the context of the oft-described 'general strike' of 1842, which had originated in the decision of mineworkers in Staffordshire in mid-July to make a stand against ongoing wage reductions, a mood of resistance which later spread to other groups of workers in the Midlands and the Northern counties (for a comprehensive treatment of the 'general strike', see Jenkins 1980). In a letter to the Home Secretary Sir James Graham, the concerned Mayor of Congleton reported that the town had been 'invaded by several bodies of persons amounting to more than ten thousand individuals marching through the market place in regular procession accompanied by a Band of Music whose object was to turn out all the operatives in the various mills of the place' (HO45/242/57–8. Letter 13 Aug. 1842). We can see the cotton workers of north-west England using the same methods a few years later. In

October 1847, at Heywood near Bury, in what would prove to be a frustrated attempt to incite another 'general strike' said to be encouraged by Chartists, it was reported that 'hundreds of men, women and children' had assembled at 3:30 in the morning and with fife and drums and flags and colours paraded the streets of the town 'shouting a general turnout of factory hands' (*Liverpool Mercury*, 26 Oct. 1847: 5).

Earlier reports coming out of the cotton districts of Manchester and neighbouring towns during the acrimonious eight-week-long spinners' strike of 1818 over the perennial issue of inadequate wages told of like-minded processions with similar sub-texts.[4] These reports, though, tell of another dimension to such processions. Not just an urgent call to arms heralding the onset of battle, the columns of marching strikers also aimed to send a firm message to potential cowards, deserters and traitors, threatening retribution should they fail to do their duty. These reports reveal, too, that in such circumstances the quite disciplined and restrained ritual of the street procession could give way to methods of persuasion of a more aggressive kind. Thus, a report sent by the Stipendiary Magistrate of Manchester to Lord Sidmouth at the end of July told of spinners assembling daily in large numbers before parading the streets of the town, and of processions numbering one or two thousand arriving at a factory to 'carry off by force or intimidation though without any violent breach of the peace the hands who might be disposed to go to work' (HO42/178/430–433. Letter from James Norris to Lord Sidmouth. 29 July 1818).

When the spinners of north-west England again clashed with the master spinners on the issue of a just price for labour a few years later in December 1830, similar strike tactics to those used in the 1818 turnout can be observed. This later strike, which spread to over fifty mills in the neighbourhoods of Ashton-under-Lyne, Dukinfield and Stalybridge, and which lasted until mid-February 1831, was initially triggered by an attempt by the master spinners to impose a reduced list of prices on their workforce.[5] In late December, the Home Secretary Lord Melbourne received a letter from Manchester containing an alarming tone. The letter told of a procession of spinners departing Stalybridge and marching through Ashton and Dukinfield 'with a band of music and tri-colour banner, six or eight a-breast, taking the hands from the different mills in their progress, in some instances by force'. Before the procession reached its destination, the letter continued, it had 'extended nearly a mile in length' (HO40/26/178–9. Letter 9 Dec. 1830). Most alarmingly for the Home Office was that the correspondent claimed that some of the marching turnout spinners were in possession of pistols. A further correspondence from Manchester a few days later reiterated the same message. It told of workmen to the number of 'several thousands' marching through the towns of Ashton, Dukinfield, and Stalybridge in procession with music and 'tricoloured' flags, stopping occasionally at mills still at work, whereupon pistols were fired into the air by way of announcing their presence to operatives yet to 'down tools' and the seriousness of their intent (HO40/26/227–30. Letter 17 Dec. 1830).[6]

More assertive methods of persuasion were also in evidence in the turnouts in the cotton towns of the north-west during the general strike of 1842. During those highly volatile Summer months, reports from anxious representatives of the propertied classes told of large bodies of flying pickets sweeping through the various mill towns 'wherever manufactories are established', where on arrival at a cotton factory the column of strikers 'ordered all the hands to leave their work' (as in Hyde, Cheshire. See HO45/242/49–50. Letter 12 Aug. 1842). One can get a sense of the highly charged atmosphere of this more direct and uncompromising call to arms from the following account in mid-August from concerned authorities in Macclesfield:

> Several thousands of men and boys armed with bludgeons who had previously stopped the mills at Bollington and other places on their way from Stockport arrived in Macclesfield at 11 o'clock this morning and joined by a large assembly of weavers who left their employment yesterday proceeded in immense crowds and succeeded in stopping every factory in the town turning out the hands and putting out the engine fires.
>
> *(HO45/242/51–2. Letter 12 Aug. 1842)*

Most alarmingly for those anxious to maintain the stability of the settled order was their growing awareness that the 1842 strike wave, the flying columns of pickets, the threats to property, and the general unrest in the cotton districts of the north-west was 'not a rise for wages' but was 'the result of widespread political disaffection' (HO45/242/60–1. Memorial of the Master Spinners and Manufacturers of Stockport. 14 Aug. 1842). We will revisit the cotton towns of the north-west later in this chapter. Before we leave them, however, mention should be made of a rather novel and forceful method of persuasion used by the weavers of the north-west during their 1808 turnout in protest against reductions in the price of their work.[7] Apparently, the weavers' strike was holding firm in early July, with 'no weavers at work, and if they are found weaving, some of the spies of the mob go into their place, and bring them out by the hair of the head. So those who would work dare not do it' (*Morning Chronicle*, 1 June 1808: 3).

An air of menace, albeit with a splash of colour and a musical backdrop, also featured in the call to arms of the framework knitters of the Midlands during their heroic efforts in the first half of the nineteenth century to contain de-skilling mechanisation and maintain a just price for their labour. In May 1825, an acting magistrate for Leicestershire informed the authorities in London of large bodies of striking framework knitters parading through the villages of the County with flags and music. The aim of these parades was 'to compel a complete cessation of all work at the stocking frame till an agreement should be obtained from the master manufacturers to pay a certain price called the Statement Price, for the making of stockings' (HO52/4/120–2. Letter 12 May 1825). So concerned was this magistrate about the use of such methods by the framework knitters that he urged the authorities in London to consider legislation to halt the practice.

Almost two decades later during the 1842 general strike, the framework knitters of Leicester continued to deploy these methods of persuasion. By mid-August, framework knitters in Leicester and neighbouring villages had been swept up by the general spirit of resistance then manifesting itself in Britain's Midland and Northern counties. Hence they struck work for an adjustment to the system of punitive charges imposed on them by the small masters which acted to reduce their weekly wage to a disagreeable level. As in other districts of the nation during the strike wave of 1842, the turnout of the Leicester framework knitters was politicised by local Chartist speakers, who pressed the strikers 'to tack the Charter' to their wage grievance (*Leicestershire Mercury*, 20 Aug. 1842: 3). In an effort to promote a general turnout of the 'hands' in the town, which included 'threatening the reluctant', a parade of strikers and their families 'singing Chartist songs' and waving wands and carrying banners proceeded to perambulate the town's various streets and visit its mills, workshops, and homes and cottages where framework knitting was still carried out. Lest any waverers or 'traitors' ignore the call to arms or doubt the seriousness of the strikers' intent, the sound of the fife and drum, part of a 'small band of music' which accompanied the parade, reminded them of their 'duty' and their responsibility to the collective and the greater good (*Leicestershire Mercury*, 20 Aug. 1842: 3).

The colliers, too, often used music, sometimes improvised, to issue a call to arms to their brethren during disputes with the coal-owners. During the aforementioned general strike wave of 1842, flying pickets of colliers from Staffordshire set themselves the task of turning out all the pits in the Potteries and neighbouring districts as far as Cheshire. In one incident in late July, involving an attempt to turn out the pitmen in the Poynton district of Cheshire, a column of around 150 'strange colliers' not known in the Poynton area were observed on the top of a bank close to the Smithfield coal pit 'making signals with a sounding Rod on the conductors to beckon the colliers in the pit out' (HO45/242/4–5. Deposition of James Bain, Colliery Manager. 22 July 1842). Neither were colliers averse to utilising music, often with a military flavour, to cow waverers, discourage acts of desertion or treachery, and threaten retribution to those who broke ranks and engaged in work below the just price once a dispute had got underway.

In early July 1864, the colliers in the mining district of Dudley in the west Midlands struck work in response to an attempt by the coal-owners to reduce their wages. During what would be become a long, drawn-out five months' dispute, processions with a decidedly musical atmosphere would be one of the principal means used by the turnout colliers to discourage deserters and traitors. The range of sounds emanating from these musical processions were many and varied, and included the sounds of drums, concertinas, tin whistles, and the music of 'amateur instrumentalists' (for information on the range of musical instruments on show, see *Birmingham Daily Post*, 29 Aug. 1864: 7; and 21 Oct. 1864: 4). Another form of persuasion was musical serenading outside pits where blacklegs were working. In the earlier weeks of the strike at least, the magical power of music to tap the emotions, convey a message, and elicit a desired response was much in evidence, as the following contemporary newspaper account demonstrates:

> There is no doubt that in some instances those who were going to work were prevented by the influence of the assembled numbers from going down the

pits; but the influence used was merely that of a sort of persuasion which assumed a strong character by the great demonstrations of those on strike. Flags, banners, so-called musical instruments, shouts, and other manifestations were displayed, and it is not at all to be wondered at that these external signs of gaiety, and what they wished to be understood as triumph, had a certain effect.

(Birmingham Daily Post, 29 Aug. 1864: 7)

Not surprisingly, as the Dudley strike lengthened and the numbers of blacklegs entering the pits increased, the more festive music present during the earlier phase of the dispute was less evident. At this stage, the music of the striking colliers assumed a noticeably more martial character and emitted a more menacing tone. As often in such circumstances, the steady beat of the drums was omnipresent. By mid-October, groups of colliers were mustering at selected points in the mining districts at 4:30 in the morning to beat the drums in order 'to draw out the blacklegs' (Glasgow Herald, 12 Oct. 1864: 3). At the end of October a Superintendent of Police attached to the Dudley area, told of striking colliers assembling in an early morning that 'was dark, save for the moon' and marching columns 'four deep' headed by bands of music coming from various departure points in mining neighbourhoods like Tipton and Coseley. Police efforts to contain these processions merely resulted in 'drums beaten with greater vigour'. When the columns eventually arrived at the pits with 'the avowed intention of stopping the men going to work', the 'noise' from the beating of drums was 'so great as to cause terror to the people' in the vicinity (Birmingham Daily Post, 21 Oct. 1864: 4).

In some disputes involving pitmen, serenading with drums to the fore took place directly outside the homes of blacklegs. In March 1864, a dispute broke out at Sunderland's Monkwearmouth colliery when a number of the pitmen refused to sign the yearly bond (Newcastle Journal, 22 Mar. 1864: 2). Some pitmen at the colliery did sign the yearly bond, however, and returned to work on these terms. To those pitmen who held out for a new, and more equitable, arrangement with the colliery owners, the returning workmen were blacklegs.[8] Once again, colourful processions, musical bands 'playing lively tunes', and loud drums were conspicuous in the engagement. During one such procession in early April, 'the houses of blacklegs on the route were pointed out, and the band stopped to give them a little drumming' (Newcastle Guardian and Tyne Mercury, 2 Apr. 1864: 3).

The sound of the beating drums of some contingents of striking mineworkers was particularly menacing. The highly mobile raiders of the 'Scotch Cattle' who operated in the coal-mining areas of south Wales at various stages in the late 1820s and 1830s frequently used the beat of the drums to send a warning of retribution to come to all colliers they deemed to be traitors and turncoats. When the coal-owners and ironmasters of Monmouthshire and Brecknockshire imposed a wage reduction on their workers in the Spring of 1832 against the backdrop of a recession, the presence of the Scotch Cattle could be heard and felt by waverers and blacklegs across the valleys. On 30 March, a manager at the Blaina Iron Works in

Monmouthshire informed London that nearly the whole of his workforce had left the works the previous night 'through fear'. The waverers at the Blaina Works had been roused to this state after hearing the sounds of a drum beating and a horn blowing on the hill opposite the works at midnight (HO52/19/229. Letter 30 Mar. 1832). An intensification of noise, usually emanating from the beating of drums and the blowing of horns, was a favoured method of the Scotch Cattle, intended to strike awe into the hearts and minds of strike-breakers. So, too, was the discharging of guns and sudden visitations by night-time raiders in disguise, sometimes 'in women's clothes and with blacked faces' (for reference to instances of the latter in the previous decade, see *Morning Post*, 1 May 1822: 4).

On some occasions, the leaders of the night-time raiders had imposing horns on their heads. During the wage dispute just mentioned, a report reached Lord Melbourne's office in London in April telling of a midnight raid by a body of 250 to 300 men on a village in the colliery district of Monmouthshire where a number of blacklegs resided. Some of the midnight raiders were in disguise and some were armed with guns. The raid was conducted with military-like precision. According to the report, the Scotch Cattle raiders arrived in the village to the accompaniment of 'sudden and uncouth sounds' which rent the night air. These 'disturbers of the peace' then:

> marched in regular order three abreast, the leaders of the column having horns on their heads, and being several of them armed with guns which were repeatedly discharged, and having swept through part of the village above described, like a destroying torrent, they disappeared in a body.
>
> *(HO52/21/11–2. Letter 11 Apr. 1832)*

The call to arms once sounded, however, did not necessarily guarantee unity and discipline in the ranks or loyalty to the 'colours' once battle had been joined with the foe. Striking workers recognised that additional procedures needed to be put in place in order to ensure that all held fast to their place in the ranks and kept their nerve as the struggle ensued. As with the initial call to arms, these supplementary forms of control had an undeniable military flavour in that they mimicked military procedures, practices and rituals.

In 1810 the cotton spinners of north-west England struck work. The spinners sought an equalisation in the piece prices, which would establish parity between the piece rates in the smaller country-based mill towns and the rates in Manchester.[9] Supported by the recently formed Spinners' Union in Lancashire, the strike extended to mills in Manchester, Stockport, Hyde, Stockport, Stalybridge, Macclesfield, Bolton and Preston. For the Lancashire factory commissioner Edward Tufnell writing about the strike retrospectively in 1834, the cotton spinners conducted their strike with all the efficiency and discipline of an army in the field. Tufnell and government informants at the time even likened one of the strike leaders, a spinner named Joseph Shipley, to 'a "general in the army", the commander of thousands of willing agents, who performed his bidding with the utmost promptitude' (Tufnell

1834: 14). Even allowing for the military-like efficiency in which the strike was conducted, however, the spinners were compelled to return to work at the former piece rate. This followed four months of struggle where the spinners endured great privations in their quest for wage parity. Even Edward Tufnell, a person who was certainly no friend of trade unions, felt moved to commend the fortitude of the spinners and their families during the conflict:

> Furniture, clothes, every article of comfort or convenience that their cottages contained, was then disposed of, and these unhappy victims of their own folly underwent a series of privations, which would appear incredible to those who do not know force of pride, and the enduring pertinacity, with which the English working classes will not unfrequently remain, what they call "true to each other". The feeling deserves praise, however we may lament its misdirected energy.
> *(Tufnell 1834: 16)*

The cotton spinners of Lancashire rose again in 1818, on the back of a trade revival. The acrimonious eight-week-long spinners' strike of 1818, with its columns of marching strikers and forceful methods of encouraging compliance during the initial phase of the dispute, has already been mentioned in this chapter. As in 1810, the spinners lined up for the struggle in 1818 as would a disciplined army in times of war. On 11 July 1818 the government spy 'B', whom we met in the previous chapter, sent a report to the Home Office describing the spinners' military-like approach to the unfolding conflict. According to 'B':

> One man from Each Shop is chose [sic] by the people and he commands them he forms them in Ranks and atends [sic] them on the march and as the soal [sic] command and they obey him as Strickly [sic] as the army do their Colonel and as little talking as in a Regiment.
> *(HO42/178/13. Letter from 'B'. 11 July 1818)*

At times, the efforts of the Lancashire cotton spinners to ensure that all held fast to their place in the ranks even resembled the military ritual of muster 'by the list'. In the Spring of 1829 against the backdrop of a stagnation in trade, falling prices, and reduced profits, the master spinners in Manchester felt 'compelled' to reduce the wages of their workers. During the turnout which followed, that began in April 1829 and which dragged on until August, the Manchester cotton spinners decreed that:

> No one was to go out of his own house before nine o'clock, and each was then to proceed to his Lodge (the smaller bodies formed by each mill) [sic], and have his name registered. All, whose names did not appear there, were to be considered knobsticks.
> *(Morning Chronicle, 14 Aug. 1829: 3)*

The framework knitters of the Midlands also adopted additional military-like measures following the initial call to arms in order to forge unity in the ranks and deter acts of desertion once the battle had got underway. As with the Manchester cotton spinners, they liked to muster their troops. Even more than the Manchester cotton spinners, their practices more self-consciously mimicked the military ritual of muster by the list. In Nottingham in August 1819, a ritual conducted before and after they paraded through the town streets in formation, striking framework knitters held formal musters in a forest close to the town for the purpose of ascertaining whether any of their number had broken ranks and returned to work (Letter from H. Enfield to Viscount Sidmouth. 13 Aug. 1819. Document in Aspinall 1949: 321). Once drawn up in military formation at the appointed times, individual section leaders 'whom they call Captain' brandished lists of names to discourage thoughts of desertion.

Nor were such military-like practices confined to the Lancashire cotton spinners and the framework knitters of the Midlands. In 1815, labour unrest broke out on the north-east sea-ports over the issues of low wages and ships setting sail with 'skeleton' crews. The latter in particular helped fuel local unemployment, a situation aggravated by the economic uncertainty generated by the end of the Napoleonic Wars (see McCord 1968). The collectively inclined and formidable seamen of Shields were at the heart of the conflict, prosecuting the strike and maintaining discipline in the ranks with remarkable military-like efficiency. These measures included the military ritual of muster 'by the list' in the form of morning roll calls to identify deserters. Other measures included the granting of 'passports' to ships the seamen permitted to go to sea, the issuing of a 'ticket of leave' should any sailor need to take a temporary leave of absence from the town, and the establishment of tribunals to supervise the process and ensure that all complied with the 'laws' of the seamen. All such proceedings were overseen by a committee, 'at the head of which was a person whom they called the Admiral, and whom they implicitly obeyed' (Hill 1860: 378). The efficiency of these proceedings, emanating as they did from those occupying the 'lower' rungs of society, alarmed and occasionally even impressed members of the elite. Thus, in regard to the latter, the Home Office official John Cartwright, sent north in the late Summer of 1815 to monitor the unrest on the government's behalf, spoke of 'the adroitness with which the lower order of people accomplish the organisation and manage the machinery necessary to give effect to combinations' (HO42/146/206–209. Letter from John Cartwright to Viscount Sidmouth. 14 Oct. 1815). Evidently impressed, Cartwright was of the opinion that the disciplined measures of the morning meetings and roll calling 'are the *bond* (sic) of union' (HO42/146/206–209. Letter from John Cartwright to Viscount Sidmouth. 14 Oct. 1815).

The colliers, too, were not averse to holding formal musters along military lines to maintain discipline in the ranks once battle had been joined with the adversary. This was evident during the bitter 1831 strike in the Durham and Northumberland coalfields over the contentious issues of paying wages in 'truck' or goods, the yearly bond, the system of punitive fines, and the excessive working day for boys. During their contest with the coal-owners, the striking pitmen, according to a local magistrate, were 'roll called at stated hours, and mustered when occasion requires by signal guns', whereupon they were counted off in Sections 'under their Captain' (HO52/14/203–5. Letter to Viscount Melbourne. 19 Apr. 1831).

As we have seen, the efficiency of such measures as the muster by the list clearly unsettled the defenders of the established order. Even more alarming for the employing classes and their supporters was the picketing system perfected by workers on strike in these years. The most recurring and recognisable form of picketing was the well-organised, highly structured and disciplined arrangement set up in the vicinity of the work premises. This arrangement sought to ensure that the work stoppage was effective and was being adhered to by those participating in the turnout. This form of picketing was also designed to prevent incursions by blackleg labour. In the hands of a well-organised body of workers inclined towards collective action and disciplined union organisation, these arrangements could proceed with military-like efficiency and precision. Edward Tufnell recognised as much when he reflected on the 'system of picqueting [sic]' developed by the factory operatives of Manchester. During the course of a turnout, stated Tufnell:

> The obnoxious factory is always watched by five or six men, unknown in the immediate neighbourhood, and who, on a given signal, can be reinforced to the extent of three hundred. These picquets are regularly relieved, by night and day, with as much order and method as is observed by an army in a hostile country; and so effectual are they in producing the desired end, that an establishment is not unfrequently kept in a state of literal siege.
>
> *(Tufnell 1834: 119)*

The cotton spinners of Manchester and neighbouring mill towns, who as we saw above in the 1810 and 1818 turnouts had acquired a well-earned reputation for combativeness and trade union organisation, were at the forefront of these developments in the art of picketing. Picketing a premises in these early decades of the nineteenth century was rarely static, or indeed easy to contain by those in authority, not least because those organising the picketing were always mindful of the need to both evade the punitive anti-Combination laws and maximise the effectiveness of the action. For the authorities, pickets would acquire a sinister air. Mysterious 'strangers', neither resident in the town nor known to the town's authorities, would arrive in a town from other places to 'lurk about the different mills in small bodies' and gather in 'clusters at the street ends' never far from the picketed premises (HO42/179/398–401. Letter 14 Aug. 1818). During the 1818 strike, mill owners and local magistrates complained of picketed mills being 'beset by strangers', a system so fluid and oblique 'that those who attended one day, were replaced by others, the next' (HO42/179/382–383. Letter 24 Aug. 1818).

The efficiency of the picketing methods of the Lancashire cotton spinners was maintained even after the repeal of the Combination Acts in 1824. Tensions between the region's cotton spinners and cotton masters burst forth on a number of occasions during the late 1820s, 1830s and 1840s, as we have seen above at various points in this chapter. On one particular occasion, in late December 1828, as the spinners resolved to turn out 'to procure an advance' in wages, the Home Office was informed of the difficulties faced by the authorities in curbing picketing:

> All the mills where the men have turned out or where work is done below the stipulated price, are watched day and night and several picqueted as they call it by a pretty strong party, who take their stations in the streets adjoining, and are regularly relieved three or four times a day. These men are chiefly strangers who are brought from a considerable distance and against whom it is extremely difficult to establish a case because they can neither be identified, nor found for the purpose of executing any process upon them.
> (HO40/22/297–300. Letter 26 Dec. 1828)

'Stop and search' was another method of ensuring greater efficiency during a picketing 'lock-down' of a work premises. Mention has been made above of the fractious strike of December 1830 to February 1831 in the neighbourhood of Ashton-under-Lyne, Dukinfield and Stalybridge. A few months prior to this, in a dispute which broke out in mid-August, the operative spinners and master spinners in these districts had clashed over the issue of differential piece rates between districts and between workers engaged in the same work.[10] In the turnout that ensued, Stalybridge, where the spinners in that locality earned wages thirty to forty per cent lower than the average rates in the country, was the focal point of the dispute. As ever, the contentious issue of imported blackleg labour was an ever-present concern for the turnouts. The masters though had particular concerns of their own because a secure passage for their 'new hands' through the labyrinth of pickets could not be guaranteed. In early September, the local commanding officer with responsibility for the Stalybridge and Ashton district, Lt-Colonel Shaw, expressed concern about 'the picquetting [sic] system' then 'in full operation at Stalybridge', which was preventing the importation of 'new hands'. Such was the extent and rigour of the picketing operation near to one particular mill in the town, complained Shaw, that 'foot passengers and even carriages are stopped, and examined, in order to prevent the probability of new hands entering the place' (HO40/26/56–7. Letter from Lt. Colonel Shaw. 2 Sept. 1830).

In some disputes involving the cotton spinners of north-west England, 'stop and search' was even more rigorous. In early September 1826, the spinners of Oldham struck work in response to a depreciation in their wages against the backdrop of the downturn of 1825–6 in the wider UK economy.[11] The issue of outside blackleg labour again figured large in the dispute. The Oldham pickets responded by adopting stringent measures to counter the attempted incursions. One such measure was a round-the-clock vigil of 'watch-and-ward', which extended to stopping, searching, and closely questioning all 'strangers' seeking passage through the picket lines. The Oldham 'sentinels' left nothing to chance, even feeling the palms of the hands of those individuals who approached their picket lines to determine whether they were spinners intent on blacklegging (*The Suffolk Chronicle*, 25 Nov. 1826: 4).

Other groups of workers seeking redress in these years also felt the need to engage in fastidious acts of stop and search. The long-suffering weavers of the cotton districts of the north-west of England were also swept up in the strike wave of 1818 in which the spinners had been so prominent. Seeking an advance of 7s in the pound, the weavers of Manchester, Bolton, Stockport and other localities turned out on 31 August seeking a general stoppage of all weaving for those manufacturers unwilling to pay the advance. As thousands of local looms were 'obliged to stand still', picketing weavers locked down their respective towns to the extent that all persons 'coming into town, were stopped, and their bundles [and] baskets, examined with all the authority of custom-house officers, that no goods might be smuggled from the loom into the warehouse of the manufacturer' (*Morning Post*, 10 Sept. 1818: 2).[12]

When considering the efficiency and effectiveness of picketing, we need to be cognisant of the fact that picketing was a ritual. Those on picketing duty followed a formalised set of rules, engaged in repetitive acts of behaviour, and subscribed to codes of conduct as diligently as did those participating in rituals in other contexts. As William Reddy informs us, a picket line is no different to a wedding ceremony or a voting procedure, in that all 'are enactments of highly structured, formalised scenarios which, so to speak, prescribe motives for the participants' (Reddy 1985: 30). In a similar vein, if firm written resolutions of intent and fiery speeches at the outset of a strike helped prescribe rules and codes of conduct for the engagement to come, then the picket line did the same and more by giving these rules and codes of conduct physical form.

There is another, related, dimension to the notion of picket line as ritual. As discussed in the previous chapter, certain rituals perform a 'legal function' (see chapter 3 and particularly the argument relating to this proposed by Miller 2005). In other words, as with law, such rituals function to ensure that participants and observers are made aware of a community's system of values and moral code and to impress upon the individual the importance of remaining true to these values and moral code. Rituals, like laws, both 'serve the general goals of preserving the fabric of social co-operation and deterring the tendency that individuals would otherwise have to defect from the social compact when doing so would serve their opportunistic self-interest' (Miller 2005: 1233). Drawing on this comparison between law and ritual, the ritual of the picket line clearly communicated the values of the working community concerned in the labour dispute in question, and the moral code to be followed during the course of the engagement. Secondly, the picketing ritual assigned roles for the participants in the set-up or structure that had been established during the engagement which aimed to foster approval of these community values and codes. Thirdly, the ritual of the picket line worked to impress upon the individual the importance of remaining true to his role within the arrangement and not to deviate from this role. Fourthly, the picketing ritual aimed to build awareness of the perils that could befall both the individual and the working community should the individual opt to follow a different course to that prescribed by the community and its moral code.

In another related respect, and again as with law, the picket line presented the workman with a clear choice, that is, whether to remain on the side of 'right' and as one with the working community, or 'cross the line' into the iniquitous world beyond, the world of the master and political economy with its valorisation of the rights of the self-regarding individual over the collective. In understanding this matter, we can bring to mind the point made by Mary Douglas that when there is pressure on the social structure, when there is apprehension concerning 'transgressions' which threaten to destabilise the system, those seeking to stabilise the structure tend to exaggerate the difference between the opposing or conflictual elements (Douglas 1991:4). Thus, picket lines not only established clear boundaries, that is, physical and moral lines it was forbidden to cross; they also accentuated the distinction between the inside and the outside, right and wrong, for and against, the just and the unjust, and the sacred and the profane. In terms of the latter, the distinction between the sacred and the profane, it is worth reminding ourselves of the point made by Catherine Bell that rituals and ritual activities have a capacity to bring the sacred to the fore by almost mysteriously sacralising things, people and events (Bell 1992: 15). In this instance, the picket line worked to mark off the world of the struggle engaged in by workers and their families on strike as a separate and sacred sphere, a distinct realm that was morally superior to the profane world beyond the boundary.

We could push the analysis of the picket line even harder if we consider picketing as primarily a negative ritual. In other words, the picketing ritual places most emphasis on the issue of prohibitive behaviours and actions. As mentioned above, picketing creates boundaries, establishes lines both physical and moral that one should not cross, and marks out particular forms of behaviour and conduct as being 'beyond the pale'. In this sense, we should view picketing as another means whereby unionised workmen were able to establish and make known the taboo boundaries of the trade union world. In this sense, the picket line complemented the role played by the trade union initiation rituals that we looked at in the previous chapter in imparting certain taboos of that world. As discussed in the previous chapter and other chapters, a taboo transgression is considered more serious than a seemingly more straightforward breach of a moral obligation because of the belief that the former unleashes danger which envelops others.[13] As Sigmund Freud tells us, 'taboo expresses itself essentially in prohibitions and restrictions' of a kind that are of a more substantive nature than moral prohibitions (Freud 1919: 30–1). The action of a miscreant worker or workers in crossing a picket line was certainly a breach of something quite serious, posing danger which had the potential to envelop others. In other words, such boundary transgressions created highly dangerous situations which did not bode well for those workers seeking to prevail in a strike situation.

Picket lines are also spatial constructs. In the larger towns, and as did the strike parades discussed above, picket lines reconfigured the urban public space and allowed subaltern groups to contest, and even control for a period of time, the space of the dominant ruling groups. Thus, picket lines represented a politicising of public space, enabling hitherto marginalised groups to challenge existing mainstream power relations. Moreover, and as with strike parades, picketing arrangements which strategically and effectively appropriated the public space of the streets rendered workers in struggle and their cause visible to a wider public.

The highly structured, formalised and disciplined ritualised arrangement which featured in the public spaces of the larger towns was not the only form of picketing in evidence during the decades covered by this book. Like the more stationary picketing of workplace premises, the strategy of highly mobile picketing became a staple of many strikes in this period, a practice which seems to have come to prominence during the dark years of the Combination Acts. As with workplace picketing, it seems that the cotton spinners of north-west England were at the forefront of developments on this front. During the eight-week-long spinners' strike in Manchester and neighbouring mill towns in 1818, which we have discussed at a number of points in this chapter, blacklegs and other 'traitors' were forcibly ejected from mills and 'carried off' by 'flying mobs of a few hundreds' said to be practising a 'guerilla [sic] mode of warfare', and which 'vanished' as soon as special constables appeared on the scene (HO42/179/214–216. Letter from James Norris. 28 Aug. 1818). There are many other examples in the primary records of raiding parties involving the Lancashire spinners (as during the spinners' strike in Stalybridge, Ashton-under-Lyne, and Hyde in mid-August 1830. See HO40/26/32–3. Letter 24 Aug. 1830).

Even more than workplace picketing, this mode of picketing was highly sensitive to the strategic value of space. Mention has already been made above of the wage dispute involving the coal-owners and ironmasters of Monmouthshire and Brecknockshire and their workforce in the Spring of 1832, and the role of the Scotch Cattle in this contest. Adept use of space, speed of movement, and a capacity to elude and frustrate the forces of law and order were the characteristics of the highly mobile raiding parties of the Scotch Cattle during the 1832 dispute. Thus, in the midnight raid on the blackleg village in Monmouthshire in April 1832 mentioned earlier in this chapter, the authorities in London were informed that the raiders came 'from a distance' and when their work was accomplished 'disappeared in a body and had not been since traced' (HO52/21/11–2. Letter 11 Apr. 1832). It was the not yet fully industrialised, nor wholly urbanised, landscape of early to mid-nineteenth century Britain which helped the flying pickets of this period to pass swiftly and furtively through places and spaces *en route* to their destination.

We can get a sense of this evolving, though still largely rural, landscape and the place of the pickets within it from some contemporary accounts of turnouts in this period. One account tells of flying pickets of Staffordshire colliers sleeping at night in a hayfield adjoining a coal pit, arising at six in the morning and listening to speeches at a canal bridge, as they set about their quest to turn out the coalfields of the Potteries and surrounding areas during the 1842 general strike (*Belfast Commercial Chronicle*, 30 July 1842: 1). A report a few years earlier from a magistrate in the cloth-weaving districts of Gloucestershire in January 1826 told a similar story of earnest, highly mobile raiders moving swiftly across space, and ably utilising the landscape to aid them in their designs. The report referred to sinister and clandestine combinations amongst the cloth weavers of the County which exerted an influence over the 'lower classes of society in the district' of such magnitude 'as to almost exceed belief'. The report also told of 'outrages' orchestrated against the non-compliant during turnouts, which would see members of the combination navigating the fields, byways and rivers of the County and 'marching sometimes ten or twelve miles during the night for such purpose, and immersing themselves to the skin in water to affect their vengeance on their victims' (HO40/19/8–14. Letter 31 Jan. 1826).

We shall hear more about flying pickets in a later chapter.[14] For now, we need to focus on other phases of the contest between unionised labour and the non-compliant in their midst. Of the latter, some would refuse to obey the call to arms. Others would break ranks and flee the field of battle once hostilities had commenced. Still others would quite cynically 'cross the line' of the 'picquets' and sentinels and enter the forbidden space beyond the line. For the collectively inclined workmen, such acts of non-cooperation required a response. As we will see in the following chapters, this response was never uniform or one-dimensional and it is to these matters that we shall now turn.

Notes

1. For additional details of this turnout, see *Manchester Courier and Lancashire General Advertiser*, 14 Dec. 1844: 6. A doffer was a mill operative, usually a child owing to the nature of the work, who removed bobbins, pirns and spindles holding spun fiber, whether wool or cotton, from a spinning frame and replaced them with empty ones during the manufacture of spun textiles.
2. On trade union processions in other national contexts, see Davis 1985; and O'Reilly and Crutcher (2006). The public space of the street could also assume importance for groups operating at the other, far-right end of the political spectrum. In this regard, see Linehan 2015.
3. I am grateful to Susan Davis for flagging up the important role played by fife and drums in strikes. See Davis 1985.
4. The spinners turned out in early July. The strike ended in defeat for the spinners, who returned to work in early September. The strike and its aftermath receives extensive treatment in Kirby and Musson 1975: 18–23; and Hammond 1995: 96–109.
5. The reduced price was 3s. 9d. per 1000 hanks of No. 40s on all sizes of wheels. The operative spinners turned out for a price of 4s. 2d. for their labour. For a further and more detailed discussion of the strike, see chapter 8.
6. The presence of firearms is also mentioned in the following document. HO40/26/232. Public Notice. 17 Dec. 1830.
7. Even after toiling some fourteen hours a day, six days a week, the distressed weavers could still only earn what a contemporary newspaper account referred to as a 'pittance' of seven or eight shillings. See *Morning Post*, 28 May 1808: 4.
8. The position of the turnouts was that the yearly bond should be withdrawn and replaced with either a monthly or fortnightly bond.
9. The rate for spinning a pound of cotton, No. 40, in the country towns was 4d, as compared to the Manchester rate of 4½ pence.

10 For other matters associated with this particular turnout, see chapter 8.
11 The spinners claimed that their wages had been cut by one-third over the previous sixteen months. For a more detailed discussion of the Oldham strike, see chapter 8.
12 The strike had all but collapsed by October, due in no small degree to the government's use of legislation in the form of the Combination Acts to bring charges of 'conspiracy' against three of the principal leaders of the weavers, which eventually led to their incarceration.
13 See chapters 2 and 3 in particular.
14 See chapter 8.

References

Anon. (1831) *On Combinations of Trades*. London: James Ridgway.
Aspinall, Algernon (1949) *The Early English Trade Unions. Documents from the Home Office Papers in the Public Record Office*. London: Batchworth.
Bell, Catherine (1992) *Ritual Theory, Ritual Practice*. Oxford: Oxford University Press.
Davis, Susan G. (1985) 'Strike Parades and the Politics of Representing Class in Antebellum Philadelphia', *The Drama Review*, 29(3): 106–116.
Douglas, Mary (1991; first published 1966) *Purity and Danger. An Analysis of the Concepts of Pollution and Taboo*. London: Routledge.
Freud, Sigmund (1919) *Totem and Taboo*. New York: Moffat, Yard & Co.
Hammond, J.L. and Hammond, Barbara (1995; first published 1919) *The Skilled Labourer 1760–1832*. Stroud: Allan Sutton.
Hill, Frank H. (1860) 'Abstract of Parliamentary Report on Combinations, 1825. Seamen', in *Trades' Societies and Strikes*. London: John W. Parker & Son: 378–380.
Jenkins, Mick (1980) *The General Strike of 1842*. London: Lawrence & Wishart.
Kirby, Raymond and Musson, Albert (1975) *The Voice of the People. John Doherty, 1798–1854. Trade Unionist, Radical and Factory Reformer*. Manchester: Manchester University Press.
Linehan, Thomas (2015) 'Cultures of Space: Spatialising the National Front', in Nigel Copsey and John E. Richardson (eds), *Cultures of Post-War British Fascism*. London: Routledge: 49–67.
McCord, Norman (1968) 'The Seamen's Strike of 1815 in North-East England', *The Economic History Review*, 21(2): 127–143.
Miller, Geoffrey (2005) 'The Legal Function of Ritual', *Chicago-Kent Law Review*, 80(3): 1181–1233.
O'Reilly, Kathleen and Crutcher, Michael (2006) 'Parallel Politics: the Spatial Power of New Orleans' Labor Day Parades', *Social & Cultural Geography*, 7(2): 245–265.
Reddy, William M. (1985) 'Response to Charles Tilly', *International Labour and Working-Class History*, 27: 30–34.
Tufnell, Edward Carleton (1834) *Character, Object and Effect of Trades' Unions. With Some Remarks on the Law Concerning Them*. London: James Ridgeway & Sons.
Wood, Kirsten (2014) '"Join with Heart and Soul and Voice": Music, Harmony, and Politics in the Early American Republic', *American Historical Review*, 119(4): 1083–1116.

5

CARNIVALESQUE RITUALS

> Some of them [the workmen] exhibited so much idleness and unwillingness to attend to their duties, that three were at length discharged; upon which all the rest turned out, brought an itinerant band of music opposite the mill, and danced and played in ridicule of their employer.
>
> *(Ashworth 1854: 13)[1]*

In August 1793 in Banbury, Oxfordshire, a contingent of 200 striking shag weavers assembled outside the home of a weaver who had refused to comply with a call to turn out against a master who had 'illegally' taken on an apprentice. Soon after assembling, a number of the striking weavers entered the home of the non-compliant weaver and proceeded to seize a piece of long-napped rough cloth or shag from his loom. With each person in the contingent adorned with a green bough in his hat, the large body of striking weavers then proceeded to parade the streets of Banbury 'two and two' to the accompaniment of fifes playing and much merriment. At the head of the procession was an ass on which was mounted the appropriated shag. The proceedings concluded when the ebullient procession of weavers 'in triumph laid the shag at the door of the master to whom it belonged' (The Shag Weavers of Banbury. Letter from Robert Spillman, JP, to Henry Dundas. 25 August 1793. Document in Aspinall 1949: 19).

There are a number of interesting features associated with the Banbury strike incident which have relevance for our study. Firstly, and most obviously, is that the actions of the Banbury weavers represented an effort on the part of collectively inclined workmen to address the contentious issue of the uncooperative in their midst in a working environment that was increasingly coming under the influence of the new economics of political economy. The second point to make about the Banbury incident is that it represented a constructive effort to utilise the creative power of ritual to address the issue of uncooperative workmen. In keeping with the creative potential of ritual more generally, the Banbury strike ritual was rich and multi-layered. At one level, the Banbury ritual worked to impress upon the minds of those participating in the incident during its various phases the imperative of holding fast to the values of duty, tradition, loyalty and brotherhood associated with the trade of journeymen weavers. The Banbury ritual thus shared characteristics with other labour rituals we have looked at in previous chapters in that it brought some structure, order and control to a potentially threatening situation that had arisen in the weavers' world of work, in regard to apprentices in this case. As such, the ritual provided a frame of sorts through which this threat could be better controlled and managed. At another level, and as flagged up in previous chapters where labour rituals have been discussed, we need to see the Banbury ritual as fulfilling a 'legal function'. To briefly reiterate this point, the Banbury ritual worked to impart awareness of the community's moral code and of the necessity of remaining true to this code. We should view this ritual then, as with other labour rituals, as an element within that broader parallel system of popular justice that marginal groups establish when forced by circumstances to operate outside the formal legal framework. In this sense, and to be more precise about the way in which the ritual functioned in quasi-legal terms, the Banbury strike ritual was underpinned by the deterrent principle in that the ritual sought to convey a strong message to the wider community that acts of deviancy would not be tolerated and had consequences. Thus, although the punishment of the transgressor who refused to abide by the strike call formed a core part of the Banbury ritual, the ritual's supplementary 'legal' function had as its aim the discouragement or forestalling of acts of deviancy within the wider working community.

Probably the most interesting feature of the Banbury strike ritual, however, concerned its unambiguously non-violent nature. During the performance of their ritual the striking weavers were very careful not to inflict physical injury of any kind on the person of the non-compliant weaver. Instead, the sanction of the weavers' community was administered with the meticulous avoidance of overt physical violence in any form. In so doing, the Banbury ritual highlighted another dimension to ritual that we have yet to consider in this book. This is the capacity of ritual, if properly staged, to regulate anger and hostility, channel aggression, and neutralise the potential for violence even in circumstances of heightened tension and conflict. As such, ritual can obviate any urge to resort to more forceful methods by taming aggression and diverting it along another path. Or, to put it another way, aggression and violence is creatively sublimated into ritual (on the sublimation function of ritual, see Burke 1978: 187). Sublimation rituals, it should be said, serve the purpose of transmuting or deflecting the more base impulses, aggressive impulses in the case of the Banbury weavers, onto another 'higher' plane which is more socially and even morally and aesthetically acceptable. An additional point that should be made in relation to the careful, structured avoidance of physical violence by the Banbury weavers is that it mitigated any potential for a confrontation with state power, as well as the potential for reciprocal violence inherent in such a confrontation. Thus, despite the efforts of the authorities to curb the procession and exert control over the proceedings through the reading of the Riot Act and the arrest of a number of the marchers, the event managed to pass off relatively peacefully without the state deciding that it needed to resort to excessive violence to control the so-called 'riot'.

This sublimation of aggression into ritual and the avoidance in consequence of a potentially dangerous lapse into a destructive cycle of reciprocal violence had much to do with another important feature of the Banbury strike ritual. This was the Banbury ritual's carnivalesque nature. When considering the Banbury affair and its carnivalesque nature, we need to be mindful that carnivalesque events are usually formally structured affairs which include a number of identifiable and recurrent characteristics and themes. The first point to make in regard to this is that all participants in a carnivalesque event are assigned a role which enables each participant to act out this role in accordance with the correct performance of the ritual. In the case of the Banbury strike ritual, each of the participants in the event would have fulfilled a role in accordance with the overriding function of the ritual, namely to channel the individual and collective anger felt towards the miscreant weaver along the safer path of non-violence. Secondly, although the carnivalesque could also take a linguistic form, the public space of the street was often the site of the carnivalesque performance in that the street was the primary domain of the people. Thirdly, and in the sense that the street provided the stage for the carnivalesque performance, carnivalesque events usually featured a procession or even a pageant. In the procession, moreover, there was often an emphasis on spectacle, consciously stylised behaviour and dramatic display, in order to more effectively impart the intended message of the ritual performance. All these elements, the public space of the street, a procession, and stylised and dramatic display, were present in the Banbury strike ritual. Fourthly, as Mikhail Bakhtin tells us, an important feature of the carnivals of the early modern period, as well as the carnivalesque festivals of the later modern period, was their capacity to parody, mock, and profane things deemed sacred in a playful manner (Bakhtin 1968). In so doing, carnivals and carnivalesque events skilfully subvert power and circumvent potential clashes with the authorities. In this way, participants in carnival are able to critique the established order of things, while avoiding those punitive punishments from the state that would have invariably followed had the circumstances been different. For Bakhtin, parody is aided in this undertaking by deliberately concealing its subversive messages and mockery of the established order behind double meanings and disguise (for an excellent account of this in relation to literature, see Shinn 2002). In a related sense, carnivalesque forms and behaviour can be teasingly ambivalent, often playfully forging quirky and seemingly contradictory juxtapositions such as seriousness and satire, the sacred and the profane, order and disorder, high and low, turbulence and calm.

Carnivalesque rituals, then, gave a licence to free expression, as well as the liberty to indulge in all manner of eccentric and extravagant behaviour, even if such behaviour is viewed unacceptable in other circumstances. In regard to the Banbury incident, there was eccentricity and extravagance in abundance. Thus, and as mentioned above, the striking weavers judiciously avoided laying a hand on the offending member of their fraternity and instead administered the sanction of the community in a highly playful form which abounded with much merriment, theatre, and creative simulation.

In a further sense, the gaiety and indulgence of the carnivalesque provided a means of bursting out of the confines of convention and normalcy created by the dominant order, if only temporarily. Following Bakhtin, Peter Burke has shown that this brief moment of respite from the everyday, this 'anarchic' interlude of carnival and the carnivalesque, often took the form of an attempt to reverse the dominant order of things, albeit symbolically. Indeed, carnival was 'an enactment of the world turned upside down' which, subliminally, for those without power, may have represented a desire for the social order to be turned the right way up (Burke 1978: 185–91). Illustrations and popular prints of the early modern period, Peter Burke tells us, often featured images of the world in reverse, such as flying fish, the sun and moon on the earth, and cities in the sky (Burke 1978: 188). Early modern carnivals and later carnivalesque events also witnessed acts of reversal, such as men dressing in women's clothes and vice versa, clergy with 'their vestments on back to front', and individuals being led through town astride a donkey facing the tail (Burke 1978: 182–99).

The formal mainstream world of the state was also mockingly turned upside down by carnival and carnivalesque festivals. The formal institutions, ceremonies and rituals of the state, as with the official courts of law and state trials, would be divested of their traditional piousness and solemnity and subjected to withering parody and clowning in carnival. So, too, would formal state punishments such as public executions. Funeral ceremonies were mocked in a similar fashion. This was usually achieved through mimicry and simulation, with mock trials, mock executions and mock funerals often the order of the day in carnival and carnivalesque events. In this way, the grandeur and pretence of the state was ridiculed, and power undermined. The theme of death in particular was a persistent motif in carnival, likely because as Bakhtin claims, the theme of death and rebirth and the renewal of time was an important part of carnival (on the preoccupation of carnival and carnivalesque performances with death, see Yaneva 2012: 227–9). The irreverent mocking of the official ceremonies and rituals of the state in regard to administering justice would become a persistent theme in carnivalesque events. We can see vivid examples of this on carnivalesque occasions when the 'people' decided to administer justice on behalf of the community in circumstances where they found the formal legal system to be badly wanting.

Moving beyond the Banbury weavers, we can see the presence of carnivalesque merrymaking, mockery, and often outrageously stylised behaviour in other strike rituals in the decades covered by this book. As mentioned above, a popular item of carnival was an individual being led through the streets of the town in a mock procession astride a donkey facing the tail. This practice would also become part of the staple diet of traditional rituals of popular justice. The perceived wrongdoer on such occasions would be placed on an ass facing the tail before being led through the town or village to the great amusement of the watching crowd, often to the accompaniment of 'rough music'. According to some accounts, the donkey-ride punishment was an ancient custom which dates as far back as the first century BC, and was certainly much in evidence in plebeian communities during the medieval and early modern periods (Alford 1959: 507). The custom was also transnational, to use a modern term, it being an aspect of the charivari ritual much witnessed in locations in continental Europe such as France and Italy, and even crossing the Atlantic to the 'New World' of the Americas (see, for instance, Davis 1971; Barker 2013; and Palmer 1978).

Riding an individual accused of violating community norms was certainly a long-established act of censure in plebeian communities in England, Scotland and Wales. The practice was more common in the western and southern counties of England and tended to operate under the name of 'skimmerton riding', though there was a Welsh variant of the punishment, the *ceffyl pren* or wooden horse ritual (Thompson 1992: 4). A close cousin of skimmerton riding and the *ceffyl pren* was the punishment ritual of 'riding the stang', reputed to be more likely witnessed in the northern counties of England and parts of Lowland Scotland; stang riding will be discussed in more detail in a later chapter.[2] As we will see with the donkey-ride sanction applied by working communities during the *laissez-faire* period, these highly ritualised expressions of disapproval were targeted at those adjudged to have breached community taboos, as with a sexually promiscuous partner charged with breaking his or her marriage vows.

We can clearly observe in the riding ritual the presence of the carnivalesque. The public space of the street usually provided the forum for the event, and there was nearly always a processional element to the proceedings. There was also a strong emphasis on parody and play, dramatic display and spectacle, while the overall purpose of the ritual was to send a strong message, not only to the wrongdoer but also to the watching audience, that acts of transgression would not be tolerated by the community. By bringing parody and play to the forefront of proceedings, moreover, the event unfolded in a context which reduced the risk of a direct and potentially dangerous confrontation with the representatives of state power. In the same vein, these carnivalesque rituals of popular justice enabled those participating in the ritual to dilute and channel any aggression they may have felt towards the perceived wrongdoer by setting it in a structured and controlled framework. Thus, aggression and violence was creatively sublimated into ritual.

An additional, important point needs to be made in regard to the riding ritual, which applied to past episodes and certainly to instances involving workers in the period covered by this book. The donkey-ride ritual was more effective in addressing strike-breakers from within the local working community, those usually referred to as blacksheep, scabs or knobsticks, rather than the more reviled blacklegs who tended to brought in from other places and thus represented an external rather than an internal threat. As E.P. Thompson explained it in relation to that close cousin of the donkey-ride ritual, 'rough music', the sanction only works 'if the victim is sufficiently "of" the community to be vulnerable to disgrace'

(Thompson 1992: 10). With the blackleg 'stranger' from afar, it was usually the case that different methods, often of a more aggressive kind, had to be deployed to deal with this external threat to the structure, as we will see in later chapters. This is not to say, however, that the 'donkeying' sanction could not be brought to bear to contain blacklegging, only that it was more likely to be used to address internal threats.

In regard to riding and being 'vulnerable to disgrace', it is important to be cognisant of the strong element of shaming involved in this punishment ritual. Thus, while also accounting for the carnivalesque merrymaking which ran through the proceedings, the donkey-ride ritual represented a form of folk justice which sought to publicly shame the wrongdoer by bringing his misdeeds into the fulsome glare of public scrutiny. The attempt to induce feelings of shame in the wrongdoer, it should be said, point up that primary characteristic of shame as identified by Helen Lewis in her important study of shame and guilt. Whereas the experience of guilt is directly about the *thing* done or not done, the experience of shame directly concerns the *self*, which becomes the focus of the evaluation (Lewis 1971). The self being a social construction, shame is thus much more of an existential experience which has a discernible social dimension. The social dimension of shame and its capacity to encourage social conformity and enforce the social norms of the wider group or collective on the individual had been recognised earlier by the social anthropologist Ruth Benedict (Benedict 1946). Benedict also claimed that the sanction of shame has greater potency in cultures which are more collectivist than individualistic, as with Japan in relation to the former or the United States in relation to the latter (on this point, see Jacquet 2016: 28–9).

One aspect of these studies of shame which particularly interests us here is the notion that shame arises when there is a rupture in the social bond between an individual and the group, when a person experiences or fears social disconnection from others in the group (see also Scheff 2000: 95). Another aspect is that which suggests that shame as a means of regulating individual and social behaviour functions more effectively in a collectivist culture, as with the collectivist-orientated culture of a workers' combination. Clearly, given that the sources we have at our disposal are unlikely to yield such information, we are unable to determine whether shaming punishments such as the donkey-ride ritual succeeded in their attempt to successfully induce shame in every offender punished in this manner. What we can state with some certainty though, is that from the point of view of those administering this punishment sanction, shame inducement was very much to the fore in their deliberations.

A number of journeymen groups in our period seem to have favoured 'donkeying' as a method of punishing those within their ranks deemed to have violated the taboos of the trade. One such group was the journeymen hatters. In February 1770, the journeymen hatters of Southwark in London were embroiled in a wage dispute with the Master Hatters. In one incident during the dispute, which had all the appearance of a mock arrest and trial in the lead-up to the enactment of the punishment, a number of journeymen Hat-Dyers 'took one of their Brother journeymen into custody, whom they charged with working over hours without more pay, and for taking under Prices' (reported in the *Northampton Mercury*, 26 Feb. 1770: 2). For this infraction of the hatters' 'laws' regarding hours and pay, the offender was obliged to mount an ass and ride through all the parts of Southwark 'where Hatters are employed', as well as other streets in the city to the accompaniment of 'rough music' composed by a number of boys with fire-shovels. Lest those observing the burlesque proceedings were in any doubt as to the meaning of the ritual, an individual led the procession carrying a pole upon which was attached a label explaining the offence committed by the errant journeyman. The journeymen hatters of Southwark seem to have a long history of injecting an element of carnivalesque ridicule into their punishment sanctions. In an earlier incident in Southwark in 1696, a journeyman amongst their number found to be working below the agreed rate of pay was tied to a wheelbarrow and then wheeled in 'a tumultuous and riotous manner' through the streets of the Capital (mentioned in Webb and Webb 1920: 28).

By the early decades of the nineteenth century, with *laissez-faire* economics and the introduction of new machinery rendering the position of those working in the longer-established skilled journeymen crafts more and more precarious, the journeymen hatters continued to believe in the efficacy of the donkey-ride ritual as a means of punishing transgressors. We can observe this in a bitter labour dispute which took place in mid-1834 centred on the town of Atherstone in Warwickshire. Hat manufacturing had a relatively long-standing presence in Atherstone, having been established there since the Tudor period, though it was the manufacture of low-cost felt hats for various markets which helped place the town at the centre of the hatting industry in the west Midlands.[3] The background to the labour dispute of 1834 was the decision by one of the principal hat manufacturers in Atherstone, Joseph Willday, to move his 'manufactory' to Rugeley, a town situated some twenty-four miles distant from Atherstone in Staffordshire. It seems that this move on the part of Mr Willday was prompted by his desire to dispense with the Hatters' Trade Union, along with those in the Atherstone community associated with this union (*Staffordshire Advertiser*, 7 June 1834: 2). As part of this effort to bypass the union, Mr Willday sought to entice from Atherstone a small number of 'the most experienced and best disposed men' to instruct the non-union workforce then being assembled at Rugeley in the skills of the business. This withdrawal of the skilled personnel from Atherstone would, in the words of Mr Willday, 'not only be the means of assisting us at Rugeley' but was 'the only effective method of subduing the combination' (HO52/25/270–1. Letter 27 Apr. 1834).

Mr Willday was able to persuade at least two Atherstone workmen to follow him to Rugeley and take up a position there during what he described as 'my contest with the men, who are in combination against me'. On discovering that the two hatters had absconded in the dead of night, and having left their wives and families behind in Atherstone, the remaining Athterstone hatters proceeded to show their disapproval of this act of betrayal. The method they determined on was to make straw effigies of the men, which they then placed upon an ass and led in procession through the most public parts of the town (HO52/25/272–3. Letter 26 Apr. 1834). A procession said to comprise some several hundred persons, an accompaniment of 'rough music' in the form of much blowing of horns, and a mock execution which saw the effigies being consigned to the flames, added to the carnivalesque atmosphere of the event (HO52/25/272–3. Letter 26 Apr. 1834).[4] The ebullient behaviour of the Atherstone hatters would not have come as a great surprise to Joseph Willday, given his view that the 'hatmakers are a description of workmen much given to excess' (HO52/25/270–1. Letter 27 Apr. 1834).

The carnivalesque effigy on a donkey punishment ritual was witnessed again in Atherstone during another dispute involving members of the Hatters' union in early 1862. On this occasion, the hat manufactory of Messrs Hall and Phillips in the town provided the background to the incident. According to an Atherstone union official, the dispute arose in consequence of additional numbers of apprentices being 'forced upon us' by the firm's owners contrary to an earlier agreement, along with the imposition of a scale of prices said to be inferior to that given in the hatting trade in other parts of the United Kingdom (*Coventry Herald*, 14 Feb. 1862: 8). The firm of Messrs Hall and Phillips sought to defeat the turnout by the usual method of importing blackleg labour. The Atherstone hatters responded to this move in their time-honoured manner. Thus, on one occasion the arrival of 'fresh hands' into the town prompted the staging of a procession through Atherstone's streets and market place followed by 'hundreds of spectators'. At the head of the procession was a donkey with a masked effigy astride its back (*Coventry Standard*, 8 Feb. 1862: 3).

Another group of workers who administered community justice in this carnivalesque manner were the ribbon weavers of Warwickshire, particularly the weavers who lived and worked in Coventry and the market towns and villages which lay to the north of that city. Usually though, it was a human astride the donkey rather than an effigy. If Warwickshire was at the heart of the ribbon weaving trade in the early decades of the nineteenth century, one could also say that the region was the home of the donkey-ride sanction during the labour unrest of this period. Like other skilled journeymen in this period, the ribbon weavers of Warwickshire found the new times associated with industrialisation, new machinery, and market-driven economics unsettling and dangerous for their traditional skills and their families. In 1832, a sheriff of the city described Coventry as a place of some 30,000 to 40,000 inhabitants, consisting 'mainly of inferior people', many thousands of whom were operative weavers, a description which tells us more about the mind-set of the governing classes than of the weavers of Coventry, it should be said (HO 52/20/13/41–42. Letter from John Ralphs and Thomas Pepper, Sheriffs, Coventry. 30 Mar. 1832).

Silk ribbon weaving was one of the principal industries in Coventry and had been since the latter part of the eighteenth century (Stephens 1969). Small-scale industrial establishments and independent journeyman craftsmen and members of their family working their own single handloom in a 'top-shop', that is, a room in the top floor of their home, were the predominant industrial forms in the city during the early decades of the nineteenth century. The predominant method of payment for the weavers' work was a piece-work rate set by a standard list of prices to which all parties, whether associated with labour or capital, were meant to subscribe (see Searby 1972).

Following a brief 'golden age' for Coventry's ribbon trade in the years which immediately preceded the culmination of the Napoleonic Wars, the 'cottage-based' industrial form associated with the ribbon weavers and their families entered a difficult time arising from a number of ongoing issues and newer developments. These included the import of cheaper French ribbons, a surplus of labour, and the advance of more 'efficient' factory-based methods of production which drew on innovations such as power-run looms. The increase in competition from ribbon manufacturers in other towns in England which had embraced the new methods added to these pressures, as did the presence of a new class of employer who favoured the free-market, de-regulating principles of *laissez-faire* economics over the paternalistic model which had traditionally governed relations between the master and the weavers in the region. The fluctuating nature of the consumer market compounded the weavers' difficulties still further, as changing tastes in upper-class women's fashion periodically reduced the demand for ribbons. As Peter Searby informs us, 'unpredictability and precariousness were the dominant themes of the weaver's life' (see Searby 1972: 33). From around 1815 onwards then, Coventry's home-based ribbon weavers experienced a changing working environment which saw increasing pressure on the 'list of prices'. Arguably most concerning was the new class of master who ignored the list of prices for the weavers' work established via an agreement of 1816, and who were more willing to exploit the 'modern' industrial methods by employing half-pay apprentices and under-paid women to work the new engine power-looms.

The response of the Coventry ribbon weavers to these dangerous developments was to enter into a 'combination' through the establishment of a 'Weavers' Committee' to try to ensure compliance with the list of prices. The weavers' efforts at collective action would be heavily tinged with carnivalesque mockery and defiance as they sought to persuade the new masters and those within their own ranks to remain true to the principle of a 'fair price' for labour. In the Summer of 1819, for instance, Coventry witnessed a spate of 'riding', as masters in particular were ritually punished in this fashion 'to the amusement of some, and the great terror of others' (*Bell's Weekly Messenger*, 23 Aug. 1819: 4). On 17 August, 'several masters' were ridden upon donkeys bare backed 'for not paying a fair price', while another received the same punishment for employing half-pay apprentices. Reports from the district also told of ribbon weavers having 'amassed' several donkeys for the purpose of a renewed spate of donkey parades through the streets of the city the following day on 18 August (*Morning Post*, 20 Aug. 1819: 2). In a letter sent on 20 August, the 'Postmaster' for Coventry informed the Home Office that in his opinion the behaviour of the ribbon weavers in handing out what 'they call a little justice' was understandable given that the weavers 'have been very ill-treated by some of the masters' (Letter from the Postmaster, Coventry, to Francis Freeling. 20 Aug.

1819. Document in Aspinall 1949: 321). By early September the situation in the city had stabilised when the weavers returned to their employment following an agreement from the ribbon manufacturers to adhere to the list prices (*Manchester Mercury*, 7 Sept. 1819: 3).

Maintaining a uniform price for the ribbon weavers' labour would prove difficult, however. In July the following year, the Coventry ribbon weavers were again involved in a donkey-ride incident. On this occasion, one of their number who had taken work under price, a weaver named Amos Carver, was 'placed on the back of a donkey bedecked with ribbons' with his face towards the tail and paraded around the Coventry streets where he was 'exposed to the insults, hootings, and revilings of the mob' (*Morning Chronicle*, 18 Nov. 1822: 4). The King's Court though was not impressed by this display of popular justice of long-standing and imposed stiff punishments on twelve of the ribbon weavers involved in the affair. All the prosecuted weavers were members of a weavers' club named 'The Weavers' Fund'. As well as each being ordered to pay a fine 'to the King', nine of the defendants were sentenced to imprisonment in the House of Correction in Warwick Castle for nine months, two for a period of seven months, and one for six months (*Morning Post*, 18 Nov. 1822: 2). It should be said here, that those punishing miscreants within their ranks via the donkey sanction had historically sometimes trodden a fine line between harmless burlesque and behaviour likely to trigger alarm on the part of the authorities. Since a key judgement by judges in King's Bench based on an incident in Canterbury, Kent, in 1676 found that the skimmington ride 'constituted a riot', those at the forefront of the event often ran the risk of running afoul of the law (Ingram 1984: 101).

As mentioned, the ribbon weaving industry extended beyond Coventry to the villages and market towns that lay to the north of the city, as in the town of Nuneaton. Situated some ten miles distant from Coventry, Nuneaton was home to a population of close to 5,000 according to the 1801 Census. As with Coventry, the predominant industrial form in Nuneaton during the early decades of the nineteenth century was small-scale handloom ribbon weaving which took place in the home. Like their Coventry brethren, the Nuneaton weavers were beset with problems arising from increased competition, technological innovation, and periodic pressure on the list of prices.

Like the Coventry ribbon weavers, the Nuneaton weavers were also susceptible to the practice of 'riding' those deemed to have contravened the taboos of the trade. In September 1829, Nuneaton witnessed an outbreak of donkeying incidents. This took place against the backdrop of a turnout involving ribbon weavers in Coventry, Nuneaton and neighbouring towns and villages relating to the price lists that the weavers were seeking to uphold. In the early phase of the strike, two individuals who had taken out work at a reduced price were mounted on an ass and conveyed through the streets of Nuneaton to Attleborough, a hamlet adjacent to the town, 'amidst the revilings of the mob' (*Morning Post*, 28 Sept. 1829: 4). In another incident on 16 September, a foreman for a ribbon manufacturer in Coventry named John Taylor, then conducting some business in Nuneaton, was seized by 'a mob of five or six hundred persons'. The unfortunate Taylor was then placed upon an ass 'brought for the occasion' with his face towards the tail. The 'soft power' of carnivalesque people's justice was less in evidence on this occasion, however, as Taylor 'was pelted with filth of every description', had 'his clothes torn to pieces', and 'was twice knocked off the ass' (*Bell's Weekly Messenger*, 28 Sept. 1829: 6–7). Several ribbon weavers residing in Bedworth, a market town roughly equidistant between Coventry to the south and Nuneaton to the north, who continued working during the strike were also donkeyed, as were a man and women who also lived in the town (*Morning Chronicle*, 26 Sept. 1829: 1; and 3 Oct. 1829: 1). The punishment ritual proved to be quite contagious in Bedworth, some local bricklayers taking it upon themselves to 'donkey' two of 'their brethren' for working under price soon after the incident involving the ribbon weavers (*Morning Chronicle*, 3 Oct. 1829: 1). The deterrent principle underpinning the riding ritual was in stark evidence a few days later when several hundred striking ribbon weavers assembled on the road leading from Bedworth to Coventry. At the head of the column of weavers were two men carrying a flag bearing the inscription 'Jackass them that work'. To remove any ambiguity about the message and its intent, a donkey stood at the side of the men bearing the flag (*Morning Chronicle*, 3 Oct. 1829: 1).

The ribbon weavers of Nuneaton, Bedworth and neighbouring areas returned to work in early October having secured a readjustment of the list of prices to their satisfaction (*Leicester Chronicle*, 3 Oct. 1829: 3). Matters did not end there, however, as the courts decided to exact harsh retributive justice on those said to have subjected the foreman John Taylor to a riding in Nuneaton on 16 September. Two of the defendants accused of being at the forefront of events received prison sentences of two years with hard labour in Warwick gaol, while a third defendant received a sentence of six months' imprisonment (HO17/36/15. Trial of John Thomas, Thomas Suffolk and Joseph Moreton).

Given the increasing tendency of the formal legal system to hand down punitive punishments, it should come as no surprise that the riding ritual was less in evidence during disputes between Warwickshire's ribbon weavers and the masters in the decades after the 1820s. Additionally, leading representatives of the weavers' union, the Ribbon Weavers' Association, were showing evidence of eschewing such methods, thinking them counter-productive in terms of building wider support embracing all elements of the community. Rather, they wished to move beyond 'a time when tyrants were visited by a long-eared animal, having upon him a bunch of ribbons', and instead 'wished to appeal to man's reason and sense of justice' in resolving labour disagreements in the trade (spokesperson for the Ribbon Weavers' Association speaking at a weavers' meeting in August 1858. Cited in Searby 1972: 263). This being said, the donkey-ride ritual did not completely die out in this region of Warwickshire. In the Summer of 1833, eight weavers from Foleshill, a rural parish a few miles to the north of Coventry, were charged with 'riotous assault' involving a weaver residing in the same parish. Apparently, the accused weavers, who 'were idle for want of work and had families to support', had seized the weaver at his home for taking work 'under price' and had 'a donkey with them, on which they intended to have him put' (*Coventry Herald*, 14 June 1833: 4). Riding was still in play in the region as late as 1845. In an incident early in that year involving under-price work, an Attleborough weaver working under price was taken from his house, placed upon an ass with his face to the tail, and paraded through the streets (*Coventry Standard*, 4 Apr. 1845: 2).[5] As was becoming more frequent in such cases, stiff prison sentences were handed out to three local weavers accused of being at the centre of the affair, in this case sentences of four months, three months and two months, all with hard labour.

The neighbouring County of Leicestershire also witnessed some episodes of donkey riding during industrial disputes in the early decades of the nineteenth century, this time involving framework knitters. The resistance of the framework knitters of Leicestershire and Nottinghamshire to price cutting and de-skilling machinery during these decades has been well documented (for general accounts see, for instance, Henson 1970; Gurnham 1976; and Hammond 1995: 221–56). These forms of resistance ranged from 'soft' to 'hard' pressure. The former included petitions to Parliament for an enactment of a minimum wage or for the abolition of wide frames and so-called cheap 'cut-up work', the latter of which had inundated the market and undermined the demand for more superior hosiery work. The latter form of resistance included the more direct measures of Luddite frame-breaking (on cut-up work, see Hammond 1995: 226–7). At some point in between these two contrasting ends of the spectrum was another form of pressure, which was more carnivalesque in character. This can be observed during an episode which took place in the latter phase of the turnout of 1819, when some fourteen thousand workers in the stocking trade in Leicestershire, Nottinghamshire and Derbyshire struck for a return to a Statement price agreed by the hosiers at Leicester in 1817. In the incident in question, a hosiery dealer accused of giving out work below the 1817 Statement price was 'roughly handled' by a number of men, women and boys in the village of Burbage prior to being placed on an ass with his face to the tail 'and carried through the street in a sort of mock procession' (*The Leeds Mercury*, 11 Sept. 1819: 4). The procession was led by a workman carrying a placard inscribed with the words 'Statement of 1817'. A few days later, a stocking-maker in Belgrave, a village to the north of the County, was also donkeyed for working under price (*The Leeds Mercury*, 11 Sept. 1819: 4). The framework knitters of Hinckley, a market town in south-west Leicestershire bordering Warwickshire, were also not averse to donkeying uncooperative members of the trade, as during a dispute over labour prices in September 1829 (*The Leicester Chronicle*, 26 Sept. 1829: 3).

Although it could be claimed that the home of the donkey-ride strike weapon was the Midland counties of Warwickshire and Leicestershire, the sanction was not just confined to these counties alone, as we saw above with the journeymen hatters of Southwark. The records show that the practice was also carried on in Spitalfields in east London by the silk-weavers of that district. The 1760s were marked by turbulent labour unrest in Spitalfields. The main causes of the unrest were the falling piece-work rates and rising unemployment experienced by the weavers, arising from a number of factors and ongoing developments. These included a slump in trade, the import and manufacture of cheap foreign wrought silk, and mechanisation which was seeing handloom weaving being displaced by machine-driven multiple shuttle looms at an increasing rate (on the trade's changing character, see Page 1911).

The silk-weavers of Spitalfields used a number of strike tactics during the turbulent 1760s, as we will see in the following chapter of this book. One such tactic used to punish those within their ranks adjudged guilty of a 'misdemeanour' was to place the offender on a jackass. The *Annual Register* described this as 'a scandalous custom' of the weavers (*Annual Register* 1769: 162). We can see the same sanction being used in later disputes involving the weavers of Spitalfields. In the Spring of 1827 the weavers of Spitalfields struck work over wages. Anxious reports from the authorities in the district stated that crowds of 'refractory' weavers 'ride them' who are reluctant to obey the strike call by taking them from their dwellings 'and parade them about the streets seated upon an ass' (HO40/22/69–70. Letter 29 Mar. 1827). A foreman whose behaviour had proved 'obnoxious' to the weavers was also 'donkeyed' during the same turnout (HO40/22/67–8. Letter 29 Mar. 1827).

At this point, we should pause to reflect on an important aspect of these aforementioned punishment rituals in regard to their deliberately contrived carnivalesque atmosphere and their strong emphasis on mockery and ridicule. While there is obviously a clear intention in the riding ritual to punish through mockery and ridicule those deemed to have violated community norms and codes of behaviour, it would be a mistake to focus on this dimension of the ritual alone. Indeed, it was the very richness and complexity of charivaris that 'helped to organise a variety of experiences within a single conceptual framework' (Ingram 1984: 98). As mentioned earlier in this chapter, an important feature of the 'anarchic' distraction of carnival and carnivalesque occasions was the skilful way that those participating in these events were able to subvert formal power by mocking and inverting the established order of things, even if only symbolically in regard to the latter. This symbolic turning of the world upside down was usually accomplished by bouts of highly eccentric behaviour, bizarre acts of reversal, and the fashioning of quirky juxtapositions of seemingly incongruous elements. Given the richness and complexity of carnival, then, and its undercurrent of playful subversion, should we not look for another layer of meaning to the carnivalesque punishment rituals that we have been looking at in this chapter, a layer of meaning which goes beyond the punishment of the particular individual charged with an offence against the community? In other words, being exposed to ridicule and mockery in these carnivalesque displays was the philosophy of *laissez-faire* individualism with the ideal of the 'free labourer' at its core. This was the ideal of the 'well-disposed' workman with supposedly good habits of industry, whose only desire, according to this narrative, was to exert his 'natural' right to sell his labour in an open labour market in accordance with his individual self-interest and personal liberty. To reiterate a key theme of this book, for workers of a more collectivist persuasion the philosophy of self-interested individualism encouraged behaviour which threatened to unravel the traditional social fabric of the trade and working community. Those workers who identified with this philosophy were thus seen as dangerous collaborators in league with those forces which threatened the community's well-being and very survival. In their uniquely eccentric, anarchic and defiant way, the rituals of the carnivalesque sought to check this drift towards self-interested behaviour by exposing it to mockery and ridicule and, in so doing, restore some equilibrium and stability to the social structure. The donkey-ride seemed an appropriate instrument to undermine the free labourer ideal in this way, given, as Ilario Favretto points out, the long-standing symbolism of the donkey as a byword for stupidity (Favretto 2015: 222).

Continuing with this line of analysis, Martin Ingram tells us that part of the complex richness of charivari rituals was the creative manner in which they, through the application of the principle of analogy or correspondence, evoked contrasts between different elements within the social structure, which included different modes of behaviour (Ingram 1984: 98–9). We should thus surely seek to interpret the donkey-ride ritual as a ritual of reversal which evoked a contrast between different modes of behaviour within a community, the one permissible and the other impermissible. Placing the wrongdoer astride the donkey the 'wrong way' facing the tail sought to point up behaviour which went 'against the grain' of things, turned traditional patterns of behaviour and morality on their head as it were. Thus, one could argue that in this respect at least, the working community was not necessarily attempting to 'turn the world upside down', but merely seeking to turn the world the right way up in response to the efforts of the supporters of *laissez-faire* individualism to turn their customary world of work upside down.

That other prominent element of carnivalesque people's justice we have been looking at, rough music, can be interpreted in a similar way. As Martin Ingram points out, 'cacophony evoked a contrast between harmony and disharmony', as between the traditional harmony represented by the collective values of the community and the disharmony signified by the individualistic self-interested behaviour of the offender (Ingram 1984: 98). In a similar vein, one could interpret the discordant sounds emanating from the motley collection of instruments used by the rough musicians during turnouts as pointing up aberrant behaviour which struck a discordant note in the community. Rough music, then, shared many characteristics with the riding ritual. As part of that 'system' of folk justice which took place outside the formal legal framework, rough music stridently proclaimed the community's moral code, loudly registered disapproval of immoral acts, brought acts of wrongdoing into public view, and reaffirmed the community's informal judicial code.[6] The rough music ritual also had that capacity to dampen violence and channel aggression along a more moderate path, and to an even greater degree than the riding ritual. Other elements closely associated with the carnivalesque were present, too, like stylised gestures, props, dramatic display, parody, and play. There were some differences nevertheless. As we have seen, the donkeying sanction tended to be aimed at culprits from within the community. An important feature of the rough music performances witnessed in the labour disputes of this period is that they were directed both at wrongdoers from inside the community and at those who menaced the community from outside, that is, the blackleg stranger from afar. Another difference is that whereas the riding punishment involved some degree of rough handling of the wrongdoer, the use of physical force was nearly always absent from the rough music sanction. In that sense, the rough music sanction was a psychological punishment.

Rough music took a number of forms. Its sounds could be the product of an array of instruments or extraordinary objects, the latter of which could include pots, pans, kettles, bells, whistles, chains, and shovels. Alternatively, or as an accompaniment to the instrumental performance, rough music could involve noisy utterances of a raucous or eerie nature emanating from the 'crowd', like hooting, hissing, or even groaning. Songs with a strong component of parody and satire could also form part of the repertoire of rough music. Rough music also proved incredibly malleable and could be adapted to a number of ends. As we saw above, a rough music performance could provide a clamorous backdrop to a donkey riding. In that sense, it served as an accoutrement of a more elaborate punishment ritual. Rough music could also be performed independently. When performed independently in regard to the labour disputes that concern us, rough music could be performed as a noisy accompaniment to scabs or blacklegs going to and from their place of work. Alternatively, it could take the form of a mock serenade either directly outside the home of a perceived offender or in the vicinity of the offender's place of work. We can see the operation of rough music in all its variety by looking at a few examples in the primary records from just one year alone, namely 1844, and involving just one group of workers, mineworkers.

Relations between the mineworkers and Britain's colliery owners had become increasingly strained as 1844 approached, over a range of contentious issues which included low wages, payment by truck instead of cash-wages, the yearly bond, punitive fines, and brutal and unhealthy working conditions. Early in the year, and in a portent of things to come, the colliers of St Helen's, Lancashire, turned out in protest against low wages. During the engagement, the tactic of rough music was used to bait and ridicule blackleg labour. In early February, the *Northern Star* reported that knobsticks were regularly accompanied 'to and from the pits' by a host of 'colliers' wives, children and female friends' who were 'beating drums, frying pans, pots, and kettles, hooting, shouting, and making the most hideous noises imaginable' (*Northern Star*, 10 Feb. 1844: 2). By the Spring of 1844, relations between the mineworkers and the 'coal kings' had reached breaking point and on 31 March some 40,000 miners struck work. The 1844 miners' strike took on a national character, though arguably the heart-beat of the strike was Durham and Northumberland. During the turnout in the Durham and Northumberland coalfields, where the pitmen sought redress on a number of issues which included the yearly bond, the system of punitive fines and irregular pay, the strike tactic of rough music was much in evidence. In early June, 'large mobs' of men, women and children were said to have gathered to 'intimidate' the scabs and blacklegs as they returned home from work 'by hooting, hissing and shouting and making a great noise beating on tin cans, [and] frying pans' (HO45/266/107. Affidavit. William Longstaff. 3 June 1844).

There was a distinct ritual component to these rough music proceedings, as the scabs and blacklegs were greeted by a cacophony of noise on a nightly basis. 'Every night', stated another report from the region, nineteen local individuals who refused to join the strike 'are hissed and hooted by mobs of men, women and children' as they made their way home from work (HO45/266/108. Affidavit. John Appleby. 3 June 1844). A mock serenade of sorts directly outside the homes of strike-breakers, displaying a whole manner of harsh and eerie sounds, also featured in the 1844 dispute. Depositions from strike-breakers told of striking colliers hissing, groaning and shouting outside their homes (HO45/644/11–12. Deposition of James Defty. n.d. c. Apr. 1844). At times, the serenade could be quite perfunctory. One deposition from a strike-breaker told of a number of striking colliers coming to his house in the hours close to midnight whereupon they 'groaned at the door' before soon departing (HO45/644/13. Deposition of Nicholas Wearmouth. n.d. c. Apr. 1844).

Tactics of a similar kind were used by striking colliers further south in Killamarsh, north-east Derbyshire, when the colliery owners, Messrs. Appleby, Walker, and Co., brought in blackleg labour. In May it was reported that the 'new workmen' had to 'encounter every description of annoyance, more especially from the misguided wives of the turnouts', arising from rough music performances (*Derby Mercury*, 22 May 1844: 3). The main cause of the blacklegs' discomfort was the overture of sound which they encountered on their passage home from work discharged by a drum, fifes, whistles, kettles, pots, pans, and other similar accompaniments. Another account relating to striking mineworkers in Derbyshire tells of knobsticks being annoyed by 'performers upon tin cans and fire shovels', and of tin cans being rattled 'about the heads' of the same knobsticks by the female supporters of the colliers (*Sheffield Independent*, 25 May 1844: 5).

As mentioned above, songs of a parodic and satirical nature also formed part of the repertoire of rough music. On another occasion during the Killamarsh dispute just discussed, two 'knobsticks' on returning from work ran into around 100 men, women and children 'who struck up the well-known air "March in Good Order", seconded by yells, hoots, and groans, of the most furious description' thrown in for good measure (*Sheffield Independent*, 25 May 1844: 5). The use of song to bait and ridicule blacklegs was witnessed in another Derbyshire coalfield some 24 miles south of Killamarsh, in Belper. Low wages and the much-despised system of payment by truck seemed to be at the heart of tensions between the Belper colliers and the 'coal kings' of that district. The truck system was said to be carried on in Belper 'to a frightful extent', with some Belper mineworkers, according to the *Northern Star* report of April 1844, not having received 'money' for their work 'during the last five years' (*Northern Star*, 20 Apr. 1844: 4).[7] Labour relations in Belper worsened still further when one of the coal masters of Belper decided to dispense with union labour. This move precipitated a carnivalesque response from the several hundred members of 'The Miners' Association of Great Britain and Ireland' who refused to give up the union. 'Armed' with a drum, fife, and triangle, the union men proceeded to traverse the streets of Belper and 'being musical, they played their tunes up and down everywhere; and sometimes when they met a traitor to the cause, they sung out lustily, if the weather was fine:

> Bah, bah, Black Sheep,
> Have you any wool!' (*Northern Star*, 20 Apr. 1844: 4).

The origins of the well-known miners' anti-blackleg folk song, *The Blackleg Miner*, with its less carnivalesque and much more uncompromising lyrics, is difficult to determine, though it may have originated in the attempts of the Durham and Northumberland pitmen to curtail blacklegging during the bitter dispute of 1844.[8]

It should be mentioned as well that, beyond 1844 and mineworkers, other groups of workers also wrote songs and broadside ballads, both emotive and satirical, to amplify issues and problems specific to their particular trade, circumstances and struggles. For example, the Kidderminster carpet weavers issued as many as seventeen broadside ballads during their long-running strike of 1828 over piece rates in an effort to give emotional expression to their grievances and promote their cause by other means.[9] Satirical songs also featured in a strike in Wolverhampton in 1850 involving tin-plate workers resisting a reduction in their wages. In one such song, the *Song of a Strike*, apparently sung to the tune of *King of the Cannibal Islands*, strike-breakers or 'rats' were held up for derision, as shown by the following selection of lyrics from the song:

> They [the masters] cast honest workmen in the street,
> And catch each long-tail rat they meet,
> ...Now every maiden old and young,
> Shun every rat who now does wrong,
> They'll only lead you in the throng,
> Of slavery, not Freedom.
>
> (Kidd 1949: 77)

Satirical lines relating to miscreant workers also occasionally appeared in humorous plays performed in theatres, such as the following lines uttered in a farce at the Theatre Royal in the Haymarket in 1767 on the subject of a strike of journeyman tailors:

> Some timid Dungs (unworthy of the name
> Alike of tailor or of man; from whom
> Opprobrious rise to hurt our fame)
> Meanly descend to work for half-a-crown.
>
> (cited in Galton 1896: xli)[10]

It remains, finally, to make a few additional points regarding rough music and its more refined cousin, satirical songs. Firstly, the more coarse expressions of rough music and satirical song have that capacity to illuminate the real with humour, to make the deadly serious through collective laughter. Secondly, rough music performances and satirical songs were certainly not confined to any one particular category of worker, as shown by the few examples above. A few additional examples from north-west England involving cotton workers demonstrate this further. During a strike in Oldham in late 1825, 'knobsticks' seeking to usurp the positions of the town's cotton workers found themselves subjected to 'the din of frying-pans' (*Leeds Intelligencer*, 29 Sept. 1825: 3). Then in another incident a few years later in 1829 during the labour unrest in Stockport and Manchester which mostly involved spinners resisting a wage reduction, knobsticks were 'serenaded with the "knobstick song", and other species of annoyance' (*Sheffield Independent*, 30 May 1829: 2).[11] It seems that the 'knobstick song' had traditionally been much used by the Lancashire cotton workers to mock and ridicule strike-breakers. In an earlier incident during the bitterly contested spinners' turnout of 1818, a group of 'cotton girls' formed a ring around a knobstick and proceeded to sing a song to the encircled strike-breaker 'which they call the "knobstick song", intended to ridicule those who are not what they call fair workmen'. The presence of a 'blind fiddler' added to the carnivalesque atmosphere of the incident (*Caledonian Mercury*, 17 Sept. 1818: 4). Thirdly, we should not underestimate the capacity of all forms of rough music and satirical song to sway the reluctant and the hesitant and send a strong message to traitors. As one commentator on rough music put it during the Stockport spinners' strike of 1829 just mentioned, 'the fear of being "knobsticked", or hooted through the streets, upon the timid mind, acts with an all-powerful effect' (*London Standard*, 16 May 1829: 3). Should the various manifestations of rough music, satirical song and other variants of the carnivalesque fail to have the desired effect, however, striking workers had other forms of persuasion in their armoury, as we will see in the following chapters.

Notes

1. Ashworth cites this incident of carnivalesque defiance and mockery which took place in Preston at an unspecified date in the late 1840s or early 1850s as an example of the 'growing insubordination' of the Preston operative spinners and their tendency to 'turn out' whenever any of their brethren were discharged from employment.
2. See chapter 7.
3. One of these markets was highly dubious it should be said, in that it was associated with the slave trade in the West Indies and America.
4. It seems that a wife of one of the absent men had also incurred the displeasure of the crowd, her effigy being burnt along with the effigy of her husband. This donkey and effigy ritual is also mentioned in HO52/25/261–2. Letter 5 May 1834.
5. The incident took place on 26 February.
6. A point made by Norman Simms as applied to other contexts. See Simms 1978.
7. Mention of the truck system in Belper can also be found in the classic work by Engels on proletarian life in England in the first half of the nineteenth century. See Engels 1969: 280.
8. The following lines from the song provide an indication of the uncompromising tone of *The Blackleg Miner*:

    So join the union while you may,
    Don't wait till your dying day,

For that may not be far away,
You dirty blackleg miner!

9 The strike began in March 1828. It was precipitated by a decision by the carpet manufacturers to reduce the piece rate for weaving the principal carpet produced in the town from one shilling to ten pence per yard, which represented a seventeen per cent cut in the weavers' income. The strike ended in August in defeat for the weavers. See Smith (1979).

10 The play, in three Acts, was entitled *The Tailors; A Tragedy for Warm Weather*. The play was evidently a product of the times as the year in question, 1767, was one of heightened tension and conflict in London's tailoring trade.

11 Unfortunately, the newspaper account did not provide the lyrics of the song. The Stockport strike began in January 1829 and ended in June when the spinners were forced to concede.

References

Alford, Violet (1959) 'Rough Music or Charivari', *Folklore*, 70(4): 505–518.

Aspinall, Algernon (1949) *The Early English Trade Unions. Documents from the Home Office Papers in the Public Record Office*. London: Batchworth.

Ashworth, Henry (1854) *The Preston Strike, An Enquiry into its Causes and Consequences*. Manchester: George Simms.

Bakhtin, Mikhail (1968) *Rabelais and his World*. Cambridge, Mass.: MIT Press.

Barker, Naomi (2013) 'Charivari and Popular Ritual in 17th-century Italy: A Source and Context for Improvised Performance', *Early Music*, 41(3): 447–459.

Benedict, Ruth (1946) *The Chrysanthemum and the Sword*. Boston: Houghton Mifflin.

Burke, Peter (1978) *Popular Culture in Early Modern Europe*. London: Temple Smith.

Davis, Natalie Zemon (1971) 'The Reasons of Misrule: Youth Groups and Charivari in Sixteenth-Century France', *Past & Present*, 50: 41–75.

Engels, Friedrich (1969; first published 1845) *The Condition of the Working Class in England*. London: Granada.

Favretto, Ilario (2015) 'Rough Music and Factory Protest in Post-1945 Italy', *Past and Present*, 228: 207–247.

Galton, Frank Wallis (1896) *Select Documents Illustrating the History of Trade Unionism. 1. The Tailoring Trade*. London: Longmans, Green & Co.

Gurnham, Richard (1976) *200 Years. The Hosiery Unions 1776–1976*. Leicester:National Union of Hosiery and Knitwear Workers.

Hammond, J.L. and Hammond, Barbara (1995; first published 1919) *The Skilled Labourer 1760–1832*. Stroud: Allan Sutton.

Henson, Gravenor (1970; first published 1831) *Henson's History of the Framework Knitters*. Newton Abbot: David & Charles.

Ingram, Martin (1984) 'Ridings, Rough Music and the "Reform of Popular Culture" in Early Modern England', *Past and Present*, 105: 79–113.

Jacquet, Jennifer (2016) *Is Shame Necessary? New Uses for an Old Tool*. London: Penguin.

Kidd, Archibald (1949) *History of the Tin-Plate Workers and Sheet-Metal Workers and Braziers Societies*. London: National Union of Sheet-Metal Workers and Braziers.

Lewis, Helen (1971) *Shame and Guilt in Neurosis*. New York: International Universities Press.

Page, William (ed) (1911) 'Industries: Silk-weaving', *A History of the County of Middlesex*. Vol. 2: London: Victoria County History: 132–137.

Palmer, Bryan (1978) 'Discordant Music: Charivaris and Whitecapping in Nineteenth-Century North America', *Labour/ Le Travail*, 3: 5–62.

Scheff, Thomas (2000) 'Shame and the Social Bond: A Sociological Theory', *Sociological Theory*, 18(1): 84–99.

Searby, Peter (1972) *Weavers and Freemen in Coventry, 1820–1861: Social and Political Traditionalism in an Early Victorian Town*. PhD Thesis: University of Warwick.

Shinn, Christopher (2002) 'Masquerade, Magic, and Carnival in Ralph Ellison's "Invisible Man"', *African American Review*, 36(2): 243–261.

Simms, Norman (1978) 'Ned Ludd's Mummers Play', *Folklore*, 89(2): 166–178.

Smith, Len (1979) *The Carpet Weaver's Lament. Songs and Ballads of Kidderminster during the Industrial Revolution*. Kidderminster: Kenneth Tomkinson.

Stephens, William B. (1969) 'The City of Coventry: Crafts and Industries, Modern Industry and Trade', in William B. Stephens (ed), *A History of the County of Warwick. Volume 8, the City of Coventry and Borough of Warwick*. London: Victoria County History: 162–189.

Thompson, E.P. (1992) 'Rough Music Reconsidered', *Folklore*, 103(1): 3–26.

Webb, Sidney and Webb, Beatrice (1920) *The History of Trade Unions*. London: Longman.

Yaneva, Rozaliya (2012) *Misrule and Reversals. Carnivalesque Performances in Christopher Marlowe's Plays*. Munich: Herbert Utz Verlag.

6

MAGIC RITUALS AND TABOOED THINGS

> The carts have been stopped – but not robbed – the carman has fled his charge, the carts have been broken, and the manufactured goods and the unmanufactured material have been scattered in a damaged condition upon the high road and fields.
> (The Spitalfields Weavers' Journal, Nov. 1837: 27)[1]

In an incident which took place in the weaving district of Camlachie in Glasgow in mid-September 1824, a weaver who had taken webs from a master deemed obnoxious to the Weavers' Association and contrary to the union's wishes, found himself at odds with the local community. The incident occurred in the context of a strike by the weavers' combination then in progress against a prominent manufacturer of muslins in Glasgow, Peter Hutchinson, the strike having begun on 8 September (on the background to the dispute, see *Morning Post*, 23 Sept. 1824: 4). During the raucous affair which unfolded, an effigy of the non-cooperative weaver, George Smith, was conveyed through the various weaving villages of the district suspended from a pole with a label on its breast bearing the inscription, 'A warning to all traitors for deserting their colours' (see *Morning Chronicle*, 15 Sept. 1824: 4; and *Morning Post*, 15 Sept. 1824: 2 for further details of this incident). Mr Smith, who had also stubbornly refused to return the 'blacked' work to Hutchinson's shop, had evidently aroused the wrath of the local weavers' community given the severity of the punishment meted out to his image. As the concourse of turnout weavers and their supporters said to be in the number of 700 to 800 persons paraded the villages, the effigy was, in the first instance, lashed with a rope before the house of Smith and the houses of other 'traitors' who had 'illegally' taken work during the strike. It was then ceremonially hanged on a wooden stand specially erected for that purpose by one of the entourage who 'performed the part of the hangman in due form'. The effigy was then burnt, before the participants in the affair moved to the final act of the drama which saw what remained of 'Mr Smith' being 'torn to pieces'. The attention to detail exhibited by those who crafted the representation of George Smith was quite remarkable, his sons who witnessed the event stating that 'they might have mistaken it for their father, but for the ill-painted face' (*Morning Chronicle*, 15 Sept. 1824: 4).

Following on from our discussions in the previous chapter, it is tempting to view the Camlachie incident as but a further example of a strike ritual heavily saturated with carnivalesque play. Clearly, there was indeed a strong element of carnivalesque play present in Camlachie on the occasion in question. This being said, it is more helpful to our understanding of the incident in Camlachie if we view it through the prism of magic ritual or, more specifically, the prism of sympathetic magic. Before we proceed further, we should clarify the meaning of magic ritual and sympathetic magic. The study of magic has a rich heritage. For Jane Ellen Harrison, ritual and ritual practice always involves some form of imitation which has magical dimensions (Harrison 1913). Indeed, influenced by the work of Sir James Frazer, Harrison saw ritual as a form of sympathetic magic in that it mimics that which it desires. This could involve a desire for the pleasure of Spring to return, for nature to yield a good harvest, or for the crops to prosper. Thus, in relation to the latter, Harrison informs us, when the corn is dying due to a lack of rain the Omaha native American Indians fill a vessel with water from which a tribal member then 'drinks some of the water and spirts it into the air, making a fine spray in imitation of mist or drizzling rain' (Harrison 1913: 32–3). Or, as Sir James Frazer himself observed of the practices of some traditional peoples in the Europe of his day, 'dancing or leaping in the air are approved homoeopathic modes of making the crops grow high' (Frazer 1925: 28). For 'homoeopathic' magic, one should read imitative magic. Whatever one's choice of term, homoeopathic or imitative, such actions rendered routine in ritual practice conform to one of Frazer's principal laws of 'sympathetic magic', namely the 'law of similarity' or the principle that 'like produces like'. It should be noted at this point that there are two principal laws of sympathetic magic for Frazer, the other being the law of contact or contagion. The law of contagion claims that where there has been physical contact between things or people, a sympathetic or magical relation remains even when contact has been severed. Contagion links vary though, it should be said, according to the degree and intensity of the original contact. Whether the law of similarity or the law of contagion, the key element in both these two laws of sympathetic magic is that the magical sympathy between things and people operates at a distance, 'the impulse being transmitted from one to the other by means of what we may conceive as a kind of invisible ether' (Frazer 1925: 12).

Returning to the magical properties of ritual, as well as the imitative or mimetic faculty, emotion and desire are at the heart of magical ritual practice according to Jane Ellen Harrison, in that ritual allows for a discharge of emotion and longing. Harrison thought this an important aspect of the human condition, as well as a quality that ritual shared with art. 'We must not only utter emotion, we must represent it, that is, we must in some way reproduce or imitate or express the thought which is causing us emotion' (Harrison 1913: 34). Nevertheless, the particular and crucial property of ritual for Harrison was 'acting out' these emotions and longings, that is, representing the 'thing desired' in 'sympathetic' actions. Thus, 'to perform a rite you must do something, that is, you must not only feel something but express it in action, or, to put it psychologically, you must not only receive an impulse, you must react to it' (Harrison 1913: 35). Other scholars also recognised the role that mimesis or imitation plays in magic ritual. Bronislaw Malinowski acknowledged that magical acts typically involve a mimetic activity or action which is dramatically expressed and which aims to bring about something desired (Malinowski 2013: 51–3). Again, for Malinowski, the activity or action 'sympathetically' mimics that which is desired.

There is a further layer of meaning to rituals of sympathetic magic, including death rituals of the type which took place at Camlachie. In his magnum opus, *The Golden Bough*, Sir James Frazer provides numerous examples of peoples and communities, both traditional and more modern, participating in effigy rituals where representative images of various persons and institutions are slain, often to the accompaniment of 'rough music' and much fanfare. In some cultures, Frazer noted, one of the purposes of the effigy execution ceremony, as with 'Burying the Carnival', was to ensure some protection for the community against misfortune (Frazer 1925: 301–7). Other effigy rituals performed a similar function. Hence for some communities the 'Carrying out Death' ritual, which involved the immolation of straw effigies of Death, 'was done to ensure a fruitful and prosperous year' and provide some magical 'safeguard against pestilence and sudden death' (Frazer 1925: 308). The point of such rituals for Frazer therefore is that they sought to help the community ward off grave evils that may befall it, so as to ensure better fortune and bring forth better times. In this sense, the ritual helped to purge the community of its ills and restore a sense of equilibrium to its affairs.

If we return to Camlachie we can see that the destruction of the representation of Mr Smith conformed to one of Sir James Frazer's principal laws of sympathetic magic, that is, the law of similarity. Following Jane Ellen Harrison, the effigy punishment ritual which unfolded in Camlachie also allowed for a discharge of emotion which involved a mimetic activity that sought to bring about something desired. In this case, that which is desired is the punishment and ultimate demise, albeit symbolically and imitatively, of the traitor whose adjudged selfish and reckless behaviour was considered to pose a deadly threat to the working community and the trade. Taking our cue from the insights of Frazer regarding the 'Carrying out Death' ritual, one can also interpret such effigy rituals as purification and rebirth rituals, in that they represented an effort by the community to rid itself of potentially fatal 'epidemics' in the hope that such measures, however crude, will safeguard the community and restore good fortune to its affairs.

There are some further aspects to effigy execution rituals that we should note. The first concerns the creative capacity of effigy magic rituals to channel emotions and regulate anger in situations of conflict and tension. In this regard, magic rituals involving effigy executions shared that characteristic of sublimation with the carnivaleque rituals we looked at in the previous chapter. In other words, effigy execution rituals provided a structured framework which enabled the participants in the ritual to direct their more aggressive inclinations onto a targeted image which served as a proxy for the offending individual. In this way, the ritual allowed for a release of frustration and anger which did not involve actual physical violence. A second aspect in such rituals, like the carnivaleque punishments that featured in the previous chapter, concerns the strong emphasis on ceremony, spectacle and dramatic display. Here one should note the stress on visual extravagance, acting out and play, and the use of symbolic representations to generate meaning. Additionally, and in a related sense, there is an emphasis in effigy execution rituals on the mocking inversion of the accepted order of things, particularly the mocking inversion of the retributive ceremonial ritual of execution by the state. We will observe other such incidents below. Through the use of such parody and play, moreover, the mainstream social order and its cherished institutions are creatively subverted in a context which minimised the risk of a clash with the forces of law and order.

Before we move on to other effigy punishment episodes, it should be mentioned that there is a strong historical dimension to the ritual execution of traitors *in absentia*. Mr Smith, as we have seen, was deemed to have deserted his weaver brethren in Camlachie and engaged in behaviour of a kind which earned him the epithet 'traitor', and was duly 'executed' for his betrayal. Traditionally and historically, effigy punishment rituals have proved highly efficacious in addressing the issue of traitors and betrayal. The theme of betrayal was present with three of the most frequently ritually executed individuals in the recent and distant past, namely Judas Iscariot, Guy Fawkes and Tom Paine. According to Nicholas Rogers, the much maligned Tom Paine, whose radical predilections and supposedly 'seditious' writings had earnt him the enduring scorn of those of a loyalist 'Church and King' persuasion, was 'the most burnt-in-effigy personality' of the eighteenth century (on the latter, see Rogers 1998: 202–9). Prior to Tom Paine, probably the most oft ritually punished individual, in parts of the Christian world at least, was Judas Iscariot. Apparently, the figure of 'Jack-o'Lent', said to represent the hated Judas Iscariot, was annually consigned to the flames during the highly carnivalesque events to mark the beginning of Lent which took place in English towns and villages during the early modern period:

> A figure, made up of straw and cast-off clothes, was drawn up or carried through the streets amid much noise and merriment; after which it was either burnt, shot at, or thrown down a chimney.
>
> *(Dyer 1900: 93)*

The following point needs to be made as well in regard to perceived traitors within the ranks of the labouring classes. As with many of the carnivalesque incidents we looked at in the previous chapter, particularly the donkey-ride ritual, effigy execution rituals were more efficacious in dealing with danger emanating from within the community, as with so-called blacksheep or scab behaviour. Effigy execution rituals were less effective and much less deployed in the case of danger pressing on external boundaries, such as when blackleg labour was imported in an effort to defeat a strike.

It was not just transgressors from within the workers' ranks who were ritually punished in this fashion. We can see this in one of the earliest recorded instances of effigy execution rituals in the labour unrest of our period. Although free-market *laissez-faire* economics had not yet taken a decisive hold on working relations in the British Isles during the 1760s, the first chill winds of change were already being felt by some journeymen crafts. We can see an example of this during the long-running phase of labour unrest in the silk-weaving industry in the Spitalfields district of east London. The grievances of the silk-weavers of Spitalfields were many and long-standing. They principally related to concerns as the eighteenth century unfolded about increasing levels of mechanisation in the trade, the bypassing of traditional apprenticeship rules by masters, illegal smuggling, and rising foreign goods imports, particularly the importation of cheaper calico imports from India and French-made silks to cater for the higher end of the consumer market. To these grievances we should also add an eighteenth-century version of wage arbitrage, whereby the master acted to relocate his business to other places to reduce labour costs. All such trends, developments, and advantageous manoeuvring by capital acted to undermine traditional handloom weaving skills, working conditions, pay rates, and employment prospects.[2]

The growing discontent felt by the Spitalfields silk-weavers at the downturn in their fortunes was sometimes expressed through effigy execution rituals, though it was usually an obnoxious master and others involved in the management of labour who formed the principal target of their ire. In one incident in February 1762, the effigies of a master silk-weaver in Spitalfields and his foreman were placed in a cart and conveyed to a nearby site where they were hung upon a gallows and then burnt to ashes. The ritual punishment was administered on account of the obnoxious master so targeted having recently 'introduced the silk manufactory into Scotland, where the price of labour and provisions is so much cheaper'. Even the mainstream press admitted that such a step 'will in the end be the ruin of the Spitalfields silk-weavers' (*Ipswich Journal*, 20 Feb. 1762: 2). The ritual had all the classic elements of sympathetic magic, with a splash of the carnivalesque thrown in, which included, in terms of the latter, a no-doubt highly amused audience of upwards of 10,000 people watching the spectacle. The same fate befell another master in an effigy punishment ritual witnessed in the Spitalfields area in early October the following year. The ritual displayed a remarkably similar pattern to that of the February 1762 execution, though with a few additional parodic elements. On this occasion, a large band of striking weavers was observed parading an effigy of a master whose behaviour they judged to have breached customary practices through the streets of the district in a cart to a site of execution. About the neck of the effigy was a rope or halter, while on either side of it was a mock executioner and a coffin carried by the weavers. On arrival at the place of execution the effigy was hanged on a gibbet, after which it was burnt to ashes (the incident took place on 3 October. See *The Gentleman's Magazine* (1763) 33: 514–5). Unfortunate master silk-weavers were still being executed *in absentia* towards the end of the decade. In late September 1769 it was reported that a large gathering of Spitalfields silk-weavers had 'hung a master of their branch, in effigy, over a sign pole' (*Whitehall Evening Post*, 30 Sept. 1769 to 3 Oct. 1769:1).

By the turn of the century, with *laissez-faire* thinking more in the ascendency, wage cutting on the part of masters more prevalent, and self-interested behaviour in the workplace encouraged to a much greater degree by the proponents of political economy, disaffected working men tended to turn their attention more towards obnoxious persons within their own ranks. From this point, it was perceived traitors from within, rather than obnoxious masters, who were more likely to be the subject of a ceremonial execution *in absentia*. As with the 'demise' of Mr Smith in Camlachie, the community of working weavers tended to have a liking for the 'magical' execution of miscreants within their ranks.

Remaining in Scotland, during the opening decades of the nineteenth century the handloom weavers of Airdrie were beset by low wages, rising unemployment and the spectre of starvation, the former not helped by those amongst their number 'who are encouraging the low paying manufacturers by taking out and working their webs' (*Scottish Trades' Union Gazette*, 12 Oct. 1833: 2). By the early 1830s the Airdrie weavers were attempting in various ways, both formal and informal, 'to give a public demonstration of their sentiments'. These included heart-felt petitions to an unresponsive Parliament, lobbying for the establishment of a Board of Trade to regulate wages in the weaving trade and, when all else failed, burning effigies at the cross (see *Scottish Trades' Union Gazette*, 12 Oct. 1833: 2 on the effigy incident. On the petitions and the Board of Trade, see *Caledonian Mercury*, 6 May 1833: 1–2).

Moving southward, and almost a year following the Camlachie episode, we find that weavers from Stroud in Gloucestershire were also involved in effigy-related incidents. Against the backdrop of a turnout of the Stroud weavers for higher wages, 'riotous' assemblies and 'weavers who had refused to turnout', it was reported that 'several effigies were burnt on Stroud hill' (*Manchester Mercury*, 14 June 1825: 3). Nor were the framework knitters of Hinckley in Leicestershire averse to 'magically' executing errant workers from their community, such as when the latter took on work 'below the price'. Hence in a dispute relating to the 'just price' in September 1829, the effigy of an offending workman was ritually consigned to the flames, a demise which brought forth 'a loud shout of exultation' from the watching throng (*The Leicester Chronicle*, 26 Sept. 1829: 3). The ritual was much in evidence, too, amongst the weavers living and working in the villages and townships around Huddersfield years later in 1842, and played out with much carnivalesque gusto and merriment it should be said. The weavers in question worked in the fancy waistcoat branch of the trade. During a strike which took place in April of that year, a number of miscreant weavers whom the turnouts had 'designated blacksheep' were burnt in effigy. For the *Leeds Times* there was a subtext to these episodes beyond the mock execution of the transgressors, in that the 'vulgar parade of effigy-burning' served as 'a source of intimidation to weak minds' (*Leeds Times*, 23 Apr. 1842: 8). The fancy waistcoat weavers of Huddersfield were still immolating effigies in mid-June. On this occasion, two effigies of blacksheep were carried through the streets of the town by a number of individuals leading a gathering of some 200 persons amid 'a great noise and tumult'. The incident concluded with the effigies being ceremonially burnt in the vicinity of the homes of the blacksheep (*Leeds Times*, 3 Sept. 1842: 7–8).

Striking colliers, too, used effigy rituals to make their point. In May 1856 the Redding colliers in the Falkirk region of the Scottish coalfields turned out in protest against a twenty per cent reduction in their wages against the backdrop of falling prices said to be occasioned by economic uncertainty following the conclusion of the Crimean War.[3] It seems that effigy burning rituals were much in evidence during the conflict. On one occasion, effigies of 'some men who continued to work' during the strike were burnt during a demonstration of colliers on Redding Muir (there is an account of the 1856 strike in the *Falkirk Herald*, 4 Sept. 1926: 5). In another incident, a crowd of around 100 striking colliers assembled outside the home of a 'blacksheep' at Easter Shieldhill and proceeded to burn effigies of the offender to the accompaniment of much shouting and hissing and some missiles being thrown through the windows of the house (*Falkirk Herald*, 4 Sept. 1926: 5. See also *Falkirk Herald*, 8 May 1856: 3). Despite this creative use of ritual to gain traction in the strike, the usual blend of adverse circumstances eventually compelled the Redding colliers to return to work at the reduced rate after a twelve-week struggle. These circumstances included the extreme hardship experienced by the striking colliers and their families, the intransigence of the coal-owners, and the importation of blacklegs to undermine the strikers' efforts.

An effigy ritual, on this occasion with a more carnivalesque flavour, was also witnessed at the Denaby Main colliery, Mexborough, in the Rotherham district of the south Yorkshire coalfield during a lock-out in early 1869. In early February 1869, the manager of the colliery announced that the services of those mine-workers associated with the miners' union were no longer required on the grounds that Denaby Main was a 'free labour colliery' (*Sheffield Independent*, 6 Feb. 1869: 6). Henceforth, union men were not 'knowingly' to be employed at Denaby Main and were to be replaced by so-called free labourers. In one incident a few weeks into the lock-out in early April, the 'free labourers' who 'have supplied the places of the men on strike' were 'escorted' to work by a lively gathering of the locked-out miners and their supporters carrying an effigy and black flag to the accompaniment of a little 'rough music', the latter being chiefly performed by a tin whistle band (*Sheffield Daily Telegraph*, 9 Apr. 1869: 4).[4]

Other groups of workmen also carried out effigy executions. In early September 1834, a painter and glasier from London, 'and a member of the Trades' Unions', was charged during a dispute with Messrs Bennet and Hunt, builders of Horseferry Road, Westminster, with 'creating a mob' and 'violently assaulting' a strike-breaker. Apparently the said painter and glasier had incurred the displeasure of the courts by leading a 'hissing and hooting' 'mob' over Westminster Bridge while carrying an effigy with a rope round its neck on his shoulders. The effigy in question was undoubtedly a representation of the offending strike-breaker. It was alleged that at one stage during the disturbance, the convicted unionist shoved the effigy in the strike-breaker's face accompanied by a verbal warning that 'this is the way to serve all knobsticks' (*London Courier and Evening Gazette*, 9 Sept. 1834: 4).

Mock effigy executions also featured in a strike in Bradford in June 1845 involving woolcombers then in dispute with their employer, Messrs Rand and Ramsbotham, over the issues of pay and working conditions. Several woolcombers 'who refuse to join the strike' complained of being called 'black sheep' by the turnouts, and experiencing other forms of 'annoyance'. The latter forms of annoyance included the spectacle of striking woolcombers perambulating the streets with effigies hanging on a gallows prior to the effigies being 'publicly burnt', a tactic, in the view of the authorities, clearly 'intended to intimidate other workmen' (*Bradford Observer*, 12 June 1845: 8). More supposedly 'rational' elements within the leadership of the woolcombers' union, the Woolcombers' Protective Society, however, were more sceptical of the value of effigy executions as a strike weapon. As such, they urged their more impulsive brethren to desist from the practice 'because of the obloquy and injury which crued [sic] to the Society thereby' (*Bradford Observer*, 12 June 1845: 5).

Even cotton spinners, usually inclined towards more 'modern' forms of collective action during strike situations, occasionally resorted to effigy executions to make their point. During a strike at the mill of Messrs Hargreaves Brothers in Bolton in January 1861, a female 'knobstick' 'was burnt in effigy in front of her own house' by a party of turnout cotton operatives (*Leicestershire Chronicle*, 2 Jan. 1861: 5). Women, however, were often amongst the most active, vocal and redoubtable participants in efforts to thwart strike-breaking and build trade unionism during these decades. In the words of a *Saturday Review* columnist reporting on the colliers' strike at Wigan in the Spring of 1868, 'Penthesilea animates the strife, and, filling her apron with granite and paving-stones, does good service on the law and the knobsticks' (*The Saturday Review of Politics, Literature, Science and Art* (1868) 25: 541). Women could also inject imagination and dexterity into a strike situation. During the infamous lock-out of all workers associated with a trade union by the masters of Derby during late 1833 and early 1834, women were often at the forefront of efforts to prevent the arrival of 'new hands' into Derby to displace the locked-out unionists. In one such effort in March 1834, a group of women loyal to the union, on hearing of a 'fresh importation' of these unwelcome arrivals into the town, set to work fashioning an effigy of a black sheep, an exercise in craftwork and imagination which exemplified their talents 'in an extraordinary manner'. Once the craftwork had been completed, and the figure had been adorned with tail, 'firmly fixed upon his legs' and stuffed with wisps of straw to bring it to its natural proportions, then 'the awful ceremony of burning him took place' (*The Pioneer*, 15 Mar. 1834: 255). To enhance the dramatic impact of the ritual, the effigy burning ceremony concluded directly outside the home of the 'shepherd' tasked by the masters with importing the 'black sheep' into Derby, accompanied by the sound of 'baaing' from the watching throng which 'was deafening in the extreme' (*The Pioneer*, 15 Mar. 1834: 255).

Variations on the mock executions of effigies which comprised similar elements of sympathetic magic, notably imitative magic according to the principle that like produces like, included mock trials, mock funeral ceremonies, and mock burials. The written record is not as revealing in regard to these particular forms of sympathetic magic ritual. Nevertheless, accounts of such incidents do occasionally surface in the record. In the Summer of 1756, just before our period opens, there is an account of a mock trial of an effigy which took place in the hamlet of Newington Butts in the County of Surrey involving members of the local weavers' club. Apparently the unfortunate effigy was brought forth with due solemnity into the surrogate Court of justice, subjected to a 'long trial', and eventually executed following the sentence of death being passed by the 'people's Court' (*Gazetteer and London Daily Advertiser*, 31 July 1756: 2).[5]

Another interesting case of a mock trial occurred in Bradford on Avon in Wiltshire in May 1791. The displacement of traditional work by machinery formed the background to the incident. The latter decades of the eighteenth century and the early decades of the nineteenth century witnessed increased attempts by the clothiers of Wiltshire and Somerset to introduce a range of new machinery and other technical innovations into their industry. These included spinning jennies, flying shuttle looms, scribbling and carding engines, gig mills and shearing frames. Fearing loss of work, reductions in income and even displacement from their communities, the region's woollen workers looked on the new innovations with both fear and hostility. Thus, when a local clothier, Joseph Phelps, attempted to set up a scribbling and carding engine in his workshop in Bradford on Avon in May 1791, a number of the town's woollen workers, described in the unflattering language of the time as a 'tumultuous mob of nearly 500 persons', demanded of Phelps that he deliver up the offending machine to them. What followed next was both tragic and bizarre (*Oxford Journal*, 21 May 1791: 3). The tragic was the murderous gunfire which ripped into the assembled crowd, killing a man, a woman and a boy, and leaving others 'dangerously wounded'.[6] The bizarre concerned the eventual appropriation of the hated carding machine by the outraged multitude who proceeded to subject it to a mock trial. Sentence of death duly passed, the machine was then ceremonially burnt on the town bridge.[7]

Fast forward to October 1818 in the by then increasingly mechanised Lancashire and we find a similar incident where the implements of mechanisation met their end in a mock ceremonial manner. The ceremony grew out of a dispute concerning wage rates in the town relating to the cotton manufacturing business of Messrs. Horrockses and Co. In what transpired a body of weavers conducted a mock funeral procession in the vicinity of Gallows Hill in Preston, which culminated in the burial of a set of weaver's geerings in a grave specifically dug for that purpose. The burial was conducted with due solemnity, an oration being pronounced by a weaver at the graveside once the 'deceased' had been deposited in the ground (*Lancashire Gazette*, 10 Oct. 1818: 3).[8] The implements of machinery and production were laid to rest in a similar fashion by a body of striking weavers a few years later in Blackburn. In this particular incident in May 1829, the weavers conspired to conduct a burial in the town for a shuttle covered in a piece of calico dyed black which served as a mourning crape (HO40/23/171–2. Letter to Robert Peel. 29 May 1829).

Further north in April 1844, during the fractious dispute in the Durham and Northumberland coalfield over pay rates, regular wages, the yearly bond and the system of fines, it was an entire colliery that magically met its end.[9] The pitmen of Thornley colliery were amongst the most militant of the region's colliers and had struck work as early as 23 November 1843. In April 1844 the Thornley men were still out. To their mind, the Thornley colliery was one of the most obnoxious of the local pits in terms of the miners' grievances. The Thornley colliery also had a highly questionable safety record. In August 1841 an explosion at the colliery killed nine workers and seriously wounded many others. Most of those killed were under seventeen years of age (see *Northern Star*, 14 Aug. 1841: 6). A year later, the safety of those working the Thornley pit remained a serious issue. In August 1842, the Thornley colliers struck work in protest at having to work in the most dangerous parts of the pit with candles instead of lamps (*Northern Star*, 27 Aug. 1842: 8). By April 1844, the Thornley pitmen had exhausted their patience with Thornley colliery. In early April they attended a mock burial service read over the colliery by the clerk of the solicitor tasked by the miners' union with supporting the region's pitmen. In this strange ceremony it was frequently declared by those present that the detested Thornley colliery 'should never go to work again' (the mock burial service features in HO45/644/3–7. Letter from Rowland Burdon. 8 April 1844).[10]

If we pause to reflect for a moment on the aforementioned incidents at Gallows Hill in Preston in October 1818 and Blackburn in May 1829, it is clear that even though the implements of machinery were effectively destroyed by striking weavers, the weavers' actions cannot be so easily interpreted through the oft-used contemporary frames of reference of 'mob violence' and 'riot'. Nor do these two incidents sit comfortably in that master narrative within the historiography of 'machine-breaking', more of which a little later. In both cases, at Preston and at Blackburn, the presence of a strong performative and ritual component diluting the potential for confrontation and violence, as well as the strain of imitative magic running through the proceedings, complicates matters and should give us pause for thought in terms of applying particular terms to these incidents. If we turn to another oft-referred-to form of riot which took place during strike situations in the era of industrialisation, we can find similar examples of particular incidents during strikes which do not conform to the general narratives. This form of riot is the one described by Eric Hobsbawm as 'collective bargaining by riot' which, it should be said, he also includes under the more general heading of 'machine-breaking' (Hobsbawm 1952).

Before we turn to consider these particular incidents, these exceptions to the general rule, it is important to explain in more detail the nature of this form of riot in its various manifestations. For Hobsbawm, 'collective bargaining by riot' was more associated with the period just prior to the Industrial Revolution as well as the early decades of industrialisation. At this point, Britain's economic landscape was still characterised by small-scale units of production often centred on a domestic system of industry spatially located in villages and towns rather than the more sprawling urban environments of the later phase of industrialisation. In this earlier, slowly mutating industrial landscape, the tactic of 'collective bargaining by riot' could prove to be a highly effective means of applying pressure on often locally based masters in regard to wages and other matters. Thus for Hobsbawm, the various forms of 'wrecking' that took place under the more general rubric of 'collective bargaining by riot' were techniques of trade unionism in the period before the British economy had become more comprehensively industrialised (Hobsbawm 1952: 59). At this stage in our analysis, it should be mentioned that Hobsbawm differentiated this mode of 'machine-wrecking' from the machine-breaking which tended to reflect an opposition to the introduction of de-skilling and labour-saving machinery as industrialisation began to permeate most sectors of the economy as the nineteenth century unfolded. The latter mode of activity, of course, is more commonly associated with the Luddite destruction of knitting-frames which took place in the vicinity of the Nottingham, Leicester and Derby triangle at sustained and intermittent stages between 1811 and 1817 (see also Horn 2005). Similar methods found expression amongst the woollen workers of Yorkshire and the cotton weavers of south Lancashire between 1812 and 1813.

This second type of 'wrecking' being duly noted and observed, it is the first category of 'machine-breaking' that concerns us here, that which Hobsbawm defines as 'collective bargaining by riot'. As mentioned, this latter category of wrecking assumed various forms. This included actions directed not only against the machinery of production but also raw materials, the master's private property, and the goods and materials worked on during the stages of production. It is this latter form of 'wrecking' that is of most interest to us here. As Hobsbawm correctly states, such methods pre-date the industrial era. In this regard, we should note a so-called 'insurrection' of weavers which took place in the City of London on 9 and 10 August 1675. During the 'great mischief and disorders' which ensued, a number of houses were broken into by a 'riotous assembly' of weavers who proceeded to seize looms and goods and burn the same 'to the great disturbance of the peace' (Anon. 1675: 1–8). Remaining in the London area, we find similar methods being used during the long-running and fractious dispute in the silk-weaving trade in Spitalfields and neighbouring districts during the 1760s, referred to earlier in this chapter. As mentioned above, tensions had arisen in the trade due to a range of unwelcome developments and factors, which included the import and manufacture of cheap foreign wrought silk and the increasing habit of some masters to press down on labour costs, all of which posed a serious threat to the incomes and livelihood of the Spitalfields silk-weavers. Following the presentation of petitions to Parliament, which met with mixed success, the Spitalfields silk-weavers resorted to the methods of extra-Parliamentary direct action. One such method was 'cutting' up silk on looms worked by offending masters and strike-breaking weavers during nocturnal raids on their shops and dwellings.[11] Nor were such methods confined to the weavers of London. Here one should consider the following which occurred during a period of economic uncertainty and labour unrest in the West Country between 1756 and 1757 in clashes involving weavers in Stroud, Gloucestershire. During this so-called 'rising' of the Stroud weavers it was reported that:

> Many chains have been damaged upon the looms; some weavers have been compelled by rioters to bring home the chains they have taken out, upon the old footing; cloths have been cut and damaged upon the tenters; the shuttles have been taken away by violence, and secured in places and by persons who deserve censure; the weavers' tools have been destroyed, and other very extra-ordinary methods have been used, to prevent those who were inclined to work.
> *(Anon. 1757: 32)*

Similar methods were witnessed during labour disputes in the weaving and textile districts of England's West Country in 1718, 1724, 1726–7, 1738, and 1741 (Hobsbawm 1952: 59).

We should certainly be grateful to Hobsbawm for moving our understanding of these occurrences beyond those interpretations which have tended to characterise machine-breaking in its various forms as impulsive mindless acts of desperation. In these interpretations, machine-wrecking, whether it took the form of 'collective bargaining by riot' or Luddism, was depicted as an essentially immature form of collective action borne of almost animal-like desperation according to John H. Plumb (Plumb 1950: 150). Later historians in the wake of Hobsbawm have added even more nuance and sophistication into the study of these earlier forms of protest, rightly questioning those histories which tend to view these earlier forms through the prism of later nineteenth-century trade unionism and the meta-narratives of progress and modernisation (these later historians would include Randall 1991; Berg 1988; and Navickas 2011). In so doing, such histories were inclined to characterise these earlier forms of collective action as essentially backward-looking, primitive and ultimately aimless, and thus vastly inferior to the more rational, sophisticated and modern methods of later nineteenth-century trade unionism (for examples of the 'modernisation' school, see Tilly 1995. See also Webb 1920). With their rather strict demarcations between different historical periods, teleological assumptions about supposedly inevitable progress towards more advanced political forms, and sharp value judgements about earlier forms of protest, such interpretations betrayed something of the Whig approach to the study of historical change. For those historians who incline towards a more sympathetic portrayal of these earlier forms of collective protest, the actions of workers in this period were not regressive, mindless and impulsive. Rather, such actions were rational, considered, and usually well measured given the context and circumstances of the times and the limited power and choices that the labouring classes then had at their disposal.

One feature of these 'new histories of labour and collective action' has been to invite historians to take a more nuanced and flexible approach to collective action in the earlier phase of industrialisation and to avoid collapsing what may represent quite different and varied forms of protest into a broad, over-arching singular frame of reference like 'riot' for instance (Navickas 2011: 197). Acting on this invitation, and returning to the main theme of this section of the chapter, we find that the historical record does occasionally throw up incidents in strike situations in our period which do not sit comfortably in the master narratives of 'riot', 'collective bargaining by riot', and 'machine-breaking'. Even less do they fit that frame of reference favoured by contemporary elites and the various representatives of 'respectable' opinion in the era of liberal political economy, that of 'mob violence'. Take, for instance, the incident discussed in the previous chapter which occurred during the turnout of shag weavers in Banbury, Oxfordshire, in August 1793.[12] By way of a reminder, at one point during the turnout against a master who had 'illegally' taken on an apprentice, a contingent of striking weavers entered the home of a weaver who had continued to work during the turnout and seized the cloth that he was working on from his loom. The striking weavers then placed the cloth on an ass and proceeded in carnivalesque style to the home of the obnoxious master who had taken on the apprentice, whereupon they dispatched it at the master's door. We can observe similar incidents in other labour disputes in our period, such as the following examples from the west of England.

When the weavers of Frome in the County of Somerset clashed with the master clothiers of the town in June 1823 over wages and prices, the former determined to appropriate all work undertaken by strike-breaking labour. Following the pattern of the Banbury appropriation decades earlier, striking weavers entered the homes of those weavers working at the lower prices, seized the work, formed in procession, and carried the goods back to the premises of the master clothiers, all the while offering 'no violence to anyone in their march' (HO40/18/23–4. Letter from The Reverend Henry Sainsbury, magistrate, to Robert Peel. 12 June 1823). Nor was this practice in any way aberrant or exceptional, the town of Frome having witnessed similar acts of seizure during a turnout of weavers in protest against differential rates for the same work in January of the previous year. As in June 1823, the houses of the weavers' 'who work at the low prices' were entered, the cloth taken from the looms, and then returned 'to the clothier to whom it belonged' (HO40/17/5–6. 20 Jan. 1822). Such methods had a long ancestry in labour disputes in the west of England. In the vicinities of Taunton, Exeter and Tiverton during the labour unrest of 1725–6, circumstances exacerbated by bad harvests and uncertainty in the wider economy, striking woollen workers in the still of night entered the homes of weavers and combers working at the low rate of wages, cut the work from their looms, and proceeded to parade the seized cloth through the streets accompanied by a flag (recounted in Henson 1970: 116).

Moving forward in time to the Midland counties, we also have the intriguing incidents which occurred in Leicester in a dispute in June 1825 when bands of striking framework knitters intercepted strike-breakers and seized their goods. In one such incident, the strikers confiscated both yarn and knitting-frame before proceeding to return them to the master by setting them at his door peacefully and without violence. In a related episode, a contingent of turnouts intercepted another strike-breaker seeking to convey a quantity of knitting-frames from the warehouse to his home in a cart. Having seized the 'contraband' items, the turnouts, which included both men and women, then returned them to the warehouse in procession 'led by a man ringing a large bell' (HO40/18/252–3. Letter to Robert Peel. 17 June 1825).

How should we interpret such incidents, and in a manner which is not constrained by a reliance on such master narratives as 'collective bargaining by riot', 'machine-breaking', and certainly 'primitive riot' and 'mob violence'? As with the mock burials of machinery at Preston in October 1818 and at Blackburn in May 1829, these incidents at Banbury, Frome, Taunton, Exeter, Tiverton and Leicester are marked by the presence of a strong performative and ritual element. This presence of performance and ritual most certainly would have helped regulate some of the antagonism felt by these groups of workers towards their employers and strike-breakers and channel it down a path which obviated the need to resort to direct physical violence.

Alongside the performative and ritual element, or complementing the same, and as with the mock burials at Preston and Blackburn, we can also discern a strain of sympathetic magic running through these strike proceedings. With the incidents at Banbury, Frome, Taunton, Exeter, Tiverton and Leicester, however, we see the operation of the second of Sir James Frazer's two principal laws of sympathetic magic, that is, the law of contact or contagion. Though already mentioned, and just to reiterate, the law of contagion posits that where there has been physical contact between things or people a magical 'sympathy' or connection remains after the initial association has been severed. Distance is no barrier to the principle of contiguity according to Frazer, the secret sympathy between things and people being transmitted like a life-force or energy 'through a space which appears to be empty' (Frazer 1925: 12). As with the law of similarity, the law of contagion has both positive and negative dimensions. Examples of the former would include bridal bouquets and the supposedly lucky rabbit's foot. Examples of the latter would include an item of clothing once worn by a serial killer. The latter, it should also be said, namely negative contagious magic, falls into the category of taboo. 'The whole doctrine of taboo, or at all events a large part of it', Frazer informs us, 'would seem to be only a special application of sympathetic magic, with its two great laws of similarity and contact' (Frazer 1925: 19). Just to clarify this further, it should be noted that the properties or dangerous contagion of taboo reside in 'things' as well as persons and words. As was long established and recognised in the beliefs and customs of traditional peoples, 'things', as with words, 'may, like persons, be charged or electrified, either temporarily or permanently, with the mysterious virtue of taboo, and may therefore require to be banished for a longer or shorter time from the familiar usage of common life' (Frazer 1925: 224).

Let us return to the incidents at Banbury, Frome, Taunton, Exeter, Tiverton and Leicester. In these incidents we can see the actions of the striking workers in relation to the cloth and other materials that they seized from strike-breakers operating according to the same principles of contiguity that Sir James Frazer observed at work in the operation of sympathetic magic. Or, to be more precise, the form of contagious magic which we can see at work in these acts of appropriation is that of negative contagious magic with its association, as previously mentioned, with taboo. It has been mentioned above that in certain cases where contagious magic is seen to be at work, a magical sympathy is thought to exist between an individual and the clothes that he or she has worn. In some cases a positive magical sympathy is thought to exist, as when an admiring fan in the contemporary modern era of celebrity culture covets the acquisition of a piece of clothing worn by a celebrity or sports star. In other cases, clothing emits a negative charge and repels, as with the clothing of a child murderer or the uniform of a former SS guard who was present at one of the death camps during the Holocaust years.

We can apply the same duality of positive and negative magical sympathy to the labour process. Though more evident in the independent pre-industrial sphere of artisan craftsmanship, a positive magical sympathy can exist between the craftsman and that which his or her labour produces, whereby personal creativity and positive energy travels between the maker and the product of his or her craft. This creativity and positive energy then nestles in the product like a beautiful 'indwelling spirit' which can be felt by those who later come into contact with it. In the realm of the labour process that concerns us in this analysis, a contagious magical sympathy was also thought to exist between a strike-breaker and the product of his labour, though of a negative kind. Here the 'indwelling spirit' thought to reside in the product was perceived to be contaminating and dangerous. For the striking weavers of Banbury, Frome, Taunton, Exeter, Tiverton and Leicester, the pieces of cloth and yarn that they seized, ritually paraded in carnivalesque style and returned to the master without violence in most cases, had been defiled, being the product of the illegitimate labour of those workmen who had ignored the strike call. These materials were thus contaminated or tabooed. In this sense, the 'indwelling spirit' was wholly negative, the contagion between the workman, the materials with which he came into contact, and the product of his labour, being of a kind which aroused revulsion and contempt. Not surprisingly, even the clothes worn by strike-breakers aroused revulsion. In the 1830s in Stockport, Lancashire, for instance, it was said that the women of the town would not wash the clothes 'of any man who was a knobstick, who had any sympathy with knobsticks, or who would not oppose reduction' (*The Blackburn Standard*, 26 Aug. 1835: 8). During a labour dispute at the Monkwearmouth colliery in Sunderland in March 1864, the clothes of a blackleg pitman were smuggled out of the pit where he was working by union loyalists and burnt, so that he was 'compelled to leave the pit with nothing on but the clothes he was working in' (*Shields Daily Gazette*, 18 Mar. 1864: 2).

It is important to recognise that aside from their performative and ritual qualities, there was a particular ingredient which gave the incidents at Banbury, Frome, Taunton, Exeter, Tiverton and Leicester their quite exceptional character and differentiated them from those more frequent occurrences where the work of a strike-breaker was destroyed directly at the point of production, such as those acts of 'cutting' up silk in the looms in Spitalfields in the 1760s. This was the ingredient of spatial and temporal distance. In other words, the ingredient crucial to the principle and operation of contagious sympathetic magic in the actions taken against contaminated work and materials at Banbury, Frome, Taunton, Exeter, Tiverton and Leicester was the transmission of negative energy across space and time. At this point, as the materials and products of illegal labour were wrenched from their source or 'anchorage' in the labour process and paraded across space and time, they acquired a new status and entered the realm of negative contagious magic.

On occasions the written record brings to the fore in a quite explicit manner the awareness on the part of striking workers of the negative 'indwelling spirit' lodged in the work and materials touched by forbidden labour. In early Autumn 1846, the woolcombers of Keighley in west Yorkshire attached to the woolcombers' union struck work. The Keighley woolcombers were seeking an advance of wages on the grounds that their average weekly wage of 10s. for twelve hours per day labour was inadequate for the subsistence of their families once a number of expenses and deductions, including those for rent, rates, fire, soap, and candles, had been factored in.[13] When the Keighley masters refused to acquiesce, a fractious contest then ensued through October and November. Not surprisingly, the issue of strike-breakers and imported blackleg labour, the latter described by the pro-labour *Northern Star* as the procuring of 'the assistance of the un-principled and degraded workmen of other parts', was a concern for the woolcombers. In one particular incident in early October, a strike-breaker was thwarted in his attempts to transport 'black-sheep wool' from one of the Keighley factories in dispute with the woolcombers to his home 'a few miles' away by carters sympathetic to the woolcombers' cause. This act of collective solidarity and calculated obstruction exhibited all the aspects of negative contagious magic. The attempt to find safe passage for the 'forbidden thing' was described in some detail by the *Northern Star*:

> One fellow got a quantity [of wool] packed up, and brought it to the top of the lane leading from the factory to the high road, and placed himself in readiness for a cart to carry the forbidden thing to his home in Haworth parish, a few miles off. Many very tempting chances occurred of carts going in his direction; but his appeals and proffers of pay were all in vain. The carters declared to a man that they would not contaminate either their carts or their hands with his "black-sheep luggage", and advised him to carry it back, again, which the fellow was at last compelled to do, to the very great satisfaction of the bystanders.
>
> (Northern Star, 10 Oct. 1846: 24)

Another strike-breaker, in a separate incident in October, also ran up against the law of negative contagion. Seeking to wash a quantity of 'forbidden' wool he was working on during the strike, the unfortunate workman discovered that 'every wash-house was shut up, the combers telling him, very candidly, that there was neither soap, water, fire, nor wash-houses, in that neighbourhood, for the washing of "black-sheep wool" and the fellow had to carry it back again, a distance of some miles' (*Northern Star*, 10 Oct. 1846: 24).[14]

148 Magic rituals and tabooed things

It would of course be naïve and inaccurate to claim that all acts of seizing and parading the contaminated goods and equipment of strike-breakers passed off peacefully and were devoid of aggression in whatever form. The record does throw up instances of this latter type, though too many to mention here given the constraints of space.[15] The following incidents, though, should give one a flavour of this type of activity. The incidents in question took place during a dispute between local weavers and a master clothier named Thomas Neal in the town of Wootton-under-edge in Gloucestershire in late November 1825. The turnout was supported by the Union Society of Weavers and pivoted on the issue of irregular prices for the same work. Not surprisingly, those weavers who continued to work under price during the dispute provoked the ire of the turnouts. Some of the former were visited in their homes by bodies of turnouts led by one Joseph Wolf, a local pensioner referred to by his brethren as General Wolf. In one such incident, the strikers entered the home of a miscreant weaver. Following the forcible removal of two cassimere chains of work from the weaver's looms, General Wolf's men then formed in procession and, marching in formation, carried the chains of work to a nearby common some half a mile distant. On arrival at the common, the performance concluded when the marchers 'made a fire' and consigned the chains to the flames (discussed in the *Coventry Herald*, 9 Dec. 1825: 4). Two days later, in another incident with a distinctly military flavour, a column of weavers were observed marching through Wootton-under-edge two-by-two. Arriving at their destination, the column forcibly entered the home of a weaver working under price, seized the cloth he had been working on, 'rolled the whole up on one of the loom beams', and carried it to Thomas Neal's factory whereupon they 'cut the cloth and chain to pieces, and trod it under foot' (*Coventry Herald*, 9 Dec. 1825: 4).

Then, of course, we have 'rattening', the seizing, hiding or destroying of the tools of a recalcitrant workman as a punishment for breaking a strike or refusing to join the union. This practice had a long ancestry which can be traced back to the punishment sanctions of the English medieval craft Guilds. The seizure of tools was usually the lot of a non-compliant Guild member as a punishment for the failure to pay a fine imposed by the officials of the Guild (see Brentano 1870: 127–8). Various forms of rattening would feature in turnouts during the later 'modern' period. Mention has already been made earlier in this chapter of the 'rising' of the weavers of Stroud in Gloucestershire between 1756 and 1757, which saw the tools of 'those who were inclined to work' destroyed by the turnouts. It has been well documented that rattening was an oft-used strike weapon in the workshops and factories of nineteenth-century Britain. The practice was quite prevalent amongst certain trades and in certain localities, such as the light metal trades of Sheffield for example (in this regard, see Downing 2013). This being said, rattening was certainly not confined to one trade or one place alone, as a few examples from just one decade in our period will show. When during a strike of colliers in the Abergavenny region of Wales in June 1822 a number of the turnouts broke ranks and returned to work, they discovered that the handles of their tools had been 'burnt to a cinder having been thrust for that purpose into the burning coke-heaps' (HO40/17/296–7. Letter from The Rev. W. Powell to Henry Hobhouse. 15 June 1822). A few years later in May 1825 during a turnout of journeymen carpenters in Birmingham, the first act of the strikers, said to be in the number of 'between one and two hundred', was to make an appearance at the various shops of the masters to 'bring away' the tool chests of those workmen showing a reluctance to join the strike (HO40/18/198–9. Letter from Theodore Price to Henry Hobhouse. 11 May 1825). Two years later in June 1827, it was the journeymen shipwrights of Liverpool who utilised rattening to better prosecute their strike when they proceeded to destroy 'the utensils of some workmen in the Builders' Yards' in the vicinity of the shipyards (HO40/22/130. Letter from Lt. Colonel Jordan to Major Eckersley. 6 June 1827).

The law of negative contagious magic was not just confined to the labour, goods, equipment and tools of recalcitrant workmen. The negative contagion released by the touch or presence of offending workmen could also permeate an entire workshop, as the following example shows. In early 1824 a Parliamentary Select Committee chaired by Joseph Hume met to discuss the issue of artisans and machinery in the wider context of the developing industrial economy. In one of the sessions, which took place on 1 March, the question of 'fair' and 'foul' workshops was discussed in relation to the hat-making trade and journeymen hatters. When asked by the Committee whether a 'fair workman' would work at a foul shop, the latter defined as a workshop employing workers and engaging in work practices 'contrary to the bye-laws of the journeymen', a Manchester-based hat manufacturer named George Ravenhill replied that 'the fair workmen do occasionally come to a foul shop, but they make themselves foul by working at it' (*Second Report from the Select Committee on Artisans and Machinery*. 10 Mar. 1824: 82). The law of negative contagion could work in reverse. It was said that some union societies were so keen to prevent a knobstick from working alongside their members, it was as if the unfortunate outcast threatened to taint 'the air' of the workshop itself (*The North British Review* (1868) 95: 17).

In all the various acts of pressure brought to bear on strike-breakers that we have looked at in this chapter, whether it be effigy burning, parading or 'laying to rest' contaminated goods and equipment, or rattening, there is one important salient feature generic to all these acts of which the historian needs to be aware. This is the absence of direct interpersonal physical violence. As with much of the so-called labour violence we have looked at in this book up to now, the 'violence' used to put pressure on the hesitant, the reluctant, and the outright 'traitor' was communicated through means other than direct physical violence. On such occasions, caution, discretion and restraint were very much to the fore. On other occasions during the labour disputes of our period, however, the measures used to ensure compliance with collective norms could be much more direct, physical, aggressive and uncompromising. This less restrained form of persuasion will form the subject of the next chapter of this book.

Notes

1 The attack on the carts was prompted by undercutting by weavers in villages 'adjacent' to the city of Norwich, which was rendering weavers in the city unemployed.
2 Parliament's passing of the Second Calico Act in 1721, which banned the importation and use of calico in England, at least provided some temporary relief for the Spitalfields weavers. For additional information on the trade, see Page (1911).
3 The colliers' wages were reduced from five to four shillings per day.
4 The dispute dragged on until mid-September 1869. This being said, the fortitude shown by the miners and their families was rewarded when the locked-out unionists were re-employed at the colliery as part of the settlement to resolve the dispute.
5 This newspaper account is less revealing, however, regarding the identity and alleged misconduct of the offending effigy.
6 The killings were passed off by the discursive sleight of hand and 'gibberish laws' common to this period as 'justifiable defence'.
7 I am grateful to the following authors for this account of the mock trial. See Charlesworth, Gilbert, Randall, Southall and Wrigley 1996: 26.
8 Horrockses and Co. has a mixed legacy in terms of employment, working conditions and pay rates in this period. Although they sought to guarantee regular employment to their 'hands' even during the trade slumps of the early to mid-Victorian years, pay rates hovered consistently below the average in mills where the working conditions were said to be 'notoriously harsh'. See Dutton and King 1982: 62.
9 Other incidents relating to the 1844 strike in the Durham and Northumberland coalfield have featured in previous chapters. See chapter 5 in particular.
10 The solicitor in question was William P. Roberts, a trade union lawyer with strong Chartist sympathies.
11 For one such raid by 'a great number of evil disposed persons' said to be armed with pistols and cutlasses which occurred on 25 June 1768, see *The London Magazine* (1768) 37: 382. The use of such methods came at a high risk, an Act being passed in 1765 declaring it a capital felony to break into a house or shop with intent to cut or destroy silk in the loom in the process of manufacture.
12 See chapter 5.
13 The woolcombers calculated that following these outgoing expenses and deductions, they were left with less than 3s. 6d. per week. See *Northern Star and National Trades' Journal*, 7 Nov. 1846: 6.
14 By the end of November the Keighley woolcombers' strike had ended when the masters and workmen arrived at 'an amicable agreement' concerning their differences. See *Morning Post*, 30 Nov. 1846: 7.
15 For more violent occurrences which took place during the trade downturn and labour unrest in Manchester in 1829, see Prentice 1851: 346–51. Prentice refers to striking operatives entering various mills and 'tossing' webs and warps into the street and canal, and a street 'covered with cloth trampled into the mud'.

References

Anon. (1757) *A State of the case, and a narrative of facts, relating to the late commotions, and rising of the weavers, in the County of Glocester* [sic]. London: R. Griffiths.
Anon. (1675) *A True Narrative of all the Proceedings Against the Weavers*. London: Old Bayly [sic].
Berg, Maxine (1988) 'Workers and Machinery in Eighteenth-century England', in John Rule (ed), *British Trade Unionism 1750–1850. The Formative Years*. London: Longman: 52–73.
Brentano, Lujo (1870) 'On the History and Development of Gilds and the Origins of Trade-Unions', in Lucy Toulmin Smith and Joshua Toulmin Smith (eds), *English Gilds*. London: N. Trubner & Company: 65–199.

Charlesworth, Andrew, David Gilbert, Adrian Randall, Humphrey Southall and Chris Wrigley (1996) *An Atlas of Industrial Protest in Britain, 1750–1990*. Basingstoke: Palgrave MacMillan.
Downing, Arthur (2013) 'The "Sheffield Outrages": Violence, Class and Trade Unionism, 1850–1870', *Social History*, 38(2): 162–182.
Dutton, H.I. and King, JohnEdward (1982) 'The Limits of Paternalism: The Cotton Tyrants of North Lancashire, 1836–1854', *Social History*, 7(1): 59–74.
Dyer, Thomas Firminger Thiselton (1900) *British Popular Customs, Present and Past*. London: George Bell & Sons.
Frazer, James (1925; original editions first published in 1890, 1900, and 1906–1915) *The Golden Bough: A Study of Magic and Religion*. New York: MacMillan.
Harrison, Jane Ellen (1913) *Ancient Art and Ritual*. London: Williams & Norgate.
Henson, Gravenor (1970; first published 1831) *Henson's History of the Framework Knitters*. Newton Abbot: David & Charles.
Hobsbawm, Eric (1952) 'The Machine Breakers', *Past & Present*, 1: 57–70.
Horn, Jeff (2005) 'Machine-Breaking in England and France during the Age of Revolution', *Labour/ Le Travail*, 55: 143–166.
Malinowski, Bronislaw (2013; first published 1926) *Magic, Science and Religion and Other Essays*. London: Read Books.
Navickas, Katrina (2011) 'What Happened to Class? New Histories of Labour and Collective Action in Britain', *Social History*, 36(2): 192–204.
Page, William (ed) (1911) 'Industries: Silk-weaving', *A History of the County of Middlesex. Vol. 2*. London: Victoria County History: 132–137.
Plumb, John H. (1950) *England in the Eighteenth Century*. Harmondsworth: Penguin.
Prentice, Archibald (1851) *Historical Sketches and Personal Recollections of Manchester*. London: Charles Gilpin.
Randall, Adrian (1991) *Before the Luddites. Custom, Community and Machinery in the English Woollen Industry, 1776–1809*. Cambridge: Cambridge University Press.
Rogers, Nicholas (1998) *Crowds, Culture, and Politics in Georgian Britain*. Oxford: Oxford University Press.
Tilly, Charles (1995) *Popular Contention in Great Britain, 1758–1834*. Cambridge, Mass.: Harvard University Press.
Webb, Sidney and Webb, Beatrice (1920) *The History of Trade Unions*. London: Longman.

7

SHAMING AND DEGRADATION RITUALS

> Communicative work directed to transforming an individual's total identity into an identity lower in the group's scheme of social types is called a "status degradation ceremony".
>
> *(Garfinkel 1956: 420)*

For Harold Garfinkel, degradation ceremonies are universal to all societies, particularly given that the categories of morality, moral indignation and shame are universal properties of all societies (Garfinkel 1956: 420–4). These degradation ceremonies, moreover, assume different forms in the context of different societies and different sets of circumstances. For instance, they can assume a highly formal ceremonial character, as with those which take place in professional courts of law in modern industrial societies. Alternatively, they can be highly informal, as with the degradation rites conducted by those acting on behalf of kinship and tribal communities. Whatever the context and circumstances, both highly formal and informal degradation ceremonies have a clear purpose and generally conform to a standard set of criteria. They seek to degrade the status of a perceived wrongdoer in the eyes of the community and, in certain circumstances, seek to expel the wrongdoer from the community altogether. All such degradation ceremonies, moreover, and following Arnold van Gennep, have a distinct rite of passage format. Hence, they work to bring about a transformation to a different state of being or status of the person or persons at the centre of the rite, albeit a transition to a negative rather than a positive state as with more conventional rites of passage (see Thérèse and Martin 2010: 98; and van Gennep 1960). As such, the ritual proceeds through definite stages with a clearly discernible beginning and end stage.

When considering the transformative function of a degradation ritual, it needs to be recognised that such rituals aim to beget a *total* transformation in the identity of the wrongdoer such that the offender can no longer be viewed as a legitimate member of the community. In terms of the community and its value system, the degradation ritual thus works to confirm the wrongdoer as an atypical person engaged in atypical behaviour which stands in sharp contrast to the typical, accepted and established behaviour engaged in by members of the community. In other words, the ritual works to define the offender as not of this community in a moral sense, as someone governed by priorities and inclinations contrary to those embraced and practised by the community. As Garfinkel explains it, 'the denounced person must be ritually separated from a place in the legitimate order, i.e., he must be defined as standing at a place opposed to it. He must be placed "outside", he must be made "strange"' (Garfinkel 1956: 423). It follows from this that there must be reference in degradation rituals to what Garfinkel describes as a 'dialectical counterpart', that is, some reference to community-accepted standards and morals which stand in opposition to those of the wrongdoer. This serves the purpose of providing moral comparison, which helps bring the failings and misconduct of the denounced person into sharper focus.

Needless to say, the degradation rituals that we will be looking at in this chapter are of the more highly informal kind. Before we go on to consider such rituals in the context of the labour unrest of the decades covered by this book, there are a number of additional points to convey in regard to the characteristics of these rituals which follow on from themes we encountered in previous chapters. Firstly, in regard to all of the aforementioned points, it is apparent that along with the 'denounced person' and a denouncing agent acting on behalf of the community, the presence of an audience, moreover an audience representative of the denouncing community, is crucial to the successful functioning of a degradation ritual. The presence of the audience is essential, not least to induce feelings of shame in the offender but also to ensure that the moral lesson imparted by the sanction is not lost on the community and its members. In terms of the audience as 'witness' to the event, degradation rituals thus work to apply the 'soft pressure' of the fear of social stigma to help reinforce the prevailing moral code. In this way, a degradation ritual binds individuals to the collective, the part to the whole.

Secondly, mention of the previous point flags up the crucial role played by shaming in degradation rituals. The role played by shaming in the carnivalesque donkey-ride punishment sanction has been discussed in an earlier chapter.[1] As also mentioned in that chapter, and as outlined by Helen Lewis in her important study of shame and guilt, shame is a more powerful existential experience than guilt in that the former directly concerns the social entity of the *self*, whereas the latter concerns the *thing* done or not done (Lewis 1971). There is also a social dimension to shame, which rendered it a powerful weapon in the hands of those who believed that compulsion is necessary to bring forth righteous behaviour. In this regard, the anthropologist Ruth Benedict has flagged up the power of shame to encourage social conformity, as well as its greater efficacy in collectivist as opposed to individualistic cultures, the latter being more inclined to favour the more self-focused guilt as a means of regulating an individual's behaviour (Benedict 1946.

See also Jacquet 2016). Clearly, in a collectivist-orientated culture like a workers' combination or trade union, shame could function as a powerful means of ensuring that individual behaviour conformed to the norms of the wider collective of the trade and the working community. As with the donkey-ride sanction then, for those administering punishment sanctions of a type which sought to downgrade an offender's status within the community, shame inducement played an important role in their calculations.

Thirdly, and in a related sense, we need to see at least some of the shaming and degradation rituals that we will be looking at below as fulfilling a 'legal function' in the community. In other words, these rituals made manifest the working community's moral code and the punishments that would follow in the wake of a serious breach of this code. As with other labour rituals we have looked at in previous chapters, then, we need to recognise the relationship between degradation rituals and that parallel system of popular justice that communities of workers in this era set up to try to control internal and external threats to the community and its traditional way of life and working.

Fourthly, though the degradation episodes which feature below involved varying degrees of rough handling and aggressive behaviour on the part of those administering the sanction, the tendency was to still avoid using physical violence of a more extreme kind. Thus, as we have seen with many of the measures used against non-compliant workmen discussed in previous chapters, degradation rituals worked to dampen and contain the potential for more extreme violence by setting it within a structured framework. This being said, on some occasions, and with some groups of workers, shaming and degradation punishments assumed a particularly harsh and uncompromising character, which saw a rise in the degree of violence as a result. In these particular instances, one should be cognisant of one of the main themes of this book, namely the analogy between workers on strike and soldier combatants in war.[2] It is only by appreciating the points of overlap between the scenario of the strike and the scenario of the battlefield that one can better understand the sometimes uncompromising stance taken by striking workers towards those they believed had fled the field of combat and deserted their comrades-in-arms. It should be noted as well that degradation rituals often featured in times of war, as in certain punishments meted out to a vanquished foe by a victorious opponent.[3]

Before we turn to look at some of the more forceful and physical shaming and degradation rituals which featured in the labour disputes of our era, it is important to point out that shaming punishments did not always involve the rough physical treatment of the offender. For example, some union societies sought to compel workmen to adopt good habits of behaviour by publishing shaming Blacklists in their literature for dissemination to the wider membership. During the 1820s at least, the national union having been formed in 1821, the National Union of Tin-Plate Workers published the names of strike-breakers and other offenders in their annual reports. Thus, in the Union's Third Annual Report, covering the period 1822 to 1823, we find the following extract:

It is the custom of the times to place on record the deeds of good or bad men, both for caution and example. We, therefore, expose to public view and execration the following abominable and very notorious characters.
(MRC. MSS.101/SM/LI/4/2/1. *Third Annual Report of the National Union of Tin-Plate Workers. 29 Sept. 1822 to 29 Sept. 1823.* Cited in Turner 1934: 43)

A list of the names of a number of so-called 'miserable wretches' who had broken ranks during a strike then followed. We know, as well, that the Friendly Society of Operative Iron Moulders published the names of so-called 'Black Sheep' in their 'half-yearly' reports during the late 1830s at least. The names came with information on the particular offence, and details of the workplace at which it occurred. Usually added to this information were some pointed words of advice to the wider membership should they encounter the blacksheep, as in the extract in the following report published in early 1839:

Should any of the above honourables be fortunate enough to have occasion to take the road, you will please to bear them in mind, and treat them according to merit.
(MRC. MSS.41/FSIF/4/2/1. *The Friendly Iron Moulders' Society's Third Half-Yearly Report. May to Nov. 1838)*

For its part, the Operative Stonemasons' Society published Blacklists in their Fortnightly Returns during the 1830s, 1840s and 1850s on a regular basis. The names of strike-breakers, or so-called 'Blacks', would be listed under headings such as 'Turned Traitor At Armagh' or 'For Working In Opposition To The Society At Elland' (MRC. Friendly Society of Operative Stonemasons. MSS.78/OS/4/1/1/ 403–7. Fortnightly Return. 19 Dec.–2 Jan. 1840). The stonemasons' union knew well the power of the Blacklist to shame the 'unprincipled'. When the names of twenty-four 'Blacks' who worked during a strike in Dundee appeared on an extensive Blacklist published by the Stonemasons' Society in the Summer of 1841, the 'Dundee Blacks' were described as 'men, who, uninfluenced by principle, are not altogether lost to a sense of shame' (MRC. MSS.78/OS/4/1/4/403–7. Corrected Blacklist For The Three Societies of England, Ireland, and Scotland. n.d. c. May–June1841). There was to be no escape for those whose names appeared on the dreaded 'List'. Hence the advice from the Secretary of the national union in late 1836 was that 'we recommend the Secretary of every Lodge to get a sheet and post the names of all the Blacks thus published, in a conspicuous place, every Lodge night, that all members may know their characters' (MRC. Friendly Society of Operative Stonemasons. MSS.78/OS/4/1/1/103–5. Fortnightly Return. 30 Sept.– 14 Oct. 1836). Some stonemasons' Blacklists from this period contained the instruction that the names of strike-breakers should be inserted in the union's minute books in all the Lodges of the Society throughout Scotland, England and Ireland 'in order to be read at every General Meeting' (MRC. MSS.78/OS/4/1/

4/487. To The United Operative Masons of Scotland, England, and Ireland. n.d.). The same Blacklist, which listed the names of a number of Edinburgh stonemasons who had blacklegged during a strike of masons in London, contained the following additional comment to crank up the shaming element of the punishment:

> We further declare, that the conduct of those individuals alluded to is at once an outrage upon common sense, and a violation of all the principles of justice and humanity, inasmuch as they have acted as traitors by joining the standard of Despots, who are using every effort to enslave their workmen, and to rob them of their unalienable rights and privileges, which is the birthright of every British subject.
> *(MRC. MSS.78/OS/4/1/4/487. To The United Operative Masons of Scotland, England, and Ireland. n.d.)*

Shaming also had a long reach. On some occasions, the names of offenders would be made known to the wider public beyond the confines of the union Lodge. When five workmen broke ranks and returned to work during the 1822 tin-plate workers' wage strike in Wolverhampton, they were derided as 'rats' by the local union Society and their names and addresses were printed on posters which were then posted up in shops, public houses, and adjoining streets (Brake 1985: 79). With the stonemasons' union, the reach could be even longer. In July 1842, the Stonemasons' Society in Canada requested their brethren in England to send them a Blacklist of those who had committed strike-breaking offences in England to ensure that Canada 'is not a place in which such perfidious traitors to the cause of humanity will be permitted to hide their hydra heads' (MRC. Friendly Society of Operative Stonemasons. MSS.78/OS/4/1/4/201–4. Letter from John Worthington and Alexander Wilson. City of Toronto, Upper Canada. 23 July 1842. Cited in Fortnightly Return. 11–25 Aug. 1842). There was to be no sanctuary for the wrongdoer even in the United States, as the United States of America Masons' Society also requested a copy of the same list, which they planned to republish 'throughout the entire of this vast continent, so that should any of the serfs migrate to this country they will meet with a warm reception' (MRC. Friendly Society of Operative Stonemasons. MSS.78/OS/4/1/4/201–4. Letter from John Worthington and Alexander Wilson. City of Toronto, Upper Canada. 23 July 1842. Cited in Fortnightly Return. 11–25 Aug. 1842). A Blacklist could have a long memory, too. In mid-1853 the UK stonemasons' union published a Blacklist containing the names of literally hundreds of individuals, with details of the particular offence committed and where it occurred, covering a period from April 1853 stretching back to September 1834 (MRC. MSS.78/OS/4/1/13. Revised Black List. From September 1834 to April 1853. n.d.).

A variation on this non-physical shaming method was that in operation in Scottish collieries during the 1820s at least, whereby 'un-associated' colliers reluctant to join the colliers' combination suffered the penalty of the 'black law'. Those exposed to this 'law' found themselves shunned by other colliers in the pit at which they worked to the extent that no man would speak to them, and if their light went out underground they were obliged to return to the bank for another 'as none of the rest would give them a light' (*Perthshire Courier*, 20 Oct. 1825: 2).

Turning to more direct and physical shaming punishments, it should be mentioned that we have already encountered one example of this type of sanction in chapter 5, namely the donkey-ride sanction. While it seemed appropriate to situate the donkey-ride punishment in a chapter on the 'carnivalesque' given the burlesque atmosphere which usually pervaded these proceedings, the same cannot be said for other shaming and degradation punishments deployed in this period. At one level it is tempting to characterise that close cousin of the donkey-ride, namely 'riding the stang', as burlesque. Undoubtedly, and as with donkey riding, in a stang-ride there was an element of contrived stylised behaviour and theatre whereby the villain of the piece was ceremonially exposed to public rebuke by being paraded through the village or section of a town, sometimes to the accompaniment of 'rough music'. Only in this case, however, the mode of transportation for the offender was usually a long stout pole, rather than a donkey. Another point of comparison with the carnivalesque donkey riding sanction is that riding the stang was a custom and extra-judicial punishment of long-standing in plebeian communities and certainly pre-dates the modern industrial period (Alford 1959).

Despite some points of comparison with donkeying, the stang-ride was hardly abounding with playful carnivalesque elements like irreverent clowning and parody. Rather, rough treatment and a degree of pain were to the fore in the stang-ride, with the offender usually carried on the pole shoulder high and often for some considerable amount of time. We can observe this tendency to set aside burlesque and playfulness in an account of a riding which took place in a labour dispute in Newcastle-upon-Tyne in 1768. The dispute involved the seamen of the town and their attempts at 'raising and regulating seaman's wages'. It appears that the stang-riding sanction was widely used during the strike, being applied to ship-owners, masters, and strike-breakers. According to the Tory *Newcastle Courant*, and making allowance for some political bias in the tone of the report, masters and owners of ships were 'by force compelled' to go on shore at Shields by the striking seamen to sign Preliminaries or Terms which addressed the latter's concerns regarding their wages. Those who refused to sign were then 'carried about on poles, beat, hurt, terrified, and put in Danger and Fear of their lives, and such seamen as took the accustomed Wages, they have treated in the like manner against the Peace and to the manifest Terror of the People' (*Newcastle Courant*, 28 May 1768: 2).

The seamen and keelmen of the Tyne and Wear, the latter whose role was to man the sailing barges which transported coal down river, had a long history of collective struggle and resistance. Those in positions of authority recognised that the men of the Tyne and Wear were a formidable and resolute adversary when aroused to indignation and action. John Cartwright, a Home Office official sent by the then Home Secretary Lord Sidmouth to report on labour unrest in the north-east ports in the late Summer and Autumn of 1815, informed Sidmouth that the seamen of the region 'are a body of men formidable from their courage and natural hardihood' (HO42/146/206–209. Letter from John Cartwright to Viscount Sidmouth. 14 Oct. 1815). A discernible and strong spirit of 'combination', to use the terminology of the times, had been present in the towns of North and South Shields since at least the late 1760s, as clearly demonstrated by the strike of 1768 in Newcastle-upon-Tyne mentioned above. According to one Tyne ship-owner writing in 1792, since that time the towns and ports on the river Tyne had been under the 'dominion of mobs' who illegally assemble for 'the purpose of extorting high wages from their employers', in his view 'crimes little inferior in magnitude to rioting itself' (HO42/22/196–253. Letter 3 Nov. 1792).

Part of the Tyne seamen's long history of struggle in seeking a fair remuneration for their labour involved a tendency to mete out summary rough justice to traitors in their midst. Punishment sanctions involving degradation and shaming were often to the fore on these occasions, including stang riding. When the Tyne seamen turned out for an increase in wages in November 1792, those of their brethren who did not abide by the instructions of the strike committee encountered rough justice, one form of which was to be 'carried through the town on a pole as a sign of ignominy' (mentioned in McCord 1980: 22). In a separate incident in August the following year, seven keelmen from Sunderland and Bishopwearmouth received prison sentences of two years' duration in Durham gaol for 'violently assaulting' a fellow keelman who had turned 'informer' during a strike, by carrying him through the town on a stang (a retrospective account of this incident appeared in the *Durham Advertiser*, 1 Sept. 1854: 5). Ten years previous to this episode, the sailors of Sunderland meted out similar rough justice to traitors who had assisted press-gangs during the first American revolutionary war. A number of the said informers were seized in their homes, mounted on a stang, carried through the streets of Sunderland, and, while in transit, bedaubed 'plentifully with dirt' by a number of women of the town (*Durham Advertiser*, 1 Sept. 1854: 5).[4]

Stang riding also featured in the 1815 unrest on the north-east ports. Degradation rituals of various types were much in evidence during the 1815 strike as we will see at other stages in this chapter, so it would be helpful to provide some context for what would become a fractious and long-running dispute. Following on from the troubles of the late eighteenth century in the north-east ports, the years 1803 and 1811 witnessed strikes by the keelmen of the Tyne and Wear in protest against the activities of press-gangs during the Napoleonic Wars, and in 1809 against rising prices. The year 1815 brought further unrest in the north-east due to rising unemployment amongst seamen consequent upon the end of the Napoleonic Wars (for a detailed account of the strike, see McCord 1968). The grievances of the seamen of the Tyne and Wear in 1815 pivoted on a number of issues. Firstly, there was a concern about the number of 'foreign' sailors being employed while local sailors were in want of employment. Secondly, there was resentment felt towards the ship-owners for exploiting the pool of unemployed 'surplus labour' by driving down wages. Thirdly, and an issue which probably generated the most indignation since it exacerbated the unemployment situation, the seamen were opposed to ship-owners making their voyages with smaller crews. Instead of the ratio then in operation of three men and a boy for every 100 tonnes, a practice carried over from the Napoleonic Wars, the seamen pressed their claim for a ratio of six men and a boy for every 100 tonnes. The strike, which began in the middle of August, concluded towards the latter part of October with the seamen gaining some concessions from the ship-owners, particularly in regard to the Wear ship-owners consenting to an agreed manning scale for each vessel going to sea (McCord 1968: 138). In his communication to Viscount Sidmouth in mid-October, with the strike still in progress, John Cartwright, whom we met above, felt inclined to comment on the remarkable degree of organisation and cohesion displayed by those prosecuting the strike:

> Your Lordship will have before learnt that when mechanics have struck for wages or the redress of real or fancied grievances, they seem at once to have arranged every grade of authority necessary to enable them to act with unity.
> *(HO42/146/206–209. Letter from John Cartwright to Viscount Sidmouth. 14 Oct. 1815)*

One 'grade of authority' which enabled the Tyne and Wear seamen to act with unity during their particular turnout was that which derived from the system of discipline and punishment that they set up during the strike. Though it be certainly and understandably offensive to twenty-first-century sensibilities, degradation punishment rituals formed a core element of this system. As mentioned, riding the stang was one such punishment as we will see below. In a deposition of 17 October which eventually found its way to the Home Office, a local ship-owner named William Coppin described an incident he claimed to have witnessed in mid-September involving striking seamen in North Shields. In the said incident, the striking seamen 'blacked the faces of certain men as a punishment for certain offences'. In a similar incident in North Shields, another group of seamen put tar and paint on the face of an individual as a punishment for an offence. Resistance in such circumstances appeared unwise it seems. Consequently, when he resisted, the 'man whose face was so painted was put upon a pole and carried to different parts of the town' and then to fields beyond the town where he was deposited in a less than ceremonial manner (HO42/146/109–110. Deposition of William Coppin. 17 Oct. 1815).

Before we leave the seamen of the northern upper reaches of England, mention should be made of a stang-riding incident involving seamen in Whitehaven, Cumbria, on England's north-west coast in October 1825. The incident came in the wake of an announcement by one of the principal shipbuilders in Whitehaven of his intention to employ only non-union labour. On hearing of this, some forty pro-union apprentices employed at the shipyard greeted the arrival of one such 'scab' to work at the yard by mounting him upon a pole and riding him through some of the streets of the town. Having ridden the 'obnoxious stranger' in this manner 'without any very great regard for delicacy', the apprentices then ate a hearty breakfast before proceeding to mete out similar treatment to another scab (*Cumberland Pacquet*, 25 Oct. 1825: 2).

According to some scholars, riding the stang tended to be more confined to the northern counties of England and parts of Lowland Scotland (see, for instance, Alford 1959: 508; and Thompson 1992: 4). While this may be true of pre-industrial, plebeian communities, there is ample evidence that the very public, and often painful, stang-ride sanction was also in use during labour disputes in the more southern counties of the British Isles. We are grateful to Benjamin Franklin for leaving us with an account of one such incident during the strike of river workers on the London ports in the Spring and Summer of 1768. As Peter Linebaugh put it, 'starvation stalked the City in 1768' (Linebaugh 2003: 309). Soaring food prices would see the price of bread double and the price of meat increase by a third. Food riots followed, as did attempts at collective action by London workers like sailors, shoemakers, tailors, coopers, lightermen and coal-heavers to secure a fairer return for their labour. The Irish coal-heavers who offloaded coal from the Thames barges were at the forefront of this struggle. Militant, aggressive, and favouring direct action in their efforts to secure a more tolerable wage for their exceedingly arduous and ill-paid labour, the Irish coal-heavers had a low tolerance level for blacklegs and scab traitors in their midst. While penning a letter to the American Loyalist Joseph Galloway in mid-May 1768 during the height of the labour unrest, Benjamin Franklin observed a 'great mob of coal porters' in the street 'carrying a wretch of their business upon poles to be ducked, and otherwise punished at their pleasure for working at the old wages' (Benjamin Franklin to Joseph Galloway. 14 May 1768. Reprinted from Franklin 1818: 163–4). Other 'confederacies' of London workers also favoured utilising the stang-riding punishment sanction. In June 1772, journeymen hatters in an unspecified London borough were said to have seized one of their number for 'working under price' and carried him 'astride on a pole' through several streets of the area accompanied by 'every mark of ignominy and insult' (*Morning Chronicle and London Advertiser*, 26 June 1772: 3).

Remaining in the southern portions of the United Kingdom, we also have the well-documented 'ride' of the shipwright James Tuckfield in Bristol on 30 September 1826 (Gorsky 1994). The broader backdrop to Tuckfield's ride was the economic downturn of 1825–6 in the wider UK economy which, amongst other problems, saw a slump in the export market to the Americas, which invariably impacted trade in the Bristol ports. The master shipbuilders in Bristol reacted to these changing economic circumstances in a predictable fashion by reducing the shipwrights' wages from 30s to 24s per week, a move which precipitated a turnout of the men in July 1826. James Tuckfield had formerly belonged to the union, the Bristol shipwrights' association which was in the vanguard of the strike, and had initially struck work with his fellow shipwrights. By late September, however, Tuckfield had broken ranks when he accepted work at the reduced rate. To his fellow shipwrights, Tuckfield was a 'rascal for working under wages' and for 'selling all us shipwrights' as one striking shipwright put it (*The Bristol Mercury*, 6 Nov. 1826: p.4). Tuckfield's punishment for this betrayal proved to be particularly painful for him. For almost six hours he was carried in procession on a nine-feet-long pole by a contingent of striking shipwrights through various streets of Bristol. During the course of Tuckfield's riding ordeal, his face was covered with soot from a chimney-sweep's soot-bag. In addition to this indignity, a ticket was attached to Tuckfield's back with the word 'Black' written on it to leave the watching audience in no doubt as to the nature of the wayward behaviour which had occasioned the punishment. As was usually the case, the formal judicial system of the state proved that it could trump the quasi-legal sanctions of the workers in regard to the severity of sentence it handed down to those adjudged to have committed a wrong. Five of the shipwrights who participated in the riding were charged with conspiracy, riot and assault, with two of that number receiving jail sentences of three months and the remaining 'conspirators' receiving prison terms of nine months with hard labour.

The deployment of the stang-riding sanction to register collective disapproval of errant behaviour seems to have been quite common amongst workers in the west of England. Along with the journeymen shipwrights of Bristol, woollen cloth workers in the west of England counties of Somerset, Wiltshire, Devon and Gloucestershire had traditionally subjected perceived deviants within their ranks to a pole-ride. This was a stang-ride with a difference, however, for following the riding the miscreant was tossed into a pond or canal. 'Cool-staffing', as it was termed, was the oft-used mode of punishment in this region to try to ensure that all complied with an agreed rate of pay.

The wages of the weavers of the West Country during the eighteenth century were subjected to the same financial chicaneries which affected the pay of workers in other trades in this period. Ever-greater quantities of work were required for the same rate of pay, there were periodic reductions in price by artful masters, punitive deductions were imposed by masters for damaged or allegedly damaged work, while wages were frequently paid in goods charged at exorbitant prices. To combat this and other iniquities, incipient trade unions came into being in the early decades of the eighteenth century in the form of trade clubs, as with the cloth workers of Gloucestershire (Minchinton 1951). In relation to pay and working conditions, part of the remit of the trade clubs was to petition Parliament to enforce the Elizabethan Acts relating to a fair rate of wages, the number of apprentices entering the trade, and the custom of seven years' apprenticeships applied to workers entering the woollen trade. Needless to say, as the eighteenth century unfolded, the woollen workers of the west of England also had ongoing concerns about the introduction of new machinery which posed a threat to their livelihoods, particularly as regards the use of gig mills and shearing frames. The west of England woollen workers also sought redress through violent direct action when the need arose and when other more formal avenues had been denied or closed to them.

In regard to maintaining a fair rate of wages, cool-staffing was much in evidence in the West Country in the eighteenth century, particularly during phases of heightened labour unrest. As Gravenor Henson informs us, 'every person who worked beneath the usual rate, was seized upon, and put upon the cool-staff, that is, seated astride a long pole, mounted upon men's shoulders, and held up to the derision of the populace' (Henson 1970: 116). 'Several' of those who contrived to take work below the usual agreed rate were cool-staffed during the labour unrest of 1725–6 against the backdrop of a looming economic depression and bad harvest (Henson 1970: 126). Economic depression, hardly helped by the onset of the Seven Years' War, returned in 1756 to again blight the woollen trade in the west of England. In this context, the woollen workers pressed Parliament to pass an Act authorising the justices to establish a list of prices setting out agreeable piece rates for weavers' work. At the same time, the weavers 'downed tools' to help improve their bargaining position. The threat of cool-staffing was omnipresent during the strike of 1756. During the engagement, the weavers of Stroud in Gloucestershire issued a warning to any weaver tempted to enter into an agreement with the master clothiers to take work at the lower rate. Should any miscreant be so enticed, 'the weavers of each parish are fully resolved to meet in a body and car him on the wooden horse, and throw him into his master's mill pond' (cited in Minchinton 1951: 134–5). The custom of cool-staffing as a means of enforcing compliance with an agreed rate of pay certainly proved resilient amongst the weavers of the western counties. The custom was still in evidence during the early decades of the nineteenth century. When cloth weavers in Stroud struck work on 29 April 1825, primarily over the issue of payment for work undertaken, striking weavers would visit the strike-breaker's home 'and take the beam out of the offender's loom and mounting him astride it, take him to the nearest mill pond or canal and tumble him into it' (Loosley and Southgate 1993: 19–20).

To return briefly to the more conventional stang-ride, it seems that the practice of punishing transgressors in this manner persisted amongst West-Country workers well into the Victorian period. We have a record of an interesting incident at a chemical works in Dean Forest in 1852, where a number of workmen aroused the ire of their fellow workers by working on Christmas Day. When a few of the miscreants refused to pay a fine imposed on them by their brethren for this violation of that most sacred day in the Christian calendar, they were duly 'horsed' by being placed astride a pole and carried about the works (*The Bristol Mercury*, 10 Apr. 1852: 2).

As mentioned in the opening paragraphs of this chapter, a degradation ritual aims to degrade the status of a person deemed to be out of step with the values and norms of the community, and to bring the offender's misconduct and shame to the attention of the wider community. Degradation rituals also have a rite of passage structure and hence a transformative function. In other words, they work to effect a transformation in the offender to a different state of being or status of a quite negative kind. To cite Harold Garfinkel again, the denounced person must be ritually placed 'outside' the community in some way; 'he must be made "strange"' (Garfinkel 1956: 423). The latent aspect of a degradation punishment ritual thus worked to establish and confirm difference. Sitting astride, and balanced precariously on, a long pole mounted on the burly shoulders of local workmen and being conveyed around town in this manner certainly performed this function. In this way, the stang-ride ensured that the denounced individual was 'made strange' in the eyes of the community, and was confirmed as 'different'. Being deposited in water by being cool-staffed performed a similar function of ensuring that the offender was made strange and thus rendered different. In both these degradation punishments, stang riding and cool-staffing, there was clearly some attempt made by those enforcing the punishment to alter the physical appearance of the transgressor in some way. In some cases the physical appearance of the transgressor was altered in a quite marked and dramatic fashion, which added to the victim's humiliation. Thus, in the case of seamen in North Shields during the strike of 1815 there was the 'blacking' or painting of the face of a person about to be 'ridden' through the town. The face of the Bristol shipwright James Tuckfield, too, was 'blacked' in a similar manner, though in this instance with soot rather than tar or paint as in the North Shields case. A ticket pinned to Tuckfield's back with the word 'Black' written on it served to reinforce his differential status in the eyes of other members of the community. The vast majority of the additional degradation punishments that we will be looking at in the following paragraphs of this chapter also contrived to bring about an alteration in the physical appearance of the offending person.

Before we look at these other variants of the degradation ritual, we need to dwell a little longer on the punishment of face blacking. We have already seen above that the strike of seamen in the north-east ports in the late Summer and Autumn of 1815 was notable for its high degree of unity and organisation. As mentioned previously, the seamen were helped in this regard by the system of discipline and punishment that they established to help prosecute the strike. Degradation punishment rituals, which included stang riding and face blacking, as we have seen, were prominent in this system. Indeed, a remarkable feature of face blacking during the strike, presumably administered with paint, is that the punishment was highly formalised, it being prescribed in the rules of the turnout seamen. Notwithstanding the highly restrictive and punitive anti-union Combination Laws then in operation, the seamen of the Tyne and Wear were highly organised and issued Articles which established a set of rules that were binding on all seamen involved in the strike. Article IV stated that a person in the seamen's Body found breaking the strike by boarding a ship 'shall have his jacket turned, his face blacked, and [be] marched through town' (Tar 1815: 8). Similar treatment was visited upon those who did not attend the regular morning muster of the seamen (HO42/146/246–50. Memorial to Lord Sidmouth from the General Committee of the Shipping Interest of the Port of Newcastle-upon-Tyne. 17 Oct. 1815). We know that the striking seamen did mete out this punishment during the 1815 dispute. As mentioned above, William Coppin witnessed several instances of face blacking, as he explained in his deposition. There is also an incident in the same strike involving a seaman named James Lincoln. Lincoln was seized from a sloop by striking sailors who 'blacked his face' for some infraction of the seamen's rules, which probably had much to do with the vessel he had been aboard (details of the incident came out a few years later. See *Durham County Advertiser*, 19 Aug. 1820: 4). In another variation on the face blacking punishment, any seaman refusing to play his part in the strike of 1815 was blacked and then 'put on a tree, for public example' (Tar 1815: 7).

An even harsher punishment than face blacking with paint during the 1815 seamen's strike was tarring and feathering. As with face blacking, this highly degrading punishment ritual was prescribed in the Articles of the seamen's Body. Quite correctly deemed to be more punitive than face blacking with paint, the punishment of tarring and feathering was to be carried out following more serious infractions of the seamen's Rules. Thus, Article III stipulated that on the third occasion of a seaman missing his muster, 'he shall be tarred and feathered'. Article IV stated that the same fate would befall a seaman previously punished by having his face blacked should he be found on board a 'blacked' ship on any future occasion. Article VI let it be known to spies and informers that they would be treated in a similar manner (Tar 1815: 8). The evidence has not been forthcoming in regard to many instances during the 1815 strike where this punishment was administered to the letter. The Home Office official sent by Sidmouth to report on the 1815 strike, John Cartwright, whom we met above, claimed that 'many' who failed to attend the morning muster were tarred and feathered, though this has been difficult to corroborate by reference to other sources (HO42/146/206–209. Letter from John Cartwright to Viscount Sidmouth. 14 Oct. 1815). This being said, we do have the testimony of William Coppin referred to above. Coppin's testimony mentions tar, though not feathers, being applied to the face of an offending seaman prior to this person's stang-ride around town. What can be verified is that the extremely punitive punishment of tarring continued as a strike weapon in the armoury of the seamen of the Tyne and Wear for many decades after 1815. We can see this from a report of an open-air meeting of striking sailors in Sunderland in February 1843, the seamen having turned out in protest at a reduction in their wages. In addressing the gathering of striking sailors, the speakers urged all present to 'stick true' to their cause and beware the 'scabbed sheep' amongst them, while threatening tarring and feathering to any inclined to break the strike (*Caledonian Mercury*, 20 Feb.1843: 4). It is highly likely that, as was probably the case in 1815, the deterrent principle underpinning the sanction had the desired effect as to my knowledge no cases of tarring and feathering have come to light in this dispute.

The same cannot be said, however, for a strike involving the seamen of the Tyne and Wear which took place a few years later in early 1851. In late January, the seamen of Shields, Sunderland, Hartlepool, Seaham and other northern ports turned out ostensibly for an advance in wages. Though low wages were obnoxious to the seamen and their families, a more serious bone of contention during the turnout was the Mercantile Marine Act, which had recently passed into law. The seamen found many of the clauses contained in the Act's various articles objectionable, which they felt were prejudicial to their pay and working conditions. They also abhorred the numerous highly rigorous rules, regulations and restrictions which reduced the British sailor 'to the condition of a slave', and resented the pressure that they were being put under by the shipping authorities to sign the articles (*Newcastle Journal*, 15 Mar. 1851: 8). As such, the seamen sought repeal of the most obnoxious clauses of the Act, not least those relating to the system of penalties fixed by the Act. These penalties included such punitive and 'degrading' fines as the forfeiture of one day's pay for not being cleaned, washed and shaved on Sundays, one day's pay for swearing or using improper language, and one day's pay if late on board following expiration of leave. The strike was a long and contentious one. Blackleg labour was used in an effort to break the strike, while in March the Board of Trade infuriated the seamen by reneging on an earlier assurance to the strikers that the most obnoxious clauses of the Act would be repealed (*Newcastle Journal*, 15 Mar. 1851: 8). There was also a number of instances of tarring and feathering during the dispute, as some of the more militant of the seamen applied every means to enforce discipline within their ranks and thwart blacklegging. It should be said though, that this was contrary to the instructions of the committee of the seamen's union. In one incident in Shields on 16 February, a blackleg about to board a vessel bound for London was seized by a 'mob' of around 100 striking seamen and 'roughed up' before being rolled in the mud and tarred (*The Standard*, 19 Feb. 1851: 3). Apparently, it was reported that the latter act was performed by a 'female' who poured coal tar over the victim's face, a deed for which she received a prison sentence of 36 days (*The Standard*, 19 Feb. 1851: 3). Around the same time, in an incident which may have been related to the mud and tarring incident just mentioned, the concerned authorities in North Shields informed London that 'two foreign sailors were tarred on entering the town' as the 'obstinate' seamen continued to use 'every means in their power to prevent owners getting crews' (HO45/3472G/78–80. Letter 16 Feb. 1851). The contest rumbled on into April. In mid-April the Home Office received another anxious communication from the region, on this occasion from the Mayor of Tynemouth, telling of a 'riot' at Shields during which 'a Scotch sailor was tarred and feathered' (HO45/OS3472G/179–81. Letter 17 Apr. 1851).

Although it seems that the degradation ritual of tarring was part of the longstanding strike culture of the seamen of the Tyne and Wear, the seamen of that region did not have a monopoly on the practice. The seamen of Hull also took exception to the Mercantile Marine Act and turned out to oppose it at the same time as the Tyne and Wear seamen. To help better promote the objects of the strike, which were to secure the abolition, or at least the modification, of the Act and discourage any of their number from 'scabbing' by signing the articles relating to the Act, the Hull seamen formed a union society called the Sailors' Friend Society. While petitioning the House of Commons was a favoured strike method of the Hull seamen, they were not averse to using more robust methods of persuasion, one of which was tarring strike-breakers. Accordingly, a member of the union strike committee who broke ranks and signed the articles was tarred and 'rather roughly handled' by a 'mob of seamen' to dissuade him from proceeding to sea aboard a 'blacked' ship (*The Hull Packet and East Riding Times*, 22 Feb. 1851: 5). Similarly, the records show that seamen, whether from the Tyne and Wear or other ports, did not have a monopoly on that other highly degrading punishment ritual whereby a person's face was blacked with paint or some other unpleasant substance. For example, during a turnout in Liverpool in late November 1826 two journeymen bricklayers were charged with assaulting and 'blacking' the face of a fellow bricklayer for taking work under price and strike-breaking (*Liverpool Mercury*, 1 Dec. 1826: 6). The city of Liverpool witnessed a similar incident a few years later in September 1833. On this occasion Liverpool magistrates consigned three journeymen painters attached to the union to Kirkdale jail for three months each 'on the treadmill' for daubing paint over the face of a 'blacksheep' within their ranks for refusing to join the union (*Dublin Morning Register*, 12 Sept. 1833: 3).

We should also reflect on the symbolism present in face blacking with paint, as well as the more extreme measure of tarring. Both degradation punishments brought to the fore, and to mind, and in an acute and aggressive form, the arbitrary association between the colour black and malevolence, which had deep-seated historical roots. As we saw in a previous chapter, from the medieval period the word and colour black became encumbered with all manner of unfortunate derogatory connotations, entering both consciousness and discourse as a symbolic representation of things evil, wicked and foul. This was sharply contrasted with the word and colour white, as symbolic of things pure, innocent and clean.[5]

Another degradation punishment contrived to shame and humiliate the victim to a high degree was that whereby a strike-breaker was stripped of his clothes. Once again, we find this extreme form of rough justice being practised by the seamen of the river Tyne. During the turnout of late 1792 referred to above, a letter reached the Prime Minister's office from a Tyne ship-owner. The letter stated that, amongst other matters concerning the strike, sailors found to be breaking ranks were being driven naked through the town of North Shields by large crowds of striking seamen (HO42/22/196–253. Letter 3 Nov. 1792). This was not an isolated incident. A few days previously, three seamen said to be 'not quite punctual' at meetings of the strikers were stripped naked and 'made to walk in that situation' through the main street of South Shields and 'round the Market Place' (HO42/22/198–199. Letter 1 Nov. 1792).

The seamen of the Tyne were not alone in resorting to this highly demeaning measure in strike situations. We can find evidence of striking mineworkers, and often mineworkers' wives, engaging in the practice when they felt the need arose. This was certainly the case when many of Britain's mineworkers 'downed picks' in the Spring and Summer of 1844. As mentioned in previous chapters, the dispute pivoted on the issue of a range of injustices, which included payment by truck, low wages, punitive fines, the cottage system, and the yearly bond which prevailed in many pit communities in the north of England. In one incident in early April at a colliery owned by Messrs. Field, Cooper and Co., in Worsborough, Barnsley, south Yorkshire, a strike-breaker was stripped naked by striking colliers assisted by a number of women described by the local press as 'a disgrace to their sex'. The unfortunate 'blacksheep' was then compelled to make his way home in this condition for a distance of half a mile, accompanied by a crowd of around 100 persons (*Derbyshire Courier*, 6 Apr. 1844: 2). Even this was not the end of the matter for the unfortunate man, in that his naked body was also smeared with dirt.

It is worth reflecting on this latter phase of the degradation punishment involving the aforementioned Worsborough strike-breaker, namely 'dirtying'. 'Dirtying' has its roots in traditional charivari-like rituals of folk justice of long-standing. In this particular punishment, the victim is smeared with dirt, garbage, and various other forms of 'filth' which are to hand (for instances of 'dirtying' in early modern England, see Ingram 1984: 82). Needless to say, some of these substances would have given of a most unpleasant odour, which would have added to the victim's humiliation and rendered him even more 'different' to those present in the watching throng. It seems that the ritual punishment of 'dirtying' in strike situations has proved to be quite resilient, even surviving into the twentieth century as evident during labour unrest in post-1945 Italy (see Favretto 2015: 218–21).

Returning to the labour unrest in Britain's mining communities in 1844, we find that the 'dirtying' incident in Worsborough was not an isolated occurrence. In other incidents in the south Yorkshire coalfield in July, in the vicinity of pits at Thurgoland and Silkstone, a number of blacklegs were waylaid and 'stripped stark naked' by striking colliers and their supporters. As in Worsborough, women were much in the vanguard of the proceedings. In one such episode a strike-breaker was stripped almost naked, pelted 'all over with dirt and sods', and made to walk ahead of a procession of some 200 strikers and their supporters shouting out 'Bah! Blackseep!' to leave onlookers in no doubt as to the purpose of the punishment ritual (*Northern Star*, 20 July 1844: 5).

As we saw in a previous chapter, and following Martin Ingram, an important aspect of the richness of charivari-like rituals relates to the creative way that such rituals evoke contrasts between different values and modes of behaviour within society through the application of the principle of correspondence.[6] In this manner, it is surely permissible to read the symbolism of dirt and 'dirtying' in degradation rituals in these labour disputes as evoking a contrast between purity and impurity. Hence, the former represented the honourable struggle of the collectivised mineworkers to redress the many injustices which blighted their lives, while the latter pointed up the self-regarding and polluting behaviour of blacklegs, which to the mineworkers amounted to the worst type of betrayal.

'Dirtying', though, did not feature in every incident where those adjudged to have betrayed the miners' cause during the great strike of 1844 were divested of their clothes. In the north Derbyshire coalfield in late June, a blackleg working at the Cottam colliery was seized by a number of women 'who stripped him naked and left him to wander home in that condition' (*Derbyshire Courier*, 29 June 1844: 3). Neither was this shaming sanction confined to scabs and blacklegs. During the turnout in the Durham and Northumberland coalfields, a coal agent narrowly escaped being stripped of his clothes (HO45/644/37. Letter 12 Apr. 1844). The threat of being stripped naked should one blackleg and betray the mineworkers and the union was omnipresent in the Durham and Northumberland coalfields. During the turnout of Durham and Northumberland pitmen in the early months of 1831, a printed broadside 'went the rounds' which contained a poetic but clear warning to blacklegs:

But I will tell his travels here
As he went from the binding;
They stript him there of part of his clothes,
And left his skin refining.
But remember you that come
Unto Seghill to bind,
You may think upon the man
That we have treat so kind.

(The song was entitled The First Drest Man of Seghill *and features in Colls 1977: 107)*[7]

If we can decode the symbolism of dirt and 'dirtying' as hinting at a contrast between purity and impurity, then it may not be beyond the bounds of possibility to read another of the more prominent degradation rituals of this period as a rite of purification which sought to symbolically cleanse the wrongdoer of the sin of strike-breaking. Here one is referring to the ritual punishment of immersion in water used to shame and punish strike-breakers. As with other degradation rituals we have looked at up to now, water punishments were a highly public form of humiliation and shaming and certainly performed the function of ensuring that the offender was rendered 'strange' in physical appearance by the ordeal. We have already observed that an important component of cool-staffing involved tossing the offender into a pond or canal. A water punishment was not always dependent on the presence of a pole or the spectacle of a riding, however. During the cloth weavers' strike of 1825 in Stroud, Gloucestershire, referred to above, strike-breakers were routinely seized by strikers, hoisted upon the shoulders of some, and then ducked in fish ponds, thrown into a brook, or 'soused' in a river (a few such incidents are mentioned in HO40/18/227–8. Letter 7 June 1825). In one instance, the local magistrate thought he should put a stop to the practice by swearing in a number of special constables. The magistrate's effort was to no avail, however, as several of the special constables, in a quirky reversal of the natural order of things, were duly 'arrested' by the strikers and subjected to 'a cold ablution in the Stroud Canal' (*Derby County Chronicle*, 16 June 1825: 3). In another incident, as many as fourteen weavers residing in the weaving village of Frogmarsh who refused to turn out were ritually ducked by a visiting party of striking weavers. An eighty-year-old weaver from the same village who had not joined the strike was also ducked in a pond. In this instance though, and in an interesting variation on the ritual, mercy and forbearance were the order of the day. The strikers apologised profusely to the elderly weaver for the 'unavoidable' punishment that they were about to visit upon him for his misdeed before proceeding to enact the punishment, 'without violence', and with the utmost sensitivity for his advanced years. Thus, as well as the apology, the elderly man was encouraged to drink half a pint of gin prior to his immersion in the pond to help dull the shock of the impact. The forbearance of the striking weavers did not stop there. On conclusion of the ritual, the elderly weaver was provided with a change of dry clothing, which he was urged to hurriedly put on in order to help preserve his modesty and health (*Morning Chronicle*, 10 June 1825: 4). The state proved less forbearing towards the practice of ducking though. In the aftermath of the turnout, a number of persons were charged with various acts of 'riot and disturbance' relating to the strike. Amongst those charged were weavers accused of ducking strike-breakers, some of whom received punitive prison sentences ranging from three months to two years (Loosley and Southgate 1993: 44–7).

Another group of workers who seemed to have a predilection for ducking strike-breakers were the mineworkers of the west Midlands. In the late Spring of 1822, the pits and iron works in the districts of Wolverhampton, Bilston, West Bromwich, Wednesbury, Sedgley, and Dudley were virtually at a standstill owing to a turnout of colliers and other mineworkers. The turnout came on the back of an economic downturn in the iron trade and the decision of the iron and coal masters of the region to reduce the wages of the men. At the core of the dispute, however, was the detested system of payment by truck, where the workmen were compelled to accept two-thirds of their wages in goods such as sugar, meat, bacon, flour, soap and candles. Through these means, as even an officer of the Walsall Troop of cavalry admitted in a letter to the Home Office, 'an unreasonable large profit' accrued to the coal and iron masters, adding to the sense of injustice felt by the workmen (HO40/17/220–1. Letter 5 May 1822). Favoured strike tactics of the turnouts, in what would prove to be a fractious dispute, included cutting the ropes to the pits and 'ducking and half-drowning those who are disposed to work' (HO40/17/220–1. Letter 5 May 1822). Those lined up to resist the colliers were prepared to use more lethal force, however. On 29 April during a disturbance outside one of the local pits, a collier named John Robson was shot and mortally wounded by a soldier on horseback. A few days later, the striking colliers issued a leaflet condemning the shooting. The leaflet stated that 'whatever be the motives of the masters in using such severity towards their servants is a mystery which none but themselves can explain' (HO40/17/217. Leaflet. May 1822).[8]

Almost ten years later, in December 1831, the colliers of the west Midlands were again in dispute with their employers over the issue of wages. A managing director of an iron works in the vicinity of Staffordshire told of his workforce, though 'satisfied with their earnings', being 'forced to abandon their work by the ferocious conduct of the neighbouring colliers connected with the Union' (HO44/24/327. Letter for the information of Lord Melbourne at the Home Office. 8 Dec. 1831). Part of the 'ferocious conduct' included immersing strike-breakers in water. At the start of December, a manager of a works in Corngreaves near Dudley described the fate of strike-breakers in his employ:

> Our men were willing to continue at work but a party of ferocious fellows of eight hundred came yesterday and fetched the men out of the pits and threw them into an adjoining pool and threatened death to anyone opposing them. The colliers are now parading the country armed with bludgeons.
>
> *(HO44/24/328. Letter 1 Dec. 1831)*

Reports from the region in the later part of December told of striking colliers from Bilston descending on the collieries of the Earl of Lichfield in the vicinity of Walsall. On arrival, the striking colliers compelled strike-breakers to ascend the pits whereupon many of the latter were then ducked in the canal (*Staffordshire Advertiser*, 10 Dec. 1831: 4). Some ten years later during a turnout in August 1842 against the backdrop of the 'general strike' which had spread to a number of industrial sectors in the United Kingdom, the Bilston colliers, many of whom had been recently subjected to short-time working, were still ducking strike-breakers, this time in reservoirs (*Durham County Advertiser*, 5 Aug. 1842: 2. On the general strike, see Jenkins 1980).

Though seemingly much used by these groups of workers in these districts, water punishments were not exclusively confined to the Stroud weavers and the mineworkers of the west Midlands. There are accounts of colliers in the Potteries ducking strike-breakers during a strike in the turbulent Summer of 1842, which followed an attempt by a local coal-owner to reduce the men's wages. Some elements of the mainstream press put the strike down to the Chartist principles that they claimed were making considerable headway amongst the colliers of the Potteries. These Chartist principles, opined the press, were creating 'disaffection in the minds of the colliers', as well as 'exciting the turnouts to adopt active measures of resistance' (*Derby Mercury*, 20 July 1842: 3). In various skirmishes during the Potteries turnout, strike-breakers were pulled out of the pits and then ducked in engine pools and ponds (see *Derby Mercury*, 20 July 1842: 3; and *Freeman's Journal*, 18 July 1842: 4). In another incident in the same strike, two strike-breakers discovered loading carts with coal were dragged away to 'pits of water' lying nearby and 'made to dip over head' (*Derby Mercury*, 20 July 1842: 3).

Workers on the Tyne also ducked strike-breakers. In late 1822 there was another bout of labour unrest on the Tyne, involving the keelmen on this occasion, which was sparked by the issue of the quantity of coal carried downriver by the keels. On one occasion during the turnout, in response to blacklegs being drafted in to defeat the strike or 'stick' as it was termed, striking keelmen forcefully removed an entire crew of these unwelcome strangers from their keel. The strikers then 'dragged' the blacklegs to the south side of the river, and ducked them (*Bell's Life in London and Sporting Chronicle*, 17 Nov. 1822: 3).[9]

The punishment of immersion in water was even more extreme with some groups of workers, as the Parliamentary Select Committee on Artisans and Machinery which met in 1824 was informed. The Select Committee was told that Liverpool journeymen shipwrights were so desirous of ensuring that a spirit of union was maintained amongst them that on one occasion a number of shipwrights 'not belonging to the club' were visited on the ship where they worked and literally thrown overboard into the two-and-a-half feet of water round the vessel, along with their working tools (extracts from the Select Committee findings feature in Webb Trade Union Archive. A/1/177–8. Trade Unionism. Shipwrights. Liverpool 1823–4). Water punishments were also visited upon 'knobsticks' in Manchester during turnouts. This usually took the form of the victim being borne away to the canal and literally thrown in by the striking operatives, which was the fate of a number of knobsticks during the power-loom weavers' strike of 1829 (*Durham County Advertiser*, 12 Sept. 1829: 4). Remaining in the north-west of England, a variant of the water punishment degradation ritual took place in Stockport in early June 1818 in the context of the power-loom weavers turning out for an advance in wages. The dispute was a bitter and fractious one, which saw blacklegs being drafted in to defeat the strike and 'rioting' strikers fired upon by soldiers, resulting in the former sustaining a number of injuries from gunshot wounds and one death (Hammond 1995: 95). In such an atmosphere, blacklegging was clearly frowned upon to say the least. In one incident in early August, a number of young women found to be blacklegging were taken to a pump and 'pumped upon' by a group of turnouts, the latter including both women and men (H042/179/281–282. Letter 1 Aug. 1818).

Turning the coat or jacket of a strike-breaker inside out or around was another degradation punishment ritual witnessed in our period. As with face blacking, tarring, dirtying, and ducking in particular, turning the coat of the scab or blackleg was highly symbolic. Coat turning was a sign of treachery, turning on one's brethren, turning one's back on the community, going over to the enemy's camp, or to 'turn tail' and flee the field of battle at the sight of the enemy's formations. As such, the ritual evoked a contrast between order and chaos, the inside and the outside, loyalty and betrayal, duty and negligence, and courage and cowardice. We have already seen above that the seamen of the Tyne and Wear were alive to the symbolic value of coat turning, even going so far as to include the sanction in the Articles that they issued during the 1815 strike to discourage vacillating and outright strike-breaking. Thus, to restate the sanction, Article IV stipulated that those discovered breaking the strike by boarding a ship 'shall have his jacket turned, his face blacked, and [be] marched through town' (Tar 1815: 8). This was no idle threat. The Tyneside ship-owner William Coppin claimed to have seen the punishment meted out to a number of miscreant seamen during the strike. Coppin also witnessed three carpenters, who had obviously incurred the displeasure of the strikers in some way, taken round the town of North Shields 'with their jackets turned' (HO42/146/109–110. Deposition of William Coppin. 17 Oct. 1815).

The sanction was also applied during labour unrest in Lancashire, as during a dispute in Rochdale in May 1829 involving weavers employed in the town's woollen and flannel 'manufactories'. Following wage reductions by some masters in the town, the weavers sought to apply pressure on the obnoxious masters to abide by an approved scale of prices through Luddite methods of machine-breaking. In one particular assault on a local mill, the 'mob' took some time out from destroying loom-machines and other implements of production by driving all those found to be working at the factory into the streets with their coats turned inside out (*Lancaster Gazette*, 9 May 1829: 3). As was all too frequent in incidents of labour unrest in our period, the sanctions emanating from those representing property were infinitely more brutal. According to press reports, eighty-five shots were discharged by soldiers seeking to restrain 'rioters' attempting to rescue some

172 Shaming and degradation rituals

of their brethren from a 'lock-up' following the arrest of the latter (*Lancaster Gazette*, 9 May 1829: 3).[10] This use of lethal force by the state resulted in four deaths and twenty-five persons wounded, some of whom had to have limbs amputated arising from the injuries that they received. Not all the wounds were inflicted by gunshot; some were inflicted by sabre and bayonet.

The workers of the north-west of England were involved in another episode of coat turning two years later, in early 1831. On this occasion it was cotton spinners administering the sanction. An attempt by the Spinners' Union centred in Manchester to prosecute a series of rolling strikes in various cotton mills in the region in an effort to establish a price for their labour higher than that offered by the 'cotton lords' of the district formed the background to the incident. Whereas the masters insisted on a reduced price of 3s. 9d. per 1000 hanks of No. 40s on all sizes of wheels, the cotton operatives held out for a price of 4s. 2d. When the strike began in December 1830, some 18,000 spinners and other operatives working in fifty-two factories in Stalybridge, Dukinfield, Mossley and Ashton-under-Lyne had ceased working (Jevons 1860).[11] In early January 1831 it was reported that a flying picket of some 600 cotton spinners emanating from Ashton-under-Lyne, some of whom were carrying bludgeons, had descended upon the cotton works of Messrs. John and William Sidebottom and Co. of Millbrook, Longdendale, in the County of Chester, where a portion of the workforce had broken ranks and returned to work at the reduced price. According to the report, and in a clear parallel with war and the capture of prisoners of war, the strikers entered the works, 'forcibly wrested the men from their employment and marched them along with them as prisoners – bound in cords and having their coats turned inside out' (HO52/8/486–9. Letter 4 Jan. 1831). We know from another source that the matter did not end there. To amplify the betrayal and shame of the turncoats, the strikers inscribed the obnoxious masters' price of 3s. 9d. on their backs with chalk (Jevons 1860: 476). The disgrace of the captured 'prisoners' was compounded still further when they were then paraded 'in this condition through the Districts' as a marked warning to other potential turncoats. When the prisoners were eventually released from their 'captivity', they were warned that 'Death and Destruction' would be visited upon them should they return to work at the low rate of wage (HO52/8/486–9. Letter 4 Jan. 1831).

Riding the stang, face 'blacking' with paint, tarring, being stripped naked, water punishments, and coat turning were the most oft-used degradation rituals in the strikes of our period. There were others though, albeit never so frequently in use as the aforementioned. Nevertheless, these other degradation rituals are certainly not without interest. In all such instances, the strike-breaker was displayed or paraded in some form or another before an audience composed of members of the community. As mentioned at the start of this chapter, along with the 'denounced person' and a denouncing agent acting on the community's behalf, the presence of an audience representative of the denouncing community is a crucial component of a degradation ritual. By way of a reminder, the presence of a representative audience had a dual function. Firstly, it helped reinforce the prevailing moral code of the community by ensuring witnesses to the punishment. Secondly, the presence of a disapproving audience increased the likelihood of shame being felt by the victim. We have seen above in some incidents involving coat turning and being stripped naked that parading the strike-breaker through the streets of the town was a common occurrence. In some strike situations though, strike-breakers were simply paraded through the town without the added indignity of having their coat turned or being shorn of their clothing. We have a record of one such incident during a wage dispute involving calico-printers in Glasgow in mid-February 1834. Following the importation of blackleg labour to break the by then six-month-long strike, striking workers responded by physically removing blacklegs from a number of print-works at which they were employed. The forceful removal of the blacklegs from the work premises, however, was but a prelude to the next and most important stage of the proceedings, which was to parade the offenders through the various districts of the city so as to bring their wrongdoing to the attention of a wider public (*Derby Mercury*, 12 Feb. 1834: 2). On occasions, parading the blacklegs through the streets of the town as a mark of shame and displeasure was the precursor to them being forcibly expelled from the district altogether. In an incident which took place during labour unrest in the mining districts of north Wales in the Summer of 1831, a flying picket of some 400–500 colliers from Holywell visited a colliery near the town of Mold. The colliery in question had incurred the displeasure of the flying picket by taking on non-union blackleg labour from Anglesey. Arriving at daybreak to better escape detection by the authorities, the pickets 'forcibly' compelled the blacklegs to discontinue their work, then paraded them through the town of Mold, before literally driving them out of town in the direction of Anglesey (HO52/16/89–90. Letter 6 July 1831).

As mentioned earlier in this chapter, some punishment rituals used to shame strike-breakers assumed a particularly harsh and uncompromising character which bring to mind punishments meted out to deserters or traitors in time of war. Such punishments are quite understandably unsettling when viewed from the perspective of the more convivial labour relations and moral landscape of the twenty-first century. Take for instance the method used to shame and punish a number of strike-breaking seamen during the labour unrest on England's north-east ports in 1815. This long-running and bitter dispute has figured at a number of points in this chapter in the context of discussing stang riding, face blacking, tarring and feathering, and coat turning. Arguably, and if we can rely on the account of the Home Office official John Cartwright, an even greater degree of indignity was heaped upon three non-compliant seamen in Sunderland during the turnout. According to Cartwright, the unfortunate men were placed in a 'hastily constructed' pillory and exposed to public derision in that manner for 'some hours' (HO42/146/206–209. Letter from John Cartwright to Viscount Sidmouth. 14 Oct. 1815). Then we have the following degradation punishment involving striking journeymen rope-makers in Liverpool in 1825. This particular shaming rite went through a number of stages. The opening stages involved the dragging of three strike-breakers from their place of work, placing them in a cart brought along for that purpose, tying their hands together, and attaching a placard to their bodies bearing the inscription

174 Shaming and degradation rituals

'Black-sheep'. The next stage of the ritual saw the captives being paraded through the town in this condition. The final stage saw the cart making its way through the watching crowds followed by a concourse of people 'shouting in the most tumultuous manner', whereupon the unfortunate strike-breakers were then pelted with mud and 'missiles' to add to their evident discomfort (reports of the incident can be found in HO40/18/389. Combination. 1825; *Birmingham Journal*, 19 Nov. 1825: 4; and *Manchester Courier and Lancashire General Advertiser*, 12 Nov. 1825: 3).

The journeymen of Liverpool seemed to have had a liking for displaying offending workmen in an open cart. The 1824 Parliamentary Select Committee on Artisans and Machinery was informed of one such incident in Liverpool in an unspecified year involving journeymen carpenters. During the incident, a number of 'strangers' composed of Irishmen and Welshmen engaged in 'illegal' pedlar work, contrary to the wishes and rules of the workers' combination, were seized by the unionised carpenters and placed in an open cart. They were then conveyed out of town in that manner to a place along the 'north shore', whereupon they were set upon their way with a warning to 'keep out of the town' (*First Report from Select Committee on Artisans and Machinery*. 23 Feb. 1824: 223). Another form of humiliating the wrongdoer by openly parading him through the streets of the town was witnessed during the early weeks of the great Preston 'ten per cent and no surrender' lock-out of October 1853 to May 1854.[12] In this case, the victim was conveyed not by cart through the town streets, but, in an exercise no less injurious to personal pride, was carried aloft on the shoulders of individuals through the streets in the midst of a vast multitude of strikers and their supporters (*The Standard*, 7 Nov. 1853: 1). There is also the somewhat unconventional shaming parade that a strike-breaker had to endure during a turnout of seamen in Whitehaven, Cumbria, in mid-July 1841. On this particular occasion, the offending workman was compelled by the strikers to parade the streets of the town clothed in sheepskin (HO45/48/3–4. Memorial of the owners and masters of vessels of Whitehaven. 19 July 1841).[13] Villages, as well as sea-ports, small towns and larger urban districts, could also be the scene of shaming parades targeted at those found to have engaged in strike-breaking. Some such parades could be heavily stylised. Thus, in some villages in Lancashire during the 1820s, those recognised as strike-breakers were 'chaired' through the village with knobsticks in their hands (Anon. 1831: 37).

Then we have the particularly unpleasant punishment meted out to a non-union shipwright by the unionised journeymen shipwrights of Liverpool, which initially came to light in evidence given to the 1824 Parliamentary Select Committee on Artisans and Machinery. The punishment was carried out in the immediate aftermath of the incident mentioned earlier in this chapter, when a number of shipwrights were apprehended on the schooner where they worked and thrown overboard for 'not belonging to the club'. One of the offending shipwrights survived being tossed into the water, only to be seized by the union men, whereupon:

> they put a pair of slings round his body and hooked the main topsail holyards [sic] to the slings, and took the part of a hand pump to beat the slings together

upon his body, and beat him also upon the head with the same instrument most severely.

(extracts from the Select Committee findings feature in Webb Trade Union Archive. A/1/177–8. Trade Unionism. Shipwrights. Liverpool 1823–4)[14]

This was not the end of the matter. Even more degradation was heaped upon the unfortunate man when his persecutors proceeded to hook the slings attached to his waist to the fore-holyards of a vessel lying nearby, hoisted him a certain height off the deck of the ship, 'let go the schooner's topsail holyards' and 'swung him right across' the vessel's deck whereupon 'he fell into the next yard' (these additional details of the incident can be found in Rathbone 1860: 482).

Degradation punishment rituals clearly represented a notching up in the degree of coercion and violence used against those accused, as the trade union activist George Howell once put it, of having 'fled into the enemy's camp to fight against his own comrades' (Howell 1973: 84). During moments when the contest between labour and capital in strike situations became most acute, the antipathy felt towards perceived deserters and traitors within the workers' ranks deepened and assumed an even more menacing character. This rise in the level of resentment usually intensified as the nature of the struggle between worker and master increased. This next and more violent stage in the contest between pro-union workmen and those they deemed to have 'fled into the enemy's camp' will form the subject of the following chapter of this book.

Notes

1 See chapter 5.
2 A more detailed discussion of this relationship between strikes and war can be found in the Introduction to this book.
3 A potent example here would be the humiliating parade of around 60,000 German Wehrmacht prisoners-of-war through the streets of Moscow by the Red Army in July 1944.
4 The ridings were said to have taken place on 13 February 1783.
5 See chapter 2. See also Joyce 1981.
6 See chapter 4, and Ingram (1984: 98–9).
7 The 1831 mineworkers' strike is discussed in chapter 3 of this book.
8 The leaflet mistakenly referred to the victim as J. Roberts. For additional details on the shooting of Robson, see *Worcester Journal*, 9 May 1822: 4.
9 The report stated that the blacklegs were also beaten with sticks. See also *Saunders's News-Letter*, 21 Nov. 1822: 1.
10 A six-year-old boy was also shot and killed, though not by direct gunfire.
11 Tensions ran exceedingly high in the cotton towns during this period. In one particularly disturbing incident, the son of a Hyde cotton manufacturer named Thomas Ashton was shot and killed by an unknown assailant. Attempts were made to implicate the cotton spinners' union in the murder but according to the 'official report' into the murder there was not 'the least proof' for this charge. See Hammond 1995: 134–5.
12 For a brief summary of the origins of the lock-out and a discussion of blacklegging during the dispute, see chapter 2. For a comprehensive coverage, see Dutton and King 1981.

13 The turnout originated in an attempt by the ship-owners of the port of Whitehaven to reduce the seamen's wages. See *Carlisle Patriot*, 31 July 1841: 2.
14 A holyard, or the better known term halyard, is the strong rope on a ship used to hoist or lower a sail, ladder, yard or flag into position.

References

Alford, Violet (1959) 'Rough Music or Charivari', *Folklore*, 70(4): 505–518.
Anon. (1831) *On Combinations of Trades*. London: James Ridgway.
Benedict, Ruth (1946) *The Chrysanthemum and the Sword*. Boston: Houghton Mifflin.
Brake, Ted (1985) *Men of Good Character. A History of the National Union of Sheet Metal Workers, Coppersmiths, Heating and Domestic Engineers*. London: Lawrence and Wishart.
Colls, Robert (1977) *The Collier's Rant. Song and Culture in the Industrial Village*. London: Croom Helm.
Dutton, H.I. and King, JohnEdward (1981) *Ten Per Cent and No Surrender. The Preston Strike 1853–1854*. Cambridge: Cambridge University Press.
Favretto, Ilario (2015) 'Rough Music and Factory Protest in Post-1945 Italy', *Past and Present*, 228: 207–247.
Franklin, William Temple (ed) (1818) *Memoirs of the Life and Writings of Benjamin Franklin. Vol. II*. London: Henry Colburn.
Garfinkel, Harold (1956) 'Conditions of Successful Degradation Ceremonies', *American Journal of Sociology*, 61(5): 420–424.
Gorsky, Martin (1994) 'James Tuckfield's "Ride": Combination and Social Drama in Early Nineteenth Century Bristol', *Social History*, 19(3): 319–338.
Hammond, J.L. and Hammond, Barbara (1995; first published 1919) *The Skilled Labourer 1760–1832*. Stroud: Allan Sutton.
Henson, Gravenor (1970; first published 1831) *Henson's History of the Framework Knitters*. Newton Abbot: David & Charles.
Howell, George (1973; first published 1891) *Trade Unionism New and Old*. Brighton: Harvester Press.
Ingram, Martin (1984) 'Ridings, Rough Music and the "Reform of Popular Culture" in Early Modern England', *Past and Present*, 105: 79–113.
Jacquet, Jennifer (2016) *Is Shame Necessary? New Uses for an Old Tool*. London: Penguin.
Jenkins, Mick (1980) *The General Strike of 1842*. London: Lawrence & Wishart.
Jevons, William A. (1860) 'An Account of the Spinners' Strike in Ashton-under-Lyne in 1830', in Report of the Committee on Trades' Societies Appointed by the National Association for the Promotion of Social Science, *Trades' Societies and Strikes*. London: John W. Parker & Son: 473–478.
Joyce, Joyce A. (1981) 'Semantic Development of the Word Black: A History from Indo-European to the Present', *Journal of Black Studies*, 11(3): 307–312.
Lewis, Helen (1971) *Shame and Guilt in Neurosis*. New York: International Universities Press.
Linebaugh, Peter (2003) *The London Hanged. Crime and Civil Society in the Eighteenth Century*. London: Verso.
Loosley, John and Southgate, Kenneth (1993) *The Stroudwater Riots of 1825*. Stroud: The Stroud Museum Association.
McCord, Norman (1980) *Strikes*. Oxford: Basil Blackwell.
McCord, Norman (1968) 'The Seamen's Strike of 1815 in North-East England', *The Economic History Review*, 21(2): 127–143.

Minchinton, Walter (1951) 'The Beginnings of Trade Unionism in the Gloucestershire Woollen Industry', *Transactions of the Bristol and Gloucestershire Archaeological Society*, 70: 126–141.

Rathbone, Philip H. (1860) 'An Account of Shipwrights' Trades' Societies in Liverpool, the Tyne and Other Ports', in Report of the Committee on Trades' Societies Appointed by the National Association for the Promotion of Social Science, *Trades' Societies and Strikes*. London: John W. Parker & Son: 479–520.

Tar, A. (1815) *An Impartial Account of the Late Proceedings of the Seamen of the Port of Tyne*. Newcastle-upon-Tyne: K. Anderson.

Thérèse, Sandrine and Martin, Brian (2010) 'Shame, Scientist! Degradation Rituals in Science', *Prometheus*, 28(2): 97–110.

Thompson, E.P. (1992) 'Rough Music Reconsidered', *Folklore*, 103(1): 3–26.

Turner, Francis (1934) *History of the Liverpool Society of Sheet Metal Workers and Braziers from 1802 to 1920*. Liverpool. Unpublished manuscript.

van Gennep, Arnold (1960; originally published 1909) *The Rites of Passage*. Chicago: University of Chicago Press.

8

RETRIBUTION

> A system of vengeance or retribution (as they call it) [sic] is much talked of amongst the seditious.
>
> *(HO42/179/135–136. Letter 5 Aug. 1818)*[1]

In early August 1853, a violent incident took place during a strike of dyers and fustian finishers at the works of James Crompton and Company in Pendleton, Manchester. The strike in question had begun on 1 July when the dyers and finishers turned out for an advance of wages. By the start of August a resolution to the dispute between the master and his workforce seemed some way in the distance, a situation hardly helped by an earlier decision of the former to draft in 'new hands' to fill the places of the striking operatives. Up to that point the strike had witnessed a few sporadic instances of violence but then, on 2 August, the dispute took a particularly violent turn. On that day, a large contingent of strikers to the number of around sixty to seventy individuals armed with staves and pieces of logwood launched an audacious attack on Crompton's works. On entering the yard, one group of the assailants rushed into the dye-house and proceeded to 'beat all who were at work in it', while another group moved swiftly through other parts of the works to apprehend and assault the remaining new hands in a similar manner. In the words of the mainstream press, the new hands were 'most violently and cruelly beaten', and that 'the only object of the assailants appeared to be to inflict personal chastisement upon Messrs. Crompton and their men; for they made no attempt to damage any property' (*Morning Post*, 5 Aug. 1853: 7).[2]

How should the historian understand the violence of 2 August 1853, which was undoubtedly very aggressive and specifically targeted at individuals with an intent to inflict harm? Before we look more closely at the violence of 2 August it would be helpful to say what it was not. Up to this point in this book, we have looked at a range of measures deployed by unionised workers to address the issues of strike-breakers and other categories of non-compliant workmen in the ranks. Many of these measures took a ritual, even stylised form. The measures adopted by striking operatives on 2 August in Pendleton shared none of these characteristics, however. On 2 August there was a notable absence of carnivalesque ritual, no attempt to address the problem of the strike-breakers by resort to mockery, parody and theatrical display. There was no burlesque laughter or audience present on 2 August, while the playing of 'rough music' seemed far from the thoughts of the assault group of turnouts as they surged through the premises of the Crompton works in search of blacklegs. Nor did the striking dyers and finishers seek to punish the new hands 'sympathetically' by recourse to magic ritual. Hence there was no elaborate attempt to hang or burn the images of the blackleg strangers in effigy. Nor were the strike-breakers subjected to elaborate degradation rituals. Rather, the manner of dealing with errant workers on 2 August was shorn of all such displays, and was instead more direct, crude, aggressive, and included the conscious use of overt physical violence.

When one examines the violence of 2 August 1853 closely, one can clearly discern the strain of retributive justice running through it.[3] Broadly speaking, the theory of retributive justice is composed of a number of key elements. First of all, retributive justice theory posits that it is morally acceptable and even necessary for a healthy functioning society to punish acts of wrongdoing and that this will ultimately benefit society. Second, the punishment should be proportionate to the crime committed. Third, and following on from the previous point, the wrongdoer should suffer some hurt in proportion to the wrong he inflicted, as in the concept of an eye-for-an-eye. Fourth, the retributive punishment restores a sense of equilibrium in regard to the victim of the offence and the wrongdoer. In other words, the punishment should serve in some way to compensate the victim for the crime done and thereby help re-establish the state of affairs between the parties that had prevailed hitherto. Fifth, as mentioned, some degree of suffering, as well as shame, is unavoidable in retributive punishments as 'debts' are paid and justice is done and seen to be done. Sixth, some forms of retributive justice involve the use of physical violence to a certain degree depending on the circumstances and the nature of the offence committed. Seven, retributive punishments tend to increase in severity when wrongdoing is seen as intentional, and when the act of wrongdoing induces a high level of moral outrage within the wider community (see Bastion, Denson and Haslam 2013). Eight, retributive punishments can, in certain contexts and circumstances, provide a cathartic release for the community from the anxiety and pent-up anger occasioned by the wrongdoing (Wood 2012: 416). Finally, it follows from all of the above that deterrence and rehabilitation are not the main preoccupations of retributive justice. Not surprisingly, acts of retributive justice in labour disputes which comprised many of the key elements just mentioned, particularly awareness of intentionality, a high degree of moral outrage, the use of some degree of physical violence, and cathartic release, were more likely to be directed at the category of non-cooperative workman deemed to have committed the most serious offence, namely the new hand or blackleg.

There is an additional aspect to the retributive violence of 2 August 1853 that we should also note. While it may be tempting to follow the contemporary mainstream press in dismissing the violence of 2 August as the mindless actions of a 'mob' of turnouts and 'delinquents' as one press account put it, the historian needs to be rightly cautious of interpretations which over-represent the supposedly negative traits of crowds and crowd behaviour (*Daily News*, 4 Aug. 1853: 5). As discussed in the Introduction to this book, there is a tendency in such interpretations to characterise crowds, or 'mobs' in the language of the contemporary press, as innately chaotic, unstable and irrational. In the same vein, when collective gatherings appear in circumstances of heightened political tension, they are denounced as a regressive form of political expression engaged in by irresponsible 'primitives' and deviants with no moral compass to guide behaviour. Such characterisations claimed that collective gatherings were irrational and deviant in other ways, in that this represented a mode of behaviour which was inconsistent with society's true course of development which followed the civilising path of reason, modernisation, enlightenment and progress.

Unfortunately, the striking workers who assailed Crompton's works and violently attacked the new hands on 2 August 1853 have not left behind a written record as to their thought-processes and motivation both prior to and after the attack. Nevertheless, judging by the sequence of events that unfolded prior to the assault, as we will see below, from the perspective of the assailants it is very likely that the violence directed against blacklegs on 2 August seemed eminently rational, and even morally defensible. In seeking to conceptualise this mode of violence in this way, we should certainly be grateful to those earlier scholars who effectively challenged the view that crowds were mere collections of primitives, deviants, marginal types, or impressionable dupes who too readily lapsed into violence and brutality on entering the 'mass'. For instance, in her classic account of religiously motivated crowd violence in sixteenth-century France, Natalie Zemon Davis tells us that during times of conflict, crowds usually had a strong sense that what they are doing was reasonable, legitimate and moral given the circumstances which formed the background to these events (Davis 1973: 91).[4] According to this view, crowds are often 'prompted by political and moral traditions which legitimise and even prescribe their violence' (Davis 1973: 53). These traditions, moreover, tend to be organic to the community rather than external to it. In a related sense, some scholars argue that rather than seeing violence as a marginal and pathological phenomenon, it needs to be seen as 'integral and inevitable' in human social and cultural relationships (see Whitehead 2009). We should thus be careful not to view much of the collective violence which has marked the course of history in moments of crisis as somehow being external to a community and its traditions and moral concerns, as being unrepresentative of the community and visited upon it by a few delinquents from within.

The notion of collective violence as rational rather than pathological has received support from certain theoretical perspectives within the discipline of sociology, such as resource mobilisation theory. According to an important strand of thinking within this perspective, when developing their tactics and making their challenge to existing power relations, those participating in collective action are highly sensitive to the existing conditions which prevail at any one time as they attempt to accomplish movement goals. As rational-choice social actors with clear goals in mind, movement activists are thus mindful of both the advantages and disadvantages of political action in any given context and base their decision on whether to act on the relative benefits to be gained from action as opposed to inaction (see Buechler 1993).

As we will see from the 2 August Pendleton turnout, the strategic and tactical decision-making of the striking dyers and finishers did not proceed in a random and aimless manner. Judging by the sequence of events and strike tactics deployed, it appears that the turnouts did weigh their options when formulating their tactics based on the context and circumstances which presented themselves at any one time. Hence, newspaper accounts tell us that the initial response of the turnouts to the incursion of the new hands was moderate and restrained. At this point in the engagement, a system of 'picqueting' was set up at the entrance of the Crompton works, which aimed to peacefully confer with the new arrivals to persuade them to return from whence they came. During this stage of the proceedings, the turnouts 'entirely abstained from violence, and only used persuasion' (*Morning Post*, 5 Aug. 1853: 7). Rather than agree to cease the blacklegging, however, these tactics merely provoked an aggressive response from the 'new workpeople' who challenged the pickets 'to fight' (*Daily News*, 4 Aug. 1853: 5). In this sequence of evolving tactics, it appears that the resort to the more aggressive option of retributive violence witnessed in the storming of the Crompton works to violently expel the blacklegs emerged in response to the failure of earlier tactics to achieve the desired end. As mentioned, these earlier tactics included constructing a picketing system designed to attempt to peacefully persuade the new hands to return home. When this 'soft' pressure failed to halt the incursion of blackleg labour and matters appeared to be turning decisively in favour of the masters, a more aggressive and even desperate strategy was deployed in an attempt to retrieve the situation.

We can bring these aforementioned factors into even sharper focus if we turn to consider another turnout exhibiting some similar features to the Pendleton strike, which took place some years earlier in 1826 in the nearby district of Oldham. Before turning to the Oldham dispute, it is worth clarifying the most salient of these aforementioned factors. Most importantly, it needs to be recognised that a resort to physical violence in labour disputes can emerge sequentially and is very likely to have had its roots in some form of rational evaluation of developing circumstances on the part of the striking operatives. It should also be recognised that an organic relationship can sometimes exist between a community and certain acts of collective violence, which is implicit in the community's moral traditions. It is worth clarifying a few additional matters. Even more than the Pendleton violence of August 1853, the Oldham turnout shows that labour violence can change its form and increase in intensity in circumstances of heightened and accelerating tension in strike situations. In such circumstances, actions taken against offending workmen could assume a more direct and retributive form without the need for resentment to be mediated via other, more elaborate, means of the type we have looked at in previous chapters. It should be flagged up as well that this more direct retributive violence was usually deployed on occasions when the dangers to the community associated with acts of strike-breaking had accumulated and become particularly acute.

In late December 1826, the Home Secretary Robert Peel received a letter signed by a number of master spinners from Oldham telling of a turnout of operative spinners then underway in the town (HO40/21/352–6. Letter 21 Dec. 1826). The turnout in question, which extended to nine of Oldham's mills, had begun in earnest in early September in consequence of a decision by the masters to reduce the wages of the spinners by fifteen per cent, a reduction which the workmen argued followed a cut of one-third in their wages over the previous sixteen months.[5] The economic downturn of 1825–6 in the wider UK economy and a general attempt at wage reduction by the master spinners throughout Lancashire provided the backdrop to the wage cuts in Oldham, and the turnout which followed. The letter to Robert Peel was extensive in length and is particularly revealing in regard to the tactics used by the turnouts to try to thwart attempts by the masters to defeat the strike through the use of blackleg labour.

Very shortly after the commencement of the turnout, at some point during early to mid-September, three of the principal masters in the town made the decision to draft in blackleg labour, mainly from other parts of Lancashire, to fill the places of the striking operatives. As the letter to Peel stated, 'against this measure of supplying their places with new hands, the whole combined efforts and attention of the turnouts was directed' (HO40/21/352–6. Letter 21 Dec. 1826). These efforts took a number of forms and seemed to follow a discernible pattern. In the first instance, the turnout spinners sought to disrupt the flow of blacklegs into Oldham by applying 'soft' pressure in the form of 'annoying the new spinners with threats and insults' as the latter arrived in the town and went to and from their new places of employment. Secondly, when the 'soft' pressure of verbal 'threats and insults' failed to halt the influx of new arrivals, the turnouts opted for a different approach. At this point, they attempted to inject a performative element into their endeavours by parading 'in dense and strong numbers' before the three mills which had taken in the blacklegs, a method of proceeding which the Oldham masters admitted 'has a most strong and intimidating effect on a workman' (HO40/21/352–6. Letter 21 Dec. 1826). During the later weeks of October, as the offending mills 'still continued to fill fast with new workmen', the turnouts responded by adopting a third strategy in an effort to wrest the initiative from the masters. In the words of the master spinners, the turnouts decided to pursue 'another and more effectual plan of operations by putting the said mills into a state of blockade' by placing 'a strong guard of their body around the respective mills', both day and night. We know from other sources that this picket was comprehensive, wide-ranging and effective. The picket extended to the rural 'task-scapes' beyond the mills in question, that is, to the various fields and country lanes on the periphery of the Oldham urban landscape (on the role of 'task-scapes' in industrial conflicts in this period, see Navickas 2011). In these outlying fields and lanes, the Oldham turnouts kept up a round-the-clock vigil of 'watch-and-ward' to halt further incursions of blacklegs into the offending mills and to prevent supplies reaching those blacklegs already in the mills who were now sleeping on the premises. Henceforth, all seeking to enter the township were stopped, searched, and closely questioned as to their business. This mode of scrutiny even extended to feeling the palms of the hands of 'strangers' to determine whether they were spinners by trade about to embark on blacklegging (*The Suffolk Chronicle*, 25 Nov. 1826: 4).

Then in early November, a fourth strategy, the character of which forms the main concern of this chapter, came into focus. For the Oldham master spinners communicating with Robert Peel, the tactic about to come into view was 'of a more desperate character than ever was adopted by the turnouts' up to that stage in the strike (HO40/21/352–6. Letter 21 Dec. 1826). At around 7pm on the evening of 7 November, a body of some 500 turnouts suddenly appeared before the premises of Collinge and Lancashire, one of the offending mills that had brought in blackleg labour. A party of the turnouts then broke off from the main body and began scaling the wall surrounding the mill, said to be the height of 11 or 12 feet. On gaining entry to the mill, the party then proceeded to force the lock of a door within the walls so as to gain access to the mill gates. From there, the party advanced towards the mill gates, which they then forced open by means of a mattock, crowbars, and sundry other instruments which they had brought with them for this purpose, in order to let in the main body of the turnouts. Once they had gained entry, the large body of Oldham turnout spinners then spread out in all directions throughout the large grounds of the mill taking in the yard and the staircases. They then 'went in search of the new spinners who, as many as could, had concealed themselves in order to avoid the fury of the mob' (HO40/21/352–6. Letter 21 Dec. 1826). Concealment proved but a temporary respite, however, as the obnoxious 'strangers' were all discovered and forcefully dragged out of the mill. As they were being ejected from the mill, many of the blacklegs, according to the Oldham master spinners, were ill-treated in the 'most barbarous' manner (HO40/21/352–6. Letter 21 Dec. 1826).

Having succeeded in forcefully driving the blacklegs from the mill of Collinge and Lancashire, the body of turnouts then made their way to 'the other side of the Highway' where another of the offending mills which had taken in blackleg labour was located. At this second mill, the mill of John Lees and Sons, a scenario similar to that which had unfolded at the mill of Collinge and Lancashire was played out. This saw the mill gates being surmounted, locked doors being forced open with heavy instruments, and groups of turnout spinners advancing determinedly through the mill in search of concealed blacklegs. On this occasion though, the turnouts carried lighted candles to assist their passage through the mill, and to better illuminate its darker recesses. As with the blacklegs at the mill of Collinge and Lancashire, attempts at concealment proved futile. The various hideaways were soon discovered and the 'obnoxious' strangers were apprehended and forcibly dispatched from the mill.

It needs to be noted as well that ejecting blacklegs from the mills was but one stage of the process of seeking to eradicate the perceived danger posed by the influx of new hands. What then followed was the physical removal of the blackleg threat from the town of Oldham altogether. Making allowance for some of the more exaggerated and hysterical descriptions in contemporary newspapers, it seems beyond doubt that a greater degree of physical violence was used at this stage of the drama. Hence, the 'strangers' were literally chased out of town 'by crowds who continued to maltreat them most cruelly' as they ran along the lanes and through the fields beyond town in order to escape (*Belfast Commercial Chronicle*, 15 Nov. 1826: 2).

Leaving aside the matter of the audacious nature of the tactics deployed by the Oldham turnouts at this stage of their struggle, the matter which particularly concerns us here is the role played by physical violence in these events. It should be mentioned here that 7 November was not the first occasion that the Oldham turnout had seen violence. This being said, these particular instances of violence, witnessed early in the contest at the start of October, were of a sporadic nature and mostly directed at property. The premises of one of the offending mills employing blacklegs was assailed with repeated 'volleys of stones' in one incident, while the windows of the dwelling houses of two of the master spinners at the centre of the dispute were broken by stones thrown by a number of individuals in another (HO40/21/352–6. Letter 21 Dec. 1826).[6] The form of violence on show in the events of 7 November, however, was of a different order and included a retributive component targeted at blacklegs in particular. Additionally, everywhere one looks in relation to the storming of the Oldham mills one can see some form of rational calculation at work. Hence, the violence was not random, chaotic or aimless. Rather, the violence was controlled, highly structured and carefully directed at specific targets. We can see this clearly from the calculated manner in which the turnouts accomplished their daring entry into the mill, to the systematic way in which they then went in search of the concealed blacklegs. The events at Oldham demonstrate further that the targets of collective industrial violence do not tend to be chosen at random, and physical violence if deployed is usually specifically aimed at those perceived to have caused the most offence, in this case the blackleg stranger (a conclusion also arrived at by Randall 1982: 296 and 302).

Also, in a more general sense, and as in the 1853 Pendleton turnout, nor did the strategic and tactical decision-making of the Oldham turnouts proceed in a random and aimless manner. Judging by the sequence of events and strike tactics deployed, it appears obvious that the turnouts carefully weighed their options when formulating their tactics based on the context and circumstances which presented themselves at any one time. In the sequence of evolving tactics, the resort to the more aggressive option of storming the Oldham mills to violently expel the blacklegs clearly emerged in response to the failure of earlier strike tactics. As mentioned above, these earlier tactics included verbal threats, parading before the offending mills, and mass picketing which involved an attempt at the peaceful persuasion of blacklegs to return home. When this 'soft' pressure failed in its attempt to stem the flow of blacklegs and the turnouts appeared to be losing ground in the contest, a more aggressive and even desperate strategy was adopted in an attempt to wrest the initiative from the masters.

Furthermore, the events at Oldham on 7 November should caution us against seeing acts of violence in labour disputes in the decades covered by this book as somehow being unconnected to the wider community and its moral concerns. Thus, when a number of the Oldham turnouts arrested for their part in the 'riots' managed to procure bail, they were not shunned by the community on their return home. Indeed, far from it, as they were accompanied home on their release from incarceration by a Band of music and 'immense numbers of people shouting and dancing and indulging in all the extravagance of insolent triumph', as the Oldham master spinners put it (HO40/21/352–6. Letter 21 Dec. 1826). To the evident dismay of the Oldham masters reporting on the home-coming, by the time the released prisoners arrived back in Oldham the numbers gathered from the community to welcome their home-coming had swelled to 'several thousands, completely filling the streets'. If this was not enough, and as if to leave no one in doubt as to where their allegiance lay, the huge crowds 'set up the most riotous shouts and exhibited the most rancorous and exulting spirit' as they passed the houses of several of the Oldham master spinners involved in the dispute (HO40/21/352–6. Letter 21 Dec. 1826).

All the above being said, and beyond recognising that the resort to physical violence emerged sequentially in the Oldham dispute and is very likely to have emerged as a result of striking operatives engaging in some form of rational calculation of developing circumstances, some theoretical perspectives have been criticised for 'over-rationalising' the recourse to violent tactics on the part of outsider groups. Thus, resource mobilisation theory, for instance, has been accused of placing too great an emphasis on resources and organisational matters and assuming too close a relationship between tactics and results, to the detriment of other considerations which may problematise the decision-making of the actors engaged in collective violence (Sharman Grant II and Wallace 1991). One such important other consideration concerns the manner in which employer decision-making and counter-strategies in strikes conspire to shape strikers' tactical options, which bring forth circumstances where more aggressive forms of violence are more likely to break out. Hence, in response to the 'instrumentality' of resource mobilisation theory, analyses based on 'situational' perspectives prefer to depict industrial violence 'as an emergent phenomenon, grounded in the social context and interplay of events between conflicting groups' (Sharman Grant II and Wallace 1991: 1119). In this scenario, tactics such as the aggressive use of physical violence, which may have seemed unthinkable during a strike's early stages, emerge as the only logical course of action to pursue during the dispute's later phase. In this evolving situation with employers and elites more able to determine the course of events in their favour given the greater resources at their disposal, this recourse to violence emerges as the only viable strategy for striking workers in a scenario of rapidly dwindling choices. Nor should we rule out that in such circumstances this step change in tactics in the direction of aggressive violence often emerges as a defensive measure. In such a scenario of developing and emerging employer counter-strategies, there are critical moments in strike situations which can determine whether this type of more aggressive violence will take place. For instance, when all avenues to achieving success in the turnout for striking workers have been blocked, when all strategic options had been tried and exhausted, a step change in tactics towards more aggressive and confrontational measures can emerge as a weapon of last resort, as the only option remaining, as the 'last throw of the dice'. It should be stressed in this regard as well, that aggressive industrial violence was more likely to be deployed on occasions when the danger associated with a given situation had become particularly acute.

Situations of particularly acute danger for the workers' cause usually arrived in certain circumstances. These would include those circumstances which saw a dispute lengthening in duration with seemingly no resolution in sight; when employer intransigence showed no sign of abating; when those on strike began to experience severe economic hardship and privation; when a range of strike tactics had been frustrated by employer counter-strategies; and when the terrible prospect of defeat got ever closer and seemed more likely or even imminent. As studies of strikes in other times and places have shown, in such circumstances of heightened and ever-increasing danger, the resort to more aggressive measures on the part of the workers becomes more likely (Sharman Grant II and Wallace 1991).[7] We should add as well, that in such a scenario, labour violence could assume a more daring and even desperate character. To return to the analogy between a strike and war which has featured in other chapters in this book, the actions of the workers at this stage of the contest bring to mind the desperate plight of an army facing defeat in a war. Knowing defeat may be imminent but reluctant to surrender, the workers' efforts to reverse an ever-worsening situation has all the appearance of a last-ditch stand.

In all the acute danger scenarios in strike situations, the blackleg loomed large. As we saw in a previous chapter, the blackleg was the ultimate tabooed person to collectively inclined and unionised workmen, an individual thought to emit pollution danger to a high degree.[8] As the master's definitive weapon in a turnout, the blackleg was both feared and loathed by striking workers. The importance of blackleg labour to employer strategies and counter-strategies in an unfolding strike situation can be seen in the following correspondence relating to a turnout of spinners in the Stalybridge, Ashton-under-Lyne, and Hyde districts of north-west England in mid-August 1830. The spinners in these districts struck work in response to an attempt by several spinning establishments in their neighbourhood to bring down piece rates. According to the reasoning of the masters, the piece-rate reduction was due to competition from rival low-wage districts and a trade depression. Stalybridge was the focal point of the turnout, the operative spinners in that locality said to be amongst Britain's lowest paid workers, with their wages some thirty to forty per cent lower than the average rates in the country (Kirby and Musson 1975: 104–7). The turnouts were to be supported in their endeavours to secure wage equalisation with other districts by the local spinners' Society and the recently formed Grand General Union of Operative Spinners led by its charismatic guiding-light John Doherty. Shortly following the commencement of the turnout, a number of letters were sent from Manchester by Lt-Colonel Shaw, the commanding officer with responsibility for the Ashton and Stalybridge district, to Major General Henry Bouverie, appraising the latter about the progress of the dispute. The letters are extremely interesting from our point of view because they provide an insight into the mind-set of the authorities concerning the crucial importance of blackleg labour in a developing strike situation.

On 24 August Shaw informed Bouverie that in his judgement the use of blackleg labour was essential if the masters were to prevail in what was likely to be 'a serious contest' with the turnouts (HO40/26/32–3. Letter 24 Aug. 1830). Shaw knew that the unions were acutely aware that the stakes were high in the dispute and that they recognised, as did the masters, that control over the supply of blackleg labour was the key to the outcome. As Shaw admitted, the unions recognised that if they 'allow the employment of new hands, their cause is gone, and the object of their union defeated' (HO40/26/32–3. Letter 24 Aug. 1830). The unionised workers had already beaten back one attempt by the masters early in the contest to fill their places with 'new hands'. During this early engagement, the usurpers were 'driven from their work' by a body of turnout spinners. At this early stage in this contest between capital and labour in north-west England, Shaw urged caution on the masters in terms of deploying a further batch of new hands, lest it add to the 'excitement' which already prevailed in the working-class districts of north-west England arising from the July Revolution in France. A few days later, Shaw dispatched another letter. In this correspondence he drew a link between the introduction of blackleg labour and a violent response on the part of the turnouts, particularly in the volatile atmosphere generated by the events in Paris, stating that an influx of blackleg labour at this point 'would infallibly lead to open violence' (HO40/26/46–9. Letter 29 Aug. 1830). Nevertheless, Shaw was of the view that 'ultimately' the masters 'will have no other recourse against the measures of the union but that of supplying their mills with new hands in place of those who turn out'. If the masters do not adopt this measure, Shaw continued, the union would prevail, a consequence that 'the masters see clearly', which necessitates that 'the struggle for new hands must come sooner or later' (HO40/26/46–9. Letter 29 Aug. 1830).

The letters of Lt-Colonel Shaw are interesting on a number of counts. Firstly, they indicate a readiness, far too often it seems in the early decades of liberal political economy, on the part of those who supported the new economics to resort to the use of blackleg labour in a strike situation, even at the risk of precipitating an increase in the level of industrial violence. Secondly, the letters tell of the vital importance to the masters of blackleg labour as a tactical weapon in the contest to be deployed when the circumstances were most favourable to attain the desired outcome. Thirdly, the letters highlight the awareness on the part of both sides in the divide of the crucial importance of blackleg labour to the eventual outcome of the contest.

Lt-Colonel Shaw's gloomy predictions regarding the supposed inevitability of blackleg labour having to be deployed to defeat the operative spinners of Stalybridge, Ashton-under-Lyne, and Hyde in August 1830 did not come to pass, however. In early September, the dispute was settled to the satisfaction of the spinners when the masters at the centre of the dispute agreed to an advance in the piece-rates. This victory for the operative spinners of this region was but a 'stay of execution' though. Towards the end of 1830, virtually all the master spinners of Stalybridge, Ashton-under-Lyne, Mossley, and Dukinfield entered into a combination for the purpose of presenting their workforce with a reduced list of prices. Should any amongst the operative spinners refuse to accept this reduced price of 3s. 9d. per 1000 hanks of No. 40s on all sizes of wheels, they were to be locked out. The spinners, supported by the spinners' Grand General Union led by its Secretary John Doherty, responded to the enforced abatement by insisting on a price of 4s. 2d. for their labour. Accordingly, the spinners struck work in early December, a general stoppage which eventually involved fifty-two mills in the area and around 18,000 workers.[9] According to the Hammonds, the real object of the associated master spinners in Stalybridge, Ashton-under-Lyne, Mossley, and Dukinfield in enforcing the objectionable reduced list of prices on their workforce was to provoke a confrontation with the intent of crushing the spinners' union (Hammond 1995: 132). Following a bitter contest which saw a number of very serious incidents of violence, the spinners finally succumbed to the multiple pressures that they were experiencing when the strike collapsed in mid-February 1831.[10]

There are a number of reasons for the collapse of the strike and the defeat of the spinners' union, not least the fact that the strike in the view of John Doherty was deliberately precipitated by the masters at the most inhospitable time of the year for the turnouts and their families in mid-Winter (Kirby and Musson 1975: 128). To these reasons we should also add the increasing privation of the strikers as the turnout dragged on without resolution, the failure of the spinners' union to bring about a wider more 'general strike' to help carry the day for the spinners, and the inadequate volume of relief obtained by the strikers from various sources which included strike funds (Kirby and Musson 1975: 119–52). In terms of our concerns in this chapter, however, it seems that the contest was ultimately decided by the ability and determination of the masters to procure blackleg labour to fill the places of the mills vacated by the striking operatives, as well as the willingness of the new hands to fill these places. This, at least, was the view of William A. Jevons, who produced the first detailed analysis of the strike in 1860:

> That although to some extent, probably, the men gave in from physical distress, to a great extent they were forced to a surrender by the masters being about to fill their mills with other hands, and that therefore the state of the labour market practically decided the matter in dispute in favour of the masters.
>
> *(Jevons 1860: 477)*

As was often the case in turnouts in the heyday of political economy, the price of defeat for the spinners was exceedingly heavy. As well as being forced to accept the hated price of 3s. 9d, their union had suffered a highly damaging defeat, while an estimated 300 of their striking brethren lost their employment, either because their places had been filled by blacklegs or because they had been placed on a country-wide 'blacklist' by the 'barbarous' and vengeful victorious master spinners, in the words of John Doherty. As Doherty put it in regard to the latter in an editorial in the pro-union newspaper the *Voice of the People* on 2 April 1831, the 'old hands' were to be 'turned adrift to perish in the streets and plunder in the highways. They are to be hunted down like beasts' (cited in Kirby and Musson 1975: 137).

When considering the matter of a tactical shift in the direction of more confrontational violence on the part of striking workers, which often took a retributive form, as well as the role of the blackleg in employer strategies and counter-strategies in precipitating a rise in the level of violence, we should not assume that the blackleg stranger was always a passive victim of trade union violence. Indeed, the history of the relations between workmen who favoured a collective approach to work and wages and those who followed a less co-operative path has been marked by periodic outbreaks of extreme confrontational violence. This is not to make light of the use of violence by union-inclined workers on strike, of course. Rather, it is to recognise that a confrontation could involve the use of violence by both sides, which could include using weapons. Take the following examples from Britain's tailoring trade alone. Relations in the tailoring trade between the 'legal' flints and the 'illegal' dungs, the latter tending to work by the piece and under price, were often strained to say the least. There is a report of a fierce fight between two rival groups of flints and dungs in a church-yard in an unspecified location in London in April 1764. Both groups were armed with weapons of various kinds, which resulted in a number of 'broken heads and aching bones' prior to the contest being terminated by a number of watchmen and constables 'who came to preserve the peace' (*Gazetteer and London Daily Advertiser*, 2 Apr. 1764: 2).[11]

There is another account of a 'violent affray' between flints and dungs in June 1777, on this occasion in the Bedfordbury district of London, which is said to have led to several of the combatants being 'dangerously wounded' (*General Evening Post*, 12–14 June 1777: 1). Nor was it unusual for strike-breakers to be armed with fire-arms and other lethal weapons. 'Knobsticks' working for the tabooed lower price of 3s. 9d. are said to have discharged pistols during the strike in the cotton districts of Stalybridge, Ashton-under-Lyne, Mossley, and Dukinfield in late 1830 and early 1831 discussed above (*Worcester Herald*, 22 Jan. 1831: 2). Remaining in north-west England, the pro-labour *Northern Star* claimed that many of the blacklegs brought in to thwart a turnout of millwrights, moulders and mechanics in Bury in May 1845 carried pistols 'and fire them every evening as they go along the streets' (*Northern Star*, 31 May 1845: 5). One of the strike-breakers during the same labour dispute was also charged with stabbing a young operative with a twelve-inch dagger (*Northern Star*, 31 May 1845: 5).

Nor was it uncommon for masters contesting a turnout to provide their new hands with fire-arms and other deadly weapons, ostensibly for the latter's protection and for the protection of the master's property. Thus in relation to an influx of blacklegs into Glasgow in late 1824 to help the masters defeat a turnout of cotton spinners, we are informed that 'every precaution has been taken for the safety of the new workers, who are well provided with fire arms' (*Fife Herald*, 23 Dec. 1824: 3). According to a member of the Glasgow Cotton Spinners' Operative Association, making his comments against the backdrop of the Glasgow cotton spinners' strike of 1837, the practice was commonplace:

> When a dispute takes place in a factory, and any new hands go in, those hands are armed with pistols, and allowed to go about the streets, carrying those pistols and flourishing them about, and insulting the inhabitants and the householders, and when complaints have been lodged as to the annoyance of these new hands, there was no redress obtained.
>
> (*The Operative*, 30 Dec. 1838: 12)

This course of action could sometimes have tragic consequences. At Oldham in April 1834, an operative named James Bentley was shot and killed by 'knobsticks' working at a mill deemed obnoxious to the local spinners' union (*Chelmsford Chronicle*, 18 Apr. 1834: 2).[12] The 'fresh hands' had earlier been supplied with muskets by the mill's owner. Salford, Manchester, witnessed a similar incident on 15 September 1842. In this particular incident, a young local weaver then on strike named Joshua Lyness was attacked and severely beaten about the head with picking-sticks by a number of knobstick strangers 'from other towns', the latter having been brought in to defeat the strike by the mill-owner at the centre of the dispute (*Manchester Courier and Lancashire General Advertiser*, 24 Sept. 1842: 2).[13] Lyness died from his injuries the following morning. For the *Northern Star*, the deceased was a martyr 'who had been basely murdered' (*Northern Star*, 24 Sept. 1842: 10). Not surprisingly, those sympathetic to property and capital registered a different verdict on the death of Lyness, declaring it to be 'justifiable homicide' (*Manchester Courier and Lancashire General Advertiser*, 24 Sept. 1842: 3).

Let us look at some other instances of retributive violence in our period. We have already looked at the storming of the Oldham mills in November 1826 and the Crompton works at Pendleton in August 1853 by groups of turnouts, both with the intent of forcibly ejecting and retributively punishing the blackleg intruders. Such acts were not confined to these incidents alone. Blacklegs were forcibly ousted from mills during the bitter eight-week-long cotton spinners' strike in Manchester in 1818 by 'flying mobs of a few hundreds' (HO42/179/214–216. Letter from James Norris. 28 Aug. 1818).[14] We find similar examples of parties of flying pickets raiding mills to forcibly eject blacklegs during the strike of spinners in Stalybridge, Ashton-under-Lyne, and Hyde in mid-August 1830, as mentioned above (HO40/26/32–3. Letter 24 Aug. 1830). Nor was the storming of work premises to physically dislodge blacklegs confined to the cotton towns of north-west England. In early November 1833, calico-printers in Glasgow numbering some 700 workers struck work seeking an equalisation of prices. What ensued was a long and bitter nine-month contest which followed a pattern depressingly familiar in the labour disputes of this era. The master calico-printers refused to concede ground and a few months into the strike conspired to defeat the turnout by drafting in blackleg handloom weavers to fill the places of the strikers. This move on the part of the masters in early February 1834 was the catalyst for the disturbances which followed. During the following few weeks, the turnouts attempted to contain this new threat by resorting to ever-more aggressive measures, which included the storming of printing works to eject the new arrivals. In one such assault, on 3 February, a 'mob' of turnouts said to be armed with sticks stormed a printing works at the village of Milngavie in the County of Stirling where a number of the blacklegs had been working. After having 'forcibly entered the premises', the turnouts proceeded to 'carry' away the new hands prior to marching them 'as prisoners' to Anderston in Glasgow, a distance of around eight to nine miles, where they were dispatched (*Morning Post*, 1 Apr. 1834: 1). Another account of this incident states that the so-called 'mob' which carried out the eviction was composed of some 500 persons, which included women and children, and that the 'prisoners' were formed into a procession 'amid the cheers of the multitude' prior to their long march of shame to Anderston (*Perthshire Advertiser*, 13 Feb. 1834: 2).

Not all such assaults in the calico-printers' strike were successful, however. On another occasion in early February, an assault group of some 300 striking calico-printers and their supporters, 'armed with sticks' and led by a trumpeter, staged a daring attack on a works at Anderson print-field 'with the avowed determination of taking out the new hands' (*Perthshire Advertiser*, 13 Feb. 1834: 2). Urged forward by the doughty trumpeter, the raiders managed to destroy the palisade protecting the print-field, sweep across the grounds *en masse*, and storm the premises. At that point though, the attack was repulsed by a contingent of police stationed at the works to protect both the property and the blacklegs. In the bruising sortie which ensued, injuries were incurred on both sides (*Perthshire Advertiser*, 13 Feb. 1834: 2). Despite these bold, and at times desperate, attempts to physically oust the hated 'strangers', the relentless flow of blackleg labour could not be halted. Towards the close of July 1834 the journeymen calico-printers, their families and supporters were forced to yield to the superior resources of their opponents.

Retributive clashes with blacklegs could assume numerous forms. Such confrontations could encompass measures higher up the scale of violence, such as the targeting of blacklegs in their dwellings. These could be temporary abodes like inns, which acted as staging posts prior to the new arrivals securing more permanent residence in a town. Alternatively, these abodes could be of a more permanent nature like colliery houses which the new hands had occupied in the wake of striking mineworkers and their families being evicted during a turnout. These incidents could take different forms. As we saw in the above incidents at Milngavie in February 1834 and at Oldham in November 1826, ejecting blacklegs from their place of work was often but the first stage of a process which involved an attempt to free the town from the blackleg threat altogether. We can see a similar process at work during a dispute in April and March of 1825 involving seamen in the port of Scarborough on the north Yorkshire coastline. On this occasion though, the blacklegs were dislodged from their dwellings rather than the workplace prior to being driven out of town. An attempt by local ship-owners, then in dispute with Scarborough's seamen, to procure blackleg labour from the nearby coastal town of Bridlington to man their vessels and put them to sea formed the background to the forced eviction of the unwelcome strangers (HO40/18/150–1. Letter 9 Mar. 1825).[15] On hearing of the arrival of six of the Bridlington blacklegs, a 'mob' said to number some 150 to 200 persons, which included Scarborough seamen associated with the local seamen's union, paid a late evening visit to the Inn where the Bridlington men were lodged. The Bridlington men were then pulled from the premises, dragged through the various streets of the town, and set on the road back to Bridlington. The blacklegs' involuntary journey from the Inn to the Bridlington Road was hardly a pleasant experience, as they received the occasional 'blow' to the back of the neck or side of the head from a fist or the palm of a hand. They were also warned that should they venture to blackleg in Scarborough again they would be hanged on the 'Vagrant post' in the town. Although the Bridlington men were subjected to a degree of physical violence, it was reported that none 'sustained any bodily injury'. The principle of retributive justice demanded, however, that the culprits should be enlightened as to their wrongdoing and some sense of equilibrium between the parties be restored. As such, and to add to their discomfiture and shame, the wrongdoers were cast adrift from Scarborough in the dead of night in the midst of inclement weather (HO40/18/152–3. Depositions. 2 Mar. 1825).[16]

Incidents where blacklegs were targeted in their dwellings assumed a more serious character when their dwellings were forcibly entered as a precursor to the material objects and possessions in the house being destroyed. This could include the destruction of windows, furniture and clothing. It is often difficult to determine the motivation behind these more extreme acts of retributive violence. On some occasions, when it became apparent to the turnouts that their cause was lost there may have been a motivation to exact some form of vengeance on those considered to have had some responsibility for the defeat, as with blacklegs. On other occasions, those engaged in such acts may have been seeking to apply pressure on the blackleg and his family to return from whence they came. There were occurrences of window and furniture breaking towards the close of the 1826–7 Oldham spinners' turnout which featured earlier in this chapter. As to the motivation behind these acts, they seem to fall into the former category of a desire to exact vengeance.

As January 1827 unfolded, it was becoming apparent to all intelligent observers that the Oldham spinners were facing defeat, with all the unpleasant consequences that such an outcome entailed. Against this backdrop of imminent defeat, a number of occurrences of window and furniture breaking took place. In one of these, which took place on 17 January, a body of around 200 individuals said to be 'strangers' to the town, though obviously sympathetic to the Oldham strikers' cause, arrived at the houses of a number of blacklegs who had taken up residence close to the mill where they now worked. Forcibly entering one of the houses, an advanced guard of the larger group then proceeded to break the windows of the house, destroy some of the furniture, and throw the clothes of the 'obnoxious' workman and his family out of the door (H040/22/24–5. Letter 21 Jan. 1827). It seems that the Oldham turnouts themselves did not participate in this act of retribution. An Oldham mill-owner admitted that the assailants 'were all unknown to us according to the usual practice of strange men being employed upon these acts of violence' (H040/22/24–5. Letter 21 Jan. 1827). A similar act of retribution was said to have taken place two days later on 19 January. On this occasion, 'the houses of several work people were broken into by parties in disguise', who then proceeded to break the windows of the houses and demolish the furniture with blows from an axe which they evidently brought with them for this purpose (H040/22/24–5. Letter 21 Jan. 1827). It should be said that it was not just 'new hands' that faced retributive violence of this kind. Another report emanating from Oldham at the same time told of the houses of three workmen, who had broken ranks and returned to work during the turnout, being broken into by 'the mob', who then proceeded to destroy 'all the furniture they contained' (H040/22/17–8. Letter 20 Jan. 1827).

The concerted attack on the homes of blackleg miners during the long-running Thorncliffe lock-out of 1869–70 seems to fall into both categories, in that the attackers were likely motivated both by a desire to exact vengeance and a desire to pressurise the new hands to leave the district. It would be helpful at this point to provide some background to this attack. Thorncliffe was an ironworks and colliery village in the south Yorkshire coalfield located between Barnsley and Sheffield. The lock-out originated in a decision taken on 24 February 1869 by the owners of the five collieries at Thorncliffe, namely Newton Chambers and Co., to dismiss their workforce of around 850 workers on 28 days' notice. An offer to resume their employment was forthcoming from the colliery owners at the expiration of the notice, though this was dependent on each man signing a 'contract' which effectively ensured the elimination of the union and all form of collective bargaining from the Thorncliffe pits (*Sheffield Daily Telegraph*, 9 Oct. 1869: 8). There were some outstanding recent and ongoing issues between the colliery owners and the union men working the pits in the south Yorkshire coalfield, which added to the strained relations between mineworkers and colliery masters at Thorncliffe. These included such issues as the eight-hour day, low wages, the correct and proper weighting of coal, and concerns about the 'minute-contract system' which allowed the colliery masters to dismiss their 'hands' at a moment's notice.

Henceforth, on the issuing of the 28 days' notice, Newton Chambers refused to negotiate with their workforce on such issues while the latter were 'in combination'. To add to the sense of injustice felt by the union men, all those who received notice to quit their employment and who refused to sign the 'free labour' anti-union contract were also required to give up possession of the company dwellings that they rented from Newton Chambers. In a conflict which dragged on into early 1870, the locked-out Thorncliffe mineworkers were supported in their efforts to seek redress by the South Yorkshire Miners' Association. Not surprisingly, the conflict was often acrimonious and hard fought, particularly given that blackleg miners, mostly from Derbyshire and Durham, were drafted in to fill the workplaces vacated by the locked-out union mineworkers. By mid-October 1869 it was said that around eighty blacklegs were employed at the Thorncliffe works (HO45/8370/2–5. Letter 19 Oct. 1869). This was despite efforts by the locked-out mineworkers and their supporters to persuade the new arrivals by various means, both peaceful and aggressive, to return home.

On the morning of 21 January 1870, however, and almost a year into the dispute, the conflict took a new and more ominous turn. On that morning, an attack was made on a row of cottages in the village of Thorncliffe which housed a number of blacklegs and their families. These cottages, amounting to some fifty in total, had been recently built at Thorncliffe by Newton Chambers for the sole purpose of providing dwelling places for their new hands. The main site of the newly erected double row of cottages was Westwood Row, close to the Thorncliffe collieries and situated on the Company's property. Reports of the attack on 21 January vary, with some accounts stating that as many as 600 persons launched the assault on Westwood Row, which resulted in some thirty houses being sacked (*Birmingham Daily Post*, 24 Jan. 1870: 5). Many of the assailants were said to be wearing 'grotesque disguises' to conceal their identities, which included faces either bedaubed with soot or burnt cork or painted in alternate streaks of black and white, all of which created 'an effect most hideous to behold' (*Manchester Times*, 29 Jan. 1870: 3). To add to the air of retributive menace, many of the attackers were said to be in possession of weapons, such as large sticks with pieces of scythe blades stuck in the end of them. As to the attacks on the dwelling houses themselves, this was not an exercise in restraint, nor was it characterised by the use of moderate violence. After fanning out along the row of cottages, the assailants then began smashing in doors and windows prior to bursting into the premises. On entry, they then proceeded to break chairs and tables, smash clocks to pieces with brickbats, dash crockery on floors, destroy all other breakable household goods, break up beds, and consign bed clothing to the flames (*Sheffield Daily Telegraph*, 22 Jan. 1870: 8). To demonstrate the assault's violently retributive nature, the attackers attempted to set several of the houses on fire prior to their departure, though without success. In fairness to the locked-out Thorncliffe mineworkers, they protested that they did not participate in the attack, a defence borne out to a large extent by police statements which declared that the bulk of the assailants were 'strangers' to the district (*Manchester Times*, 29 Jan. 1870: 3).[17]

How should the historian seek to comprehend the seemingly incomprehensible acts of violence witnessed at Thorncliffe on 21 January 1870? Firstly, the events at Thorncliffe tell us in no uncertain terms that labour disputes in the period covered by this book could often be brutal and unforgiving. Secondly, we cannot deny that the attack on 21 January was motivated to some extent by a desire for vengeance against the despised intruders, borne of feelings of betrayal, moral indignation, and a growing frustration at a perceived wrong which continued to fester. To the extent that there was an impulse to punish this wrongdoing and thereby restore a sense of equilibrium in regard to the victims of the offence and the wrongdoers, the attack was retributive. Thirdly, there could also have been a cathartic dimension to the attack. Hence, the forceful expulsion of the blackleg presence enabled a cathartic release of pent-up anger in a community and helped restore some balance to a social order undergoing severe strain and dislocation.

All this being said, beyond the desperation, frustration, growing anger, desire for retribution and cathartic release of emotional tension, there is a further aspect to the events of 21 January that we should also consider. Although the severity of the attack on 21 January appears shocking by the moral standards of the twenty-first century and twenty-first-century trade unionism, it would be a mistake to see this as an exercise in mindless, wanton destruction carried out by an incensed and riotous 'mob' inclined to primitiveness. It needs to be recognised that in certain circumstances the issue of home and home occupancy formed part of the class war of industrial and labour relations in this era. This was particularly so in mining communities when mineworkers and their families could be evicted from the tied cottages they rented from the mine owners as a punishment for 'refractory' behaviour, as in strikes or lock-outs. Evictions where families and furniture were tossed into the unforgiving streets and fields were much in evidence for instance during the 1832 lock-out in the Durham and Northumberland coalfields, such as at Hetton and Friar's Goose collieries in Durham.[18] The deliberate and callous use of eviction by the employers in the 1832 lock-out as a means of cowing the workforce, punishing 'refractory' behaviour, and destroying the mineworkers' union, was clear for all to see. On 14 June, some ten weeks into the dispute and close to its dénouement, the mainstream press reported that 'twenty families of pitmen, who persist in the turn-out, were ejected from their houses at Sheriff-hill colliery, near Gateshead, on Monday week' (*Perthshire Courier*, 14 June 1832: 2). To add insult and further pain to the injury, the colliery owners invoked the Vagrancy Act to prevent the evicted setting up camp in a tent in the open air, and then filled the vacated cottages with blacklegs recently brought in to replace the locked-out pitmen (Hammond 1995: 43, on the Vagrancy Act). This brutal method of gaining leverage in a strike was again much in evidence during the turnout of Durham and Northumberland mineworkers in 1844. The 1844 strike began at the start of April over a range of issues which included low and irregular pay, the yearly bond, and the system of punitive fines. The strike eventually ended in September in defeat for the miners. A few months into the dispute, the mine owners resorted to the tactic of evictions in an effort to cow the miners into submission. Friedrich Engels has left us with a telling account of the brutality of this procedure in his classic study, *The Condition of the Working Class in England*, which he penned in 1844–5:

> Thus the strike had continued well on towards four months, and the mine owners still had no prospect of getting the upper hand. One way was,

however, still open to them. They remembered the cottage system; it occurred to them that the houses of the rebellious spirits were their property. In July, notice to quit was served the workers, and, in a week, the whole forty thousand were put out of doors. This measure was carried out with revolting cruelty. The sick, the feeble, old men and little children, even women in child-birth, were mercilessly dragged from their beds and cast into the roadside ditches.

(Engels 1969: 281)

Consider also the following later account by a writer sympathetic to the plight of the mineworkers in 1844:

Often, when the [union] men were away at public or district meetings, the policemen, with their ruffian auxiliaries, would swoop down upon a village and turn all the defenceless inhabitants to the door, so that when the husbands or fathers returned, they would find their dear ones huddling together amongst their broken furniture, beneath some hedge.

(Fynes 1873: 75)

The issue of home and home occupancy also figured prominently in the class tensions of the Thornberry labour dispute. We have already seen above that the locked-out Thorncliffe mineworkers were required to relinquish possession of the company cottages that they rented from Newton Chambers. The issue of home occupancy became even more conspicuous in the conflict as the months dragged on. For much of this almost year-long conflict, the main sites of struggle for the unionists seeking to contain the blackleg threat had been the principal port of arrival for the new hands at the Chapeltown railway station, along with the routes to and from the collieries worked by the blacklegs. By January 1870, the strategic terrain of this struggle had shifted quite decisively to another location, that is, to the terrain of the home. In early December 1869, a solicitor acting on behalf of Newton Chambers penned an urgent letter to the Home Office requesting that a military force be sent to Thorncliffe to forestall an attack on the dwelling places of the new hands, which he believed was imminent (HO45/8370/8–15. Letter 4 Dec. 1869). The dwellings that the solicitor had in mind were the fifty newly built Thorncliffe cottages which housed the new hands. As so often in the labour struggles of the period covered by this book, the key to victory for either side in the dispute was control over the supply of blackleg labour. The Company's solicitor recognised this, as did his clients, and as did the workers attached to the union. As the solicitor explained it, all sides in the contest recognised that if the blackleg workers could be secured in their new abodes 'without molestation', his clients, Newton Chambers, 'will be able to carry on their collieries without the union men', and the union cause would be lost. Hence, he reasoned, the object of those associated with the union 'is to destroy the houses' and 'terrify the occupants', both as a lesson to the inhabitants and as a marked warning to others who may have had thoughts of obtaining work at Thorncliffe during the lock-out (HO45/8370/8–15. Letter 4 Dec. 1869).

The home as a site of conflict and struggle in a labour dispute featured in a lockout in the south Yorkshire coalfield in the same year as the Thorncliffe dispute, and over the same issue of union recognition. The dispute at Denaby Main colliery, which began in February 1869 and which continued for around six months, saw the arrival of blackleg labour from places such as Staffordshire. As with the Thorncliffe blacklegs, the 'wants' of the new arrivals were well catered for, which included at their place of work 'plenty of meat, bread, and beer', as well as newspapers, periodicals and books 'for those whose tastes are of a literary or inquiring character' (*Leeds Mercury*, 15 Mar. 1869: 3). In addition to these pleasures to be consumed on the colliery premises, as many of the new arrivals as could be accommodated were housed in 'unoccupied' company cottages in Sparrow Barracks about a third of a mile distant from the colliery. This new presence in Sparrow Barracks was not to go unnoticed or unrecorded, however. Evoking the historic association between the colour white and purity, those unionists who remained housed in the Barracks marked out their homes with 'a large white cross painted outside each' to distinguish them from those homes of the non-unionist '"blacks" as they are called' (*Sheffield Independent*, 31 Mar. 1869: 2).

It should be noted as well that the urge for retribution against blacklegs often burned more fiercely following a union defeat in a turnout. Mention has been made earlier in this chapter of the Durham and Northumberland mineworkers' strike of 1844. Blackleg miners who remained working in the pits at the conclusion of the six-month-long strike were made to reflect on this decision as the returning strikers 'in many instances gave way to their revengeful passions to an inordinate extent' (Fynes 1873: 109. See also Douglass 1972). A range of 'mischievous', and sometimes dangerous, 'pranks' were played upon Welsh blacklegs for instance. This included extinguishing the latter's candles as they worked and stealing their clothes, so that they 'had frequently to go home without any clothes after being hard at work all the shift' (Fynes 1873: 109–10). Another 'prank' proved to be more menacing and painful to the blacklegs. This involved a line of rope, arranged to sag a little in the middle, being suspended across the main underground roadway connecting the working areas of the pit with the 'flat', with the aim of catching some part of the blackleg's upper body as he travelled down the roadway on a tub. The journey down the steep incline of the roadway could be very precarious. As the blacklegs hurtled down the road at great speed with their heads above the tub, the rope, 'hanging down across the tramway, caught them in the faces, and often threw them on their backs' (Fynes 1873: 109).

There was another form of retributive violence in evidence during the labour unrest in the decades covered by this book that we have yet to consider. This form of violence tended to be carried out by the more militant 'physical force' elements of the labouring classes who inclined towards direct action, vigilante justice and audacious acts of exemplary punishment. It was a form of violence that was uncompromising and aggressively masculine, and often involved the use of weapons, including fire-arms, which could and did lead to loss of life, not just the lives of strike-breakers but also the lives of striking workers. At times such violence was open and visible, bursting forth when tensions in a labour dispute boiled over and could not be contained, when the class nature of the conflict was laid horribly bare, and when a strike began to assume many of the characteristics of a war. The history of employer-labour relations in Britain in our period is replete with such outbreaks, which were characterised by varying degrees of intensity and could be of long or short duration. Outbreaks of this more extreme form of retributive violence were usually associated with phases of particularly acute economic hardship or depression and tended to be less in evidence once conditions improved. It was a form of violence as well that often surfaced in periods of acute political repression. This was the point when, in the eyes of the labouring classes, the state seemed to show every willingness to exploit the laws of the land to clamp down on all efforts by workers to collectively combine to seek redress, when it was felt that successive governments in thrall to prevailing economic dogma were lining up unambiguously on the side of the masters and capital, and when Parliament repeatedly spurned labour's anguished petitions to secure a measure of emancipation through legislative means. In such circumstances more aggressive tactics often came to the fore, when it was felt by some of the more militant workmen that redress would not arrive via other means, when it became apparent that the labouring classes had nowhere else to turn other than to their own resources and methods. In this latter respect, it needs to be recognised that all movements of whatever political and ideological persuasion contain these more militant sections, whose views and choice of tactics are not necessarily representative of the wider body, nor of the movement's leadership. In this regard, this form of extreme retributive violence is as far removed as one can get from the history of formal mainstream legal trade unionism with its committee rooms, grand assemblies, peaceful lobbying of political representatives, and aspiration towards consensus and collective bargaining. Nevertheless, it needs to be recognised that this more aggressive form of workers' action is as much part of the history of labour in Britain, as well as the history of Britain's trade unions, as those other more moderate forms associated with formal mainstream legal trade unionism.

When it did not burst forth in more open and visible manifestations of violence, or 'tumult' or 'riot' to use the terminology favoured by ruling elites, this particular mode of violence went underground. In this guise it was associated with mobile, fast-moving raiding parties of small groups of men, often in disguise, who traversed byways, fields and rivers as they paid nocturnal visits to the abode of blacklegs and others deemed to be traitors to the workers' cause. Here labour violence assumed a spatial character, as the raiders exploited the power of geographical mobility to contest and establish a measure of control over space, a key determinant in the developing struggle between the forces of capital and labour as 'those who command space can always control the politics of place' (Harvey 1990: 234). As capital and the new ruling elite sought to dominate space 'for its own class purposes', primarily through the development of modern communications and transport systems, the territorial division of labour, and an increasingly fluid labour market which aided capital and broke down traditional barriers to wage speculation, then it was imperative that the labouring classes needed to do the same if they were to avoid economic impoverishment (Harvey 1990: 236).[19] As they passed swiftly and undetected through the spaces and places of the newly industrialising, though still largely rural, landscapes of early nineteenth-century Britain, the raiders seemed to act as the emissaries of a disapproving community, 'avenging angels' bringing vengeance and justice in their wake. In this guise, it was a strike tactic often shrouded in mystery and myth and one replete with oath-bound secrecy, passwords, signs, coded language, 'grotesque' disguises and mysterious and symbolic names like 'Rebecca' and 'Scotch Cattle'. Its contemporary and equally spatialised counterpart, which tended to target the machines and technology of emerging modern capitalism, were the Luddites.

One of the first manifestations of this form of extreme retributive violence in the labour disputes which feature in the period covered by this book, exhibiting both open and more clandestine elements, was the London coal-heavers' strike of 1768. The mostly Irish coal-heavers of Wapping and Shadwell in London's East End who unloaded coal from the Thames barges and hauled it ashore formed part of that class of workers who were the eighteenth-century equivalent of the 'precariat' of our own day. Although their labour helped power the late eighteenth-century London economy, the working life of the coal-heaver was encumbered by casual and uncertain work, seasonal employment, low status, arduous working conditions which sapped health and invited injury, and 'efficiencies' of work which cut unloading times and whittled away at wages. The latter were also vulnerable to enforced appropriations by coal 'undertakers', the middle-man agents who held the contract for the work. These appropriations included, as Peter Linebaugh tells us, deductions from wages of '6d. to 9d. a day for drink, 1s. to 18d. for 'Commission money', 1d. for the undertakers' drawer, 1d. for his maid and 2d. rent on the shovel per chaldron unloaded', amongst other penalties (Linebaugh 2003: 306). Voluminous pints of liquid and ale were required to compensate for lost fluid and render disagreeable work more palatable, which the coal-heavers were forced to consume at dockside taverns owned by the undertakers.

Matters came to a head in 1768 in a climate of growing industrial and political unrest in the Metropolis, fuelled by soaring food prices which saw the price of bread double and the price of meat increase by a third. To offset the rise in the price of food, and following unsuccessful attempts to lobby the coal masters by peaceful means which began in February, the coal-heavers turned out for an increase in payment per load and a better regularisation of working practices, alongside other London workers also seeking a fairer remuneration for their labour in light of the rise in provisions (Bloom 2010: 152–3). These other workers included shoemakers, tailors, coopers, lightermen, and sailors. Benjamin Franklin has left us with a vivid description of London in the late Spring of 1768 at the highpoint of the strike wave. His account highlights a political and economic structure in crisis, when class antagonisms had been laid bare and could not be contained, when industrial unrest fused with wider political tensions, and when industrial violence burst forth into something close to open rebellion against the masters, property and capital:

> Even this Capital, the Residence of the King is now a daily scene of lawless Riot and confusion. Mobs are patrolling the streets at Noon Day, some knocking all down that will not roar for Wilkes and Liberty: Courts of Justice afraid to give judgement against him; Coalheavers and Porters pulling down the Houses of Coal Merchants that refuse to give them more wages; Sawyers destroying the new Sawmills; Sailors unrigging all the outward-bound ships, and suffering none to sail till Merchants agree to raise their pay; Watermen destroying private Boats and threatning [sic] Bridges; Weavers entering Houses by force, and destroying the work in the Looms; Soldiers firing into the Mobs and killing men, women and children, which seems only to have produced an universal sullenness, that looks like a great black Cloud coming on, ready to burst in a general Tempest.
> (Benjamin Franklin to Joseph Ross. 14 May 1768. Reprinted from Sparks 1838: 401–2)

The 'river strike' that followed which commenced in earnest in April, and which effectively shut the Port of London, was brutal and bloody with deaths recorded on both sides. Unwilling to concede to the coal-heavers' terms, the undertakers and their supporters in the London authorities drafted in blackleg labour which was afforded rest and security in the taverns of Shadwell and Wapping run by the undertakers. The Irish coal-heavers did not approve. A contemporary witness tells of indignant Irish coal-heavers with drawn cutlasses in their hands parading the streets of Wapping and visiting public houses kept by local coal undertakers instrumental in recruiting the 'unregistered' blackleg labour. At one such public house, the 'Sheep and Shears', they broke several windows, pulled the frames out of the house, 'and let all his liquors out, and destroyed the goods in the house' (Trial of Thomas Gilberthorp and John Green for Murder. 18 May 1768. *Old Bailey Proceedings Online*: 5). Coal-heavers were also said to be 'mobbing in the street' in the words of another witness, as well as calling out 'Wilkes and coal-heavers for ever' and 'shaking their cutlasses together and striking them against the wall' (Trial of Thomas Gilberthorp and John Green for Murder. 18 May 1768. *Old Bailey Proceedings Online*: 4). The chief culprit in the eyes of the coal-heavers was John Green, the keeper of the Roundabout Tavern in New Gravel lane. In the words of Green, the coal-heavers told him in no uncertain terms that they 'would do for me if I did not desist in my proceedings, that was to register such people as applied' for the 'vacant' work (Trial of John Grainger, Daniel Clark, otherwise Clarey; Richard Cornwall, Patrick Lynch, Thomas Murray, Peter Flaharty, Nicholas M'Cabe, for Breaking Peace. 6 July 1768. *Old Bailey Proceedings Online*: 4). The bloody confrontation which ensued between the coal-heavers and Green at the Roundabout Tavern on 20 April has been well documented in the historiography, so there is no need to dwell on it here (Linebaugh 2003: 314). Suffice to say that as so often was the case in the bloody labour disputes of this era, the violence was not one-sided. On 20 April, Green, in his euphemistic words, poured a 'warm fire' amounting to 108 rounds upon his assailants, resulting in at least two deaths and an unspecified number of individuals wounded.

Despite the audacious visibility of their retributive violence, there was also a clandestine dimension to the actions of the Irish coal-heavers of Wapping and Shadwell. Contemporary accounts saw interconnections between the coal-heavers and the late eighteenth-century underground Irish peasant movement, the Whiteboys. In June 1768, *The London Magazine* reported that:

> Great disorders were committed by the coalheavers (mostly Irish White Boys) [sic] on occasion of the sailors taking upon them to perform the work they had refused, killing and maiming the latter, with whom they had several desperate battles.
>
> *(The London Magazine (1768) 37: 326)*

A number of authoritative accounts in the historiography have also flagged up these interconnections (see, for instance, Featherstone 2011: 73–8; and Linebaugh 2003: 318–21). The Whiteboy movement was active in Ireland at various phases between 1761 and 1785. The Whiteboys sought redress of grievances relating to expropriation of Irish lands, enclosure of common land, displacement of the rural poor from the land, rack-renting, evictions, tithe collection, and exorbitant priest dues (see Donnelly Jnr. 1978). The interconnections between the Whiteboys and the struggles of the coal-heavers in London are said to be political, associational, tactical, and spatial. In regard to these interconnections, David Featherstone has argued that there existed 'important commonalities and exchanges between subaltern politics in Ireland and England in the eighteenth century'. These interconnections were fuelled by a shared sense of grievance against increasing levels of societal inequality and new methods of economic organisation and a shared attachment to notions of customary rights or 'moral economy' (Featherstone 2002: 54). Spatially, Featherstone has flagged up the relation of the Whiteboy movement to wider transnational Atlantic routes of radical ideas, forms of association and political tactics, routes which would have found their way to London during the 1768 coal-heavers' strike. Though not the sole influences of course, the material growth in transnational commercial and trade networks, along with migratory trends which drew Irish labour into the harvest fields, workshops, ports, mines and factories of England, Wales and Scotland, both seasonal and long term, would help forge these relational interconnections.

Most interesting though, from the perspective of this book, are the other influences travelling along the transnational highway. This is the suggestion that a levelling instinct, a deep distrust of official authority, and an insurrectionary mood may have been exported via the transnational highway, linking the struggles of the displaced and aggrieved Irish with those of their dispossessed and equally aggrieved social-class 'brethren' in England, Wales and Scotland. These networks which linked spaces and places could include as well the quite distinctive forms of association and tactics known to some elements of migrant Irish labour with connections to the Whiteboy movement. These would include, in terms of the former, the culture of myth, mystery and secrecy which clandestine underground groups like the Whiteboys sought to encourage, as in the use of disguise when carrying out raids. In terms of tactics, this would include the use of vigilante justice to punish 'traitors' and the tactical deployment of a variety of methods of forceful persuasion to ensure loyalty in conflict situations. One has to be careful not to over-emphasise this interconnectedness of course, though the record does show that Irish workers were often inclined towards levelling and insurrectionary behaviour which may have some connection to these transnational 'geographies of resistance'. Irish migrant workers have been much maligned as blacklegs who pressed down on wages and undermined strike action.[20] The true picture of Irish labour is much more nuanced, however, in that Irish workers were often in the forefront of labour struggles in the decades covered by this book. Many Irish workers were staunch trade unionists and formidable adversaries in the struggle against the masters for better pay and working conditions. Irish workers often brought to a dispute a capacity for organisation, group cohesion and solidarity. This was certainly evident during the 1768 coal-heavers' strike. The coal-heavers, stated a press report in late April, 'most of them Irish, have formed themselves into several parties, go armed with cutlasses and pistols, and by means of cat-calls, in a short time, assemble a vast number together' (*St James's Chronicle*, 26–28 Apr. 1768: 1).

Shifting location and moving forward in time, we find the same characteristics present in a strike of cotton weavers in Lancashire in 1808. Against the backdrop of the contraction in trade and commerce occasioned by the Napoleonic Wars, a resulting rise in the price of provisions, and the rejection of a Bill in Parliament to establish a minimum wage for the distressed weavers, the Lancashire cotton weavers struck work in May and June of 1808. The weavers sought an advance in wages of 6s. 8d. in the pound, effectively, that is, an advance of thirty-three and one-third per cent. Official reports coming out of the cotton districts indicate that Irish weavers were key players in the attempts to prosecute the strike. In so doing, Irish weavers showed a high degree of organisation, guile, and a willingness to use forceful persuasion to discourage acts of strike-breaking. One local magistrate complained to the Home Secretary, Lord Hawkesbury, in early June that weavers seeking to return to their looms were being prevented from doing so 'by small menacing parties', most of which were composed of 'the lowest description of Irishmen, who are so well organised as to be able to elude the vigilance of the Peace Officers' (J. Silvester to Lord Hawkesbury. 2 June 1808. Document in Aspinall 1949: 98). Another report coming out of the 'disturbed' Manchester cotton districts two days later complained that:

> We have a great number of Irish weavers, who are the foremost and most turbulent in all the proceedings. A considerable fund has been, as I hear, for

some time collecting, and is now distributing, but in the whole of their proceedings, there is such secrecy and arrangement, that we find the utmost difficulty in detecting or gaining any information to found proceedings upon.
(R.A. Farington to Lord Hawkesbury. 4 June 1808. Document in Aspinall 1949: 99)

Irish weavers in the Manchester cotton districts remained 'truculent' as the strike moved into the later weeks of June. The Home Secretary was informed that during one incident in mid-June, a 'few refractory weavers, principally Irish, molested the people then at their looms, and gave hindrance in one of the districts of the town to several weavers bringing in and returning with work' (R.A. Farington to Lord Hawkesbury. 27 June 1808. Document in Aspinall 1949: 121).

The levelling and insurrectionary tendencies of Irish weavers continued to disturb the peace of mind of the property-owning classes of Lancashire beyond the strike of 1808. A report in February 1812 emanating from a Stockport magistrate's office informed the Home Secretary, Richard Ryder, that 'the weavers have latterly evinced a very restless and refractory spirit... I fear the bad spirit is kept up by some few desperate characters from Ireland that have got among the weavers here' (J. Lloyd to Richard Ryder. 26 Feb. 1812. Document in Aspinall 1949: 121). As these few examples involving Lancashire weavers show, as well as demonstrating skills in organisation and group solidarity, Irish workers were not averse to using forceful methods of persuasion to try to bring people into line in a dispute. The same characteristics were also much in evidence during the 1768 London coal-heavers' strike, as we saw above. Similar characteristics can be observed in a much later struggle of the London Irish for better pay in the London dock-strike of August 1853. Seeking an increase in pay from 2s. 6d. to 3s. per day and 6d. an hour for overtime, the dock-labourers, many of whom were Irish, 'downed tools'. As in the above disputes, Irish workers were a formidable presence in a strike situation. As one dock-labourer involved in the strike recounted, those amongst the workforce disinclined to join the turnout faced the daunting prospect of an unwelcome visit from a body of Irish labourers who 'half-murdered anyone who would not join in the dispute' (*Bucks Herald*, 20 Aug. 1853: 2).

Negative anti-Irish stereotypes circulating within the wider Victorian culture were often rolled out to try to make sense of these more forceful methods of persuasion. For the Victorian moralist and advocate of the philosophy of self-help, Samuel Smiles, writing in 1862, the 'impulse and passion' too often witnessed in strikes in Britain was due to the strong Irish presence in these turnouts, particularly amongst the leadership. Smiles thought that this 'impulse and passion' mirrored the Irishman's 'nature', and that excessive violence witnessed in some strikes, as in Glasgow in the 1830s, was likely due to the 'greater infusion of the Irish element in the operative population there' (Smiles 1862: 127).

These forms of organisation, modes of action and strike tactics, with their strong emphasis on the more extreme mode of retributive violence, were not exclusive to Irish workers of course. The historical record shows such forms in evidence at various industrial locations in the United Kingdom and at various times in the decades covered by this book. A few examples should suffice to demonstrate this. In 1802 in the counties of Wiltshire and Somerset, matters relating to the introduction of de-skilling machinery had come to a head, threatening the craft status, customary practices, incomes and even the employment of the shearmen (see Randall 1982). The journeymen shearmen or cloth dressers of the west of England who, with great dexterity and strength, hand-finished a cloth after it had been fulled, faced an existential threat to their livelihoods from the gig mill and the shearing frame, both of which in their different ways acted to dramatically reduce the time and amount of labour required to manufacture the cloth.

Some of the industrial violence in 1802, which came with the attempts at collective action on the part of the shearmen to check the encroachment of the cloth-finishing machinery into their districts, exhibited the pattern previously discussed. Armed and mobile raiding parties of men, their identities concealed behind 'blackened faces', traversed the towns of the County of Wiltshire in particular, visiting mills and other properties associated with the hated machinery, including the homes of errant master clothiers who had introduced the machines. The resulting destruction of machinery and mills by these raiding parties, who often travelled in the dead of night, was accompanied by attacks on the dwelling houses of those amongst the shearmen who refused to join the struggle. The regional press commented that 'hardly a week passes without some fresh outrage committed on the persons and property of those well-disposed shearmen who have continued in the service of the clothiers at Warminster' (*Salisbury and Winchester Journal*, 20 Dec. 1802: 4). Other reports logged the various assaults committed by the refractory shearmen. These included the firing of guns in the dead of night through the windows of the cottages of workmen who remained loyal to their masters (HO42/65/411–412. A List of Outrages Lately Committed in the Clothing Districts in the Neighbourhood of Bath. 29 July 1802). Anxious magistrates representing the towns of Warminster, Trowbridge, Westbury, Bradford, and Melksham told of 'illegal' gatherings of people 'armed with musquits [sic], pistols, swords, bayonets and other offensive weapons', driven to commit outrageous acts by an 'ignorant blindness that the machinery used by them was injurious and detrimental to the poor' (HO42/65/373–374. Letter from John Jones to Lord Pelham. 24 July 1802).

Moving north and forward in time, we can observe similar forms of organisation and strike tactics in a turnout of framework knitters in Nottinghamshire and Derbyshire in March and April 1822. The heroic and eventually doomed resistance of the framework knitters of the counties of the east Midlands to hold back the tide of de-skilling and price-cutting machinery during the late eighteenth century and particularly the early decades of the nineteenth century has been well documented (see, for instance, Henson 1970; Gurnham 1976; Binfield 2004; and Thomis 1972). In mid-March 1822, framework knitters in Nottinghamshire and Derbyshire in the cotton hose branch of the trade turned out for an advance in wages. Contemporary records of the turnout are scanty, though it appears that the turnout framework knitters paraded the various parishes and villages of the said counties in large bodies, 'threatening and intimidating during the day time all persons found at work, and destroying by night their property in serious ways' (HO40/17/151–2. Letter 16 Apr. 1822). Apparently, these nocturnal raids were not spontaneous, random or un-coordinated. London was informed that 'the plan has been to ascertain by delegates what persons were at work during the day, then to return in the night and make a grand attack on their houses with all kinds of missiles' (HO40/17/162–3. Letter 20 Apr. 1822). Though planned, co-ordinated and certainly intimidating, it should be said that no injuries were sustained by the occupants of the dwelling houses, and there is certainly no evidence of fire-arms being used in these attacks.

The same cannot be said for the raiding parties of colliers which periodically made an appearance during strike situations in Britain's coalfields in the early decades of the nineteenth century. Here the forms of organisation and strike tactics conformed to the more general pattern of highly mobile underground raiding parties operating under a cloak of anonymity in the form of disguise and mythical names, and committed to direct action. Direct action included a willingness to use retributive violence in the war against blacklegging, as can be seen from the following example from Scotland. In early 1823, blackleg colliers were drafted in from Ayrshire as part of an effort by the colliery lease-holder to defeat a turnout of colliers striking over conditions of work and pay at the North Green colliery in the village of Gilmerton, a parish in the County of Edinburgh. Soon after their arrival, however, the blacklegs were dragged out of their homes and 'drawn into the fields at midnight, an assault which so completely terrified them that they would remain no longer, but returned to Ayrshire' (*The Scotsman*, 31 Jan. 1824: 7).[21] By early 1824, the acrimonious relations between the Gilmerton colliers and the lease-holder of the colliery had not improved. In January, bands of Gilmerton colliers were observed assembling in the village prior to a raid 'armed with bludgeons, pickshafts, and pistols, and disguised with sheets over their clothes, and handkerchiefs round their heads, which concealed their faces' (*The Scotsman*, 31 Jan. 1824: 7).

Such incidents need to be put in context. As always in disputes involving colliers during these decades, the stakes were exceedingly high. With defeat of their 'combination' in a strike came the inevitable loss of livelihood and home due to enforced evictions.[22] Similar strike tactics were on show in response to the arrival of blackleg labour during a turnout of colliers resisting a wage reduction in Airdrie, North Lanarkshire, in June 1832. In one incident it was reported that 'a numerous band of colliers, with their faces blackened, and armed with pistols and cutlasses, attacked a house at Whitterigg, in which several of the new workmen were lodged, and breaking open the doors and windows began an assault upon the inmates' (*Perthshire Courier*, 14 June 1832: 3). According to the report, the 'new workmen' were also armed, resulting in individuals from both sides of the divide sustaining gunshot wounds.

Further south in the coalfields of north-east England, 'new workmen' brought in to defeat a strike faced the prospect of midnight visitations from bands of striking colliers dressed in women's clothes. Hence, during the turnout of Durham and

Northumberland mineworkers in 1844 discussed earlier in this chapter, striking colliers, said to be 'very violent', with some 'going about in women's clothes', kept a constant night-time vigil on the homes of strike-breakers accompanied by warnings to the inhabitants of impending 'Rebecca visits' should they continue on their present course (HO45/644/3–7. Letter from Rowland Burdon, 8 Apr. 1844). 'Rebecca' was active in Durham even before the 1844 troubles.[23] The previous September, the pro-union *Northern Star* reported that this 'lady of principle' had made an appearance in the Durham coalfields and 'ferretted [sic] out some unprincipled blacklegs to the colliers' society, and wreaked her vengeance on their treacherous heads. It would appear that she was not well acquainted in the locality, for instead of avenging herself on the old known blacklegs, she discovered some new ones, whom she has punished' (*Northern Star*, 9 Sep. 1843: 6).

Moving south and west to the Welsh coalfields, we find the highly mobile raiders of the 'Scotch Cattle', whom we encountered in a previous chapter.[24] Like the militant Rebecca bands just mentioned, the Scotch Cattle favoured the methods of the tactical use of warning messages, direct action, physical force, and exemplary punishment as a means of encouraging compliance in a labour dispute. The Scotch Cattle made their presence known in the coal-mining districts of south Wales at various stages in the late 1820s and 1830s, usually at times of economic recession and hardship in the Welsh valleys. Stern warnings to strike-breakers were often transmitted via sinister proclamations written in red ink to symbolise blood and threatening letters conveyed to the homes of 'traitors'. Other tactics were the blowing of horns, the beating of drums, the discharging of 'hideous yells' and the firing of guns near to blacklegs' places of work. One such proclamation issued by the 'Cattle' sent the following uncompromising message:

> To all Colliers, Traitors, Turncoats and others. We hereby warn you the second and the last time. We are determined to draw the hearts out of all the men above named, and fix two of the hearts on the horns of the Bull, so that everyone may see what is the fate of every traitor – and we know them all. So we testify with our blood.
>
> *(HO52/21/17. Proclamation. 19 Apr. 1832)*

A sketch of a bull's head with two hearts fixed on the horns at the bottom of the proclamation gave strong visual and symbolic reinforcement to the written warning. Should the 'traitors' and 'turncoats' not heed such warnings, retribution would swiftly follow. Accordingly, they faced the prospect of nocturnal visits by a 'Herd' of raiders led by a 'Bull' usually with horns on his head, their faces 'blacked' with coal dirt to help conceal their identities, who proceeded to break their windows and furniture and drag them from their lodgings and 'beat them' (for evidence of such raids, see HO52/19/232–3. Letter 5 Apr. 1832; and HO52/19/216–7. Depositions of Thomas Brown and David Edwards. 7 Mar. 1832).

When the handloom weavers working in Glasgow's cotton manufacturing industry struck work in mid-November 1812 in an attempt to establish a minimum wage to curb the incessant 'speculation on the price of labour' which bedevilled the trade, it was not the Bull, Rebecca, or the ghost of the Whiteboys who threatened violent retribution to blacklegs and other accused traitors, but the 'black cat'. 'Price speculation' in the industry during the years preceding the 1812 strike, that is, wage cutting by another name, was compounded by the trade depression consequent on the French Revolutionary Wars it should be said. Faced with such pressures, the weavers of the region felt that they had no choice but to agitate for an end to 'price speculation' and the establishment of a 'uniformity of price for the same fabrics', or a minimum wage (Richmond 1824: 8). This the weavers attempted to do via peaceful, legal means, which initially met with some success when on 10 November 1812 the Justices of Peace for Lanarkshire decreed the weavers' table of prices 'moderate and reasonable'. In consequence, local magistrates were empowered to fix the rate of wages and arbitrate in circumstances where the actions of the masters regarding prices and wages ran contrary to the 10 November ruling. Unfortunately for the Glasgow weavers, however, matters did not end there. The cotton masters signalled their intention not to comply with the 10 November decision, and the weavers replied by turning out on 18 November. The strike which followed halted the production of around 40,000 looms throughout Scotland extending to Carlisle in the north of England. The turnout was remarkably solid in the main, most weavers being 'conscious of the situation in which they stood' and thus 'determined to make the last stand for their rank in society' (Richmond 1824: 27).

Not all members of the weavers' fraternity, though, grasped the higher moral purpose of the struggle, or the consequences for the weavers and their families of a failure to prevail in the contest. For those weavers of a more self-interested persuasion, it was thought judicious for them to voluntarily give up their revels and beaming machines to the weavers' collective lest they be tempted to take out work at the low rate of wages. For those who through more surreptitious means opted to ignore this advice and take work from the masters at the low prices, retribution sometimes came in the form of a midnight visit to their shop or home by the 'black cat'. Black cat visits usually entailed the smashing of the windows of the shop, and vitriol being thrown on the webs in the looms through the broken window. The attacks were preceded by warnings, which were transmitted by various means. These usually involved small groups of striking weavers visiting the shop of the offending weavers urging them to desist their 'illegal' work if they wished to forestall a visit from the black cat which was going about at night 'to frighten people who were working at the low prices' (NAS. AD14/13/8/5. Declaration of James Lang. 15 Dec. 1812). Warnings were imparted by other means, as when striking weavers were said to be 'going about from shop to shop making a noise like cats' (NAS. AD14/13/8/6. Precognition against James Lang, Patrick Grant, and Thomas McCall. 17 Dec. 1812).

There is no agreed consensus as to the symbolism and meaning of the Glasgow weavers' black cat. For some, the black cat 'signified breaking windows or injuring webs in looms' (NAS. AD14/13/8/5. Declaration of James Younger. 19 Dec.

1812). For others, the black cat signified vitriol (*Dublin Evening Post*, 2 July 1829: 3). At other times though, a link was made between cats and ridding an environment of 'vermin' and 'rats', the latter of course being one of those disagreeable epithets that collectively inclined workers assigned to strike-breakers in our period (NAS. AD14/13/8/8. Declaration of Duncan Bennet. 22 Dec. 1812; and NAS. AD14/13/8/5. Declaration of James Younger. 19 Dec. 1812).[25] This being said, and these incidents apart, given its scale, duration and the high stakes involved, the turnout, which lasted for nine weeks, was conducted in a remarkably peaceful fashion. Despite the general resolve of the strikers, the 1812–13 turnout ended in defeat for the weavers and effectively shattered the power of the handloom weavers' combinations in Scotland.

The historical record contains many other instances of the type of extreme labour violence addressed in this chapter, too many to mention here. It would not be appropriate, however, if no mention is made of the violence in the Manchester brickmaking trade and the light metal trades in Sheffield during the 1860s and 1850s. This violence took a particularly extreme form, which included the blowing up of a workman's home with gunpowder and the murder of two individuals in separate incidents. The publicity given to the 'Outrages' in Manchester and Sheffield in the mainstream press and beyond proved highly embarrassing for trade unionism, leading, as is well known, to the appointment of a Royal Commission of Inquiry into trade unions in February 1867. The following few examples from one of the eleven Royal Commission reports that were eventually published relating to the Manchester area alone show the extent of the violence and its links to local unionism.[26] The Stockport Brickmakers' Society and the Ashton-Under-Lyne Operative Brickmakers' Union were said to be involved in numerous 'Outrages' in the Manchester area during the 1860s. These 'Outrages' saw pistols being fired, work sheds set ablaze, needles and small nails being thrown into clay, and bottles containing gunpowder being thrown into the homes of masters who employed non-union labour (*Report Presented to the Trades Unions Commissioners. Manchester and its Neighbourhoods. Volume 1. Royal Commission of Inquiry into Trade Unions.* 28 Feb. 1868: viii–xvi).

The following incident is said to have involved Stockport unionists. On 17 June 1863, a gun was discharged through the window of a brickyard of a master brick-maker at Stockport Moor, the latter having employed a non-union brick-burner. The previous month, on 8 May, tools, barrows and trestles belonging to the same master brick-maker were cut to pieces, along with the destruction of 25,000 bricks caused by men trampling on them (*Report Presented to the Trades Unions Commissioners. Manchester and its Neighbourhoods. Volume 1. Royal Commission of Inquiry into Trade Unions.* 28 Feb. 1868: ix). The Manchester Brickmakers' Union was implicated in the following incidents in early 1862 relating to the business of William Alfred Atkins, a brick-maker in Cheetwood Lane, Manchester. Apparently, Atkins had incurred the ire of the union because he employed non-union labour and made bricks with machinery. Retribution came in a number of forms, which included physical attacks on the non-union workmen, the roof of the engine house on

Atkins's work premises being blown off by gunpowder, and Atkins himself being sent a letter containing a sketch of a coffin with the message that he should prepare for death (*Report Presented to the Trades Unions Commissioners. Manchester and its Neighbourhoods. Volume 1. Royal Commission of Inquiry into Trade Unions*. 28 Feb. 1868: xvii–xviii).

With the ugly violence of the Manchester and Sheffield 'Outrages', and the widespread negative publicity that came the way of the trade unions because of it, it seemed that labour relations in Britain had reached a new low. Certainly, it could be argued that the 'Outrages' represented the nadir of British trade unionism, particularly given the uncomfortable association of some local trades and unions with the violence. In other respects, however, the violence in Manchester and Sheffield, and the Royal Commission of Inquiry into trade unions which came in its wake, marked a watershed in both trade union history and the history of labour violence in the modern period up to that point. Remarkably, given the state of labour relations for the best part of the previous century, with its tendency towards mistrust, confrontation, violence and exclusionary legislation in regard to labour, the decades which followed the 1860s would see trade unions become a recognised and legitimate participant in the nation's economic and political affairs. This transformation in labour's fortunes will form part of the discussion in the following Conclusion to this book.

Notes

1 The individual who penned the letter made the comment in the context of discussing the 'spirit of combination' growing amongst the workers in north-west England.
2 James Crompton was also physically assaulted during the attack.
3 This is not to deny the presence of a retributive component within some of the other types of punishment rituals we have looked at in this book up to now, such as ducking an offending workmen in a canal for instance. Nevertheless, the retributive violence which concerns us in this chapter is more unequivocal.
4 For a similar position in the context of an industrial dispute in Britain, see King (1985).
5 This exceedingly fractious dispute raged until the end of January 1827 when the strikers were 'starved into submission'. See Kirby and Musson 1975: 43.
6 This is not say that blacklegs were not at risk of physical attack during this early phase of the dispute. Indeed, a blackleg was said to have been physically assaulted in one of the incidents of violence which occurred in early October. See HO40/21/352–6. Letter 21 Dec. 1826.
7 The study of Sharman Grant II and Wallace looked at a range of strikes in Ontario, Canada, from 1958 to 1967. See also Snyder and Kelly 1976.
8 See chapter 2.
9 The spinners of Hyde refused to turn out, it should be said.
10 These included assaults on mills employing blacklegs or 'knobsticks', shots fired into the home of a master spinner, and the murder of the son of a Hyde manufacturer.
11 The affray took place in St. Clement's church-yard.
12 Bentley left behind a wife and two young children.
13 Picking-sticks or picking-pegs were pieces of wood about three-quarters of a yard in length.
14 The strike ended in defeat for the spinners in early September. There then followed the usual bout of punitive punishments meted out to the 'refractory' workforce by the

masters, which included dismantling the spinners' combination and 'blacklisting' around 100 of the most militant of the turnout spinners.
15 Bridlington was some sixteen miles' distant from Scarborough.
16 It seems that the Bridlington blacklegs were beyond shame, however, as they attempted to return to Scarborough at a later date. On this later occasion they returned in a somewhat undignified manner, concealed in 'a covered cart'. This elaborate exercise in deception came to nought though, for the Bridlington men decided to return home when they were informed that they would have to sail to the highly unionised port of Shields, where they were convinced that their arrival would not elicit a warm welcome. For details, see HO40/18/150–1. Letter 9 Mar. 1825.
17 The shock of the attack had a tragic consequence in that it was said to have hastened the death of the wife of one of the occupants of Westwood Row, a woman named Sarah Hughes who was already severely ill with consumption.
18 See chapter 2 for details of the 1832 lock-out.
19 On 'blackleg economics', see chapter 1.
20 On blackleg labour from Ireland, see chapter 2.
21 Additional records relating to the 1823–4 Gilmerton unrest can be found at the National Archives of Scotland. Reference AD/14/24/259.
22 The will of the coal-master eventually prevailed in the conflict. Sixty Gilmerton colliers and their families were eventually evicted from their homes following the defeat.
23 The activities of 'Rebecca' in rural protests in Wales is well known of course. Bands of men disguised in women's clothing calling themselves the daughters of Rebecca were active in rural protest movements in south-west Wales during the late 1830s and early 1840s. Sometimes the 'women's clothing' would merely be composed of a bed-gown, sheet or the raider's own coat turned inside out. The heads of the Rebeccaites would also be adorned with women's large hats to which bunches of fern and heather were attached. The faces of the Rebeccaites were often 'blackened', too, while in their hands they usually carried cow horns and an intimidating array of weaponry which could include guns, pick axes or sledge-hammers. In short, the 'more grotesque' the image constructed, 'the more complete the disguise'. See *The Illustrated London News*, 11 Nov. 1843: 309. See also Rees 2011.
24 See chapter 4.
25 See chapter 2 on the 'rat' epithet.
26 In Sheffield, the Saw Grinders' Union was heavily implicated in the violence. Other unions were also said to have played some role in the violence in Sheffield. These were the Jobbing Grinders' Union; the Saw Makers' Union; the Saw Handle Makers' Union; the Sickle Grinders' Union; the Fork Grinders' Union; the Fender Grinders' Union; the Pen and Pocket Blade Grinders' Union; the Scissor Forgers' Union; the Scissor Grinders' Union; and the Nail Makers' Union. See *Report Presented to the Trades Unions Commissioners. Sheffield. Volume 1. Royal Commission of Inquiry into Trade Unions.* 1867.

References

Aspinall, Algernon (1949) *The Early English Trade Unions. Documents from the Home Office Papers in the Public Record Office*. London: Batchworth.
Bastion, Brock, Denson, Thomas and Haslam, Nick (2013) 'The Roles of Dehumanisation and Moral Outrage in Retributive Justice', *Plos One*, 8(4): 1–10.
Binfield, Kevin (ed) (2004) *The Writings of the Luddites*. Baltimore: John Hopkins University Press.
Bloom, Clive (2010) *Violent London. 2000 Years of Riots, Rebels and Revolts*. London: Palgrave Macmillan.
Buechler, Steven (1993) 'Beyond Resource Mobilization? Emerging Trends in Social Movement Theory', *The Sociological Quarterly*, 34(2): 217–235.

Davis, Natalie Zemon (1973) 'The Rites of Violence: Religious Riot in Sixteenth-Century France', *Past & Present*, 59: 51–91.
DonnellyJnr., James (1978) 'The Whiteboy Movement, 1761–1765', *Irish Historical Studies*, 21(81): 20–54.
Douglass, David (1972) *Pit Life in County Durham. Rank and File Movements and Workers' Control*. Oxford: History Workshop.
Engels, Friedrich (1969; first published 1845) *The Condition of the Working Class in England*. London: Granada.
Featherstone, David (2011) *Resistance, Space and Political Identities. The Making of Counter-Global Networks*. Oxford: John Wiley.
Featherstone, David (2002) *Spatiality, Political Identities and Environmentalism of the Poor*. PhD Thesis: Open University.
Fynes, Richard (1873) *The Miners of Northumberland and Durham*. Blyth: John Robinson.
Gurnham, Richard (1976) *200 Years. The Hosiery Unions 1776–1976*. Leicester: National Union of Hosiery and Knitwear Workers.
Hammond, J.L. and Hammond, Barbara (1995; first published 1919) *The Skilled Labourer 1760–1832*. Stroud: Allan Sutton.
Harvey, David (1990) *The Condition of Postmodernity. An Enquiry into the Origins of Cultural Change*. Oxford: Blackwell.
Henson, Gravenor (1970; first published 1831) *Henson's History of the Framework Knitters*. Newton Abbot: David & Charles.
Jevons, William A. (1860) 'An Account of the Spinners' Strike in Ashton-under-Lyne in 1830', in Report of the Committee on Trades' Societies Appointed by the National Association for the Promotion of Social Science, *Trades' Societies and Strikes*. London: John W. Parker & Son: 473–478.
King, John (1985) '"We could eat the police!": Popular Violence in the North Lancashire cotton strike of 1878', *Victorian Studies*, 28(3): 439–471.
Kirby, Raymond and Musson, Albert (1975) *The Voice of the People. John Doherty, 1798–1854. Trade Unionist, Radical and Factory Reformer*. Manchester: Manchester University Press.
Linebaugh, Peter (2003) *The London Hanged. Crime and Civil Society in the Eighteenth Century*. London: Verso.
Navickas, Katrina (2011) 'Luddism, Incendiarism and the Defence of Rural "Task-scapes" in 1812', *Northern History*, 48(1): 59–73.
Randall, Adrian (1982) 'The Shearmen and the Wiltshire Outrages of 1802: Trade Unionism and Industrial Violence', *Social History*, 7(3): 283–304.
Rees, Lowri Ann (2011) 'Paternalism and Rural Protest: The Rebecca Riots and the Landed Interest of South-West Wales', *The Agricultural History Review*, 59(1): 36–60.
Richmond, Alexander B. (1824) *Narrative of the Condition of the Manufacturing Population and the Proceedings which led to the State Trials in Scotland*. London: John Miller.
Sherman Grant, IIDon and Wallace, Michael (1991) 'Why Do Strikes Turn Violent?', *American Journal of Sociology*, 96(5): 1117–1150.
Smiles, Samuel (1862) *Workmen's Earnings, Strikes, and Savings*. London: John Murray.
Snyder, David and Kelly, William R. (1976) 'Industrial Violence in Italy, 1878–1903', *American Journal of Sociology*, 82(1): 131–162.
Sparks, Jared (ed) (1838) *The Works of Benjamin Franklin. Vol. II*. Boston: Hilliard, Gray, & Co.
Thomis, Malcolm (1972) *Luddism in Nottinghamshire*. London: Phillimore.
Whitehead, Neil (2009) 'Introduction: Humanistic Approaches to Violence', *Anthropology and Humanism*, 34(1): 1–10.
Wood, Amy Louise (2012) '"Killing the Beast": Murderous Beasts and the Thrill of Retribution', *The Journal of the Gilded Age and Progressive Era*, 11(3): 405–444.

CONCLUSION

> But when men of character, and good workmen, were proscribed and driven to desperation, and when men of bad character were employed in their places, could the Association be blamed for retaliation?
>
> *(Mr McNish, member of the Glasgow Cotton Spinners' Operative Association and delegate of the Glasgow Trades' Committee;* Morning Advertiser, *2 Feb. 1838: 3)*

By 1871, the point at which this book concludes, labour and the trade unions had begun the process of formally entering the mainstream of Britain's economic and political life. That year, 1871, saw the passing of the Trade Union Act by Gladstone's Liberal government. The Act effectively decriminalised trade unions by recognising that their purposes should not be deemed to be unlawful merely because they 'are in restraint of trade'. The 1871 Trade Union Act also accorded unions a degree of legal status through such measures as granting them the protection of the courts, allowing them to protect their funds and property by registering as Friendly Societies, and giving formal recognition to the term 'trade union'. Although the Criminal Law Amendment Act passed on the same day introduced some checks on labour by in effect outlawing picketing, labour's entry into the mainstream continued to gather pace as the 1870s unfolded.

Sensitive to the power and even the needs of labour, Disraeli's Conservatives, on replacing the Liberals in government, passed two Acts in 1875, the Conspiracy and Protection of Property Act and the Employers and Workmen Act. Both Acts further cemented the place of trade unions in the economic and political life of the nation. The former repealed the contentious Criminal Law Amendment Act of 1871, including its punitive clauses on peaceful picketing, the even more contentious Master and Servant Act of 1867, 'and all other laws that made breach of contract criminal' (Orth 1991: 143). Clearly, the status quo in labour relations prior to this point was far from satisfactory. For instance, nineteenth-century master and servant law was patently unjust. For breaching a contract of service with the employer, a worker was deemed liable to be proceeded against before a court of law and faced the prospect of three months' imprisonment with hard labour. For its part, by casting the relationship between capital and labour in terms of employers and workmen rather than the more demeaning 'master' and 'servant', the Employers and Workmen Act went some way to putting both parties on a more equal legal footing in regard to labour law (Orth 1991: 144). Through later decades to 1914, give or take the occasional set-back, legislation continued to be favourable to labour. To name but a few of the most important pieces of this legislation, the 1897 Workmen's Compensation Act provided the worker with the right of recovery for personal injury sustained at work; the 1906 Trades Disputes Act declared that trade unions could not be made liable for damages arising from strike actions, effectively overturning the 1901 Taff Vale judgement; and the 1913 Trade Union Act allowed for political spending. In addition, by this time, the principle of wage levels being established by bargaining and negotiation between parties broadly equal in law, that is, by contract, had become firmly embedded in the relations between employer and worker.

Given the marked improvements in the circumstances of labour relative to the law and the nation's economic and political life which took place during 1871 and the years that followed, how then should we assess the preceding decades of labour relations covered by this book, which were so marked by acrimony and conflict between fellow workers? The first point to make is that given the way that the nature of employer-worker relations was prescribed during the decades which preceded the 1870s, whether by the formal law or by the laws of liberal political economy, it is almost beyond the bounds of possibility to expect that labour relations would have been free of acrimony and conflict during these years, including incidents of violent clashes between unionised and uncooperative workers. For much of this earlier period, the worker was not free to combine, strike, raise funds, engage in picketing, peacefully persuade the hesitant or reluctant to help improve the lot of labour, nor vote for a political representative to raise labour's concerns in Parliament, let alone negotiate with the master as an equal to establish fair rates of pay and hours and conditions of work. Reasonable readjustments in the relations and terms between the employer and worker which addressed these iniquities would need to await the more enlightened decades after 1871, with their inclination towards arbitration procedures, conciliation agreements, collective bargaining and industrial cooperation and negotiation rather than strife.[1] Indeed, Joint Boards of Conciliation and Arbitration where employers negotiated with trade unions on equal terms would become commonplace after 1871, an arrangement that would have been inconceivable in earlier decades of the nineteenth century when *laissez-faire* thinking was predominant (Webb and Webb 1920: 337–8).[2]

Lacking, too, during the bleak decades for labour before 1871 was a legal system which worked to help resolve the tensions and disagreements between unionised and uncooperative workmen in a fair and balanced manner which was sensitive to the concerns and grievances of the former. If anything, to the labouring classes, the legislature seemed to be giving free rein to the new unregulated and impersonal market-driven economics of liberal political economy, which was ever-pressing down on wages and degrading their conditions of life. To the workers' mind, the master and his supporters in the legislature seemed embarked on a quest to subject labour to the will of capital unrestrained, render labour subservient to the stern and uncompromising logic of political economy. So, too, with the forces of law and order, whereby the unionised workman 'was regarded by the constable and the magistrate as something between a criminal vagrant and a revolutionist' (Webb and Webb 1920: 325).

In this quest to render labour compliant to capital, the various types of uncooperative workman loomed large, but particularly the blackleg. A person not of the community, the blackleg was seen as the callous and unprincipled 'stranger' from afar who threatened to infect the trade and community with the contagious blight of low wages, non-unionisation, de-skilling, loss of status and independence, and new more alienating ways of working. At a related though broader level, the blackleg was viewed as the advance guard of threatening economic change, a person who carried the destabilising influences of liberal political economy into the trade and community. As a stalking horse for the new philosophy, the blackleg seemed to represent and embody its worst elements, not least the ethos of self-interested individualism which eroded the cherished union principles of brotherhood and mutual support in the affairs of work and life. Not surprisingly then, unionised workers saw the blackleg stranger as crucial to employer strategies and counter-strategies during a turnout. He was despised in his role as the master's ultimate weapon in a contest with the unionised workers, a bludgeon used to enforce a wage reduction, defeat a strike, teach the workforce a lesson, and dismantle the union if necessary. In some instances in the wake of a calamitous defeat for the workers, the blackleg helped the victorious master drive the most 'refractory' of the strikers from their jobs, trade, homes and communities, along with their families. In short, for unionised workers the blackleg represented the structural violence of liberal political economy made manifest.

In another, though related, respect, the blackleg signified the unwillingness of the master and capital to formally negotiate with labour. Or, to put it another way, the blackleg represented capital negotiating with labour by other means. All too frequently during these long decades the recourse to the 'new hand' was the master's preferred mode of resolving disagreements with his workforce. Looked at from the other direction, the recourse to acts of coercion and even violence against non-compliant workmen signified labour negotiating with capital by other means. In other words, these abrasive methods represented the informal regulation of the price of labour by the labouring classes in the absence of formal legally sanctioned institutional frameworks within the mainstream system to enable reasonable negotiation on these matters to take place. In a similar vein, these abrasive and sometimes punitive methods represented the informal application of a system of popular justice in the absence of formal judicial process and a fair and equitable legal system.

This book has attempted to move beyond the comfort zone of many of the standard histories of British trade unionism. In so doing, it has sought to address the imbalance in these standard histories by refusing to view the coercion against non-compliant workmen, which included acts of physical violence, as something separate to the 'true' history of trade unionism. However unsettling, it is important that this matter is not treated as a sub-text in the history of the struggle of collectively inclined working people to build trade unions. There has been a tendency in some of the earlier classic heroic 'forward march of labour' histories in particular to render the awkward issue of interpersonal violence within labour relations marginal or even invisible, confine it to the 'back pages' of trade union history, or characterise it as a rather embarrassing phenomenon unrelated to 'real' trade unionism. This tendency to avoid awkward, delicate, offensive or embarrassing topics is certainly not confined to trade union history.[3] Nevertheless, some strands of labour history have been content to side-step the issue, and instead gravitate around more comforting narratives and more reassuring and less controversial factors to explain the story of labour's advance and eventual entry into the mainstream of the nation's economic and political life.[4] These include the labour movement's painstaking efforts to build more efficient, rational and 'modern' forms of organisation; the charisma, courage and intelligence of inspirational leaders; martyrological traditions of heroic sacrifice; the proliferation of provincial trade councils from the 1850s onwards; the holding of grand conventions to craft enlightened policy; the shift from local to national societies; the building of so-called 'New Model' unions inclined towards arbitration and 'respectability'; and righteous struggles to lobby a grudging state and Parliament to recognise labour's legitimate right to have a proper stake in the nation's economic and political affairs.[5]

It follows from the above observations, and a point made many times in this book, that given the circumstances of the times, and particularly the absence of formal mechanisms which would have provided opportunities for all sides to engage in meaningful negotiation to resolve differences, we should not view the coercive methods used against non-compliant workmen, even when this took a violent form, as indicators of irrationality or primitive backwardness on the part of those who engaged in such actions. Such methods were not traits of an earlier time that were destined to disappear as the historical process moved through its various stages in the direction of modernisation, reason and peaceful progress. This arrival at the point where arbitration and collective bargaining moved into the mainstream, and aggression and violence against uncooperative workmen was no longer to the fore, was not pre-determined or inevitable. This changed state of affairs did not emerge as if via a process of natural necessity brought on by the force and pressures of a particular set of historical circumstances which logically favoured the advance of modernisation and responsible legal trade unionism. These circumstances, it was assumed, driven by the imperatives and iron laws of the modernisation and civilisation process and pressures emanating from the economic base, brought forth an inevitable consequence. This was the transition to more mature forms of political behaviour and thus the next 'stage' of trade union consciousness more in keeping with the modern circumstances of regulating wages and working conditions via the rational procedures of collective bargaining, consensus and arbitration agreements. In such circumstances, it is assumed, the abrasive methods and ugly violence of the early period of labour history, logically out of step with the new times, simply and 'naturally' faded away.

Rather, these coercive methods and violence 'faded away' once all sides, but particularly the more enlightened members of the employing and governing classes, realised that the status quo in labour relations before 1871 was no longer tenable. That is, when it became glaringly apparent that confrontation, restrictive laws, legal persecution, exclusionary politics and punitive punishments were becoming counter-productive and that the labouring classes were deserving of a 'seat at the table' in matters pertaining to the regulation of the conditions which concerned them, such as work and wages. It is with some irony that one should reflect on the fact that it was the extreme trade union-implicated violence witnessed in the light metal trades in Sheffield and in the Manchester brickmaking trade during the 1860s, which included cans of gunpowder being thrust down the chimneys of the homes of 'knobstick' saw grinders or put in the troughs of their grinding wheels, which marked an important moment in bringing all sides to an awareness that a new way had to be forged in labour relations beyond confrontation and violence and that this should be reflected in changes to the law (on the violence in Manchester, see *Report Presented to the Trades Unions Commissioners. Manchester and its Neighbourhoods. Volume 1. Royal Commission of Inquiry into Trade Unions.* 28 February 1868. On the Sheffield violence, see Downing 2013).

The public outcry in the wake of the Manchester and Sheffield 'Outrages' was instrumental in the appointment in February 1867 of a Royal Commission of Inquiry into trade unions. Though damning in regard to the trade union-related violence against non-union workmen that was brought to light, the Commission recommended that the rights of workers to combine should be properly reflected in law, setting in train a process which led eventually to the legal recognition of trade unions, a principle enshrined in the Acts of 1871 and 1875 referred to above.[6] As a caveat to the above, it should be pointed out that the final report of the Commission which came out in 1869 did acknowledge that, despite the 'immense increase of unionism', the 1850s and 1860s had witnessed a fall in instances of trade union-related violence, the aforementioned trades in Manchester and Sheffield notwithstanding. This was judged to be particularly the case with acts of extreme violence such as 'incendiarism or machine breaking', vitriol throwing, and 'actual attempts on life or limb' (*Eleventh and Final Report of the Royal Commissioners Appointed to Inquire into the Organisation and Rules of Trades Unions and Other Associations. Volume 1.* 1869: xxxiii–xxxiv). In adding this caveat, it is important not to lose sight of the fact that in some parts of Britain before the more enlightened legislative period of the 1870s, that aspect of labour relations that we have been looking at in this book was in a parlous state. Take the following account from the northern mill town of Ashton in regard to the highly conflictual and dangerous atmosphere which prevailed in the manufacturing and mining districts of north-west England in the 1860s:

> If Parliament cannot contrive to strengthen our county and municipal arrangements for maintaining order, it will wake up one day to find civil war raging over half the north of England. In those vast hives of humanity, the mining and manufacturing cities, with their narrow streets and fierce population, there are plenty of elements of combustion – one alone, the quarrel between unionists and non-unionists, is of the most dangerous and widespread character.
>
> *(Ashton Weekly Reporter, 23 May 1868: 7)*

In saying all of the above, this is not to claim that all forms of compulsion and violence against uncooperative workmen, whether extreme or otherwise, magically disappeared after 1871. Against the backdrop of an acute downturn in trade and wage reductions during the early years of the 'Great Depression', incidents of violence against blacklegs featured in the nineteen-week strike of cotton workers in north Lancashire in 1878 (King 1985). Violence against non-unionists also occurred with the onset of so-called 'New Unionism' from 1889, which saw large swathes of lower paid and semi-skilled and unskilled workers such as dockers, gas workers, shipyard labourers, chemical workers, and general labourers being recruited into trade unions.[7] Militant anti-blackleg violence involving the 'new trade unionists' is reported to have taken place during this period in strikes involving dock-workers in London, Liverpool and Cardiff, and gas-stokers in south London and Manchester (Howell 1973: 140). Nevertheless, in the view of some informed observers, the extent and degree of coercion and violence used against so-called 'free labour' workmen in these strikes was not of the same order as the decades before 1871 (Howell 1973: 140). Also, whereas acts of personal violence and intimidation did not completely disappear in strike situations in the immediate decades after 1871, they were much less in evidence when considered in comparison to the all-too-frequent incidents of violence which occurred in labour disputes in the years between 1760 and 1871. It seems, too, that one would need to search long and hard in the record to find acts of extreme retributive violence similar to those we looked at in a previous chapter of this book in the immediate decades after 1871 at least.[8] The pro-liberal trade unionist George Howell, writing in 1891, stated that 'the history of industrial warfare has been singularly free from actual outrage for a period of twenty years' (Howell 1973: 159–60). The socialist Annie Besant, writing around the same time as Howell in 1890, concurred with this assessment. According to Besant, after the legal shackles had been removed from labour after 1871 and 1875, the:

> outrages disappeared, and rational argument took the place of explosions. A knobstick or a blackleg may still, now and then, in times of great excitement

be threatened or even used with violence; but such incidents are rare, and rarest of all with the firmly organised unions.

(Besant 1890: 23)

While it could be argued that these forms of extreme violence were already on the wane during the 1850s and 1860s, as the 1867 Royal Commission of Inquiry into trade unions acknowledged, it seems that the more favourable legislative climate within which labour operated after 1871 finally drew the curtain on this mode of violence, at least in the decades that immediately followed 1871. An era which saw the throwing of cans of gunpowder down the chimneys of the homes of knobstick workers in Sheffield in 1866 and, at another time and place, the discharging of guns near to blacklegs' places of work in the coal-mining districts of south Wales in the 1830s by mysterious mobile raiders calling themselves the Scotch Cattle, it seems had passed.

Even considering the more extreme forms of compulsion that we have looked at in this book, that is, acts of direct physical violence against uncooperative workmen, how damaging was this to the cause of labour between 1760 and 1871? Was this violence, in the various forms that it assumed, an obstacle on the pathway to trade unionism, a deviation from the standard route, a discomfiting 'bump in the road' on the journey towards labour's eventual entry into the mainstream of the nation's economic and political life? At one level, this violence certainly alarmed so-called respectable middle-class opinion, and most likely delayed an invitation to labour to participate in the nation's economic and political affairs. The Webbs are surely correct to point out that when the trade union movement put its 'best foot forward' in the form of giving a platform to skilful and articulate negotiators such as Robert Applegarth, William Allan, Daniel Guile, Edwin Coulson, George Odger, T.J. Dunning, Henry Broadhurst, John Prior, George Howell, George Shipton, Alexander MacDonald, John Kane, William Dronfield and Alexander Campbell amongst other unionists, to promote the case for peaceful and moderate trade unionism, the cause of labour was considerably advanced (Webb and Webb 1920: 233–40). This being said, and while recognising the contribution of moderate 'responsible' trade unionism to the cause of labour, should the historian completely dismiss the violence of the decades between 1760 and 1871, viewing it simply as an encumbrance to labour's advance? Of course, one needs to take a critical stance towards the violence, most obviously the more extreme forms of retributive violence that we looked at in an earlier chapter, particularly when judged against the moral standards of twenty-first-century trade unionism.[9] Nevertheless, the more astute scholars of violence have shown that history has taught us on innumerable occasions that in certain contexts and circumstances and under certain conditions, violence can have beneficial uses and can even be justified, with actors in such situations constantly rationally weighing up and calculating the values involved in any given scenario prior to embarking on a course of action (Runkle 1976).[10] Thus, for instance, actors in these situations could weigh up whether their engagement in violent actions will curtail an evil act, thwart the possibility of a greater evil being inflicted, or bring forth a greater good. Similarly, actors are often faced with the difficult choice of weighing up whether the resort to violence is the only option remaining to save a community, a way of life, or an existing set of values. In such circumstances, 'violence may be done with great reluctance as a call to duty' (Runkle 1976: 382). To decline to act in such circumstances is itself a choice which can be productive of even greater evil and, as such, can represent a serious abdication of moral responsibility. Such calculations, making these balanced judgements, is certainly not easy, as we have seen on many occasions in this book when violence featured in a labour dispute. The resort to violence by workers on strike only occurred, in many instances during our period, when the danger associated with a given situation had become so grave, and when all other more peaceful strategies for achieving success in the turnout had been rejected or run aground. In such scenarios, violence emerged as a weapon of last resort, as the only choice left to stave off a potentially disastrous situation.

Beyond the circumstances of a particular strike situation, and at a more general level, one also needs to reflect on the real possibility that the often fierce and sometimes ugly battle waged against perceived internal enemies in the form of waverers or blackleg interlopers most likely helped trade unionism to stay afloat in extraordinarily dangerous times for working people and their families. The stakes were indeed exceedingly high. These perceived internal enemies were even seen to pose an existential threat to unionism itself, with the many dangers that this implied. As a cotton spinner informed the 1838 House of Commons Select Committee on workers' combinations, 'without a union our wages would be reduced to nothing' (cited in Lushington 1860: 392).

The violence may have had justifiable uses to labour in other, though related, ways. As mentioned in the Introduction to this book, and when discussing retributive violence, the use of violence could sometimes be cathartic for the working community, providing an outlet for a release of anger and a corresponding lessening of emotional tension. This release of tension can work to relieve pressure on the social structure, particularly at times of acute instability and change, as when Britain's working communities were struggling to transition to a more industrial and market economy during the decades of the late eighteenth and nineteenth century. René Girard's thinking on cathartic violence is not without interest here (on Girard's thoughts more generally, see Girard 1977; Girard 1987; and Hodge 2011). Clearly, the profile of the uncooperative strike-breaker during labour disputes does not conform to Girard's classic image of the scapegoat, the scapegoat for Girard being an entirely innocent surrogate victim picked out because of his atypical persona, or supposedly 'victimary signs', which markedly differentiated him from the group and made him vulnerable to attack. Nevertheless, Girard's point that the focus on and expulsion of a presence deemed deviant, disagreeable and polluting can have a cathartic effect and act to stabilise a fragmenting community is not without relevance to the study that we have undertaken. As with Girard's innocent sacrificial scapegoat, the removal of the hated blackleg stranger, in particular through an act of forceful expulsion, rids the community of the perceived contamination and restores tranquillity to the social order.

It should be noted as well that labour violence, as we have seen on many occasions in this book, was often reconfigured in the language of a just war, a reframing of the conflict which also aided the cause of labour in difficult times. The fight against both external and internal enemies cast in the language of a just war against a well-resourced and often cruel opponent helped strengthen the bonds of union, helped forge that sense of collective identity and comradeship that was the essence of unionism. For many unionists, acts of violence against perceived deserters and traitors viewed through the prism of a just war also served to give a sense of meaning and even legitimacy to what would have been seen in other situations as immoral acts. Understanding the struggle against a seemingly uncaring and exploitative economic system through the frame of war also helped instil discipline in the ranks, put all concerned on alert, and reminded potential waverers of their duty to the higher cause of the collective and the trade to which they belonged. Additionally, and if Georges Sorel is to be believed, a workers' strike, particularly if protracted and hard fought, had that rare capacity to inject a heroic quality into a struggle, as well as bring forth an 'epic state of mind' in the participants (Sorel 1941: 294). Fully understanding such a disposition and state of mind is not easy to grasp from the standpoint of the essentially peaceful and moderate trade unionism of the twenty-first century. A struggle against the uncooperative non-union workman conducted through the lens of war certainly bemused those who penned the final report of the 1867 Royal Commission of Inquiry into trade unions. The Commission was informed that unionists 'regard workmen who stand aloof from the union with a feeling akin to that which defenders of their country have towards a citizen who deserts to the invaders for the sake of better pay' (*Eleventh and Final Report of the Royal Commissioners Appointed to Inquire into the Organisation and Rules of Trades Unions and Other Associations. Volume 1.* 1869: xviii).

Lest we are in any doubt as to the quite extraordinary nature of labour relations in Britain in the period covered by this book, it would be appropriate to conclude this book by recounting the details of the following violent affray which took place in the vicinity of the Eccles district of Manchester in May 1843. The affray in question, between striking workers and blacklegs, is fascinating, not least because it provides a vivid example of the always fractious, frequently ugly, often violent, and sometimes bloody nature of labour relations in Britain during these decades. It also graphically brings to light the correlation between a workers' strike and war. A strike of brick-makers at the brick-croft of Messrs. Pauling and Henfry some three months previously and the decision of the masters to replace the men with blackleg labour formed the background to the affray. The affray ensued when a 'mob' of turnouts said to be armed with blunderbusses, pistols, bludgeons, pickshafts and other weapons launched an assault on the brick-croft premises under the cloak of darkness at 11.00pm. The blacklegs for their part were also armed with an array of blunderbusses, guns and pistols. What then followed was a ferocious fire-fight between the armed combatants lasting about 15 minutes which, according to contemporary reports, resulted in 'several' of the attackers being 'wounded', some possibly fatally (*Derby Mercury*, 24 May 1843: 4; and *Sherborne Mercury*, 20 May

1843: 2). When their armed assault on the brick-croft had been repulsed, the attackers effected their retreat, 'at the command of one who acted as their leader', carrying their wounded with them (*Derby Mercury*, 24 May 1843: 4). The survivors of the assault then reassembled in orderly columns at a point on the road towards Eccles some distance from the brick-croft. Here the military ritual of muster by the list came into play as the survivors were called over by the roll, which was performed at the command of 'No. 1, get your men together', 'No. 2, get your men together', and so on and so forth issued by their 'divisional leaders'. The roll call having revealed that several of their original number were missing, the 'six regular divisions' with their 'leaders' at the forefront of each column, then marched off in regular order towards Eccles (*Derby Mercury*, 24 May 1843: 4).[11]

Notes

1 This being said, a more accommodating attitude towards the labouring classes can be discerned before 1871, most notably with the 1867 Reform Act which granted the franchise to the artisan in the towns and cities.
2 The friction between employers and their workforce did not miraculously disappear with the establishment of Joint Boards of course, though this did represent a marked improvement on the confrontational relationship of previous decades.
3 A similar tendency has been noted in the study of folk-beliefs and folk rites. See Simms 1978: 176.
4 Examples here would again include Webb and Webb 1920; Cole 1948; and Pelling 1963.
5 In terms of exceptional leaders, here one would have in mind, for example, John Doherty, the Lancashire cotton-spinners' leader; John Gast, the leader of the Thames shipwrights; Gravenor Henson, the Nottingham framework knitters' leader; and Thomas Hepburn who led the mineworkers of the Tyne and Wear during the early 1830s. To this brief list we should add the leading lights of the so-called 'Junta', Robert Applegarth and William Allan, both being influential during the third quarter of the nineteenth century in steering the union movement towards a more conciliatory stance towards capital. This is not to underestimate the contribution of exceptional leaders, and the various other factors of course, all of which certainly helped labour emerge into the later decades of the nineteenth century and beyond, unbowed and undefeated.
6 The final deliberations of the Commission came in two forms. A Majority Report proposed that trade unions should be granted legal recognition in certain limited respects, whereas a Minority Report recommended the complete legalisation of unions. Other enlightened recommendations by the Commission included the establishment of Boards of Conciliation.
7 Total trade union membership is said to have doubled between 1889 and 1891 to around 1.5 million members.
8 See chapter 8.
9 On retributive violence, see chapter 8. In a similar vein, we should be rightly very critical of those instances in the labour disputes of these decades when women strike-breakers were physically assaulted by male strikers.
10 Obvious examples of justifiable violence from recent history would include the fight against Nazism, and the struggle at various stages between 1975 and 1999 of the islanders of East Timor against the Indonesian military occupation.
11 Twenty-three bricklayers were later arrested on suspicion of being involved in the gunfight, most of whom were said to belong to the brick-makers' union, the Brickmakers' Operative Association. See *Leeds Mercury*, 27 May 1823: 7. Prison sentences of twelve months with hard labour were later handed down to nine of that number.

References

Besant, Annie (1890) *The Trades Union Movement*. London: Freethought.
Clark, Anna (1995) *The Struggle for the Breeches. Gender and the Making of the British Working Class*. Berkeley: University of California Press.
Cole, G.D.H. (1948) *A Short History of the British Working-Class Movement, 1789–1947*. London: Allen & Unwin.
Downing, Arthur (2013) 'The "Sheffield Outrages": Violence, Class and Trade Unionism, 1850–1870', *Social History*, 38(2): 162–182.
Girard, René (1987) *Things Hidden Since the Foundation of the World*. Stanford: Stanford University Press.
Girard, René (1977) *Violence and the Sacred*. Baltimore: Johns Hopkins University.
Hodge, Joel (2011) 'Why do Humans Commit Violence? Violence, War and Rioting in the Modern World and René Girard's Mimetic Theory', *Compass*, 45(3): 3–12.
Howell, George (1973; first published 1891) *Trade Unionism New and Old*. Brighton: Harvester Press.
King, John (1985) '"We could eat the police!": Popular Violence in the North Lancashire cotton strike of 1878', *Victorian Studies*, 28(3): 439–471.
Lushington, Godfrey (1860) 'Abstract of Parliamentary Report on Combinations, 1838. Cotton Spinners', in Report of the Committee on Trades' Societies Appointed by the National Association for the Promotion of Social Science, *Trades' Societies and Strikes*. London: John W. Parker & Son: 389–393.
Orth, John V. (1991) *Combination and Conspiracy. A Legal History of Trade Unionism, 1721–1906*. Oxford: Clarendon Press.
Pelling, Henry (1963) *A History of British Trade Unionism*. London: MacMillan.
Runkle, Gerald (1976) 'Is Violence Always Wrong?', *The Journal of Politics*, 38(2): 367–389.
Simms, Norman (1978) 'Ned Ludd's Mummers Play', *Folklore*, 89(2): 166–178.
Sorel, Georges (1941; first published 1905) *Reflections on Violence*. New York: Peter Smith.
Webb, Sidney and Webb, Beatrice (1920) *The History of Trade Unions*. London: Longman.

INDEX

abatements 35
Allan, William 218, 221; *see also* 'Junta', the
Applegarth, Robert 218, 221; *see also* 'Junta', the
apprenticeship system 25–6, 29, 32, 34, 38, 39, 55, 59, 69, 136, 161

Bakhtin, Mikhail 114–15; *see also* carnivalesque strike rituals
Besant, Annie 13, 217
'black cat' visits 207–8; *see also* weavers' strike, Glasgow (1812–13)
'black law' 156–7
Blacklists
　master's Blacklists 189, 210
　shaming Blacklists 71, 154–6
Bloch, Maurice and ritual theory 86, 88–9
Broadhurst, Henry 218
Brontë, Charlotte 9
Burke, Peter 115

Caine's mark and betrayal 61–2, 63, 64, 66, 74
Carlyle, Thomas 9
carnivalesque strike rituals 112–29; *see also* Bakhtin, Mikhail
Carpenter, Edward 88
catharsis 19, 179, 195, 219
charivari rituals 116, 124–5, 167; *see also* 'donkeying'
Chartism 98, 100, 150, 170
Chase, Malcolm 11, 74, 82–3
Clarke, Charles Allen 64, 71

coat turning 171–2, 173; *see also* degradation rituals
'collective bargaining by riot' 141–3; *see also* Hobsbawm, Eric
cool-staffing 161–2, 163, 168; *see also* riding the stang *and* water punishments
Cutts, Henry 5

Davis, Natalie Zemon 180
degradation rituals 152–75
'dirtying' 167–8, 171; *see also* degradation rituals
Disraeli, Benjamin 9, 212
Doherty, John 4, 187, 188–9, 221
'donkeying' 115–25, 135, 153, 157; *see also* charivari rituals
Douglas, Mary 19, 54–5, 58–9, 60, 62, 71, 73, 81, 108; *see also* taboo theory
Downing, Arthur 7, 11, 148, 216
Durkheim, Emile 81

effigy rituals 119, 129, 132–3, 134–40
Emsley, Clive 9, 11–12
Engels, Friedrich 129, 195–6
expiation 19

Favretto, Ilario 125, 167
flints and dungs 50, 189
flying pickets 99–100, 109–10, 172, 173, 190–1; *see also* picketing system
food riots 11–12, 160
Frazer, Sir James 19, 133, 134, 145; *see also* sympathetic magic

'free labourer' ideal 39–41, 46–7, 69, 124–5, 138, 193, 217
French Revolution 18, 36, 44
French Revolutionary 'mob' 9
Freud, Sigmund 19, 61, 91–2, 108; *see also* taboo theory

Garfinkel, Harold 152–3, 162; *see also* degradation rituals
Gaskell, Elizabeth 9
Gast, John 221
General Strike of 1842; *see* strikes, lock-outs and general labour unrest
Girard, René 219
Gladstone, William Ewart 212
Grand National Consolidated Trades' Union 56
Guild craftsmen and value system 24, 55, 74, 91, 148

Harrison, Jane Ellen and ritual theory 133–4; *see also* sympathetic magic
Henson, Gravenor 161, 221
Hepburn, Thomas 4, 221
Hobsbawm, Eric 27, 141–3
Hodgskin, Thomas 39
Howell, George 63, 71, 175, 217 218
Hume, Joseph 37, 149
Huskisson, William 31

Ingram, Martin 125, 167
Irish migrant labour 13, 38–9, 51–3, 54, 66, 174, 201–3
Irish strikers 199–203

'Junta', the 221

Labour Party 6
Le Bon, Gustave 11
Linebaugh, Peter 11, 31, 160, 199, 201
Lovett, William 79, 80
Luddism 83, 123, 142, 143, 171, 199

machine-breaking narrative 141–3, 144, 145
Malinowski, Bronislaw 134; *see also* sympathetic magic
McGregor, Angus 2, 4–5
Melbourne, Lord 8
mercantilist theory of wages 33; *see also* wage fund theory
military muster by the list in strikes 6, 103–5, 163–4, 221
mineworkers
    and bond system 13, 50, 51, 75, 101, 104, 110, 126, 141, 166, 195

and 'tommy shop' system 27, 50, 75, 169
'mob' theory 9–10, 141, 144, 145, 180, 195
    psychological theories 10–11
    sociological theories 11, 180–81, 185
'moral economy' 11–12, 17, 201

Napoleonic Wars 28, 33, 51, 104, 120, 158, 159, 202
Navickas, Katrina 11, 19, 143, 183
'New Model' unionism 7, 215
'New Unionism' 217

oath-taking 14, 76–92, 199
Owen, Robert 79
Owenism 30, 79

Paine, Tom 135
Palmerston, Lord 96
Parliamentary commissions, committees and inquiries
    1824 Parliamentary Select Committee on Artisans and Machinery 43, 149, 170, 174
    1837–41 Royal Commission of Inquiry into the Condition of the Hand-Loom Weavers in England and Wales 8–9, 35
    1838 House of Commons Select Committee on Workers' Combinations 219
    1867 Royal Commission of Inquiry into Trade Unions 10, 208, 209, 216, 218, 220
Parliamentary legislation
    1563 Statute of Artificers 24–5, 26, 36, 39, 161
    1718 Royal Proclamation against lawless Clubs and Societies of weavers and woolcombers in Somerset and Devon 36
    1721 Second Calico Act 150
    1721 Tailors' Combination Act (Westminster and Greater London) 36
    1726 Weavers' Combination Act 36–7
    1749 Clothing Trade Workers' Combination Act 36
    1765 Silk-Weaving Industry Act 37
    1768 Tailors' Combination Act 36
    1773 Silk-Weaving Trade (Spitalfields) Combination Act 36
    1777 Hatters' Combination Act 36
    1792 Silk-Weaving Trade (Spitalfields) Combination Act 36
    1796 Papermakers' Combination Act 36
    1797 Unlawful Oaths Act 79

1799–1800 Combination Acts 8, 36, 50, 109, 111, 163
1813 Wage-Regulation Repeal 39
1814 Apprenticeship Repeal 39
1824 Vagrancy Act 195
1850 Mercantile Marine Act 164–5
1867 Master and Servant Act 212–13
1867 Reform Act 221
1871 Criminal Law Amendment Act 212
1871 Trade Union Act 212
1875 Conspiracy and Protection of Property Act 212
1875 Employers and Workmen Act 212–13
1897 Workmen's Compensation Act 213
1901 Taff Vale ruling 213
1913 Trade Union Act 213
Peel, Robert 85, 182, 183
picketing system 105–10, 181, 182–3; see also flying pickets
Primitive Methodism 75; see also Ranter preachers

Randall, Adrian 7, 11, 12, 143, 150, 184
Ranter preachers 75; see also Primitive Methodism
Rappaport, Roy and ritual theory 89
rattening 148–9
'Rebecca' bands 199, 206, 210
Rennie, James 2, 5
resource mobilisation theory 180–1, 185
retributive justice theory 179
retributive violence 178–209, 218; see also violence, theories of
riding the stang 116, 157–61, 162–3; see also cool-staffing
Riot Act 52, 114
rites of violence 19
'rough music' 97, 116, 118, 119, 125–9, 134, 138, 157, 179

sacralisation and the sacred 30, 55, 60–1, 73–92, 108, 114
'Scotch Cattle' raiders 101–2, 109, 199, 206, 218
Senior, Nassau William 8–9, 38, 40
Sheffield light metal trades 6–7, 148, 208, 216; see also 'Sheffield Outrages'
'Sheffield Outrages' 7, 16, 208–9, 210, 216 218
skimmerton riding 116; see also 'donkeying'
Smiles, Samuel 203
Smith, Adam 8, 30–1, 40
Society for the Diffusion of Useful Knowledge 21

Sorel, Georges 18, 220
stang riding; see riding the stang
Steiner, Franz 19, 60; see also taboo theory
strikes, lock-outs and general labour unrest
  1756–7 weavers' labour unrest, Stroud 142–3, 148, 162
  1760–9 silk-weavers' labour unrest, Spitalfields 37, 44, 123–4, 136–7, 142, 146, 150
  1768 coal-heavers' strike, London 160, 199–202
  1768 seamen's strike, Tyne and Wear 94, 157–8
  1784 fullers' strike, Exeter 29
  1791 woollen workers' labour unrest, Wiltshire and Somerset 140
  1792 seamen's strike, Tyne and Wear 158, 166
  1793 weavers' strike, Banbury 112–14, 144, 145, 146–7
  1795 fullers' strike, Exeter 29
  1802 shearmen's labour unrest, Wiltshire and Somerset 12, 204
  1808 cotton weavers' strike, Lancashire 99, 110, 202–3
  1812–13 weavers' strike, Glasgow 43, 206–7
  1815 seamen's strike, Tyne and Wear 104, 157–9, 163–4, 171, 173
  1818 cotton-spinners strike, Manchester 29, 44, 83–4, 98, 103, 105, 107, 109, 129, 190
  1819 framework knitters' strike, Leicestershire, Nottinghamshire and Derbyshire 123
  1819 ribbon weavers' strike, Coventry 120–1
  1819 weavers' strike, Carlisle 84
  1822 framework knitters' strike, Nottinghamshire and Derbyshire 204–5
  1822 keelmen's strike, Tyneside 170
  1822 mineworkers' strike, west Midlands 169
  1822 and 1823 weavers' strike, Frome 144.
  1823–4 mineworkers' strike, Gilmerton, Edinburgh 205, 210
  1825 framework knitters' strike, Leicester 144–5
  1825 weavers' strike, Stroud 137, 162, 168
  1826 shipwrights' strike, Bristol 160–1, 163
  1826–7 cotton spinners' strike, Oldham 106–7, 111, 181–6, 192–3

Index

1827 silk-weavers' strike, Spitalfields 123–4
1829 carpet weavers' strike, Kidderminster 128, 130
1829 framework knitters' strike, Hinckley 123, 137
1829 ribbon weavers' strike, Coventry and Nuneaton 121–2
1830 cotton spinners' strike, Stalybridge, Ashton-under-Lyne, and Hyde 186–8
1830–31 cotton spinners' strike, Stalybridge, Ashton-under-Lyne, Mossley, and Dukinfield 98, 106, 172, 188–9
1831 calico-printers' strike, Lancashire 30
1831 mineworkers' strike, Durham and Northumberland 4, 75, 84–5, 92, 104–5, 167–8
1831 mineworkers' strike, west Midlands 169–70
1832 mineworkers' lock-out, Durham and Northumberland 50–1, 53, 92, 195
1832 silk-dyers' strike, Salford 68
1833–4 calico-printers' strike, Glasgow 191
1833–4 trade unionists' lock-out, Derby 44, 78, 139
1834 hatters' strike, Atherton 118–19
1836 stonemasons' strike, Carlisle 49
1836 stonemasons' strike, Huddersfield 2
1838 boot and shoemakers' strike, London 67
1841–2 stonemasons' strike, new Houses of Parliament, Woolwich Dockyard and Nelson's Column 67
1842 General Strike 97–100, 109, 170
1842 stonemasons' strike, Glasgow 59–60
1843 brick-makers' strike, Eccles, Manchester 220–1
1844 doffers' strike, Rochdale 94, 95–6, 97
1844 mineworkers' strike, Barnsley 166
1844 mineworkers' strike, Belper 127–8
1844 mineworkers' strike, Durham and Northumberland 51, 126–7, 128, 141, 167, 195–6, 197, 205–6
1845 bakers' strike, Belfast 58
1845 woolcombers' strike, Bradford 139
1846 woolcombers' strike, Keighley 147, 150
1850 stonemasons' strike, Grimsby Docks 65
1851 seamen's strike, Tyne and Wear 164–5

1853 dock-workers' strike, London 203
1853 dyers and fustian finishers' strike, Pendleton, Manchester 178–9, 180–1, 209
1853 mineworkers' strike, Wigan 53
1853–4 cotton operatives' lock-out, Preston 21, 52, 53, 174
1854 seamen's strike, Tyne and Wear 94–5, 96
1857–9 Northamptonshire boot and shoemakers strike 16, 21
1859 mineworkers' strike, west Fife 65
1859 weavers' strike, Hyde 30
1861 cotton spinners' strike, Bolton 139
1862 hatters' strike, Atherton 119
1868 mineworkers' strike, Wigan 53–4
1869 mineworkers' lock-out, Denaby Main colliery, Mexborough 56–7, 71, 138, 197
1869–70 mineworkers' lock-out, Thorncliffe 18, 66, 71, 193–7
strike processions 94–8, 100–101, 112, 114, 118–19, 123
stripped naked 166–8, 173; see also degradation rituals
sympathetic magic 133–4, 136–7, 140–49; see also Frazer, Sir James

taboo theory 17, 19, 60–1, 91–2, 108, 145–7
talebearing 65, 69
tarring and feathering 164–6, 172; see also degradation rituals
Thompson, E.P. 11, 27–8, 35, 116, 160
Tolpuddle Martyrs 79
'tommy shop' system 27, 35, 49, 50, 65, 75
Tufnell, Edward 77–8, 79, 80, 86, 102–3, 105
Turner, Victor and ritual theory 89

van Gennep, Arnold and ritual theory 85–6, 152
'Victorian values' 9–10
violence, theories of 6–19, 218–20

wage fund theory 33–4; see also mercantilist theory of wages
water punishments 168–71, 174–5; see also cool-staffing
Watt, James 31, 41–2
Webb, Sidney and Beatrice 6, 7, 79–80, 218
Whiteboy movement 201–202; see also 1768 coal-heavers' strike, London
women in labour disputes 2, 21, 38, 53, 98, 120, 122, 123, 126–7, 139, 145, 146, 158, 165, 166, 167, 171, 191, 196, 221